ARISTOTLE'S ANTHROP

This is the first collection of essays devoted specifically to the nature and significance of Aristotle's anthropological philosophy, covering the full range of his ethical, metaphysical, and biological works. The book is organised into four parts, two of which deal with the metaphysics and biology of human nature, and two of which discuss the anthropological foundations and implications of Aristotle's ethico-political works. The essays range over topics from human nature and morality to friendship and politics, including original discussion and fresh perspectives on rationalism, the intellect, perception, virtue, the faculty of speech, and the differences and similarities between human and non-human animals. Wide-ranging and innovative, the volume will be highly relevant for readers studying Aristotle, as well as for anyone working on either ancient or contemporary philosophical anthropology.

GEERT KEIL is Professor of Philosophy at Humboldt University of Berlin. He is co-editor of *Vagueness in Psychiatry* (2017) and *Vagueness and Law* (2016).

NORA KREFT is Assistant Professor of Philosophy at Humboldt University of Berlin. Her areas of research are moral psychology, philosophy of love, and ancient philosophy.

ARISTOTLE'S ANTHROPOLOGY

EDITED BY

GEERT KEIL

Humboldt University of Berlin

NORA KREFT

Humboldt University of Berlin

CAMBRIDGE
UNIVERSITY PRESS

University Printing House, Cambridge CB2 8BS, United Kingdom

One Liberty Plaza, 20th Floor, New York, NY 10006, USA

477 Williamstown Road, Port Melbourne, VIC 3207, Australia

314-321, 3rd Floor, Plot 3, Splendor Forum, Jasola District Centre, New Delhi - 110025, India

79 Anson Road, #06-04/06, Singapore 079906

Cambridge University Press is part of the University of Cambridge.

It furthers the University's mission by disseminating knowledge in the pursuit of education, learning and research at the highest international levels of excellence.

www.cambridge.org
Information on this title: www.cambridge.org/9781316642627
DOI: 10.1017/9781108131643

© Cambridge University Press 2019

This publication is in copyright. Subject to statutory exception and to the provisions of relevant collective licensing agreements, no reproduction of any part may take place without the written permission of Cambridge University Press.

First published 2019
First paperback edition 2021

A catalogue record for this publication is available from the British Library

Library of Congress Cataloging in Publication data
NAMES: Keil, Geert, editor.
TITLE: Aristotle's anthropology / edited by Geert Keil, Humboldt-Universität zu Berlin, Nora Kreft, Humboldt-Universität zu Berlin.
DESCRIPTION: 1 [edition]. | New York : Cambridge University Press, 2019. | Includes bibliographical references and index.
IDENTIFIERS: LCCN 2018047256 | ISBN 9781107192690 (hardback) | ISBN 9781316642627 (pbk.)
SUBJECTS: LCSH: Aristotle. | Philosophical anthropology.
CLASSIFICATION: LCC B485 .A675 2019 | DDC 128.092–DC23
LC record available at https://lccn.loc.gov/2018047256

ISBN 978-1-107-19269-0 Hardback
ISBN 978-1-316-64262-7 Paperback

Cambridge University Press has no responsibility for the persistence or accuracy of URLs for external or third-party internet websites referred to in this publication, and does not guarantee that any content on such websites is, or will remain, accurate or appropriate.

Contents

List of Contributors	*page* vii
Acknowledgements	ix

Introduction: Aristotle's Anthropology	1
Geert Keil and Nora Kreft	

PART I HUMAN BEINGS AS RATIONAL ANIMALS — 23

1	Aristotle on the Definition of What It Is to Be Human *Christian Kietzmann*	25
2	Speech and the Rational Soul *Ian C. McCready-Flora*	44
3	Aristotle's Peculiarly Human Psychology *Elena Cagnoli Fiecconi*	60
4	The Planetary Nature of Mankind: A Cosmological Perspective on Aristotle's Anthropology *Christof Rapp*	77

PART II HUMAN NATURE IN THE LIGHT OF ARISTOTLE'S BIOLOGY — 97

5	Is Reason Natural? Aristotle's Zoology of Rational Animals *James G. Lennox*	99
6	Spot the Differences! The Hidden Philosophical Anthropology in Aristotle's Biological Writings *Jörn Müller*	118
7	Aristotle on the Anthropological Difference and Animal Minds *Hans-Johann Glock*	140

vi *Contents*

PART III ARISTOTLE'S MORAL ANTHROPOLOGY 161

8 Why Human Virtue Is the Measure of All Virtue 163
Kathi Beier

9 Aristotle on Friendship and Being Human 182
Nora Kreft

10 Aristotle on the Possibility of Moral Perfection 200
Christoph Horn

PART IV ARISTOTLE'S POLITICAL ANTHROPOLOGY 219

11 Political Animals and Human Nature in Aristotle's *Politics* 221
Joseph Karbowski

12 Political Animals and the Genealogy of the *Polis*: Aristotle's
Politics and Plato's *Statesman* 238
David J. Depew

13 The Deficiency of Human Nature: The Task of
a 'Philosophy of Human Affairs' 258
Dorothea Frede

Bibliography 275
Index 291

Contributors

KATHI BEIER is Junior Fellow in Philosophy at the Max Weber Centre for Advanced Cultural and Social Studies at the University of Erfurt.

ELENA CAGNOLI FIECCONI is Lecturer in Philosophy in the Department of Greek and Latin at University College London.

DAVID J. DEPEW is Emeritus Professor of Communication Studies at the University of Iowa and was previously Professor of Philosophy at California State University, Fullerton.

DOROTHEA FREDE is Professor Emerita of Ancient Philosophy at the University of Hamburg.

HANS-JOHANN GLOCK is Professor of Theoretical Philosophy at the University of Zurich.

CHRISTOPH HORN is Professor of Practical Philosophy and Ancient Philosophy at the University of Bonn.

JOSEPH KARBOWSKI is Visiting Assistant Professor of Philosophy at the University of Pittsburgh.

GEERT KEIL is Professor of Philosophy at the Humboldt University of Berlin.

CHRISTIAN KIETZMANN is Assistant Professor in Philosophy at the University of Erlangen.

NORA KREFT is Assistant Professor in Philosophy at the Humboldt University of Berlin.

JAMES G. LENNOX is Professor of History and Philosophy of Science at the University of Pittsburgh.

viii *List of Contributors*

IAN C. MCCREADY-FLORA is Assistant Professor of Philosophy at the University of Virginia.

JÖRN MÜLLER is Professor of Ancient and Medieval Philosophy at the University of Würzburg.

CHRISTOF RAPP is Professor of Ancient Philosophy at the Ludwig Maximilian University of Munich.

Acknowledgements

We wish to thank Gelareh Shahpar, Noah Nasarek, and Martin Günther for their invaluable assistance in preparing the final manuscript and compiling the bibliography and index. Eric J. Engstrom meticulously copy-edited the Introduction and three chapters (1, 6, and 10). His work was funded by the Fritz Thyssen Stiftung. Christof Rapp read a draft of the Introduction and made a number of very valuable suggestions. We are also grateful to an anonymous reader for Cambridge University Press whose helpful comments significantly improved the manuscript. Throughout the editing and publication process, it was an immense pleasure to work with Hilary Gaskin, Marianne Nield, and Sophie Taylor at Cambridge University Press.

Introduction
Aristotle's Anthropology
Geert Keil and Nora Kreft

1 Is There Even Such a Thing?

One might well wonder whether there is such a thing as 'Aristotle's anthropology'. Isn't the title a blatant anachronism? The term 'anthropology' was not in use in ancient philosophy. And Aristotle might have resisted the label for philosophical reasons, too. Let us begin by addressing these concerns.

(a) The term 'anthropology' was not used before the sixteenth century. The Latin-Greek word 'anthropologia' is said to have been coined by the German philosopher, theologian, and physician Magnus Hundt in 1501. Late in the sixteenth century, the humanist philosopher Otto Casmann defined 'anthropologia' as 'doctrina humanae naturae', thus consolidating the philosophical use of the term.[1] Nowadays, the English term 'anthropology' encompasses a wide array of loosely connected academic subjects. The Oxford English Dictionary defines 'anthropology' as 'the comparative study of human societies and cultures and their development'. The sub-entry 'physical anthropology' adds 'the study of human biological and physiological characteristics and their evolution'. In fact, many university departments of anthropology host biological and medical sciences, over and above the social and cultural study of people and places. Trying systematically to relate this wide array of subjects to Aristotle's investigations of human beings does not seem promising. As James Lennox remarks:

> The Anthropology Department at my home institution consists of four major divisions: Archaeology, Social and Cultural Anthropology, Medical Anthropology and Physical Anthropology. It would be a puzzling and ultimately fruitless enterprise to try and figure out whether any of Aristotle's many investigations of human beings would find a home in any of these categories.[2]

[1] 'Anthropologia est doctrina humanae naturae. Humana natura est geminae naturae mundanae, spiritualis et corporeae, in unum hyphistamenon unitae particeps essentia' (Casmann 1594, 1).
[2] Lennox, Chapter 5, 99.

(b) In German-speaking philosophy, the situation is a little different because the term 'anthropology' is often coupled with the epithet 'philosophical'. The phrase 'Philosophische Anthropologie' denotes a distinctively philosophical field of enquiry, i.e. a philosophical investigation of the 'anthropological difference' that sets humans apart from other animals.[3] More narrowly, the term denotes a particular school of thought that emerged in the first half of the twentieth century. Max Scheler and Helmuth Plessner wrote influential books on human nature, partly building on Kant's and Herder's groundwork, while taking into account biological, sociological, and psychological research. The 'philosophical anthropologists' tried to carve out a core structure that integrated the different aspects of human beings that were being studied, largely in isolation from each other, by the various human sciences. But, apart from occasional references to Aristotle's hierarchy of vegetative, sensitive, and rational capacities, they did not engage with Aristotle's thoughts on human nature.

(c) Aristotle wrote no treatise on human nature. At least the *Corpus Aristotelicum* contains no book entitled *Peri physeōs anthrōpou* or *Peri anthrōpou*. The phrase that comes closest in his work is 'hē peri ta anthrōpeia philosophia' (*EN* X 10, 1181b15), i.e. 'the philosophy of human affairs', or 'the philosophy of human nature', as Ross translates it. Aristotle uses this phrase in a comment on the architecture of his practical philosophy: in the concluding section of the *Nicomachean Ethics*, he announces that his investigation of the principles of legislation will complete 'the philosophy of human affairs'. Hence, the phrase is used in order to bind together his ethics and politics as a coherent enterprise of practical philosophy.[4] On the face of it, this is not a descriptive investigation into human nature, but a normative project that tries to identify the ways in which human beings should conduct their lives and organise their communities.

(d) Aristotle definitely had enough material for a book on human nature, but instead of collecting it in one treatise he preferred to scatter it throughout his writings. He discusses human nature extensively and frequently, but under various headings, ranging from biology to metaphysics. (Likewise, within contemporary philosophy, the study of human nature is not an established subfield, but a shared concern of at least the philosophy of mind and action, metaphysics, moral psychology, the

---

[3] We use the term of art 'anthropological difference' interchangeably with 'human–animal difference'.
[4] The phrase is discussed in Frede's Chapter 13, 268–9.

Introduction

philosophy of biology, and the philosophy of religion.) Aristotle's study of human nature even extends to practical philosophy, because humans, unlike other animals, need to cultivate their virtues in order to live well. Such a heterogeneous discipline, if it is one, does not fit into Aristotle's classification of the sciences. Accordingly, the topic of anthropology is orthogonal to the classification of his works, as it is to the research agenda of Aristotle scholarship.

(e) A possible reason for Aristotle not establishing a distinct science of human nature is his view that a science of some X has to be built on a definition of X. And, although he famously characterises the human being as a *zōon logon echon*, it is controversial whether the phrase is meant as a definition in his sense of the term. The phrase does follow the scheme of *genus proximum* and *differentia specifica*, since *logos* isn't shared by any other animal. But, for Aristotle, definitions do more than that: they capture essences.

While specifying a unique feature (an *idion*) of some natural substance is one thing, capturing its essence is quite another. Given the strict requirements Aristotle sets for essential definitions in his *Organon*[5] and in *Metaphysics* Zeta, there is reason to doubt that he regarded any *idion* or any combination thereof as amounting to a definition of human essence. Essences, unlike mere *idia*, are supposed to explain whatever they are essences of. In the *Metaphysics*, Aristotle wonders 'wherein consists the unity of that, the formula of which we call a definition, as for instance in the case of man, two-footed animal; for let this be the formula of man. Why, then, is this one, and not many, viz. animal *and* two-footed?' (*Met* VII 12, 1037b11–13, transl. Ross/Barnes).[6] So, among other things, definitions have to establish a particular kind of unity between their terms in order to do their explanatory work. Aristotle's view in *Met.* Zeta is that, in a correct *dihairesis*, the ultimate *differentia* of a thing constitutes the *logos tēs ousias*, its essential definition. Counting *zōon logon echon* as such a definition requires further argument then. And there are reasons to doubt that the non-biological characteristic of possessing *nous* can work as a *differentia* that defines a biological species. What needs to be shown is that the formula *zōon logon echon* meets the unity condition.

Optimistic as Aristotle is about the prospects of finding definitions for various substances, he may be less optimistic when it comes to defining

---

[5] See *Top.* I 8, 103b7–16 and VI 6, 143a29–b10.
[6] An interesting question is how serious Aristotle is about the idea of defining humans as 'two-footed animals', which is often taken to be a joke. See Kietzmann, Chapter 1, 28.

GEERT KEIL AND NORA KREFT

human beings. At least this is what Kietzmann argues in his contribution to this volume. According to him, Aristotle is worried about a severe tension inherent in the phrase – a tension between the terms '*zōon*' and '*logon echon*' that stands in the way of a unified definition. Kietzmann concludes that there can be no proper and separate science of human nature for Aristotle:

> Human beings belong to two completely different ontological realms and, therefore, must be investigated by two different kinds of sciences: humans as animals are investigated by physics, and, more particularly, by zoology, whereas humans as rational beings are investigated by theology.[7]

This is controversial, however, and other contributors to this volume are more sanguine about a unified study of human beings. For one thing, one might deny or at least qualify the premise that, for Aristotle, a science of X requires a proper definition of X. In many contexts, 'nominal' definitions that build upon *idia* may suffice (this would also depend on what Aristotle means by 'science' in different contexts). Secondly, even if one agrees with the premise, perhaps possessing logos *is* the required ultimate difference that makes *zōon logon echon* an essential definition and there is no tension after all. Also, the idea of a *hybrid* science that combines human characteristics established by both natural science and practical philosophy might not be ruled out for Aristotle. All of this remains to be debated.

In calling this book 'Aristotle's Anthropology', we have set aside concerns about terminological anachronism. And, in light of the controversy just mentioned, we also do not wish to commit to ascribing to Aristotle an anthropology in the sense of a proper and separate science of human nature. Instead, the aim of this book is to study the various intriguing and sometimes curious observations Aristotle makes about human beings. He was obviously deeply interested in whether there is such a thing as a human nature and, if so, what it consists of. In many of his major works, he considers the 'anthropological difference', i.e. traits that set humans apart from other animals. For example, in addition to being 'rational animals', humans are also characterised as 'political animals'. According to the pertinent passage in the *Politics*, we are not the only political animals, but the *most* political of all. What does he mean by 'most political', and why and how is this related to being rational?[8] In other places, he points out further uniquely human features: humans are the

---

[7] Kietzmann, Chapter 1, 25.

[8] Although 'mallon' could also be translated as 'rather' instead of 'more'. This would change the claim in interesting ways (see below).

Introduction 5

only animals capable of *self-induced agency, active memory, anticipation of the future, happiness, laughter,* and *true friendship.* He also observes that their physique is strikingly different from that of any other species, in particular because humans have *free hands* and an *upright posture.*

The relations between these various characteristics are underexplored in the literature. This book aims to fill this lacuna: it wants to shed light on these relations and explore their importance for the rest of Aristotle's philosophy. Consider the above controversy again, for instance, and assume for a moment that Aristotle doesn't believe in the possibility of a unified account of human beings. What would this mean for his ethics? Without a definition, are we also unable to specify the human *ergon*? If that is so, then what precisely is going on in his ethical writings when he appears to be doing precisely that?

2 'Man Alone of All Animals': Aristotle on Continuity and Discontinuity

Recent philosophy has seen a revived interest in the question of what distinguishes humans from other animals. This interest was partly stirred up by the emerging interdisciplinary research field of human–animal studies. In the philosophy of mind, we have witnessed the establishment of a new subdiscipline called 'the philosophy of animal minds'.[9] Both within and outside of philosophy, the anthropological exceptionalism of otherwise diverse thinkers such as Aquinas, Descartes, Herder, Kant, and Hegel has fallen out of favour. In recent debates on the anthropological difference, a new terminology has been suggested: '*Differentialists* maintain that there are categorical differences separating us from animals; *assimilationists* maintain that the differences are merely quantitative and gradual'.[10] Most participants in the recent debate sympathise with assimilationism.[11]

Aristotle's position on this issue is hard to pinpoint. Both assimilationists and differentialists will easily find support in his writings. In many places, Aristotle insists that human traits and abilities are continuous with those of other animals. The resemblances he finds include physical, emotional, and intellectual qualities:

---

[9] See the brief overview in Glock, Chapter 7.   [10] Ibid., 143.
[11] Dissenters who make a strong case for discontinuity between human and non-human minds include Davidson (1982), Tomasello and Rakoczy (2003), Premack (2007), Penn et al. (2008), and Penn and Povinelli (2012).

GEERT KEIL AND NORA KREFT

> For just as we pointed out resemblances in the physical organs, so in a number of animals we observe gentleness or fierceness, mildness or cross temper, courage or timidity, fear or confidence, high spirit or low cunning, and, with regard to intelligence, something equivalent to sagacity. Some of these qualities in man, as compared with the corresponding qualities in animals, differ only quantitatively; that is to say a man has more of this quality, and an animal has more of some other; other qualities in man are represented by analogous qualities: for instance, just as in man we find craft (*technē*), wisdom (*sophia*) and insight (*synesis*), so in some animals there exists some natural capacity akin to these. (*HA* VIII 1, 588a16–31, transl. Thompson)

The view that many differences between the capacities of humans and other animals are either merely quantitative or to be understood analogously accords well with Aristotle's general notion that nature proceeds little by little (*kata mikron*). He maintains that all living things can be arranged in a single *scala naturae* and, accordingly, even leaves room for intermediate steps in his tripartite classification of plants, animals, and humans: marine invertebrates such as *adscidians* (sea squirts) and *testacea* (seashells), he argues, stand between plants and animals.[12] This is to be expected:

> In fact nature passes continuously from soulless things into animals by way of those things that are alive yet not animals, so that by their proximity the one seems to differ very little from the other. (*PA* IV 5, 681a11–14, transl. Lennox)[13]

It is worth noting that this continuity thesis goes slightly beyond the gradualism that the *scala naturae* metaphor expresses. Literally speaking, both the *scala naturae* and the medieval metaphor of the *great chain of being* posit discrete steps or links in a chain. Genuine continuity, by contrast, does not. A truly continuous transition has no steps. A continuity thesis that deserves its name abandons steps or degrees in

---

[12] *GA* I 23, 731b and III 11, 761a; *PA* IV 5, 681a.

[13] See also *HA* VII 1, 588b4–17. Aristotle's continuity thesis is in obvious tension with his essentialist metaphysics. The concern is that 'the continuity of kinds in Aristotle's biology overthrows the theories of essentialism and classification of the logic and metaphysics' (Granger 1985, 186). Some scholars argue that Aristotle actually allows for organisms that 'dualise' (Peck's translation of the Aristotle's term *epamphoterizein*), in the sense of sharing essential properties of more than one kind and, hence, participating in different, overlapping kinds. Others argue for a weaker reading of the continuity thesis. According to Granger (1985), the difficulty of neatly classifying 'dualisers' is merely epistemic: Since nature proceeds *kata mikron*, as Aristotle says, often 'it is impossible to determine the exact line of demarcation, nor on which side thereof an intermediate form should lie' (*HA* VII 1, 588b4–6). On dualisers, see also Pellegrin (1987) and Müller, Chapter 6, 121.

Introduction 7

favour of a seamless transition. In ordinary parlance, the phrase 'matter of degree' is ambiguous between both readings.

The differentialist picture, i.e. anthropological exceptionalism, also finds support in Aristotle. Even in his biological works, he makes repeated use of the phrase 'man alone of all animals', and sometimes it serves to introduce features that don't even have analogues in other species. Some of these features were mentioned above: only human beings stand erect, make equal use of both hands, are capable of deliberation and decision, or can recall the past at will.[14] In *De Anima*, Aristotle describes the most striking case of an *idion* that has no analogue in the animal kingdom: the intellect (*nous*) is uniquely human, comes from outside (*thyrathen*),[15] is not associated with a specific bodily organ, and does not belong to the proper study of natural science. It is by virtue of their *nous* that humans partake in the divine. But this partaking is imperfect and temporary:

> [I]f human beings are active in theoretical thinking they activate what is the best and the most divine portion within them and thus attain a small and limited piece of the kind of life that the divine intellect enjoys without interruption and limits.[16]

The partly divine nature of the active intellect makes humans belong to two distinct realms, as it were, and seems to belie the continuity thesis. And so perhaps the either-or question of whether Aristotle favours a differentialist or an assimilationist view of the anthropological difference is oversimplified. What we need is an exegetically plausible reconciliation of the continuity thesis in his natural philosophy and his metaphysical view that the active *nous* 'comes from outside', whatever that means exactly.[17]

3 The Transformation Thesis

A fresh approach to this challenge is the 'transformational' view of what sets humans apart from other animals, in short: the *transformation thesis*.[18] Roughly speaking, the idea behind this thesis is that a new character's arrival on the scene can change everything. According to the transformation thesis, human beings' rational faculties are not a mere addition to

---

[14] *PA* IV 10, 686a27–29; *HA* II 1, 497b13; *HA* I 1, 488b24; *HA* I 1, 488b25.
[15] *DA* III 4/5; cf. *GA* II 3, 736b27–28 and 737a10.   [16] Rapp, Chapter 4, 90.
[17] Frede (Chapter 13, 260) argues that *thyrathen* 'does not mean that reason is bestowed by some supernatural power', but only 'that it is not contained in the semen and does not develop organically, for there is no organ of reason', as Aristotle says in *GA* II 3, 737a10.
[18] Section 3 is authored solely by Geert Keil.

'lower' capacities they share with other animals, but rather convert those capacities into something substantially different.[19]

Take perception (*aisthēsis*): Both human and non-human animals are capable of sensation. All animals have sensory organs, even if some species have to get by only with a sense of touch (*DA* II 3, 414b4). In humans, however, sensory impressions give rise to *perceptual judgements* with *propositional contents*, which in turn depend on the possession of the required *concepts*. Perceiving that such-and-such is the case goes far beyond having sensory impressions. Propositional perception requires additional abilities – abilities that, as Davidson famously argues, non-linguistic creatures lack:

> However, speech is not just one more organ; it is essential to the other senses if they are to yield propositional knowledge. Language is the organ of propositional perception. Seeing sights and hearing sounds does not require thoughts with propositional content; perceiving how things are does, and this ability develops along with language.[20]

Speech, according to Davidson, transforms the faculty of seeing sights and hearing sounds into something substantially different: into the distinctively human faculty of grasping truth-apt propositions.[21] When applied to Aristotle, the suggestion is that the possession of *logos*, and in particular the rational soul's capacity to actively apprehend forms, transforms the other mental capacities in a similar way.

We find no explicit and general statement of the transformation thesis in Aristotle. What we do find are particular instances of this line of thought. Cagnoli Fiecconi (Chapter 3) explores the transformation thesis with respect to imagination. Non-human animals are capable of imagination

---

[19] 'Transformative theories of rationality contrast with *additive* theories, which hold that the capacities which make us rational can be added to capacities for perception and voluntary movement that remain essentially similar to those of nonrational animals. ... What rational and nonrational animals 'share', on this view, is not a separable *factor* that is present in both, but a generic *structure* that is realized in different ways in the two cases' (Boyle 2017, 114–15). For an exposition of the transformation thesis, as advocated by the Pittsburgh philosophers Sellars, Brandom, and McDowell, see Glock, Chapter 7, 155–57. The Pittsburgh philosophers interpret both Aristotle's and Aquinas's hierarchical models of capacities along the lines of the transformation thesis.

[20] Davidson (1997, 22). Perception is also McDowell's and Boyle's primary example: 'a *transformative theory* of rationality ... takes the nature of our perceptual capacities themselves to be affected by the presence of rationality, in a way that makes rational perception different in kind from its nonrational counterpart' (Boyle 2017, 114).

[21] For a critique of the view that animals are confined to object perception, without being capable of perceiving facts and, in general, 'without encompassing that-ish intentionality and, hence, truth conditions', see Glock, Chapter 7, 151.

Introduction 9

in some sense, but human *phantasia* has a wider cognitive range as a result of its cohabitation with reason and thought:[22]

> Despite the similarities with non-human animals, humans are peculiar because in them non-rational cognition and desire cooperate with the rational part and with *logos*. ... Humans have a peculiarly expanded non-rational perceptual and desiderative range. This difference in sophistication is not merely a matter of enhanced discriminatory capacities: humans also have the peculiar ability to exercise deliberative *phantasia* at will and the peculiar ability to synthesise many *phantasmata* into one.[23]

According to the transformation thesis, being able to exercise *phantasia* at will and to synthesise many *phantasmata* into one is not a mere addition to an otherwise unchanged ability.

Another case in point would be *desire*. Both human and non-human animals have desires, but a human desire, as Rabbås interprets Aristotle,

> is not a mere urge or impulse towards a certain object; rather, the desire itself partly consists in a logically structured representation of the object as connected in a certain way to its appropriation and the satisfaction of a need. Only a rational creature – a *zōon logikon* – is capable of such representation, and in such creatures even the most basic desires, such as the desire for food and drink, are structured representations of this kind. That is how in human beings reason, *logos*, is not something added on to the desires that we share with animals, with the further difference that we have the capacity to step back from and take a stand towards these desires; rather, reason fundamentally transforms these desires themselves and makes them rational desires, or the desires of rational creatures.[24]

Rabbås explicitly formulates the transformation thesis that he attributes to Aristotle:

> But while it is, in some sense, true to say that we share these activities and functions with the lower kinds of organism, they are *transformed* when they are part of human life, and that is because the way we perform these activities is informed by reason.[25]

Memory and *anticipation of the future* are further cases in which 'being informed by reason' also transforms those abilities that humans seem to

---

[22] See Cagnoli Fiecconi, Chapter 3, 64–5.   [23] Ibid., 61 and 60.

[24] Rabbås (2015, 101). For a similar interpretation of Aristotle's doctrine that whatever is desired is desired under the guise of good (*quidquid appetitur, appetitur sub specie boni*, as the schoolmen codified *DA* III 10, 433a28–29), see Boyle and Lavin (2010).

[25] Rabbås (2015, 100).

share with other animals. According to Aristotle, both abilities are shared in a sense by non-human animals, albeit not in another.[26]

The transformation thesis about the anthropological difference has a number of advantages. It can, first, serve to explain certain ambiguities and tensions in Aristotle's comparisons of humans and other animals. Take the notion of agency. In his ethical works, Aristotle says that humans are the only animals capable of agency, while in his biological works he also attributes actions (*praxeis*) to non-human animals.[27] Obviously, he sometimes uses *prattein* and *praxis* in a relaxed sense and sometimes in a more demanding sense. In the more demanding sense, only conduct that is both self-initiated and responsive to reasons counts as agency. These requirements, however, are not mere additions to an otherwise unchanged ability, but make a huge difference for a being's agential powers. Now, in many contexts it may not matter much in exactly what sense of *praxis* ants or bees can perform *praxeis*. Yet, when discussing the anthropological difference, it matters crucially.

The transformation thesis may also help defuse the ill-defined either-or question of whether the mental abilities of human and non-human animals differ in kind (qualitatively) or in degree (quantitatively): They can differ in kind in one sense, and be gradual in another (of which more below). Such a disambiguation strategy could account for the coexistence of Aristotle's gradualist and his non-gradualist claims about the anthropological difference. The passage in the *Politics* mentioned above can serve as an example: Aristotle states that 'man is more of a political animal [*mallon politikon*] than bees or any other gregarious animals' (*Pol.* I 2, 1253a7–8, transl. Jowett/Barnes).

On the face of it, comparative phrases like 'more of', 'in a greater measure', 'to a higher degree', or 'to a greater extent' are indicative of a gradualist view. But, in his subsequent explanation of what the higher degree of the *zōon politikon's* being political consists of or is due to, Aristotle makes a number of claims that are anything but gradualist. He states (a) that man alone possesses speech, (b) that speech serves a uniquely

---

[26] 'Many animals have memory, and are capable of instruction; but no other creature except man can recall the past at will' (*HA* I 1, 488b25–26; cf. *Mem.* 2, 453a7–14). While 'we say that some even of the lower animals ... have a power of foresight with regard to their own life' (*EN* VI 7, 1141a27–29, transl. Ross), 'mankind alone becomes expectant and hopeful for the future' (*PA* 669a20) in a demanding sense, because hope (*elpis*) requires imaginative anticipation of a future good.

[27] See *EE* II 6, 1222b18–20; *EN* VI 2, 1139a19–20; *HA* VIII 1, 588a18.

Introduction 11

human purpose, and (c) that it requires or presupposes uniquely human cognitive abilities:

> Nature, as we often say, makes nothing in vain, and man is the only animal who has the gift of speech [*logos*]. And whereas mere voice [*phonē*] is but an indication of pleasure or pain, and is therefore found in other animals . . ., the power of speech is intended to set forth the expedient and inexpedient, and therefore likewise the just and unjust. And it is a characteristic of man that he alone has any sense of good and evil, of just and unjust, and the like, and the association of living beings who have this sense makes a family and state. (*Pol.* I 2, 1253a8–18)

The transformation thesis can help to alleviate the tension between the quantitative comparison Aristotle makes ('more political') and the qualitative differences he in turn provides as evidence. On the face of it, claiming that humans are more political than other animals is an assimilationist's statement, while claiming that humans alone, qua possessing speech, are able of perceiving moral qualities, which is in turn required to build a *polis*, amounts to differentialism. Distinguishing between a more and a less demanding sense of the ability to communicate eases the tension: both bees and humans communicate in some sense, both live in communities in some sense, but the uniquely human faculty of propositional speech that involves conventions (*synthēkai*) makes a difference that also transforms the way of living together: roughly, from being merely gregarious (*agelaios*) to genuinely living together in the sense of sharing thought and action (*suzein*), and being capable of deliberating about the common advantage (*koinon sympheron*).[28]

This is not to say that one couldn't explain this passage in other ways. A simple kind of differentialism can account for Aristotle's conclusion in a straightforward way: since non-human animals lack reason, a conventional language, and moral perception, they cannot build a *polis*, period. A simple differentialist reading can also invoke the alternative translation of '*mallon*' mentioned above: the adverb could also mean 'rather' instead of 'more' or 'to a greater measure', in which case Aristotle isn't saying that human beings are *more* political than other animals, but that they are better

---

[28] See *EN* IX 9, 1170b10–14; *Pol.* III 6, 1279a17–22. In principle, 'simple' differentialism has no problem with the coexistence of gradualist and nongradualist claims about the anthropological difference, as long as they don't concern the same qualities. Differentialists can argue that their preferred categorical difference *explains* other, merely gradual differences. However, arguably, the transformation thesis can explain away the tension between Aristotle's gradualist and his nongradualist claims more elegantly.

candidates for politicality (for need of a better word[29]), or that the word '*politikon*' in its proper sense applies only to humans. After all, Aristotle explicitly says that animals can't build a *polis* (*Pol.* III 9, 1280a32). So, if '*mallon*' means 'rather' and if '*politikon*' refers exclusively to the *polis*, there is no tension to be explained away, because the impression of gradualism ('more political') does not arise in the first place.[30]

Back to the transformation thesis, which might also be attractive regardless of Aristotle. In recent research on animal mentality, we have witnessed heated debates about which of the mental abilities regarded as being uniquely human are also shared by other animals.[31] If, say, dolphins and chimpanzees pass the mirror self-recognition test, then don't they possess self-consciousness? Yes and no, says the transformation thesis. And if other animals share so many allegedly human-specific abilities, then doesn't animal mentality differ from human mentality only in degree? Again, yes and no. It all depends on whether the mental predicates in question are used univocally or equivocally, or rather, how salient the differences in semantic implications are, how relevant they are deemed in the given context, and how closely related the disambiguated readings remain. What lesson is to be drawn from the apparent stalemate between well-founded gradualist or 'assimilationist' and well-founded 'differentialist' claims about animal mentality? I suggest that, if we reckon with linguistic ambiguity, particularly with Aristotle's *pros hen* ambiguity, and with 'transformative' interpretations of the anthropological difference, the original question should be revisited. Differentialists, we have heard, 'maintain that there are crucial qualitative differences separating us from animals', while assimilationists 'maintain that the differences are merely quantitative and gradual'.[32] Now what exactly is the difference between a vast gradual difference and a qualitative difference? Is this a well-defined alternative? Linguistically, what exactly is the difference between a highly general term with a broad and heterogeneous range of

---

[29] There is no noun that corresponds to the adjective 'political', either in Greek or in English, as Frede (Chapter 13, 259) observes.

[30] Christof Rapp suggested this reading to us. For further interpretations of this key passage for Aristotle's anthropology, see McCready-Flora (Chapter 2), Karbowski (Chapter 11), and Depew (Chapter 12).

[31] This might be due to positions people take on the moral status of other animals. But these normative issues call for a separate treatment. Being either an assimilationist, a differentialist, or a transformation theorist about the anthropological difference does not commit one to any particular position in animal ethics, and vice versa.

[32] Glock, Chapter 7, 143.

Introduction 13

application, and a slightly polysemous term? Can any linguist or philosopher of language tell? Is there a fact of the matter?

Natural languages, including ancient Greek, do not harbour enough common nouns to express the fine-grained distinctions between closely related mental faculties that are sorely needed in the philosophy of animal minds. Expressions such as *agency, intention, imagination, belief, memory,* or *consciousness* are not discriminate enough for the purpose of distinguishing human from non-human abilities. Arguably, our inherited mentalistic vocabulary is tailor-made for the fully developed phenomenon: for the mental capacities and performances of adult specimens of our species. All cases that fall short of that paradigm — infants, non-human animals, artificially intelligent robots – put us in a quandary. This is why the philosophical and psychological literature on animal mentality bristles with modifier phrases such as 'rudimentary kinds of', '(not) in a full-blown sense', 'preliminary stages of', 'at least simple forms of', and the like, as well as with comparatives like 'to a higher degree' or 'to a lesser extent'. These modifiers and comparatives grade the degree of possession of mental abilities, and of the applicability of the respective predicates.

Assimilationists often invoke the fact that most if not all mental abilities come in degrees. According to the transformation thesis, however, differences between human and non-human animals' abilities can be gradual in one sense, while being substantial in another. They appear gradual as long as the same ordinary word – *perceive, act, remember,* etc. – is used for both human and non-human abilities and performances. They appear substantive or qualitative when we disambiguate the word and individuate more finely the different *concepts* that the word expresses.

Now, assimilationists deny precisely that mental predicates express different concepts when applied to humans and to other animals. Glock finds it 'absurd to deny *tout court* that higher animals endowed with sense-organs are capable of perception', and to endorse 'as-ifness' about animal perception. These formulations, however, slightly misstate the issue. 'Transformative differentialists', as Glock aptly calls them, will readily grant that the concepts remain closely related. It is no orthographic coincidence that we call both human and non-human perception 'perception', and yet, we are not referring to precisely the same capacity. While all perceivers share 'the capacity to gather information about the proximal and distal environment with the aid of sense-organs',[33] a kind of perception that gives rise to perceptual judgements with propositional contents, or to

---

[33] Ibid., 156.

the apprehension of forms, is qualitatively different from a kind of sensory experience that does not.

Still, it would seem that the transformation thesis does not represent a conciliatory position, arbitrating between assimilationism and differentialism, but in fact amounts to differentialism, even to a strong form of it. Surely it does in the Pittsburghian 'transformative differentialism' that Glock's criticism primarily targets. Transformative differentialism, though, is not committed to this particular version. It doesn't have to think of non-human perception as some kind of 'as-if perception', for example. For, saying that non-human animals perceive things in a slightly (or not so slightly) different sense of 'perception' is compatible with granting that they do perceive things, rather than just 'as-if-perceive' them. And so in the form presented here, the transformative differentialist's disagreement with a tenable form of assimilationism appears quite subtle, given that Glock himself grants that '[p]erceiving *amounts* to something different in conceptual and non-conceptual subjects. It has different preconditions and implications . . .. But this does not imply that "perception" *linguistically means* something different in the two cases'.[34] This is where the matter stands: assimilationists who are alive to different implications of ascribing mental capacities object that transformative differentialists go further in diagnosing subtle ambiguities of the respective mental predicates. I predict that, at the end of the day, when all of the findings from animal psychology are in, much of the dispute between assimilationism and differentialism will boil down to sophisticated semantic questions of ambiguity, of linguistic vs. non-linguistic implications, focal vs. non-focal meaning, the thin line between highly general and polysemous terms, and semantic vagueness.

In order to seriously attribute the transformation thesis to Aristotle, one would have to examine closely how differences between species 'with respect to the more and less' (*to mallon kai hētton*) relate to correspondences 'by analogy' (*HA* I 1, 486a26–b8 and 486b17–21). One would have to take into account his treatment of analogy in the *Organon*, his discussion of *pros hen* ambiguity[35] and his frequent use of phrases such as '(not) in the proper sense' (*kurios, haplos*). Exploiting Aristotle's systematic treatment of analogies, ambiguities, continuities, and other challenges to clear-cut classifications is, I suggest, a promising route to a more thorough

---

[34] Ibid., 156.
[35] See for example *Cat.* I, 1a1–15; *SE* 4; *Met.* IV, 2, 1003a34–b19; *Poet.* 21, 1457b7–34.

Introduction 15

assessment of his views on the anthropological difference. The task is worthwhile, but beyond the scope of this brief introduction.

Let us finally turn to the issue of *vagueness*, which is all too often neglected in discussions of the anthropological difference and the transformation thesis. Vague terms, it is said, draw no sharp boundary between their extension and their anti-extension. They tolerate marginal changes, admit of borderline cases, and give rise to the paradox of the heap – i.e. the paradox that you can 'prove', by a series of incremental arguments (if 1,000 grains of sand make up a heap, then so do 999 grains, as do 998, etc.), that a single grain of sand makes up a heap. The problem with soritical reasoning is that the conclusion is patently false, while it is notoriously difficult to pinpoint the fallacy, or the source of the paradox.

It is tempting to build an argument for assimilationism on the insight that cognitive abilities come in degrees. Briefly reflecting on soritical vagueness, however, should make us resist the temptation. Continuity as such, nowadays buttressed by an appeal to biological evolution, does not speak for assimilationism any more than the existence of borderline cases speaks for the non-existence of clear cases. The lesson to be drawn from the Sorites paradox is that the non-existence of a sharp cut-off is compatible with the existence of clear cases. The difference in cognitive abilities between amoebae and humans is as clear as can be. Obviously, continuity in the *scala naturae* and smoothness of transition, up to virtual indistinguishability between neighbouring elements in a Sorites series, can go along with striking differences between beginning and end points. Technically speaking, similarity is not a transitive relation. Tiny differences can 'add up' to significant ones, even if the cases are all-too-similar when presented pairwise. The differences in mental capacities between humans and other higher animals might be a case in point, given that our closest relatives in the animal kingdom are extinct. Aristotle did not need Darwin to notice and to be impressed by the natural continuities between species. And he was well aware that the existence of borderline cases does not speak against the existence of clear cases. He was duly, but not overly impressed by natural continuities, not taking his observation that 'nature passes continuously from soulless things into animals' (*PA* IV 5, 681a11–12, transl. Lennox) as a reason to overthrow his tripartite classification of plants, animals, and humans.

Now, unlike the classical examples of vague predicates ('heap', 'bald', 'red'), mental predicates do not merely exhibit vagueness *of degree* along one dimension. They exhibit *multidimensional* or *combinatory* vagueness as well, i.e. 'indeterminacy as to just what combination of conditions is

16 GEERT KEIL AND NORA KREFT

sufficient or necessary for the application of the term'.[36] Combinatorially vague terms have multiple conditions of application, and the question of which properties an object must possess in order to fall under the term has no definite answer. For example, is it true to say that a robot 'perceives' its environment if its electro-optical sensors enable it to react differentially to changes in its surroundings? Some answer in the affirmative, others in the negative. Here is where the transformation thesis comes into play: in their natural habitat, mental abilities do not come along one by one, but always in combination. Perceptual skills are embedded in a living being's species-specific profile of further abilities. These abilities interlock with each other, both factually and conceptually. In humans, exercising mental abilities is 'informed by reason' (if you let me get away with this turn of phrase), to the effect that 'lower' abilities are characteristically transformed into modes that other animals, let alone artefacts, do not share in a strict sense. If we keep using the linguistic expression, the slight transformation of its meaning, and the concept it expresses, may go unnoticed. This is why the deceptively simple either/or question of whether an amoeba is capable of perception is ill-defined, as is the question of whether a certain difference in a mental ability is either gradual or substantial.

Or so the transformation thesis says. One must of course argue for (or against) its exegetical adequacy and its fruitfulness on a case by case basis, as some chapters in this book do.

4 Overview

The book is organised into four parts, two of which deal with the metaphysics and biology of human nature, while the other two discuss the anthropological foundations and implications of Aristotle's ethico-political works.[37]

4.1 Human Beings as Rational Animals

The chapters in the first part deal with fundamental and definitional questions in Aristotle's anthropology. Does he ever actually define what a human being is? Which of the specifically human traits he mentions are essential and which ones accidental? What is it to be a rational animal? Did

---

[36] Alston (1964, 87–88).

[37] This overview is partly extracted from the chapters' introductory or summarising sections, hence makes ample use of the contributors' own wording.

Introduction   17

Aristotle endorse both a 'lingualist' conception of rationality and a rationalist conception of language? How are we to understand his view that the active intellect comes from outside (*thyrathen*) and partakes in the divine? Does the idea of a 'rational animal' ultimately make sense within his theoretical framework?

In the opening chapter, Christian Kietzmann observes that, although Aristotle often mentions rationality as a differentiating characteristic of human beings, he nowhere defines the essence of what it is to be human in these terms and offers no systematic treatise on human nature. This is no accident, argues Kietzmann, for given Aristotle's requirements for definitions, there can be no such thing as a unified definition of what it is to be human. For Aristotle, human beings are ontologically divided. They belong to two distinct realms and must be investigated by two different kinds of sciences. There is no common ground, argues Kietzmann, between the zoology of human animals and the theological metaphysics of rational beings, hence no place for a systematic anthropological treatise in Aristotle.

Ian C. McCready-Flora also proceeds from the formula *zōon logon echon*: 'Tracing what, in Aristotle, separates humans from other animals (what makes us *the* rational animal) leads one straight to *logos*', he observes. *Logos*, however, is a highly ambiguous term. McCready-Flora explores the exact relationship between rationality and human speech in Aristotle. His main thesis is that the relationship is less intimate than often assumed. He argues that Aristotle regards the faculty of speech as a *means* deployed to serve rational cognition, and that being merely a means bars speech from being the rational-making feature. Still, language is not *incidental* to the rational soul. Humans have it, according to McCready-Flora's interpretation, for the same reason animals have senses and mental capacities – it helps them live well.

Elena Cagnoli Fiecconi's chapter examines Aristotle's view of the peculiarly human psychology by locating human cognition between animal and divine cognition. Humans share a non-rational part of the soul and non-rational cognitive faculties with non-human animals, and they share a rational part of the soul and rational cognitive faculties with god. What makes human cognition unique, according to Cagnoli Fiecconi's reading of Aristotle, is that the rational and the non-rational parts of the soul coexist and cooperate in human souls. The example of imagination (*phantasia*) illustrates the transformative effects of such cooperation. Cagnoli Fiecconi further explains how this cooperation meets the 'peculiarity criterion' in Aristotle's ethics, according to which ethicists and political scientists should focus on aspects of the soul that are peculiarly human: the peculiarly human psychology, interpreted along the lines she suggests, meets the peculiarity criterion, because the rational and non-rational parts of the human soul are built to cooperate.

Christof Rapp adds an original perspective on the position of human cognition sandwiched between animal and divine cognition. He draws attention to a passage in Aristotle's *De Caelo* that is not intended to address anthropological questions, but rather unfolds a comparison between celestial bodies and living beings. According to Rapp, the passage reveals some of Aristotle's deep presuppositions about the position of human beings in the cosmos. The speculative analogy Rapp explores is this: of all celestial bodies, it is the planets whose nature is most akin to that of humankind. Just as the earth and its immediate cosmic neighbours cannot attain the highest good, i.e. uniform, regular, eternal, circular movement, human beings cannot attain their highest good, i.e. continuous excellent activity of the intellect. This analogy supports the diagnosis of an ambivalence of the human condition for which there is also independent textual evidence: compared with plants and non-human animals, humans enjoy the privilege of having access to the divine realm and sharing the highest good. Owing to their complex nature, however, they have to struggle and to engage in manifold activities, just as the planets have to make complex movements, both with no chance of ever reaching the ideal.

4.2 Human Nature in the Light of Aristotle's Biology

The chapters in the second part assess the anthropological relevance of Aristotle's biological works. What is the connection between Aristotle's metaphysics of human beings and his observations about their biological design? Do the detailed physiological and psychological observations add up to identifying a *differentia specifica* of the human species? How are we to understand Aristotle's view that reason is not a proper object of zoological investigation, and how does it relate to his general 'gradualist' view that humans are part of the *scala naturae*? Which mental capacities do humans have in common with at least some non-human animals? Does Aristotle endorse a 'transformative' approach to the human–animal difference, according to which our rational faculties alter the nature of the lower mental capacities that we only seemingly share with other animals?

James G. Lennox begins by focusing on a tension within Aristotle's anthropological views. On the one hand, Aristotle includes humans as an integral part of his comparative zoological study of all animals. On the other hand, he claims that our most distinctive features, the capacity to reason and deliberate, are not proper subjects for the science of nature (*PA* I 1). Lennox argues that this tension is only apparent given that Aristotle restricts the mandate of the natural scientist to investigating natural *kinēsis* and *genesis*. Reason cannot be studied naturalistically because it is not the source of any of the three sorts of natural change Aristotle distinguishes. Still, the systematic study of human beings plays a central role in Aristotle's zoological investigations, Lennox argues, as a standard of comparison in a number of respects that he discusses in turn. One of his results is that, for Aristotle, even being a political animal in the sense described in the opening chapters of the *Politics* is a broadly 'biological' category.

Jörn Müller's chapter aims at 'unearthing the hidden philosophical anthropology in Aristotle's biology'. Müller discusses three challenges to the project of (re-)constructing an overarching philosophical anthropology from Aristotle's comparative zoological observations: first, no collection of random information on human physiology and psychology will amount to a definition of human essence; second, Aristotle's biological gradualism challenges the search for a qualitative difference that sets humans apart from all other animals; and, third, vital parts of the latter enterprise seem to be beyond the reach of the biological writings (which was Lennox's concern as well). Müller argues that these challenges can be met if we take into account Aristotle's *teleological essentialism*, according to which a biological species' functions (*erga*) permeate both its physical make-up and its way of life, including the particularly human task of actively leading a *good* life, as described in the ethico-political works. The picture that emerges is one of a functionally ordered interplay of various differences that contribute to human flourishing, instead of one big anthropological difference that Aristotle does not offer.

Hans-Johann Glock discusses the contributions Aristotle has made to a field known today as 'the philosophy of animal minds': do at least some non-human animals have minds comparable to those of humans? Glock's main focus is on a substantive philosophical issue that cannot be answered via exegesis of the primary texts, i.e. the question of whether Aristotle got animal minds *right*. Glock argues that Aristotle's legacy is ambivalent as regards its merits. On the positive side, Aristotle recognised that humans are animals, established a 'capacity approach' to the mind, adequately described numerous important similarities and differences between human and non-human animals, and was alive to the special character of human societies. On the negative side, Aristotle and/or his disciples overestimated the importance of language, confined the mind proper to the intellect, and incoherently denied belief to higher animals while crediting them with perception. Glock also takes issue with the 'transformative' approach to the anthropological difference inspired by Aristotle, on grounds that it leads to an absurd 'as-ifness' about animal perception.

4.3 Aristotle's Moral Anthropology

The third part of the book discusses Aristotle's conception of the good human life. What is specifically human 'goodness' and 'badness'? Can human beings achieve moral perfection or are they tragic figures who will ultimately fail in this pursuit? Why are human beings the only animals capable of proper *eudaimonia*? Why do they have to cultivate virtues in order to live well when other animals do not? Is friendship a uniquely human relationship, and why do humans need friendship in order to be *eudaimon*?

Kathi Beier argues that the common and popular functionalist reading of Aristotle's conception of virtue is a misreading. Instead, she claims that Aristotle presents a non-functionalist, psychological conception. According to Beier, Aristotle thinks of virtue primarily as *human* virtue, meaning that only human virtue is virtue in the real sense of the term. The so-called virtues of other things, including those of other animals, are at best virtues by analogy. For Beier, this marks a crucial difference, not only between Aristotle's and Plato's respective conceptions of virtue, but also between Aristotle and some of his successors in modern virtue ethics.

Nora Kreft argues that, according to Aristotle, only human beings are capable of what he considers to be 'proper' friendship. Other animals can have relationships that resemble proper friendship in some ways, but they also fall short of it in some central respects. She goes on to argue that being capable of proper friendship is not just a uniquely human feature, but an essential one insofar as having friends is part of what it is to actualise the human form for Aristotle. She claims that this is because, in order to actualise *nous*, human beings need to share *nous*-activities, and they can do so with and only with proper friends.

Christoph Horn wonders whether or not human beings can become perfectly good. Is Aristotle's paradigmatically virtuous agent someone who permanently and infallibly executes morally correct actions? Or does the *spoudaios* sometimes and/or to some extent perform imperfect, perhaps even evil deeds? If the latter, Aristotle's *spoudaios* would be close to Plato's figure of the *philosophos*. Contrary to a view recently developed by H. Curzer, Horn argues against the latter and in favour of the former

Introduction

position. According to him, Aristotle's view points in a Stoic direction, rather than a Platonic one. Human beings are not 'tragic' figures, but capable of real moral perfection. If we take into account that Aristotle uses '*spoudaios*' (as well as '*phronimos*', '*agathos*', and other terms he uses to refer to the perfectly virtuous agent) in more than one sense, we can explain the passages in which he seems to allow for imperfections in the *spoudaios*.

4.4 Aristotle's Political Anthropology

The fourth and final part is concerned with the anthropological foundations and implications of Aristotle's political philosophy. What is the difference between being merely a social animal and being a political one? What does Aristotle mean when he says that humans are more political than non-human animals? Is he using the same sense of 'political' in the *Politics*, the biological works, and the *Nicomachean Ethics*? Finally, what exactly is the 'philosophy of human affairs', and are human beings able to build the ideal *polis* or not?

Joseph Karbowski draws on Aristotle's biological works for further insights into his *Politics* and the conception of human nature contained therein. Karbowski takes Aristotle to be working with the same broad conception of politicality in the *Politics* that was introduced in *Historia Animalium*. And he argues that this conception has two important implications that have been overlooked in the literature: first, broad political species naturally divide into functionally distinct subgroups; second, the members of these subgroups exhibit natural morphological and psychological differences that are coordinate with their distinct roles in the community. One crucial benefit of this interpretation is that it renders intelligible Aristotle's postulation of psychological differences between human beings and illuminates the place of those who, in his view of human nature, he considers to be 'natural slaves' and 'women'. Read in this way, Aristotle's endorsement of the existence of natural slaves and women and his views about their abilities do not threaten the coherence of his conception of human nature, as has often been supposed. Instead, they betray his acceptance of a rather complex, hierarchical anthropological theory. (Still, it goes without saying that Aristotle's views on these matters are awfully mistaken for other reasons – metaphysical, biological, moral, etc. – and that we cannot nowadays accept his defence of natural slavery and the subjection of women.)

David J. Depew reconstructs key arguments of Aristotle's political theory as a dialogue with Plato's *Statesman*. He argues that viewing the

Politics in this light clarifies why Aristotle takes the *polis* to be the most authoritative, comprehensive, and complete of all human forms of association. The reason lies in the naturally end-like character of shared leisure-time activities. The *polis* alone can make the enjoyment of leisure possible for all citizens, and this is the very point of *polis* life: 'the polis does not exist only for the sake of living, but living well' (*Pol.* III 9, 1280a30–32) – it is the most end-like of ends. In Aristotle's eyes, Plato's political theory doesn't capture this, in part because Plato's way of applying the method of dichotomous division doesn't allow him to sufficiently distinguish between merely gregarious and political animals. In other words, according to Aristotle, Plato's political theory is based on a mistaken picture of human politicality.

Dorothea Frede argues that Aristotle doesn't share Protagorean worries that sociability is not part of the natural human endowment, and that the art of building communities is a supernatural gift that separates humans from other animals. But, even though Aristotle displays general confidence in the natural sociability of human beings, this does not mean that he regards the ordering of political communities as an easy task. Because there is no natural uniformity to the human *telos*, as there is in the case of other living beings, 'getting it right' cannot be taken for granted. In the *Politics*, Aristotle provides what, in the *Nicomachean Ethics*, he proclaims to be 'the master science of life' and the completion of the 'philosophy of human affairs'. He does not identify specific laws of ideal and less-than-ideal states, but he tries to outline their basic structures and principles. The political philosopher, according to Aristotle, does not compete with the legislator or statesman. Rather, his groundwork and his teaching will enable politicians to design the suitable laws and to rise to the task of ordering the community even in the face of the difficulties. Unlike Plato, Aristotle believes that building the ideal *polis* is an ultimately realistic goal for human beings.

PART I

Human Beings as Rational Animals

CHAPTER I

Aristotle on the Definition of What It Is to Be Human

Christian Kietzmann

According to a philosophical commonplace, Aristotle defined human beings as rational animals. When one takes a closer look at the surviving texts, however, it is surprisingly hard to find such a definition. Of course, Aristotle repeatedly stresses that he regards rationality as the crucial differentiating characteristic of human beings, but he nowhere defines the essence of what it is to be human in these terms. What is more, Aristotle's abundant remarks about human nature are scattered throughout his texts, and he offers no systematic treatise on human beings.

In this chapter, I will argue that this is no accident, and that the two facts are linked: Human being as an object for systematic explanation simply doesn't fit neatly into Aristotle's conception of the sciences: no single science covers the essence of human being. And, since definitions fix the basic terms for each science and serve as explanatory principles within them, it follows that 'human being' cannot be defined.

This is how I will proceed: I will first argue that Aristotle nowhere defines human essence (Section 1), and then I will say a few words about the place of definitions in Aristotle's thought more generally (Section 2). In light of these remarks and Aristotle's statements about uniquely human characteristics and their explanation, I will identify the most likely candidate for such a definition (Section 3). However, it will turn out that, by Aristotle's lights, humans cannot be defined in this way because human being belongs to two completely different ontological realms and, therefore, must be investigated by two different kinds of sciences: humans as animals are investigated by physics and, more particularly, by zoology, whereas humans as rational beings are investigated by theology (Section 4). I will then explain what qualifies the human intellect as a subject of inquiry for theology (Section 5). Finally, I will draw the conclusion that, for Aristotle, humans are ontologically divided and that, therefore, there can be neither a science of humanity nor a unified definition of what it is to be human (Section 6).

25

1 Does Aristotle Anywhere Define Human Being?

I begin with the question of whether there are passages in which Aristotle defines human being as a rational animal, or rational living being – as a *zōon logon echon*. The main contender for such a passage is a famous text from the beginning of the *Politics*. Here, Aristotle employs the formula and uses it to explain an otherwise puzzling human characteristic. This is the passage usually invoked when a definition of humans as rational animals is ascribed to Aristotle:

> Now, that man is more of a political animal than bees or any other gregarious animals is evident. Nature, as we often say, makes nothing in vain, and man is the only *zōon logon echon*. And whereas mere voice is but an indication of pleasure or pain, and is therefore found in other animals (for their nature attains to the perception of pleasure and pain and the intimation of them to one another, and no further), the power of *logos* is intended to set forth the expedient and inexpedient, and therefore likewise the just and the unjust. And it is a characteristic of man that he alone has any sense of good and evil, of just and unjust, and the like, and the association of living beings who have this sense makes a family and a state. (*Pol.* I 2, 1253a7–18)[1]

According to Aristotle, there are many gregarious animal species, such as horses and cows, and some among them form associations, such as bees, ants, and humans. However, the associations formed by humans are unique in that they are held together by a shared sense of justice and a shared awareness of the common good that is served by this association. This shared sense and awareness is made possible by human *logos*, which is likewise unique to human beings. So, for Aristotle, what explains the characteristic and unique form of sociality that we find in human life, i.e. families and states, is another uniquely human property, the possession of *logos*. Only man is a *zōon logon echon*, and, therefore, only man is a *zōon politikon* and a *zōon oikonomikon* in the specific sense of these terms that is characteristic of human beings: they alone live in city-states and proper households.[2]

Does this passage prove that Aristotle defined human beings as rational animals? I don't think so, for two reasons. First, he doesn't talk about reason or rationality here, but rather about speech. Aristotle explicitly contrasts human *logos* with mere voice. The sound-making of non-human species is

---

[1] Unless otherwise noted, Aristotle's works are cited from Barnes's *Revised Oxford Translation*.
[2] Compare Cooper (1990) and (2010) for a lively description of the specific way in which humans share goals and, therefore, form communities of kinds unheard of among other animal species.

merely expressive, indicating pleasure and pain. But indicating these states is not yet communication; it is no exchange of ideas. By contrast, human speech transports concepts, and makes possible the exchange and the sharing of ideas, such as conceptions of what is good and evil, and what is just and unjust. So the distinction Aristotle is interested in is that between animal voice and human speech. And, while speech and reason are closely related to one another, for speech articulates conceptually structured thoughts, they are, nonetheless, different things.[3]

My second reason for doubting that our passage offers a definition of humans as rational animals is that the formula of man as *zōon logon echon* does not seem to be intended as a definition. All Aristotle says is that *logos* is unique to humans, and that it is a feature that can explain another characteristic feature of humans, namely their specific sociality. He nowhere claims that the explanatory feature amounts to a definition – that it lays down *what it is to be human*.[4] It is more plausible to assume that, here, Aristotle is pointing out a characteristic (*idion*) property of humans and uses it to explain another characteristic property. And, although every defining property is *idion*, not every *idion* property is part of a definition. It may be something that itself stands in need of further explanation. If these considerations are legitimate, it is doubtful whether our text is evidence for the thesis that Aristotle defined humans as rational animals.

Furthermore, there are several passages in Aristotle's logical and metaphysical works where he does state a definition of what it is to be human. However, in those passages Aristotle consistently defines humans as two-legged animals.[5] One such text is from book VII of *Metaphysics*, in which Aristotle, in the course of bringing up the question of the unity of essence and definition, gives the example of human beings:

> Wherein consists the unity of that, the formula of which we call a definition, as for instance in the case of man, two-footed animal; for let this be the formula of man ... [T]he differentiae present in man are many, e.g. endowed with feet, two-footed, featherless. Why are these one and not many? (*Met.* VII 12, 1037b11–23)

---

[3] See McCready-Flora (Chapter 2) for further discussion of this passage in *Pol* I 2 and the relation between speech and rationality in Aristotle.

[4] In *EE* VII 10, 1242a22f, Aristotle talks of man as both *zōon politikon* and *zōon oikonomikon*. It is obvious that this cannot be intended as a fundamental definition of human essence.

[5] These passages include: *Cat.* V, 3a9–15, 21–25; *DI* XI, 21a15; *APo* I 14, 79a29; I 22, 83b3; II 4, 91a28; II 5, 92a1; II 6, 92a29–30; II 13, 96b32; *Top.* I 7, 103a25–28; V 4, 133b8–11; *Phys.* I 3, 186b25–30; *PA* I 3, 644a5–11; *Met.* IV 4, 1006a32–b3; VII 12, 1038a4; VII 15, 1040a16.

For the purposes of his discussion, Aristotle provisionally defines man as a two-footed animal – provisionally, because what he says, as he is careful to point out, is to be understood as a stipulation that will serve as an example, and not as his last word on the matter. Furthermore, he adds that the human has many differentiae, i.e. distinguishing features that somehow enter into the definition, not merely two-footedness, but also footedness and featherlessness. When they enter properly into a definition, these features somehow form a unity with the other parts of the definition. The essence to be captured is one, a unity, and, therefore, the parts of the definition taken together must likewise form a unity, and not merely a list of many items. Aristotle's question is how they do this.[6]

What this passage has in common with the others in which Aristotle gives a definition of human beings is that Aristotle is concerned with logical and not with anthropological questions. The definitions he gives serve purely illustrative purposes. They are meant to provide examples for, e.g. his discussion of the question of the unity of definitions. It is, therefore, easy to think of them as *mere* examples which do not express any systematic commitment on Aristotle's part.[7] It is even tempting to take them as a joking, tongue-in-cheek reference to debates in Plato's academy.[8]

As we have seen, Aristotle doesn't define human beings as rational animals, and when he does state a definition, albeit as a logical example, he talks about humans as two-footed terrestrial animals. What does that mean? Why doesn't Aristotle define humans straightout as rational animals, as we have come to expect of him? At this point, someone may suggest that the only reason we don't find a definition of humans in Aristotle's texts is that he isn't interested in defining animal species.[9] Humans are then no exception, because Aristotle's scientific programme doesn't aim at defining species, and so isn't interested in defining humans either. However, there are good reasons to think, on the contrary, that Aristotle does have this aim. For instance, he criticises dichotomistic approaches to definition for their

---

[6] Compare his final solution to the problem in *Met.* VIII 6, 1045a7ff., where the example reappears.
[7] For such a reaction, compare Jansen (2010, 159–60).
[8] For Plato's definition of humans as featherless biped land-dwellers, see his *Statesman* 266e. According to Diogenes Laertios, Diogenes of Sinope reacted to this definition in the following way: 'Plato had defined Man as an animal, biped and featherless, and was applauded. Diogenes plucked a fowl and brought it into the lecture room with the words, "Here is Plato's man". In consequence of which there was added to the definition, "having broad nails"' (*LEP* VI 4).
[9] Pierre Pellegrin argues that Aristotle is interested in animal parts and not in animal species; see e.g. Pellegrin (1985). For a forceful refutation, compare Lloyd (1996, 54–55), and Lloyd (1991, 375–80).

Aristotle on the Definition of What It Is to Be Human

inability to give correct accounts of animal species.[10] There, he apparently approves in principle of the intention, finding fault only with the way it is pursued. What is more, given the close link between *to ti ēn einai* (essence) and *ousia* (substance), and Aristotle's consistent adherence to the thesis that *ousiai* are first and foremost individual animals, we should expect definitions of animal species, and not of single organs or organic systems, to be of ultimate interest in his zoology. And if Aristotle seeks to define animal species, we should expect him to define humans, given the central importance he confers to humanity in his zoology.[11]

Thus, we may conclude that it would be desirable for an Aristotelian scientist to give a definition of what it is to be human, even if Aristotle himself doesn't provide such a definition. So what could that definition be? As a first step towards an answer, let us clarify Aristotle's conception of definition.

2 Definition and Explanation

What role do definitions play in Aristotle's conception of science, and what does he demand of a good definition? For Aristotle, definitions have the form of a universal predication: they say that some attribute A belongs to all B, where A and B are concepts, and B is the concept of the species to be defined. Obviously, however, not every universal attribution to a species term is a definition of that term, but only an attribution that grasps the nature or essence of the species. In order to codify the *what it is to be* for a species, a proper definition must, therefore, fulfil some further requirements. Aristotle's remarks suggest the following four:

(a) Firstly, the terms of the definition must be *convertible*. A proper defining term A must be such that not only all Bs are A, but also all As are B. In other words, the terms A and B must be *coextensive*. Definitions must be extensionally adequate, i.e. the defining property must cover each and only those particulars that belong to the species to be defined.

(b) Secondly, the defining properties must be characteristic (*idion*) for the species in question. Not only must all Bs be A and *vice versa*, but this must hold of necessity. In other words, the terms A and B must be *necessarily coextensive*. This requirement ensures that an

---

[10] *PA* I 3, 642b30, 643a7, 643a17, 643b1–2, 644a10–11.
[11] Aristotle treats humans as models and points of comparison for other species; see *HA* I 6, 491a19–21 and *PA* II 10, 656a3–14.

explanation starting from a definition proceeds from the thing's nature and not just from some accidental property that all members of the species, and only these members, happen to have.

(c) Thirdly, the definition must have explanatory power,[12] for a definition encompasses those characteristic properties of a species that explain its other characteristic properties. Such an explanation – a demonstration (*apodeixis*) – shows that the characteristic properties to be explained belong to the species because of its essence or nature, and, therefore, with necessity.

(d) Fourthly, the terms of the definition must be taken from those that are characteristic of the science within which the definition is given. Aristotle thinks of sciences as sets of concepts that are hierarchically interrelated through explanatory syllogistic patterns. His idea seems to be that these bodies of concepts must be self-contained in order to be truly explanatory: sciences are concerned with specific kinds of objects, for which specific terms are required. Of course, there may be some overarching logical, metaphysical, methodological, and explanatory principles that recur in several sciences. Still, what makes a science *one* is its subject matter and the characteristic terms that are needed in order to properly grasp this subject matter.

These remarks show the importance for Aristotle of the explanatory function of definitions. He thinks of definitions as *archai*, as starting points, of scientific explanations. They are, as it were, the unexplained explainers within an Aristotelian science. We will later return to Aristotle's point that definitions are always in some sense relative to a single science.

From the central explanatory role of definitions derives a second, taxonomic function. By grasping the explanatory characteristics of a species, a definition systematically relates that species to other species. The definition codifies what the species in question has in common with other species and what distinguishes it from them. This is visible in the form a definition exhibits: on the one hand, it subordinates the species to a genus, thereby relating the species to other species that likewise fall under the genus; on the other hand, it demarcates the species in question from the other species falling under the same genus by means of specific properties that belong only to this species and not to the others. However,

---

[12] Compare *DA* II 2, 413a12–15: '[I]t is not enough for a definitional account to express as most now do the mere fact; it must include and exhibit the cause also'.

Aristotle on the Definition of What It Is to Be Human

both genus and specific difference – and thereby similarity and contrast – are supposed to form a unity in the definition, and the question of how this is possible is an important topic for Aristotle in his logical and metaphysical works.

When we ask how to define a species, the Aristotelian scientist must keep these requirements of definitions in mind. Aristotle considers the requirements of necessary extensional adequacy and of explanatory power to be especially useful. The scientist should first establish facts about which characteristic properties a given species possesses, and then try to come up with the best possible explanations for these facts. Definitions will then develop quite naturally: the essence of the species in question will consist in the explanatorily most basic and most pregnant properties of that species.[13] So, when we ask how to define human beings within an Aristotelian science, we should first identify the characteristic properties of human beings, and then establish an explanatory order among them.[14]

3 The *Idia* of Human Beings and Their Explanatory Order

What is *idion* for humans, according to Aristotle? There are numerous claims, scattered throughout his works, about the features that make humans unique in the animal kingdom, or that humans exhibit to the highest degree among all animal species. These include bodily features: for instance, only in humans is the belly hairier than the back (*HA* II 1, 498b20–21; *PA* II 14, 658a16–25); humans are the only animals with a proper face (*PA* III 1, 662b19–22; *HA* I 8, 491b9–11); and humans exhibit the greatest multiformity of parts (*PA* II 10, 656a3–14). But they also include specifically human activities: for instance, humans possess the most finely discriminating sense of touch (*DA* II 9, 421a20–22); only humans engage in thinking, calculation, and reasoning (*DA* III 10, 433a11–12, and *Met.* I 1, 980b26–27); and only humans act (*EE* II 6, 1222b18–20). These and the other features Aristotle mentions are material for a scientific understanding of human beings. Properties like these enter into explanations, either as *explananda* or as *explanantia*. And, in a complete scientific understanding of human beings, these explanations will form a hierarchical order, such that eventually certain characteristic properties of humans will explain, directly or indirectly, all the rest.

---

[13] This seems to be the message of Aristotle's programmatic remarks in *DA* I 1, 402b16–403a2.
[14] Aristotle explicitly remarks that humans are a species in *PA* I 1, 645b25.

32 CHRISTIAN KIETZMANN

What explanatory patterns emerge? A central class of explanations concerns bodily features, which are explained as realising soul functions. The idea is that bodily parts are designed in such a way that they serve a certain function, and serve it best. The kind of necessary connection that underwrites functional explanation is hypothetical necessity: a property A is hypothetically necessary for all B if some end C can only be attained for Bs (i.e. if Bs can only be C) if A belongs to all B.[15] For instance, a saw can only fulfil its function of sawing if it is made of hard and sharp material like iron. Only if the property of being made of such material belongs to all saws can the property of being able to saw also belong to them.[16] Aristotle seems to think that *idion* properties of bodies can usually be understood as serving one function or another: a heuristic principle of his science of nature is that 'nature makes nothing in vain'.[17]

I will discuss in greater detail one interesting example of an explanation of specifically human bodily design in terms of function. This example is Aristotle's explanation of humans' upright posture through their divine nature and essence, which consists in their ability to understand and think. Here is the relevant passage in full:

> Mankind . . ., instead of forelimbs and forefeet has arms and what are called hands. For it alone of the animals is upright, on account of the fact that its nature and substantial being are divine; and it is a function of that which is most divine to understand (*noein*) and to think (*phronein*). But this is not easy when much of the body is pressing down from above, since the weight makes the intellect and the common sense sluggish. For this reason, when their weight and bodily character becomes excessive, it is necessary that their bodies incline towards earth, so that for stability nature placed forefeet beneath the four-footed animals, instead of arms and hands. For it is necessary that all those able to walk should have two hind limbs, and such animals become four-footed because their soul is unable to bear the weight. (*PA* IV 10, 686a25–b2, transl. Lennox)

In accordance with Aristotle's usual explanatory pattern in terms of hypothetical necessity, this explanation has two parts: Aristotle first identifies a formal characteristic of humans, and then explains their upright posture as hypothetically necessary for realising this form. The formal characteristic is

---

[15] Hypothetical necessity is introduced in *Phys.* II 9 and *PA* I 1 and helpfully discussed by Cooper (2004).

[16] The example of the saw occurs in *Phys.* II 9, 200a10–12, a similar one of an axe in *PA* I 1, 642a9–11.

[17] The principle that 'nature makes nothing in vain' is fundamental and pervasive in Aristotle's physical writings: *Resp.* 10, 476a11–15; *PA* III 1, 661b18–25; *IA* 2, 704b12–17; *GA* II 5, 741b4; *GA* V.8, 788b20–25; *Pol.* I 2, 1253a8–9.

Aristotle on the Definition of What It Is to Be Human 33

that human nature or substantial being, i.e. what it is to be a human being, is divine. In other words, humans are not merely one animal species among many others and, thus, the subject matter of a natural scientific understanding. They have another side beyond their animality, for they are divine, and this is what characterises them formally or substantially. Their divine nature or essence is evident in the fact that they engage in understanding and thought.

Now, what must be the case for this to be possible? How must humans be arranged, physiologically speaking, such that they can understand and think? Aristotle seems to believe that a necessary physiological precondition for understanding and thinking is that not too much weight presses down on the heart. However, the details of this claim are difficult to understand and only intelligible in light of some background assumptions Aristotle states elsewhere. Here is an interpretation of what Aristotle might have had in mind: He thinks that understanding requires *phantasmata*, mental images. He repeatedly stresses that we 'never understand without *phantasmata*' because 'the *noētikon* understands the forms in *phantasmata*'.[18] This needn't mean that understanding *consists* in the exercise of *phantasia*. In fact, it cannot mean that, because *phantasmata* are *kinēseis*, and Aristotle denies that understanding consists in a *kinēsis*.[19] However, the occurrence of *phantasmata* can, nevertheless, be a *precondition* of the activity of understanding. For Aristotle, understanding what, say, a triangle is entails being able to imagine a triangle and conceive of that imagined triangle in a certain way: you think of it as a paradigm of triangularity, and thus as standing in for the *eidos* of triangles (*Mem.* 1, 449b32–450a6). *Phantasmata* come from the *phantastikon*, the part of the soul responsible for imagination, which is part of the *aisthētikon* or perceptual part of the soul. The organ with which the *phantastikon* is correlated is the heart (*PA* II 1, 647a25–b8).[20] So Aristotle's idea seems to be that, when too much weight presses on the heart, the *phantastikon* which has its seat there is impeded in its operation and becomes tardy.[21] And since understanding and thinking depend on imagining, understanding and thought are impeded, too. To avoid this, there must be little weight pressing on the heart. In animals with a bulky body above the heart, thinking and understanding are seriously impeded, so much so that they seem to lack understanding

---

[18] *DA* III 7, 431a14–18; III 7, 431b3–4; *Mem.* 1, 449b32–450a1. See also *DA* III 8, 432a9–10.
[19] Compare *DA* III 3, 428b11–12: '*Phantasia* seems to be some kind of *kinēsis*'. For the denial, see Section 5.
[20] For the heart's role in perception, compare Lloyd (1978, 222–24).
[21] Compare his explanation for why we fall asleep at *PA* II 7, 653a10–19.

34 CHRISTIAN KIETZMANN

altogether; and because of the bulkiness of their upper parts, these parts incline towards the ground, which is why these animals have four feet.[22] By contrast, humans have a light upper body, which is further propelled upwards by heat coming from the heart, so that the body's weight doesn't press down too much.[23] Thus, humans have an upright posture.

This is one important example of how Aristotle thinks the functions of the human body's parts account for their design. These functions are fixed by the different capacities for life activities whose unity is the human soul. Is there an explanatory hierarchy among these activities? If so, we need to look to the highest activities, i.e. to those on which all the others depend, in order to establish what humans first and foremost are.

In *Nicomachean Ethics* I, Aristotle distinguishes between two parts of the soul, one which has *logos* and one which does not. The non-rational part is common to all animals, both human beings and other animal species. It comprises faculties of sensation and locomotion, as well as the nutritive powers of growth and digestion (*EN* I 7, 1097b34–1098a6).[24] Aristotle elsewhere notes that the presence of higher faculties in a species imply the presence of the lower ones. For instance, beings with a perceptual capacity will also have nutritive capacities, presumably because the latter stand in the service of the former by providing for the necessary preconditions of their exercise.[25]

According to *EN* VI, the rational part also has two parts of its own: the *epistēmonikon*, which is concerned with theoretical understanding and aims at truth and knowledge, and the *logistikon* or practical part, which is concerned with action, and aims at practical truth and a good life. The practical part of reason contains knowledge of how to produce things, that is, the different *technai* which enable their possessor to engage in *poiēseis* of this or that kind. However, since such productive actions are never chosen for their own sake, but are always supposed to contribute to a good life, the possession of *technai* depends on the possession of a further faculty,

---

[22] Aristotle sometimes ascribes *phronēsis* – which I have here translated as 'thought' – to animals other than humans. See Coles (1997) for an extended discussion and an (to my mind somewhat too) optimistic view of Aristotle's outlook on animal thought.

[23] As Aristotle had explained earlier on: 'This is also why human beings alone among animals are upright; for the nature of the prevailing heat produces growth from the middle according to its own movement' (*PA* II 7, 653a30–33, transl. Lennox).

[24] See also *DA* II 3 on the nutritive, the perceptive-locomotive, and the rational soul.

[25] Compare *DA* II 3, 414b28–415a14 for the containment relations among the different parts of the soul. Interestingly, Aristotle states that these containment relations hold for faculties up to and including those responsible for reasoning (*logismos*) and discursive thought (*dianoia*). However, he explicitly excludes the intellect: 'The consideration of theoretical *nous* is another matter' (*DA* II 3, 415a12–13).

Aristotle on the Definition of What It Is to Be Human

practical wisdom (*phronēsis*), which enables their possessor to deliberate and choose with a view to correct ends. The theoretical part of reason contains bodies of material knowledge about different subject matters, e.g. physics or theology, which have the explanatory structure described in *Posterior Analytics*. Such understanding knowledge depends in turn on having insight into the essences of the things the respective sciences deal with. Possessing such insight means to have understanding, i.e. to have an intellect (*nous*).[26] So within the two parts of the rational soul, we find a kind of hierarchical order. In the *logistikon*, *technai* are in the service of the good life, and thus are dominated or 'ruled' by *phronēsis*, which deliberates correctly about what is conducive to our good life. In the *epistēmonikon*, *epistēmai* depend on insight into the essences of the objects with which the sciences are concerned, and thus on *nous*.

In *EN* X 7, Aristotle famously announces that the two parts of the rational soul are ordered hierarchically. The activities of the *logistikon*, he argues, are inferior to the activities of the *epistēmonikon*. True being and the ultimately good life for human beings doesn't consist in the practical life, which is an exercise of *phronēsis* and ethical virtue, but in the theoretical life. It consists in the full activity of the highest part of the *epistēmonikon*, in the contemplation (*theōrein*) of the essences of things.

Given these hierarchical orders, we must say that all human life activities are ultimately in the service of contemplation. For this reason, *nous*, which is the human capacity that is fully exercised in contemplation, is ultimately the defining characteristic of what it is to be human. Every other human capacity must be understood as standing in the service of *nous*. This explains why Aristotle tries to account for many of the peculiar properties of the human body in terms of human rationality. Since the body serves as a tool for the soul, we should expect the possession of reason to have repercussions on how the human body is designed. As we have already seen, Aristotle explains human two-leggedness by means of hypothetical necessity through the intellect. Similarly, he explains the uniqueness of human hands by their serving as a tool of tools, and thus by human intelligence (*PA* IV 10, 687a2–687b23);[27] and he makes several rather speculative remarks about the human body as the most natural body, presumably because he thinks of it as serving as a tool for understanding, whose articulation in members somehow mirrors the objective world order revealed by *nous*.[28]

---

[26] For *nous* as the grasp of essences, compare Frede (1996) and (2008).
[27] Note, however, that Aristotle does not speak here of *nous*, but rather of *phronēsis*.
[28] See *PA* II 10, 656a9–14. Compare also *IA* 4, 706a19–20, and *HA* I 15, 494a26–494b1.

36   CHRISTIAN KIETZMANN

Given the role Aristotle assigns to definitions, and to *nous* when it comes to understanding what human beings are, we should expect Aristotle to define humanity as *zōon noon echon* – as the essence-grasping animal. However, as we will see in the next section, there are also strong reasons to think that such a definition is impossible within the framework of Aristotelian science.

4   Are Human Beings the Subject Matter of a Single Theoretical Science?

Recall Aristotle's requirement that definitions be given within one science employing terms that come from the body of concepts of this science, or from a superordinate science. Why does Aristotle require this? The unity of a science is achieved through the unity of the *genos* under which its terms fall (*APo* I 28, 87a36–38). And Aristotle insists that there are no genus-crossing demonstrations, i.e. no demonstrations that employ terms from different *genē*: 'One cannot ... prove anything by crossing from another genus – e.g. something geometrical by arithmetic' (*APo* I 7, 75a38–39). So we should expect a definition to contain only terms that fall under the *genos* delimiting the reach of the science in which that definition serves as a first principle.[29]

If there is a definition of what it is to be human, we must ask, then, for which science it serves as an explanatory starting point. In *Metaphysics* VI, Aristotle distinguishes between three kinds of theoretical science in accordance with their subject matter. His criteria for this distinction are whether the objects of the sciences are subject to change or not, and whether they are ontologically independent (*chōriston*) or dependent. This gives us three sciences: *physics* (or *natural science*) deals with changeable and ontologically independent objects, *mathematics* with unchangeable and ontologically dependent objects, and *theology* with unchangeable and onto-logically independent objects (*Met.* VI 1, 1026a7–23).[30]

A definition of human being would have to be a starting point for a science that corresponds with one of these three broadest sciences. No doubt

---

[29] However, Aristotle also stipulates an important qualification: sciences are hierarchically ordered through the containment-relations of their delimiting *genē* – there are subordinate and superordinate sciences. A subordinate science may be able to establish a fact, but unable to demonstrate why it holds of necessity, whereas a superordinate science may be unable to get hold of the relevant fact, but able to give a demonstration for it; compare *APo* I 13, 78b34–79a7.

[30] There is no science of changeable and ontologically dependent objects – in other words, there is no science of accidents. There cannot be such a science, because facts concerning accidents do not have the universality and necessity that is a precondition of scientific intelligibility.

Aristotle on the Definition of What It Is to Be Human 37

the most likely candidate here is physics. For one, humans are changeable objects – they are subject to change in the categories of substance (coming-to-be and passing-away), of quantity (growth), of quality (alteration, which occurs e.g. in perception) and of place (locomotion). And, second, humans are ontologically independent – they are proper substances and not accidents of substances, in the way that mathematical objects such as geometrical figures or quantities are. Does this mean we should expect a definition of humans in the science of physics? For this to be the case, all characteristic properties of human beings would have to be graspable by the definition of what it is to be human, and all these characteristics would have to be terms of a single science subordinate to physics.

However, Aristotle denies that all properties of human beings are investigated by physics. This comes out in a passage from the methodological treatise at the beginning of *De Partibus Animalium*. This is a work of physics, a work that deals with the bodily constitution of living beings and aims at explaining the properties of several different kinds of bodily organs through their function. Relevant functions are given in an account of the life activities that the organs are to serve. Such an account is an account of the soul. At one point, Aristotle wonders whether all of the soul is subject matter for natural scientific explanation. In other words, Aristotle wonders whether all life activities fall within the ambit of a science that investigates the being of changeable and ontologically independent objects:

> [O]ne might puzzle over whether it is up to natural science to speak about all soul, or some part, since if it speaks about all, no philosophy is left besides natural science. This is because intellect is of the objects of intellect, so that natural science would be knowledge about everything. For it is up to the same science to study intellect and its objects, if they truly are correlative and the same study in every case attends to correlatives, as in fact is the case with perception and perceptible objects. However, it is not the case that all soul is an origin of change, nor all its parts; rather, of growth the origin is the part which is present even in plants, of alteration the perceptive part, and of locomotion some other part, and not the rational; for locomotion is present in other animals too, but thought in none. So it is clear that one should not speak of all soul; for not all of the soul is a nature, but some part of it, one part or even more. (*PA* I 1, 641a33–641b9, transl. Lennox with alterations)

Here Aristotle gives two arguments for excluding *nous* from the study of the science of natures. First, to study *nous* means to study not only its capacity, but also its objects, i.e. the intelligible forms. This is so because the capacity of *nous* is in this respect similar to the capacity of perception: both are defined as what they are by their full activities, and the fully actualised exercise of these activities is identical with their objects.[31] According to this picture, humans have the capacity to understand the things around them, to grasp their essences, and, correlatively, these things have in them the potential to be understood, to be grasped with respect to what they are. To fully exercise one of these two capacities is at the same time to fully exercise the other. For a human being to understand the essence of a horse, say, is *ipso facto* for horses to be understood with respect to their nature or essence. But, if this is right, then *nous* and intelligible forms belong together in such a way that one cannot understand or investigate *nous* in its full activity without at the same time investigating the essences grasped by it. And, if to understand *nous* is to understand it in its full activity, we cannot understand it fully without understanding all intelligible forms, i.e. without understanding everything there is. Therefore, if *nous* were a proper object of natural scientific investigation, natural science would be a science of everything – which would be, as Aristotle seems to think, plainly absurd. So natural science cannot be concerned with *nous*.

Aristotle's second argument presupposes that natures are origins of change and rest. Therefore, only those parts of soul that are principles of change can reasonably be investigated by natural science. But not all of the soul is a principle of change. The changes living things undergo are growth, alteration, and locomotion. These are respectively located in the vegetative, perceptive, and, as we might say, locomotive parts of soul. But *nous* overlaps with none of them. It is not an origin of change, because it is not responsible for growth, alteration, or locomotion, and that for which it is responsible, namely theoretical understanding, is not a change at all.[32] Therefore, *nous* is not a nature in Aristotle's sense, and thus no proper object of natural science.

That *nous* is not a topic for physics follows from the nature of thought: one cannot understand thinking without its object, and thinking is not a change. Since *nous* is not an ontologically dependent object, like the abstract objects of geometry, it is not a topic for mathematics either.[33]

---

[31] I take this to be the message of the difficult passages in *DA* III 4–5, where Aristotle works on the assumption that the perceptual grasp of perceptible properties as it had been laid out in the preceding chapters can serve as a model for understanding the intellectual grasp of intelligible forms.

[32] Aristotle makes and defends this claim in *Phys.* VII 3, 247b1–248a9.

[33] Aristotle explains the ontological dependence of mathematical objects in *Met.* XIII 1–3.

Aristotle on the Definition of What It Is to Be Human   39

The only science that is left is theology: *nous* is a theological term insofar as it is unchanging and ontologically independent.[34] It is noteworthy that Aristotle here and elsewhere talks about *nous* as divine, ascribing divinity to humans because and insofar as they have *nous*. His thought must be this: humans are divine, and thus the proper subject matter for theology, *qua* their possession of *nous*.

5   Why Is *Nous* Divine?

But what is it that makes *nous* divine? Going by Aristotle's classification of the sciences, we can already say this much: *nous* is divine insofar as it is ontologically independent and not subject to change. But to what extent is *nous* independent and not subject to change? In his theological speculations in *Metaphysics* XII, Aristotle ascribes the properties of eternity and life to God (*ho theos*). As a living thing, God is ontologically independent; and, as an eternal being, God is not subject to change. In this context, Aristotle equates God's activity with thought thinking itself, and God thus with *nous*. But why should we think of *nous* as having these properties in the first place? And do the properties of ontological independence and unchangeability apply to *nous* in general, or only to divine *nous* and not to its finite human cousin?

Let us consider the first question. In *De Anima* III, Aristotle takes his account of perception as a model for understanding the activity of *noein*. According to this model, perceivers have a capacity to perceive (e.g. to see), to which corresponds a capacity in objects to be perceived (e.g. to be seen). When I see a red blotch on my shirt, my capacity to see is fully active; at the same time, the blotch's visibility is fully active. These activities are identical: there's only one activity of seeing, which is also the activity of being seen. When we apply this model to understanding, we obtain a similar structure. Thinkers have the capacity to grasp the essence of things, i.e. they have *nous*, to which corresponds a potentiality in objects to be understood with respect to their essence. Having an essence, Aristotle seems to think, means *ipso facto* being intelligible in this way. When the thinker understands the essence of an object, the thinker's *nous*, and the object's essence, are active together. This double activity is understanding (*noein*). The full activity of

---

[34] The importance of the ontological independence of *nous* might account for Aristotle's frequent worries about whether *nous* is detachable (*chōriston*) or not; cf. *DA* I 1, 403a8; I 4, 408b18–25; II 2, 413b4–24; II.3, 415a12; *GA* II 3, 736b21–28. That worry reflects the question of where *nous* is to be located in the Aristotelian taxonomy of sciences.

40 CHRISTIAN KIETZMANN

nous is therefore identical with the full activity of the intelligibility of things. And, since the intelligibility of a thing is its essence, and its essence is the thing's being, the full activity of *nous* is identical with the full activity of the being of the thing that is being understood (*DA* III 5, 430a20–21). In this sense, *nous* becomes everything that it understands. And since there are no limits to what *nous* can understand, in the way there are limits to what can be perceived, the fully active *nous* that manages to understand everything 'becomes everything' (*DA* III 5, 430a15). This result – that *nous*, when fully active, is *in some sense* identical with everything there is – is evidently intriguing for Aristotle. It must be a truly marvellous, divine thing that is able to achieve this feat!

The parallel between perceiving and thinking notwithstanding, Aristotle emphasises that thought differs from perception in a crucial respect: it is not a change. When you engage in the activity of perceiving, you change in some respect: perception is an alteration of sorts.[35] But when you engage in the activity of understanding something you do *not* change: knowledge and understanding are *not* alterations (*Phys.* VII 3, 247b1–248a9). *Nous*, whose being consists in understanding, thus fulfils Aristotle's first criterion for divine objects: it is beyond change.

Since understanding is not an alteration, it does not involve a material transaction between the thinker and her thought's object. Understanding, therefore, is not passive, being activated by something outside itself. It is self-activating (*DA* II 5, 417b24–25) or, as later philosophers put it: it is spontaneous. Where there is no material transaction, no medium is needed for interceding between a thinker and thought's object.[36] For the same reason, understanding need not involve an organ. And it better had not, because the material composition of sense organs inevitably limits what the sense can perceive; but understanding is unlimited (*DA* III 4, 429a18–27).[37] Given this threefold independence of understanding from objects different from itself – no activating object, no medium, and no organ – *nous* and its activity is in a supreme sense ontologically independent.

This answers the first question I introduced above, in what sense *nous* is beyond change and ontologically independent. Let us now return to the

---

[35] *DA* II 5, 416b34–35, and II 4, 415b24; compare also *DA* I 5, 410a25–26. For discussion, see Burnyeat (2002).

[36] However, in *DA* III 5 he mentions the active *nous* as an *analogue* to a medium in the case of understanding.

[37] Compare also *GA* II 3, 736b21–30. The provenance of this thought is Platonic: see *Theaetetus* 184d8–185e9, and also *Phaedo* 65d–67b for an argument to the effect that we cognise many things that cannot be perceived, and that the body is in fact a hindrance to proper thought (Plato, 1997).

Aristotle on the Definition of What It Is to Be Human   41

second question, whether every kind of *nous* is divine. This question is urgent because Aristotle seems to think that human *nous* and, therefore, human contemplation (*theōria*) differ from God's, as it were, pure or fully divine *nous* and *theōria* in several respects. Aristotle notes that humans contemplate only for limited stretches of time since they get tired, whereas God's intellect contemplates forever (*Met.* XII 7, 1072b14–26). In other words, for humans, there can be knowledge without contemplation, whereas for God's *nous*, knowledge and contemplation always go together. Presumably the reason humans get tired while thinking is that their contemplation depends on the imagination, and, therefore, indirectly on perception and memory, which are tied to a bodily organ, namely, the heart. So if the heart is suitably materially affected, this will have consequences for perception, memory, and *phantasia*, and, therefore, also indirectly for understanding. According to Aristotle, the heart's activity is prone to be affected by paralysis caused by certain vapours emanating from food. This paralysis is what we know as sleep.[38] So human understanding and contemplation, in contrast to God's, depends on imagination, thus on the heart as the central bodily organ of the perceptual–imaginative faculty, and, therefore, is prone to being impeded and even interrupted by sleepiness.

This point opens into a more general difference between human understanding and God's understanding. For Aristotle, human understanding comes in three levels of activity, whereas God's understanding is always fully active.[39] Humans are born with passive *nous*, a potential to acquire knowledge, which they actualise through learning or inquiry. In other words, they must be taught or must engage in inquiry and reasoning in order to acquire knowledge of definitions. This process of knowledge acquisition brings the first potentiality that is passive *nous* into the first activity that is habitual knowledge or understanding. But, even where such understanding is present, it is not always fully active in contemplation. Humans don't contemplate their knowledge about essences all the time, but only intermittently. That is to say, in humans the second potentiality that is habitual knowledge of essences is not always exercised in the second activity that is contemplation. By contrast, these distinctions collapse when we come to God's intellect, whose activity of being consists essentially in incessant fully actual contemplation.

---

[38] These vapours are first hot, which is why they ascend to the brain, where they are cooled, before descending again to the heart. For the physiology of sleep, compare *PA* II 7, 652b10–20 and *Somn.* III, 456a30–458a32.

[39] For the distinction of levels of actuality, see *DA* II 5, 417a22–b28 and the commentary in Burnyeat (2002). For the full activity of God's intellect, see *Met.* XII 9.

Do these differences between a human intellect and God's intellect undermine my point that, for Aristotle, human understanding is something that transcends our animal nature, that it is something divine? I don't think so, because the differences I have mentioned don't touch the salient features of *nous* which make it divine. Those features are shared by human *nous* and God's *nous* alike. Three things make *nous* in general divine: First, in understanding, a thing's intelligibility and a thinker's intellect are active together; in understanding everything, the intellect, thus, in a sense becomes everything. Second, understanding is not a change. Third, *nous* is in three senses ontologically independent: understanding is not activated by an external object, it does not presuppose a medium and it does not consist in the activity of some organ. All three of these features make *nous* divine, and they apply to both human intellects and God's intellect. We should, therefore, conclude that the former is divine in the same sense and to the same degree as the latter is.

6 There Cannot Be a Complete Definition of What It Is to Be Human

From the point of view of Aristotelian theoretical science, human being emerges as a kind of being that has each of its two feet in a different ontological domain – one in the realm of natures, and one in the divine realm of the intellect. Being ontologically divided in this way, human being apparently cannot be investigated by a single science. On the one hand, humans are studied as animals by natural science, which must remain silent concerning the divine side of humanity. On the other hand, humans are studied as intellects by theology, at the price of abstracting from their being embodied animals. This should be reflected in a definition of what it is to be human. There cannot be a unified definition that grasps everything in human essence. There can only be partial definitions: one of the intellectual side of what it is to be human, which is given in theology; and one of the animal side, which is given in physics, and more precisely in biology or zoology. Perhaps human being as two-footed animality is at least a plausible contender for the latter definition.[40] No

---

[40] Compare *IA* 4, 706a19–20, and *HA* I 15, 494a26–494b1, where Aristotle says that human bodies are 'most natural' because their directions are most articulated and mirror the objective directions of the universe. This includes the differentiation into left and right, upper and lower, and front and back, which is expressed in upright bipedity.

wonder, then, that Aristotle never wrote a treatise on humans, and that his remarks on humans are scattered throughout the Aristotelian corpus! For systematic reasons, there can be no Aristotelian science of humanity that takes into view humans as a whole. We, therefore, find nowhere in the Aristotelian corpus a unified definition of what it is to be human.[41]

[41] I presented earlier versions of this chapter at the Berlin conference on 'Aristotle's Anthropology' and at the Universities of Halle/Saale, Leipzig, and Marburg/Lahn. I am grateful to the audiences for valuable feedback and discussion. I would also like to thank Kathi Beier, Wolfgang Detel, Kosta Gligorijevic, Franziska Herbst, Geert Keil, Nora Kreft, Anselm W. Müller, Aaron Shoichet, and Christiane Turza for helpful comments on earlier drafts.

CHAPTER 2

Speech and the Rational Soul

Ian C. McCready-Flora

Aristotle embeds humans in the natural order, while also affirming human specialness. We differ much more from non-humans than they do from each other, and the difference lies in our *cognitive* capacities. Humans understand, deliberate, deduce ... the list goes on. These are not brute facts, but obtain in virtue of some feature of the human soul. What soul-feature, then, explains our cognitive specialness? Call it 'rationality'. Whatever it turns out to be, very likely it will not be what makes humans the *best* at this or that. Aristotle makes plenty of *those* claims as well. Humans are the smartest (*phronimōtatoi*), the most political, the most imitative.[1] Such comparisons presuppose something *shared*, a dimension along which we can make comparisons without homonymy or abuse of language.[2] Rationality might explain *some* human preeminence, but no preeminent-making feature will *thereby* be the rational-making feature. Our exquisite sense of touch, for instance, is one reason we are the smartest animal.[3] Touch is, however, the *animal-making* feature, not the rational-making one.

Nor will we find the answer among high-level *perfections* of reason: demonstrative knowledge, practical wisdom, grasping essential definitions, contemplating eternal truths. We share with god the comprehending soul (*nous, to noētikon*, etc.) that enables such achievements, and achieving them honours the god within.[4] All the more reason to set our sights lower:

---

[1] Smartest (for example): *DA* II 11, 421a19–23 (q.v. below at n. 3); *GA* II 6, 744a30–31; *PA* IV 10, 687a8–14 (q.v. below in main text). Most political: *Pol.* I 2, 1253a7 (q.v. below in main text). Most imitative: *Poet.* 4, 1448b6–9.

[2] See Labarrière (2005a) for this apt, but rarely-made observation.

[3] *DA* II 11, 421a19–23, abridged: '... and due to humans' having this sense [sc. touch] to the highest degree of precision ... and for this reason as well [humans] are the smartest animals'. All translations are my own.

[4] So *EN* X 8, 1177b30–35: 'If understanding [*nous*] is a thing divine compared to the human, so then will the life according to it be divine compared to human life. But we shouldn't heed those who bid us, because we are human, to think on human things, nor on mortal things because mortal, but instead to the extent possible make ourselves *immortal* and when it comes to living do everything according to what is strongest in us'.

Speech and the Rational Soul

Aristotle's account of the divine mind in *Metaphysics* Λ has little to say about human mental life. God forms no beliefs, reads no signs, deploys no reckoning. Human rationality, then, is absolutely unique. Beliefs in particular are piecemeal and fallible; thoroughly non-divine, yet still beyond any non-human. This makes belief and the like central to any accurate picture of rationality in Aristotle, who furthermore is at pains to distinguish belief from the imagining (*phantasia*) that accounts for intelligent behaviour in non-humans. This amounts to comparing the highest form of non-rational cognition to the lowest rational form. Tracing what restricts belief to humans also, therefore, traces the rational/non-rational divide. Knowing is divine, but it's believing that makes us human.[5]

Except maybe not. Tracking what, in Aristotle, separates humans from animals usually leads one to *logos*, and belief is no exception. The word has a broad semantic field, but language and speaking are central to it. There is reason to think *logos* denotes our ability to speak even where – *especially* where – it grounds human/animal distinctions.[6] Plato, often Aristotle's inspiration, yokes thought and talk: Timaeus calls *logos* (also *nous*) the immortal soul that sends *messages* down to the spirited part, while in the *Theaetetus* beliefs (*doxai*) represent asserted conclusions in a soul's discourse with itself.[7] Aristotle, furthermore, draws many of his rational/non-rational comparisons in rhetorical or speech-implicating terms.[8] So, if animals cannot form beliefs because they cannot be *persuaded*, and that because they lack *logos*, the right conclusion seems to be that the power of speech (or some facet thereof) is the rational-making feature, assuming that way of talking stays apt when *logos* denotes speech.[9]

---

[5] I pursue this line of inquiry in McCready-Flora (2013; 2014).

[6] Osborne (2007, 64–67) notes that language is central to our conception of the human, especially if linguistic prowess transforms our experience. See also the chapter on *logos* in Newmyer (2016).

[7] See *Tim.* 70b3–8, 71a3–5 and esp. *Tht.* 190a. Note however *Tim.* 37b3–8, where *logos* is 'carried along within what moves itself [sc. the immortal soul] *without speech or sound*' before, nonetheless, being 'proclaimed … in the entire soul'. The thought/talk connection, then, is messy in Plato as well.

[8] Examples: *Rhet.* I 10, 1370a25–28, where 'rational' (*meta logou*) desires are for what we get 'persuaded' to want; *EN* VII 2, 1145a31–1146b2, where the akratic cannot be 'persuaded' and the vicious person can, with resolution of the puzzle at *EN* VII 8, 1151a11–14 (also in rhetorical terms); and *DA* III 3, 427a18–24, where dumb beasts (*thēria*) cannot form beliefs because they cannot 'have been persuaded' (*tōi pepeisthai*), and this because they lack *logos*.

[9] This claim, whether as a conclusion, presupposition, or corollary, enjoys broad and influential agreement in the literature. Labarrière (1984, 30–34, with elaboration in Labarrière (1993b) and Wedin (1988, 150–57)) put the point most explicitly, but see also Osborne (2007), Newmyer (2016) and Anton (1995, 2–4), who collects some earlier references. Sorabji (1993) mentions the so-called rhetorical criterion for belief, tracing it to the work of Labarrière and Fortenbaugh. Foster (1997, 31) distinguishes the 'non-linguistic grouping together of sense-perception' that smart

46 IAN C. MCCREADY-FLORA

The present study rejects that conclusion from its strongest down to its weakest form. Strongest: the faculty of speech just *is* the rational-making feature. Weaker: one particular speech-relevant ability – manipulating convention-bound symbol systems ('symbolic prowess' for short) – is the rational-making feature. Weaker still: rational cognition depends on some speech-relevant ability, as a necessary condition, in its deployment. All such views are false: for Aristotle, *no* aspect of speech grounds or constitutes rationality. The argument:

(1) If something is a means deployed to serve rational cognition, then it is not the rational-making feature. (*a fortiori* from close reading of *On the Parts of Animals* IV 10.)

(2) Speech – including symbolic prowess – is a means deployed to serve rational cognition. (Close reading of *On Sophistical Refutations*)
   Therefore,

(3) Speech is not the rational-making feature. (from 1 and 2)

The present study also, with respect to premise (2), determines that symbolic prowess, in particular, is what separates human speech (*logos*) from other animal communication. It also examines a passage from *Politics* I 2 that provides the best possible grounds for claiming that speech for Aristotle is the rational-making feature. Close reading sustains no such claim. None of this entails, however, that language is *incidental* to the rational soul. Humans have speech for the same reason animals have distal senses, imaging and desires – it helps them live well.

Here is something that holds, regardless of how speech relates to rationality: the power of speech must be distinct from whatever capacities it actuates or helps to realise. This matters because Aristotle argues that cognitive capacities are *prior in explanation* to the means a creature deploys to realise them. Language, we will see, is a crucial (albeit non-essential) *means* to rational activity. Aristotle argues for the general claim during a debate with Anaxagoras about the relationship between hands and intelligence:

> Anaxagoras anyway says humans are the smartest animals due to having hands, but it's reasonable instead to say that we get hold of hands due to being the smartest. For hands are a *tool*, and nature always portions each

---

animals do with 'propositional understanding', the realm of reason. Goodey (1996), on the other hand, thinks Aristotle never claimed there *was* a rational-making feature in the present study's sense, but, nonetheless, assumes *logos* would have referred to language, had it played that role. More recently, Moss (2014) offers 'explanatory account' as the core meaning of *logos* in Aristotle, complete with the linguistic connotation of 'generating and following' explanations.

Speech and the Rational Soul

thing – the way a smart person would – to who can use it. For it is more fitting to add flutes to flautists than flute-skill to flute-holders. (*PA* IV 10, 687a8–14)

This intriguing line of thought sets the stage for a retort (*PA* IV 10, 687a24–b26) against those who think humans weak and defenceless.[10] What matters right now is the grounds on which Aristotle rejects and reverses Anaxagoras's proposal. Call it Cognitive Priority: a creature's having some cognitive power explains their having the means to realise it.[11] This entails that our preeminent intelligence must explain why we have hands, not the other way around. The flute analogy reveals the argument's moving parts. Flute-playing is a skill (*technē*), a complex cognitive disposition aimed at making things. To deploy that capacity, you need tools (i.e. a flute) distinct from the disposition itself – this can include body parts. The flute case, furthermore, exemplifies a hierarchy of value from which Aristotle derives Cognitive Priority. It satisfies some propriety (hard to discern the force of *prosēkei* here, but it clearly expresses a pro-attitude) to give flutes to flautists rather than make a flautist out of anyone holding a flute.[12] 'For 'tis better', comes the further premise, 'to append what is lesser to what is greater and more commanding, but not what is worthier (*timiōteron*) to what is less-than' (*PA* IV 10, 687a14–16).[13] That last claim applies to any two conjoinable things, so provided flute-skill is worthier and more commanding than flutes, the 'flutes-to-flautists' conclusion follows.

Flute-skill only matters, of course, because it clarifies Cognitive Priority, whence flows the refutation of Anaxagoras. Barring patent *non sequitur*, flutes are to flute-skill what hands are to intelligence.[14] Aristotle confirms this when he claims that hands are *tools* – *meta-tools*, in fact, for fashioning a variety of tools. Intelligence, then, is the worthier, more commanding *cognitive* disposition, hands its accoutrements. From Cognitive Priority, it

---

[10] A trope in Greek folk anthropology, seen e.g. in Protagoras's Great Speech, esp. *Prot.* 321c–d.

[11] Aristotle denies that a (fully-formed) creature might have some capacity but lack the means to realise it. Any such case would entail that nature acts in vain. See esp. *DA* III 9, 432b21–23 and *Pol.* I 2, 1253a7–18 (q.v. below in main text).

[12] On *prosēkei*: Aristotle often uses it to say something like 'one would expect …', a judgement of evidence rather than propriety: *DA* I 5, 411b14–17, for instance. It cannot mean that in our *PA* passage, though, for that would make the argument circular; such a distribution would only be 'what one would expect' were it settled that nature portions wisely, but Aristotle offers the fittingness claim to *prove* that nature portions wisely.

[13] My archaism renders Aristotle's gnomic aorist (Smyth 1920, §1931). The subject of the sentence cannot be nature herself because, again, that would make the argument circular (see n. 12 above on *prosēkei*).

[14] *phronimōtaton* ≈ 'having the most *phronēsis*', though *phronēsis* cannot denote the *logos*-entangled, virtue-entailing state that it does in the ethical works.

48   IAN C. MCCREADY-FLORA

follows that we have hands because of the preeminent intelligence which allows us to put them to good use. Anaxagoras wrongly hangs the more valuable cognitive state on their instrumental means. Cognitive capacities are 'more commanding', according to Aristotle, because the powers they confer determine what form the means must take. If Cognitive Priority holds, any evidence that speech is a *means* to realise or aid rational cognition is thereby evidence that speech is not the rational-making feature. Humans may well rely on speech to actuate their rational capacities (as flautists will often require flutes to exercise their skill). Speech might even be how individuals *develop* their rational capacities in the first place, just as people cannot become flautists without spending time holding flutes. Still, no facet of the power of speech can ground or shape rational cognition *as such*.

If I am wrong about all that, and Aristotle holds the contrary view, we should expect *Politics* I 2 (specifically 1253a7–18) to be where he evinces it most clearly. For he argues therein that humans are the *most political* animal because we have *logos*, and his reasoning turns on the *cognitive* features cleaving animal voice from human discourse (on which more below). The passage well-read, however, commits him to no speech-based view, which should make us doubt he holds such a view. The text in relevant part:

> It's clear why humans are more political than every honeybee or herd animal. For nature, we say, does nothing in vain, but humans alone among the animals have speech (*logos*). So while voice is a *sign* of the painful and pleasant, and for this reason belongs to other animals (for their nature has gotten as far as having an awareness of pain and pleasure and signalling those things to each other), speech is suited to revealing what helps and harms, and so also the just and unjust. For this, other animals aside, is special to humans – having an awareness (*aisthēsis*) of good and bad and just and unjust and so forth. And sharing *those* things makes for a household and city.

Human sociality puts other animals to shame thanks to our gift of speech and (call it) *ethical awareness*. The argument turns on what sort of communication humans and beasts (honeybees too, I guess?) can undertake, so *logos* must here denote the power of speech. Suppose (non-trivially) that ethical awareness proxies rationality, and the argument seems to commit Aristotle to the view that speech is the rational-making feature.[15] Reason as follows: proper cities happen when relevant people (i.e.

---

[15] Though non-trivial, this assumption is plausible enough: see for instance Salkever (1990, 105–6) and the discussion of practical reasoning in Moss (2014). If ethical awareness is *not* a good proxy for rationality, that only helps my case, for then *Pol.* I 2 is not even *prima facie* grounds to attribute a speech-based view of rationality to Aristotle.

Speech and the Rational Soul

not slaves and other subalterns) converge on matters of goodness, justice, help, and harm. Sharing conceptions of the good/just/etc. *essentially* involves verbal exchange, speaking, and listening until enough lines up to keep society running. The only ethically aware creatures just so happen to be the only ones equipped to so converge. Happenstance beggars belief: something must explain the overlap. A tight dependence relation explains most plausibly: being trained-up for discourse on the good/just/etc. *constitutes* ethical awareness. From this it follows that speech is our rational-making feature: reason flowers only in discursive practice, and to be rational just *is* to more-or-less competently deploy some shared language about the good/just/etc. or what have you.

This reading has some allure, aided by the glamour of live and thorny issues (e.g. the Sapir-Whorf hypothesis or MacIntyrian linguistic relativity).[16] It gets the argument wrong, though. The text would only evince the view that speech constitutes ethical awareness – and rationality by proxy – were Aristotle out to prove human uniqueness for either or both. He reasons *from* the uniqueness of both, though, *towards* neither. Aristotle instead purports to explain why (*dihoti*) humans are the *most political*. Speech puts humans at the top because proper cities happen only when people converge on matters of the good/just/etc. Speech is the only way to so converge (excepting blind luck), so the most political creature will be one that is (a) aware of the good/just/etc. and (b) can share that awareness with other creatures so aware. The argument well-read, therefore, alleges no dependence of ethical awareness on the power of speech. Aristotle *does* conclude (comes the retort) that speech is how proper cities happen *from* the premise that only humans are ethically aware.[17] If the argument relies, via suppressed premise, on speech being the rational-making feature, this inference must be where that assumption does its work. Here is how: suppose first that ethical awareness *depends* on speech. The content of ethical awareness is shaped, then, by some convention-bound symbol system.[18] A creature cannot experience things *qua* good, just, or harmful

---

[16] Though the argument given above is my own creation, it distils consensus (largely unargued) on the meaning and relevance of the passage. See, for instance, Mulgan (1974, 443–45), Keyt (1987: 71–73), Salkever (1990, 74–81), and especially Trott (2014, 85–89).

[17] I make little of the switch from *sēmeion* in animals to *dēloun* in humans; beast-sound can 'reveal' things as well (*DI* I 2, 16a26–29, q.v. below in the main text). This against, for instance, Labarrière (1984, 30–34) and Trott (2014, 84, 89–92).

[18] Aristotle says suggestively at *EN* VIII 11, 1161b6–7 that a certain justice (*ti dikaion*) is open to every human (slaves explicitly included) due to their being able to share in 'law and convention' (*synthēkēs*, cf. *kata synthēkēn* as the source of symbolic meaning). Aristotle is talking about explicit *agreements* and contracts, but that metaphor must be what guides his thinking about symbols, for he

50   IAN C. MCCREADY-FLORA

without accessing the symbol system, whence it follows that speech is suited to revealing (*epi to dēloun*) the objects of ethical awareness to others who share the symbol system. So the argument (at least a vital lemma thereof) *is* after all premised on the view that the power of speech constitutes ethical awareness, from which it follows that reason is essentially linguistic.

The argument baffles, though, if it so relies on a speech-dependency claim. Aristotle's *oun* (no compound; *men* pairs with *de* at a14) means the substance of the proffered speech–voice comparison *follows* from the claim that humans alone have speech. He then, however, adduces unique awareness as a *further consideration* in favour (a15: *gar*). If the power of speech constitutes ethical awareness, though, that further claim is a logical consequence of the unique-language claim, and so adds no evidential weight. For it to serve Aristotle's purpose, the unique-awareness claim must be logically independent of the unique-language claim, which it cannot be if ethical awareness depends on speech. Perhaps the unique-awareness claim is rhetorical flourish, not an independent premise: the proposal still fails on substance. For the whole argument proceeds from the claim that *nature does nothing in vain*, meant to rule out a (possible) case wherein humans have a cognitive capacity (ethical awareness) that lets them form proper cities, but lack the means (speech) to do so, making them stunted *by design*.[19] If humans *didn't* have *logos*, nature *would* have acted in vain, so human speech confirms nature's wise soul-craft. If ethical awareness depends on speech, though, it confirms nothing of the sort and the argument is invalid. For withholding speech in such a case would also withhold ethical awareness, with humans no more stunted than any gregarious beast. One might respond that a world without city-forming creatures would be vanity. This recalls Timaeus' assertion that the universe just *needs* to contain all the creatures it does in order to be 'sufficient'.[20] Averting vanity does, for Aristotle, involve an optimific natural order (the

---

    never (so far as I can tell) disambiguates or offers a specifically *semantic* sense of convention. See further Kretzmann (1974), Wheeler (1999, 197–204), Carson (2003, 201–7), and especially chapter 5 of Noriega-Olmos (2013).

[19] This point applies even to humans who do not live in developed cities. Depew (1995, 178–80) rightly notes that, for Aristotle, humans live different lives in different places, not all of them in *poleis*, though he errs in attributing the range of lives to a range of 'relationships to rationality', which presupposes that reason depends on city-forming speech. See also Kahn (1992, 377–79), who argues that *logos* (*nous* as well) is *constituted* by language and culture.

[20] *Tim.* 41b7–c2: 'The three mortal kinds are yet unborn, but so long as these have not come to be the universe will be unfinished. For it will not have *every kind* of animal in it, which it must (*dei*) if it is to be complete enough.'

Speech and the Rational Soul

odd monstrosity aside), but nature *as a whole* is not something to optimise over and above its constituent natural kinds.[21] The Maker, says Timaeus, optimises nature *tout court*, while for Aristotle (who posits no Maker) optimal nature supervenes on its optimal parts. Adding or removing some natural kind (then solving for coherence in the resulting cosmos) would not make nature *as a whole* better or worse.

The vanity of nature is a series of *local* questions, then, and averting local vanity requires giving creatures the means to realise their cognitive capacities. 'If, then, nature neither acts in vain nor omits any necessity', Aristotle argues elsewhere, then if the motive soul were one with the sensitive soul (a live possibility at this point in the argument), '[immobile animals] would have body parts for moving around', but they do not (witness the sponge) so those two soul-parts cannot be one and the same (*DA* III 9, 432b21–26). Human speech faculties, we have shown, are the *means* nature has given us to realise our ethical awareness (the attendant, worthier cognitive capacity) and through that our power to make proper cities happen (worthier still). It follows from Cognitive Priority, then, that ethical awareness explains why we can talk, not the other way around. The speech–voice comparison at a11–13 confirms this, for it reveals the *relevant respects* of the human–animal distinction.[22] There Aristotle makes two claims: animals are (a) aware of things *qua* pleasant and painful and (b) able to communicate about the objects of that awareness. This ability to indicate pleasure and pain (but not the good/just/etc.) furthermore *explains* (a11: *dio*) why animals vocalise.[23] So animals are not aware of pleasure and pain *because* they can make certain meaningful sounds to each other, but vice versa. Given Cognitive Priority, this is what we should expect. The human case is strictly parallel, so we have no reason to think the relationship between communication and cognition is what distinguishes the two cases. What distinguishes them instead is *what* human speech reveals, and how that expanded reach lets us (and only us) form proper cities. This confirms that the argument relies on no

---

[21] Aristotle evinces such a view most clearly in *IA* I 1, 704b15–18, where he cites it as a guiding principle for natural inquiry: '... that nature does nothing in vain, but always from possible things [does what is] best regarding each animal kind concerning its nature'. Nature brings about what is best, in other words, by perfecting each kind.

[22] My translation in relevant part: 'So while voice is a *sign* of the painful and pleasant, and for this reason belongs to other animals (for their nature has gotten as far as having an awareness of pain and pleasure and signalling those things to each other), speech is suited to revealing what helps and harms ...'.

[23] See also *DA* III 13, 435b24–25: the animal has 'hearing to have something signify to it and a tongue to signify something to another' (Reading the last clause with Ross, against Torstrik).

52   IAN C. MCCREADY-FLORA

dependence between ethical awareness – nor rationality by proxy – and the faculty of speech.

That is mere absence of evidence, one might object, and furthermore ignores the *real* difference between animal voice and human speech. What might that be, though? We must isolate human speech from other animal noise, which proves intriguingly difficult. An animal's voice differs from mere noise (cowbells and coughing) because it means something. Meaning something takes more than the ability to relay information to a receptive creature; you need a *content-bearing* mental state, though the relation between sound and soul is unclear:

> ... but the thing doing the striking must be ensouled as well as [do the striking] along with *some imaging* (*meta phantasias*), for of course voice is a sort of meaningful sound. (*DA* II 8, 420b31–33)[24]

Aristotle's premise (*gar*) states a definition, from which it purports to follow that the sound an animal makes is *voice* only if (*dei* here ≈ *anagkē*) accompanied by (*meta* + genitive) some occurrent mental state. The conclusion yokes said state to the *striking* that produces sound, not the sound itself. The relevant relation cannot therefore be 'semantic', one of token signifiers to signified. Nor is mere cooccurrence enough, for that would not make the sound *mean something*.[25] If I cough while thinking of dinner, the sound does not thereby denote my hunger or some facet of the daydream. Instead, the content of the image must somehow *cause* the striking and shape the resulting sound so as to render the mental state detectable by means of the sound. So related, voice betokens mental state the way things *sēmantikon* of health indicate healthy states.[26] This applies even to dumb beasts, so the relevant difference cannot be that speech is soul-shaped.

Speech must, then, call on human-only cognitive resources. An early stretch of *On Interpretation* confirms this; the resources needed to form words lie beyond the beasts, though the argument is obscure:

> [I say 'meaningful] by convention' because no word exists *by nature*, but rather when a *symbol* arises, since even inarticulate sounds – like beasts' – reveal something, but none are words. (*DI* I 2, 16a26–29)

---

[24] Reading *empsychon* with Biehl, Torstrik and most recently Shields, against Ross' conjecture.

[25] For further issues about this passage and its context – especially on the question of human exclusivity – see Labarrière (1993b, 250–54). For a recent, comprehensive treatment of Aristotle's psychosemantics – the present study has little to say – see Noriega-Olmos (2013).

[26] See *Met.* K 2, 1061a5–7 and *Top.* I 15, 107b8–12. Alexander (*in Top.* 105.2 Wallies) offers examples such as inflammation and shortness of breath – as does Philoponus (*in de An.* 206.14 Hayduck) – which supports my understanding of *sēmantikon*.

Speech and the Rational Soul

From the premise that no *inarticulate* sounds are *words* – however meaningful (*deloun* here ≈ *sēmainein*) – Aristotle concludes there are no *natural* words. This to explain why (per *DI* a20) vocal sounds *must* be conventional signs to even be words.[27] The argument needs more than the text gives us, though. The conclusion contrasts *natural* significance with *symbolic* mediation, suggesting a suppressed premise to the effect that there are no natural symbols. The stated premise, however, mentions neither symbols nor convention, stressing instead that beast-voice is 'inarticulate' (*agramma*). The argument must, therefore, to avert *non sequitur*, connect symbolic mediation to articulation. Not *just* articulation, though, since birds can do it too:

> And some make noise, some have no voice and still others vocalize; among those [who vocalize] some have language, others are inarticulate, and some are chatty, others quiet; some sing, others are song-less. (*HA* I 1, 488a31–34)

Given no yawning gaps, this taxonomy implies that all articulate voice is language (*dialekton*), since language and inarticulate voice mutually exclude. Birdsong is *dialekton*, though. Aristotle's claim that 'those [birds] have language (*dialekton*) to the greatest extent who have a broad tongue' presupposes it. So birds articulate, and not homonymously, for he mentions people in the same breath as the only linguistic mammals.[28] Birdsong, moreover, is a robust communicative exchange: Aristotle calls it *hermēneia*, thereby grouping it with regimented philosophical debate and the expression of knowledge-conferring definitions.[29]

Comes the retort: this does not entail birdsong is *words*, since there can be natural articulate sounds but no natural words. It cannot, however, follow from there being no natural symbols that humans acquire language through *no natural capacity* at all. That would entail a supernatural

---

[27] Conventional signs as opposed to *natural*, which nowadays we would call 'evidence'. See for instance Grimaldi (1980, 384), who correctly notes that most of the signs Aristotle cares about are natural, though it seems wrong to say that he discusses only instrumental and not formal signs, given his interest in linguistic signification.

[28] All this at *HA* IV 9, 536a20–23, which includes the embedded quote in the last sentence, and then a32–b3 for the human comparison.

[29] The attribution itself is at *PA* II 17, 665a35–b1: 'And all [sc. many-voiced birds] use their tongues for the purpose of communicating with each other ...'. See also *SE* IV, 166b10–14 for the term applied to dialectical debate and, for defining, *Top.* VI 2, 139b13–15. Little should hang on this pattern of terminology, though: Aristotle uses *hermēneia* but seldom, and never refers to the treatise we know as *peri hermēneias* (i.e. *De Interpretatione*) by that name. Unclear, then, whether something systematic guides his usage, but at least he saw nothing ludicrous about grouping humans and birds this way.

psychology (in the vein of, say, the *Timaeus*) that Aristotle likely rejects.[30] The claim is rather that no particular *form of words* arises by nature.[31] Dealing with symbol systems, while natural for humans, is also highly plastic: the environment moulds particular deployments. Anyone learning another language after childhood – or teaching a child to read – can so attest. The same goes for birdsong, though:

> And some little birds do not vocalize in song the same as their parents, should they be reared away from home and listen to other birds singing. At the same time, the nightingale has been seen *instructing* its youngling, implying that *language* and voice are not similar *by nature* but rather are able to be *moulded* (*plattesthai*). And though people vocalize the same, their language is not the same. (*HA* IV 9, 536b14–20)

Birds *learn* how to *talk*, their ability to sing natural but highly plastic. Aristotle elsewhere observes that avian vocal exchange is intricate enough that 'there even seems to be instruction (*mathēsis*)' going on between them.[32] This plasticity entails that conspecifics do not sing the same song by nature. The cited human phenomenon – linguistic diversity emerging from shared phonics – is relevantly similar, he implies, to variation in birdsong. Birds communicate and acculturate each other and so do humans.[33] None of this, then, is what isolates human speech.

Of course not! says the objector: birdsong plasticity does not entail that the moulding in question amounts to their buying into some *conventions*. Conventions require the parties represent both the substance of the agreement *and* the other party's abiding by them (plus maybe the other's party's awareness that *you* abide by them, and so on), which goes way beyond picking up what others around you are singing. That must, then,

---

[30] Now is not the time to defend this reading of Plato, but note that *immortal* souls pre-exist the visible world on Timaeus' account, and so have no explanation in terms of the triangle-based elements that constitute it, which is just to say they receive no explication in terms of fundamental physics (nor can they). Many have, furthermore, alleged that Aristotle's thoroughgoing naturalism breaks down at *DA* 3.5, the 'maker mind' being immortal and detachable from the body. If so, *and* if thoughts (as argued in Noriega-Olmos 2013, ch. 4) are what words refer to, then symbolic prowess would be non-natural in an interesting sense. Policing that sector of logical space lies outside the present study.

[31] This is consistent with the claim in Kretzmann (1974) – adumbrated in Wheeler (1999) – that vocal sounds (including words) are as a kind significant by nature, since a sound can naturally be the sort of thing that means something without by nature meaning what it does.

[32] *PA* II 17, 665a34–35, which immediately follows the quote above which calls birdsong a form of *hermēneia*.

[33] Osborne (2007, 98) puts the point extremely well: the 'imprinting process' by which humans acquire linguistic and conceptual prowess just does not seem that different from how other creatures get whatever cognitive prowess they have. For more details, about birds especially, see Bodson (1996).

Speech and the Rational Soul

be what separates speech from birdsong: the power to adopt and manipulate convention-bound symbol systems. Call it 'symbolic prowess'. If symbolic prowess is not the rational-making feature or a *sine qua non* for rationality, nothing about speech is, because that (surprisingly) is all that separates speech from birdsong.

Time, then, to see whether it is the rational-making feature. Symbolic prowess is an inborn *cognitive* capacity. Maybe it causes ethical awareness, maybe not, but it *does* enable *logos, logismos, syllogismos*, etc. Access to speech (properly conceived) remains a necessary condition for rationality, since symbolic prowess enables speech, and immersion in the world of speech is what develops and refines a creature's symbolic prowess.[34] Humans will not learn to talk if you never expose them to symbols, and such deprivation has cognitive consequences.[35] From this it follows that all rational cognition is mediated by symbols. For if symbolic prowess is the rational-making feature, there will be no rational thinking that does not call upon symbolic prowess. Aristotle, however, rejects that last claim; some rational cognition is *not* so mediated, whence it follows that *nothing* about speech is the rational-making feature.

I derive this view from close reading of passages in *Sophistical Refutations*. Using words to mediate inquiry introduces the 'subtlest and most common' form of error:

> For since it is not possible to discuss (*dialegesthai*) by moving around the things themselves (*pragmata*), we instead use words in place of things as *symbols*, and think that what happens in words happens also in the things themselves, like those who reckon (*logizomenois*) with stones. (*SE* I, 165a6–10)

It is crucial to note that manipulating symbol systems and applying the result to conclusions about things themselves is not *itself* what causes the error. Truth-tracking symbolic manipulation is instead like moving stones around to do arithmetic. Externalised calculation (*calculus* = 'little stone') does not *constitute* mathematical cognition. Stones aid cognition, but moving them around is not *what it is* to do the math. Nor, presumably, is the ability to grasp the convention by which stones stand in for

---

[34] So Wedin (1988: 153–55) against Ax (1978). More recently, Moss (2014) maintains the centrality of language, since having *logos* is a matter of 'generating and following explanatory accounts', which are verbal items.

[35] Aristotle evinces such a view at *Sens.* I, 437a12–17. Hearing contributes 'the greatest share' to intelligence (*phronēsis*), but only incidentally through its being the channel by which we receive *logos* (here likely denoting speech). This explains (*dioper*), he adds, why those blind from birth are smarter than those deaf from birth (!!).

numerical units: a person could be great at doing sums, but baffled by moving stones around. Stone-moving is, therefore, a *means* to realise some distinct arithmetic capacity. All this applies *mutatis mutandis* to words:

> So just as those untalented at moving stones around get misled by those who know, *in the same way* too, when it comes to arguments, those untried in word-power reason awry both discoursing themselves and listening to others. (*SE* 1, 165a13–17)

The similarity claim here is emphatic: verbal naïfs go wrong *in the same way* that leads to bad stone-movers getting cheated. Mathematical error, though, is not what separates marks from their money. What the hustlers understand (*epistēmenōn*) and weaponise is how to move stones (*psēphous pherein*). Marks get hustled instead because they pin their reckoning to the stones, even when they stop tracking mathematical operations. This often yields the wrong answer, but not always: compare an at-sea algebra student who panics during a test, deploys some inapt rote method, and just happens to write down the correct answer. All this entails that what lets the hustlers cheat is an *instrumental* failure distinct from the cognitive capacity to do sums. If the inept stone-mover suffers instrumental failure and the same goes for word-novices, then the errant word-novice also suffers instrumental failure. He endorses, that is, some non-truth-tracking symbolic manipulations and thereby reasons awry.

What Aristotle suggests in the quote above is that symbols are tools to realise cognitive work. This means the relationship between those symbols and the powers we realise in deploying them answer to Cognitive Priority, whence it follows that rationality explains symbolic prowess, but not vice versa. If symbolic prowess does not explain rationality, then it is not the rational-making feature. An objector here intrudes: that is way too much to press out of this text. The general *capacity* to symbolize is what makes us rational, not any particular symbol system. Otherwise we cannot explain how the flailing word-novice still achieves something no cow or bird ever could. So, reason is still essentially linguistic because constituted by orderly manipulation of *some* symbol system or other.

More text repels the objection. The passage comes several Bekker pages later, but Aristotle has returned to discussing how forms of words (*lexis*) can lead us astray:

> It's for this reason as well that [this error] should be put among those due to the word (*lexin*), first because the error happens more to people inquiring with others than by themselves (for inquiry with another happens through statements (*logōn*), while on one's own it happens no less *through the thing*

itself); secondly, even on one's own it happens that one gets deceived [*sc.* by the word] when one carries out the inquiry based on language (*logou*); the error moreover [arises] from similarity, and the similarity [arises] from the word [used]. (*SE* VII, 169a36–b2)

The distinction drawn here between joint inquirers and solo thinkers – the latter do not require linguistic mediation – makes it impossible to maintain that symbolic prowess is the rational-making feature. Aristotle aims here to explain why equivocation, which happens when someone gets misled by irrelevant lexical features (hence *tōn para to schēma*), should thereby be reckoned among the ways that language itself leads us astray. For you see, people are more likely to fall into such a trap when inquiring with others. Humans are not telepathic, and must pipe any joint inquiry through shared symbols.[36] *Logōn* here is plural, so it cannot denote the *faculty* of speech as at *Pol.* I 2 – nor can the singular at b1, since the topic is language as artefact, not the cognitive capacity – but that changes nothing. Solo thinkers are less vulnerable because they do not always deploy symbols in their inquiry. They can, and when they do are as error-prone as joint inquirers. Aspects of the symbol system explain the confusion (so the 'similarity [arises] from the word'), which Aristotle takes as additional evidence that the error is due to *language* and solo contemplators can in principle avoid it.

Far from constituting rational cognition, then – only humans can inquire; solo thinkers engage in a distinctively rational activity – symbolic mediation is not even *necessary* for it.[37] Solo thinkers do what Aristotle previously said was impossible for those involved in discussion: inquiry through the thing itself (*di' autou tou pragmatos*; cf. *auta ta pragmata* at 165a6). Yet, solo and joint inquirers are doing the same kind of thing. It would make no sense to compare the two otherwise. One might respond that both solo and shared inquiry depend on symbolic mediation, but the solo case less obviously than the shared case. Perhaps joint inquirers are *aware* that their thinking depends on symbols, while for solo thinkers who do not subvocalise, this easily escapes their notice. Never mind that such an explanation would make it *less* likely for joint inquirers to get misled by symbols, being aware of them, while Aristotle claims the opposite. Such a reading founders on the claim that solo thinkers proceed *no less* through the thing itself, implying they *do* sometimes work through symbols. Anyone who figures things out by writing them down can so attest. The

---

[36] Cf. *Pol.* I 2 on why city-building requires speech.
[37] Aristotle commits to the view that only humans inquire at *Mem.* II, 453a11–13.

58   IAN C. MCCREADY-FLORA

difference cannot, therefore, lie in whether one happens to be speaking or writing. All this proves that discourse – the power of speech *qua* source of symbolic prowess – is not the rational-making feature. Language expands the power of reason, but does not constitute it.

How, then, does speech bear on the rational soul? Symbolic prowess is not the rational-making feature, but speech inheres in the rational soul for the same reason and in the same way imagining, pleasure/pain, and desires inhere in the animal soul. The animal-making feature (what separates us and cows from plants) is *sense-perception*: animals take in content-bearing representations of the world and plants cannot.[38] With perception comes the power to retain and deploy perceptual traces (*phantasia*), to feel good or bad about the world and to want (esp. to attain the pleasant and to avoid the painful). Those additional capacities let animals keep living and live *well.*[39] Humans likewise have the faculty of speech so that we might live a *good* human life. It does not follow from this, though, that speech is the rational-making feature. One might want to dismiss all this: cute analogy, but not Aristotle's view. If that is really the distinction he wanted to make, surely he would have made it *in those terms*. He does not, which tells against the whole reading.

My response is to deny the minor premise. Aristotle never puts it just this way, but he might as well, for it follows from what he says by reasoning he accepts. Take *Pol.* I 2: humans are the most political *because* we alone have what it takes to form proper cities, and we reach our full potential only within such cities. Symbolic prowess, then, enables the active social life that *constitutes* the best (non-contemplative) life, perfection of which makes us properly *human.*[40] So, speech is necessary to live a *good* human life. Speech also contributes to the best human life bar none: the contemplative. Though still social (contemplators need not be hermits), the contemplative life is not *essentially* social (the way political life is) because symbols need not mediate contemplation, which is thinking 'through the thing itself' if anything is. The political life is inconceivable without constant discursive exchange, but not so the contemplative, even

---

[38] *DA* II 12, 424a32–b2 gives Aristotle's explanation; plants 'have no mean' and so 'are affected along with their matter' by things like hot and cold, as opposed to taking on form *without* the matter. The present study offers no view as to what on earth this means.

[39] So *DA* III 12, 434b23–27: touch (and so taste) are 'necessary for the animal' to be an animal, but the distal senses are 'for the sake of the good condition', which entails they belong only to certain creatures who need them (i.e. ones that move around) in order to thrive. See also *DA* III 13, 435b19–22: animals have distal senses 'not in order to *be* but [to be] *well*'.

[40] I mean that almost literally. *Pol.* I 2, 1253a24–29 suggests those who cannot, or do not need to, live such a life are not human, but either beasts (though presumably not gregarious beasts) or gods.

Speech and the Rational Soul

one full of friendship and conversation. None of that, however, makes symbolic prowess irrelevant to the life of the mind, any more than imagining is irrelevant to a smart animal's life:

> For it is difficult to determine what is meant just the same way and what is meant differently (for the one able to do *that* is basically next door to contemplating the truth, and understands most of all how to nod along). (*SE* VII, 169a30–33)

I do not want to lean on terminology, but 'contemplate' (*theōrein*) in this passage also denotes the active exercise of knowledge that constitutes the highest flourishing (*bios theōrētikos*: cf. *Pol.* VII 2, 1324a26–29). The thought is this: verbal confusion is widespread and hard to correct. Someone who reliably makes relevant distinctions and avoids rookie mistakes, therefore, has a huge advantage (assuming, as Aristotle does, that the only valuable contemplation is of the *truth*). Excellent deployment of speech helps secure not just a human life, but the best human life. This is all consistent, however, with its not being the rational-making feature. Compare the power to retain and be affected by images: instrumental for animal wellbeing but not the animal-making feature.[41]

---

[41] Many thanks to the editors, Geert Keil and Nora Kreft, for helpful comments on an earlier draft. Thanks also to my audience at the University of Virginia, and to Robert Bolton, Victor Caston, Dan Devereux, Jessica Moss, and Jim Cargile, for their time and attention.

CHAPTER 3

Aristotle's Peculiarly Human Psychology

Elena Cagnoli Fiecconi

For Aristotle, human cognition has a lot in common both with non-human animal cognition and with divine cognition. With non-human animals, humans share a non-rational part of the soul and non-rational cognitive faculties.[1] With gods, humans share a rational part of the soul and rational cognitive faculties.[2] The rational part and the non-rational part of the soul, however, coexist and cooperate only in human souls.[3] In this chapter, I show that a study of this cooperation helps to uncover some distinctive aspects of human cognition and desire. Humans have a peculiarly expanded non-rational perceptual and desiderative range. This difference in sophistication is not merely a matter of enhanced discriminatory capacities: humans also have the peculiar ability to exercise deliberative *phantasia* at will, and the peculiar ability to synthesise many *phantasmata* into one.[4] Human rational cognition, in turn, differs from divine cognition because it can be hindered or supported by non-rational cognition. Human rational cognition also involves peculiar abilities, including the ability to direct non-rational cognition and non-rational affections by means of concentration and the appropriate kinds of pleasures, pains, exhortations, and reproofs.

Uncovering these peculiarities of human cognition is important in order to solve a puzzle about the links between Aristotle's psychology and his ethics. Aristotle thinks that ethicists and political scientists should have some knowledge of psychology and in particular of the rational part and

---

[1] *DA* III 3, 427b6–14, *EN* I 13, 1102b29 and *EE* II 1, 1219b24–26.
[2] *EN* X 7, 1177b17–1178a8.   [3] *EN* I 13, 1102b26–29, *EE* II 1, 1219b28–31.
[4] Throughout this chapter, I leave the term *phantasia* and its cognates untranslated. Imagination is a fitting translation for deliberative *phantasia*, but the translation seems less fitting in other contexts, including, for example, Aristotle's view on *phantasia*'s involvement in memory. The unity and the nature of Aristotle's views on *phantasia* are debated topics, see further Wedin (1988); Schofield (1992); Frede (1992); Nussbaum (1978, essay 5); Caston (1996b); Scheiter (2012); and Johansen (2012, ch. 10).

Aristotle's Peculiarly Human Psychology

the non-rational part of the human soul (*EN* I 13, 1102a23–28). He also endorses a 'peculiarity criterion' according to which ethicists and political scientists should only study aspects of the soul that are peculiarly human (*EN* I 13, 1102b4–13, *EE* II 1, 1219b38–39). This raises the challenge to explain how the rational part and the non-rational part of the human soul can have lot in common with the souls of non-human beings and yet meet the peculiarity criterion advanced in the ethical works. If my thesis in this chapter is correct, the rational and non-rational parts of the human soul meet the peculiarity criterion because they are built to cooperate.

1 Peculiarly Non-Rational

In the ethical works, Aristotle divides the human soul into a rational and a non-rational part. The non-rational part has two subparts. The first subpart is nutritive, 'plantlike', and shared among all living things (*EN* I 13, 1102a35–b1 and *EE* II 1, 1219b36–40). The second subpart is the seat of cognitive and desiderative faculties like appetitive desire and perception (*EE* II 1, 1219b23–25). Aristotle calls it 'the passionate part' (*to pathētikon*; *Pol.* I 6, 1254b8) and 'the desiderative part' (*to orektikon*; *EN* I 13, 1102b30). Human and non-human animals share a number of cognitive faculties and states, including perception, *phantasia*, experience, spirited desire (*thymos*), appetitive desire (*epithymia*), and memory. However, unlike non-human animals, humans can think, reason, and form beliefs.[5] This suggest that the non-rational part of the soul is shared between humans and animals: it is desiderative and perceptual, but it cannot think.[6]

Despite the similarities with non-human animals, humans are peculiar because in them non-rational cognition and desire cooperate with the rational part and with *logos*.[7] To take a closer look at this peculiarity, let us start with human perception. For Aristotle, both human and non-human animals can perceive things *as* being in a certain way. For

---

[5] See *Met.* I 1, 980a28–b28 for perception, *phantasia*, memory, and experience. See *DA* II 3, 414a29–b19 for perception and appetitive desire. See *DA* III 3, 428a20–22, *DA* III 10, 433a9–12, *DA* III 10 433n27–30, *DA* III 11, 434a6–9 for the difficult case of *phantasia*. For appetitive and spirited desire see *EN* III 2, 1111b10–13 and *EE* II 10, 1225b24–26. See *DA* III 3, 427b7–27 on non-human animals lacking thought.

[6] For this view, I follow Moss (2012, ch. 4.2) and Moss (2017), *contra* Fortenbaugh (1975, 26–30).

[7] *EN* I 13, 1102b31–35, *EE* II 1, 1219b38–1220a1. I tentatively translate *logos* with 'reason' when it is used to indicate the difference between humans and animals. On the difficulties of translating *logos* in Aristotle's moral psychology see Moss (2014).

62 ELENA CAGNOLI FIECCONI

example, we can perceive fire as hot, or food as near and available, or an object as white.[8]

Different animals have different perceptual ranges. Often, the cooperation between perception and other cognitive faculties is responsible for the expansion of a certain animal's perceptual range. For example, in *Met.* I 1, 980a28–*b*25, every animal has perception and only some have memory. Those who have memory are more able to learn (*mathētikōtera*) and can gain a little experience (*empeiria*). Gaining experience and being able to learn involve, among other things, being able to discriminate a wider range of properties. For example, some animals are better learners because they discriminate perceptually differences in articulated sounds:

> Some [sc. animals] also have a share in both some kind of teaching and learning, some from each other, some also from humans, in so far as they have a share in hearing not only sounds, but also in distinguishing perceptually (*diaisthanetai*) the difference between signals (*sēmeion*). (*HA* IX 1, 608a18–22, transl. loosely based on Thompson)

Some animals are capable of recognising perceptually different signals (*sēmeia*). This contributes to their ability to learn and, presumably, it is in part due to the fact that they have better memories. Aristotle's studies on non-human animal behaviour corroborate the suggestion that memory enlarges the perceptual range of some non-human animals: at *HA* VIII 24, 605a7–9, horses discriminate between horses they already fought and horses they did not fight yet; at *HA* IX 6, 612a3–16, goats and dogs recognise and remember which herbs induce vomiting or cure wounds, and eat them when needed.

Human and non-human perception's discriminative range can be expanded by the cooperation with different non-rational faculties and states. In the human case, perception's discriminative range can also be expanded by the cooperation with rational cognition. In Aristotle's psychological works, we find various examples of non-rational perceptual cognition that is only available to rational creatures *because* they are rational. At the very beginning of *De Sensu*, there is a description of the human ability to hear speech (*logos*):

---

[8] See *Met.* I 1, 981b10–12, *DA* II 6, 418a7–25, *DA* III 3, 428b18–29, *EN* III 10, 1118a20–23. For a similar view see Moss (2017, 130–31). These passages and the possibility of animal discriminative perception have been discussed by Sorabji (1993, 17–20, 30–40); Cashdollar (1973, 158 ff); Modrak (1987, 70 ff); and Everson (1997, ch. 5).

Aristotle's Peculiarly Human Psychology 63

> Incidentally, hearing contributes for the most part to wisdom. Speech (*logos*) is the cause of learning because it is audible, not in its own right but incidentally: for it is made of names, and every name is a symbol (*symbolon*). (*Sens.* I 1, 437a12–15, transl. loosely based on Beare and Ross)[9]

Speech is audible, though only incidentally, therefore it contributes to learning. The ability to hear names and symbols, and thereby speech, seems to be the peculiarly human version of the non-human animal ability to hear signals. Aristotle tells us little about the distinction between signals and symbols, and he even uses the words interchangeably in some passages (*DI* I 1, 16a4–9).[10] However, in this passage, he implies that speech is audible because it is composed of symbols (names) that can be discriminated perceptually. The immediately preceding lines, *Sens.* I 2, 437a10–12, can be taken to confirm this suggestion: Aristotle argues that hearing informs us both of differences in sound (*psophos*) and of differences in voice (*phonē*). The differences in articulated voice are the kind of differences one needs to grasp in order to be able to discriminate speech and symbols perceptually. After all, voice is a meaningful sound (*sēmantikos tis psophos*) at *DA* II 8, 420b33 and it is the matter of speech at *GA* V 7, 786b21. This suggests that the difference between perceptual discrimination of signals and perceptual discrimination of symbols, for Aristotle, may be relatively small. In order to perceive some sound as a symbol and not merely as a signal, the hearer must possess not only good memory and perhaps experience, but also *logos* and thought.

If this is right, names and symbols are 'incidental perceptibles' like signals. In *DA* II 6, 418a7–25 and *DA* III 3, 428b18–29, Aristotle distinguishes between proper (*idia*) perceptibles like colours, sounds, and flavours; common (*koina*) perceptibles like motion, rest, number, shape, and size; and incidental (*kata symbebēkos*) perceptibles like 'Diares' son'. Symbols and speech are not the only incidental perceptibles that can be grasped by rational animals alone: grasping other incidental perceptibles, including the paradigmatic 'son of Diares' at *DA* II 6, 418a21, may require the perceiver to be a thinker.

One may object that these cases of incidental perception do not show that humans have a broader perceptual range than non-human animals. All they show is that humans can draw inferences from perceptual experience.

---

[9] In this context, the preferred translation of *logos* seems to be speech, given that Aristotle's point is that *logos* is audible.

[10] Much more would need to be said, of course, on the relevant difference between symbols and signals. The difference that matters to me here is that, presumably, only the former require *logos* in order to be grasped.

64   ELENA CAGNOLI FIECCONI

On this view, when we hear a name or a symbol, we intellectually infer from perceptual evidence that it is a name or a symbol.[11] Even if Aristotle tells us disappointingly little on these matters, there is a persuasive response against this objection. It would be hard to see why Aristotle counted these cases as cases of incidental *perception* if what they in fact involve is drawing inferences from perceptual experience. Stipulating that incidental perception is such precisely because it involves inferences from perceptual experience would not work either, because incidental perception is available to animals who cannot draw inferences.[12]

Furthermore, the idea that thought and reason expand our non-rational discriminative range is not limited to incidental perception, but extends to common perception. When we see the sun as a foot wide (*podiaios*), we are perceiving a common perceptible: size (*megethos*).[13] As in *Theaetetus* 147*d*, here the foot is a technical measure unit and non-human animals cannot grasp technical measure units. The same applies to the common perceptible number (*arithmos*). Perhaps, for Aristotle, non-human animals can discriminate between few and many. It is, however, unlikely that he believed that discrete numbers feature in the content of their perceptions. Hence, the possession of thought renders humans capable of discriminating perceptually properties that the other animals cannot discriminate.

This analysis of the peculiarity of human perception can shed light on other faculties or capacities we share with the other animals, including non-rational desires (*epithymia* and *thymos*) and perceptual *phantasia*. Human non-rational desires are peculiar for the same reasons human perception is peculiar. In virtue of the expanded cognitive range peculiar to humans, human non-rational desires can be for objects that go beyond the perceptual range of non-rational animals.[14] For example, humans can have non-rational appetites for a specific kind of wine, or a specific type of seasoning in food. Aristotle discusses appetites of this kind in *EN* III 11, 1118*b*8. He suggests that they are different in different people and depend on the specific kinds of bodily pleasures they indulge in. These desires lie below the threshold of rationality, but they are peculiar to the human soul.

Similarly, since *phantasia* derives from our perceptual activities and *phantasmata* are perceptual remnants, a peculiarly wide perceptual range

---

[11] See e.g. Kahn (1992, 367–68).   [12] See further Cashdollar (1973, 158ff).
[13] See *DA* II 6, 418*a*17 for size as a common perceptible. See *DA* III 3, 428b3–4 and *Insomn. i*, 458b28–29 for the perceptual appearance of the sun as a foot wide.
[14] See also Whiting (2002, 188ff.) and Pearson (2012, ch. 7).

Aristotle's Peculiarly Human Psychology 65

is likely to produce a peculiarly wide 'phantastic' range.[15] The peculiarity of human *phantasia* is not limited to its expanded range. *De Anima* also suggests that the cohabitation between *phantasia*, reason, and thought characteristic of humans gives rise to a special kind of *phantasia*. Aristotle briefly describes it at *DA* III 10, 433b29–30 and *DA* III 11, 434a6–13, he calls it either calculative (*logistikē*) or deliberative (*bouleutikē*) *phantasia*, and he argues that only humans have a share in it:

> As we said, perceptual *phantasia* is found in the other animals, but deliberative *phantasia* in the reasoning animals, for to decide whether to do this or that is already the task of reasoning. And it is necessary to measure by a single standard, inasmuch as one pursues what is greater and can, consequently, make one out of many *phantasmata*. And this is the reason why [*phantasia*] does not seem to imply belief, it is because [*phantasia*] does not imply a belief that result from syllogism, but belief implies *phantasia* (*autē de ekeinēn*). (*DA* III 11, 434a5–11)[16]

Clearly, deliberative *phantasia* is peculiarly human: non-rational animals do not have it because they do not engage in deliberative calculations; divinities lack *phantasia* in general and, *a fortiori*, deliberative *phantasia*, because *phantasia* requires perception and a body (*DA* I 1, 403a8–10). It is harder to establish, however, whether or not deliberative *phantasia* is capable of reasoning on its own. If we take the implicit subject at III 12, 434a11 to be *phantasia*, in this passage *phantasia* does not imply belief. This chimes in well with the thesis that *phantasia* is non-rational, for belief is a mark of rationality (III 3, 427b7–27). However, here deliberative *phantasia* is also related to the ability to combine or synthesise many *phantasmata* into a single one, which may be taken to be an ability to engage in rational calculation.

A closer look at the role of *phantasia* in deliberation suggests that deliberative *phantasia* does not engage in autonomous rational calculation.[17] Especially in *De Anima* III 7, Aristotle writes that *phantasia* functions similarly to perception in deliberation:

---

[15] For *phantasia* and *phantasmata* as perceptual remnants, see *DA* III 3, 428b11–16, *DA* III 3, 428b30–430a9, *Rhet.* I 10, 1370a27–30.

[16] The text and its interpretation are difficult. Line a10 is corrupted, I retain '*autē de ekeinēn*'contra Cornford who has '*autē de kinei*'. *Contra* (Hicks 1907, 567), I follow Polansky (2007, 531) in taking '*phantasia*' and not '*ta alla zōa*' to be the subject at a11. For this reason, I do not follow Rodier in taking a7 to a9 as a parenthetical remark.

[17] See Moss (2012, 144–51) on the very same point and Lorenz (2006, 127).

> *Phantasmata* are similar to perceptions for the thinking soul, and whenever one affirms or denies that something is good or bad, one pursues or avoids. (III 7, 431a14–16)

> The thinking part (*to noētikon*) thinks some forms in *phantasmata*, and just as in the context of perception (*en ekeinois*) what is to be pursued and avoided is defined by it, so even outside perception, whenever it is set over *phantasmata*, it is moved. ... Sometimes, on the basis of *phantasmata* and thoughts in the soul, just as if seeing them, it calculates and plans future things with reference to the things that are present. (431b2–8)[18]

In these passages, the role of *phantasia* in deliberation is analogous to the role of perception in deliberation. *Phantasmata* are similar to perceptions and, like perceptions, they help thinkers to define what to pursue and what to avoid. The thinker's deliberative faculties are set over (*epi*) *phantasmata* and employ *phantasmata* to deliberate. *Phantasia* is employed in deliberation and calculation, but it does not engage in independent calculation, deliberation, and reasoning. Hence, assuming that these passages describe deliberative *phantasia*, deliberative *phantasia* is not an autonomous rational calculative capacity. This account can be sustained by Aristotle's remark that *phantasia* comes about either through perception (*dia aisthēseōs*) or through thought (*dia noēseōs*) in *MA* VIII, 702a19–20. If *De Motu* (*MA*) can be used to elucidate the difference between perceptual *phantasia* and deliberative or calculative *phantasia*, it implies that the two differ in origin, but not necessarily in their reasoning capacities.[19]

Even if deliberative *phantasia* does not reason on its own, we can reconstruct some of its peculiarities from Aristotle's succinct remarks on its cooperation with thought. The first peculiar aspect of deliberative *phantasia* is its connection with the ability to 'make one out of many *phantasmata*'. Even if we assume that this ability is not the same as our ability to engage in rational calculation, it is hard to establish whether it pertains to *phantasia* or to thought. The passage suggests that making one out of many *phantasmata* is the result of instrumental reasoning, because it is a consequence of our ability to take the best course of action after having measured by a single standard. On this view, the many *phantasmata* represent different means to an end, and 'making one out of them'

---

[18] I keep the same subject throughout and I take *to noētikon* to be a synecdoche for the thinker, see Hamlyn's translation (1968, 148); cf. however (Shields' translation, 2016, 64). This explains why Aristotle says that the thinking part is moved: the thinking part is moved because the thinker is moved.

[19] See further Wedin (1988, 143–45).

Aristotle's Peculiarly Human Psychology

amounts to picking a preferred *phantasma*, thus choosing the best course of action among the available ones.[20] If this is all there is to this ability, it is a peculiar feature of deliberative thought and not of deliberative *phantasia*.

The ability to make one out of many *phantasmata* may, however, be peculiar to *phantasia* in other ways. Consider the ability to combine different perceptual representations into a single complex representation. An ability of this kind does not in itself involve deliberative reasoning, though it might be natural to employ it while we deliberate. For example, we employ it when we picture to ourselves in progressively more specific detail a course of action we are about to engage in. This activity may follow a rational deliberation that employs a single criterion to determine the best course of action. Imagine a deliberator who decides to visit her friend, having deliberated that it is the best way to fulfil her goal to benefit a friend. If she has decided to walk to her friend's house, she might combine different particular *phantasmata* or appearances (of herself travelling, of herself moving by foot, of herself moving on land) into the unified appearance of herself travelling on land by foot. This unified appearance encompasses all the practical details of the means she has chosen to employ in order to achieve the goal of benefitting her friend. If the capacity to make one out of many *phantasmata* is the capacity to put together unified complex appearances, then it accompanies deliberation, but it is not itself a kind of rational calculus.[21]

A second peculiar aspect of deliberative *phantasia* is that it is voluntary. Since we generally engage in deliberation at will, deliberative *phantasia* is the kind of *phantasia* we can exercise whenever we want to (*hotan boulō-metha; DA* III 3, 427b15–24). Aristotle's account of voluntary action in the ethical works sheds light on voluntary mental acts like deliberation, recollection, or *phantasia*. For example, in *EE* II 8, 1225b30–32 some thoughts (*dianoiai*) are involuntary (or not up to us) in the same way as actions are involuntary, which suggests that other thoughts are voluntary (or up to us) in the same way as actions are voluntary.[22] Voluntary actions are, by definition, actions whose origin is in an agent who is not ignorant about the particular circumstances in which she is acting (*EN* III 1, 1111a22–24).

---

[20] This option is discussed in Polansky (2007, 529–30).

[21] For this interpretation of the ability to make many *phantasmata* into one, see Philoponus' *Commentary on Aristotle's De Anima* 592. 10–20 and 593. 1–4. On different possible interpretations of this unifying ability of *phantasia* see Moss (2012, 147–9) and Lorenz (2006, 127).

[22] Corcilius (2009) analyses voluntary thoughts as embedded in voluntary actions, for an independent analysis of the voluntariness and autonomy of human thought see Wedin (1989).

68   ELENA CAGNOLI FIECCONI

Similarly, there are voluntary mental acts, like recollection, of which we are aware and whose origin is in us. In this case, the relevant contrast is with perception, whose origin appears to be in external objects.[23]

This account of voluntary mental acts suggests that both human and non-human animals can exercise *phantasia* voluntarily. Unlike perception, *phantasia* does not require external objects, because *phantasmata* are perceptual remnants that our perceptual organs somehow retain (*DA* III 3, 429a5). Often, non-human animal *phantasia* has an external cause and is, therefore, involuntary. It may arise as a response to external perceptual stimuli that stir up and an ordered series of *phantasmata*. For example, *EN* III 10, 1118a23 explains that lions only appear to enjoy the sound of oxen, because what they really enjoy is eating oxen. A plausible interpretation of this passage is that hearing oxen gives rise to an associated *phantasia* of eating oxen that is then connected to pleasure.[24] The source of this leonine *phantasia* is external, and the *phantasia* is, therefore, involuntary.[25] In other circumstances, however, non-human *phantasia* has internal sources, for example when its active exercise is embedded in an animal's voluntary and purposive behaviour. A thirsty animal may envisage the route to the closest water pool, even if no external stimulus has given rise to the series of appearances associated with drinking.[26] More controversially, an animal confronted with a practical problem or obstacle may voluntarily envisage a way to overcome it.

However, there is something distinctive about the voluntary exercise of *phantasia* involved in peculiarly human recollection and deliberation.[27] When we deliberate about something or try to recollect something, we do not merely act for a purpose, but we set ourselves a particular kind of goal that in itself involves the exercise of *phantasia*. Deliberation has the purpose of figuring out and envisaging the most efficient means to our ends. Recollection has the purpose of calling to mind a *phantasia*, it is a kind of rational search for *phantasmata* stored in the soul.[28] This suggests

---

[23] On recollection originating from us or our soul, and perception as originating from something external, see *DA* I 4, 408b15–18. On thought being up to us because its objects are internal and perception not being up to us because its objects are external, see *DA* II 5, 417b23–25.

[24] See further Pearson (2012, 41–47); Lorenz (2006, 128–37) and Warren (2014, 15).

[25] Dreams, too, may be explained in a similar fashion. They arise from perceptual changes stored in the peripheral sense organs which travel to the heart and become active because of sleep. See *Insomn. iii* and Lorenz (2006, 154–57).

[26] In *MA* VII, 701a29–33 Aristotle describes a process of this sort, although it is not obvious that he has in mind a voluntary exercise of *phantasia*.

[27] See *HA* I 1, 488b24–26 on deliberation and recollection as peculiarly human.

[28] *Mem. ii*, 453a14–16 and the voluntarily constructed memory aids (*mnēmonikoi*) at *DA* III 3, 427b15–24.

that humans exercise *phantasia* for its own sake or for the sake of *phantasia*-involving thought. Peculiarly human voluntary *phantasiai* are not oriented to external purposes, they are not embedded in other kinds of purposive behaviour, and they seem specific to activities that involve speculation and research.[29]

This analysis of deliberative *phantasia* uncovers the peculiar voluntary exercises of human *phantasia*. It also shows that human *phantasia* has the distinctive ability to create a complex unified *phantasma* out of many distinct *phantasmata*. If the discussion so far is correct, then, while human perception, desire, and perceptual *phantasia* differ from their non-human counterparts in a discriminative degree, human deliberative *phantasia* can engage in activities that are not accessible to non-human animals. A similar difference will arise in the discussion of the peculiarity of human rational cognition and desire. Human rational cognition is in a sense less sophisticated than divine cognition because it requires the cooperation of non-rational cognition. However, humans are capable of peculiar intellectual activities that have the specific purpose of directing their non-rational part of the soul.

2 Peculiarly Rational

For Aristotle, the most important rational faculty is thought (*nous*). Thought can take different forms, engage in different activities, and be in different states. These include practical knowledge, scientific knowledge, false or true belief, reasoning, and deliberating (*DA* III 3, 427b6–14).[30] Humans and gods have thought, but non-human animals lack it.[31]

Aristotle also thinks that, just like cognitive faculties, desiderative faculties can be rational. He discusses at least two types of rational desires: decision (*prohairesis*) and wish (*boulēsis*).[32] Decision is peculiar to humans: it is the result of deliberative thought oriented to action. Divinities neither

---

[29] This kind of deliberate and voluntary mental activity may be the one that, according to Warren (2014, 17), is involved in peculiarly human expectation and recollection.

[30] Burnyeat (2008) argues that *nous* shouldn't be identified with ordinary thinking. However, at *DA* III 3, 427b6–14 thought and thinking (*nous* and *noein*) include high intellectual achievements and lower level reasoning. Burnyeat's argument may apply to Aristotle's account of active nous in *DA* III 5, but it cannot apply to, e.g. *DA* III 3 where *nous* includes false belief.

[31] On animals lacking thought, see *inter alia DA* III 3, 427b11–14. On thinking being shared by humans and gods, see *inter alia EN* X 8, 1178b22–32.

[32] On decision see *EN* III 3, 1113a21–15, on wish see *DA* III 9, 432b4–7, *Rhet.* I 10, 1369a3–4, *EE* II 10, 1225b25–26. Note, however, that, in *Pol.* VII 15, 1334b17–25, Aristotle attributes wish to the non-rational part of the soul.

deliberate about action nor engage in action. Their only activity is intellectual contemplation (*theōria*; *EN* X 8, 1178b8–25).[33] The gods, however, might have a share in rational wish. After all, Aristotle says in *Met.* XII 7, 1072b31–1073a3 that divine intellectual contemplation is the best activity. Divinities, presumably, are aware that contemplation is the best activity. This thought, combined with the pleasure of contemplation (*EN* X 7, 1177a22–27), may be the source of a rational wish to continue to contemplate.[34]

As this preliminary analysis already suggests, there are different ways to spot the differences between rational cognition and desire in humans and in divinities. First, human rational cognition and desires are often directed at something that is completely outside the concern of divine cognition: action. Hence, for Aristotle, only humans engage in practical thought. Second, human rational cognition is peculiar because it requires, at least most of the time, the cooperation of *phantasia*.[35] The cooperation between thought and non-rational cognition will be at the centre of this chapter's focus. However, some aspects of this cooperation are relevant for practical cognition too.

Let us start from the idea that humans cannot think without the aid of *phantasia*. The thesis that thought requires *phantasia* is endorsed, first, for practical deliberative thought.[36] At *DA* III 7, 431a14–16, Aristotle argues that *phantasmata* necessarily accompany thought whenever a thinker is concerned with assessing, pursuing, and avoiding good or bad things. At *DA* III 8, 432a7–14, the thesis is extended to theoretical thought. It applies more specifically to thoughts about mathematical and physical objects. Similarly, at *Mem. i*, 449b30–450a9, Aristotle argues that we need *phantasmata* in order to think about mathematical entities (quantities). He compares the use of *phantasmata* in thought to the use of diagrams in geometry. Just as geometers make use of only some of the relevant features of their diagrams, thinkers are concerned with only some aspects of the *phantasmata* they put before their eyes as they think. Nevertheless, both

---

[33] See below for discussion, and see Menn (2012) for an introduction to Aristotle's theology and divinities.

[34] A few lines before, in *Met.* XII 6, 1072a26–30, Aristotle argues that desires and wishes are consequent on thinking that something is good.

[35] In the famously obscure *De Anima* III 5, Aristotle discusses the divine agent intellect. It is disputed whether or not humans have a share to the agent intellect. If they do, presumably they can at least sometimes think without the aid of *phantasmata*. Precisely because the agent intellect is strictly speaking divine and humans can at most have a share in it, its study lies outside the scope of this chapter. See further Burnyeat (2008), Caston (1999), and Cohoe (2016).

[36] At *DA* I 1, 403a8–10, the thesis that thought requires *phantasia* is suggested, but not endorsed.

Aristotle's Peculiarly Human Psychology 71

geometers and thinkers need diagrams and *phantasmata* as aids to their proofing and reasoning.

Interpreters disagree about the exact function of *phantasia* in practical and theoretical thinking: according to some, *phantasia* is necessary for all thinking[37]; according to others, it underlies only some exercises of our thinking faculties[38]; Even if the details of the collaboration between thought and *phantasia* are hard to establish, this collaboration points towards at least two peculiar aspects of human thought. First, human thought can be aided by *phantasia* in particular, and also by non-rational cognition in general. This is already evident in the role assigned to *phantasia* in deliberation and mathematical proofs. In addition, it is evident from the role played by perception and *phantasia* in the ascent to the first principles of knowledge. Both in the *Metaphysics* I 1 and in the *Posterior Analytics* II 19, knowledge comes about with the aid of non-rational perception, *phantasia* and memory.

The second peculiarly human effect of the collaboration between thought and *phantasia* is that human thought can be hindered by *phantasia*, by non-rational cognition, and by certain bodily changes: at *DA* I 4, 408b18–28, the decay of thought sometimes connected with old age is associated with bodily changes brought about by disease and drunkenness; at *DA* III 3, 429a5–8 emotions, sleep, and illnesses can 'cover over' or 'cloud' thought; in *Insomn. ii,* 460n3–16, emotions like fear, love, and anger prompt us to make mistakes in our rational judgements. Aristotle does not say explicitly that the connection between human thought and *phantasia* explains these impediments to thought. However, he repeatedly emphasises the close connection between *phantasia*, perception, bodily movements, and affective reactions. *Insomn. iii* (*inter alia*) clearly shows that bodily movements and affections can influence and impair the workings of *phantasia*. It is, therefore, plausible to believe that Aristotle would have appealed to the fact that thought requires *phantasia* in order to explain why it is hindered by non-rational psychophysical affections.[39]

A second peculiar aspect of human thought in its cooperation with non-rational cognition is specific to the domain of practical thought. It concerns a peculiar activity of human rational cognition and not merely the necessary support rational cognition requires from non-rational cognition. Practical

---

[37] Caston (1998); Wedin (1988, 140–41); Modrak (1987, 122–23, 130–31).   [38] Cohoe (2016).
[39] Aquinas, for example, attributes to Aristotle precisely this view in his *Sentencia Libri de Sensu et de Sensatu*, l. 2 n. 4 (cf. Cohoe 2016, n. 45).

72 ELENA CAGNOLI FIECCONI

thought, for Aristotle, produces commands addressed to non-rational desires and non-rational cognition. The production of these commands and their effectiveness is important in the works on ethics and political science. At *Pol.* I 6, 1254b5–10, for example, the best possible condition of body and soul involves the thinking part ruling the non-rational emotional and desiderative part.[40] Elsewhere, the rational part persuades the non-rational part out of its bad desires and it also governs action:

> The [sc. non-rational part] with appetites and in general desires shares [in reason] in a way, in so far as it both listens to it and obeys it. This is the way in which we are said to listen to reason from father and friends, as opposed to the way we [sc. give the reason] in mathematics. The non-rational part also [sc. obeys and] is persuaded in some way by reason, as is shown by admonition, and by every sort of reproof and exhortation. (*EN* I 13, 1102b31–1103a3)

In this passage, rational cognition engages with non-rational desires by means of admonitions (*nouthetēseis*), reproofs (*epitimēseis*), and encouragements (*paraklēseis*). By analysing these kinds of commands, we can understand better the peculiar strategies that enable the rational part to communicate with the non-rational part. Reproofs (*epitimēseis*) and exhortations (*paraklēseis*) are closely connected with the fine (*to kalon*) and the shameful (*to aischron*). At *EN* X 9, 1180a5–12, exhortations are contrasted with punishments and correctives. Unlike punishments, they give guidance to people who are already inclined towards the fine and who already take pleasure in acting well. Exhortations encourage these people to pursue the right things by characterising them as fine.

Epitimēsis, for Aristotle, can refer to different things. For example, in *Top.* VIII 11, 161b19, an *epitimēsis* is just an objection to a given argument. In *Rhet.* I 1, 1355a27 and *EN* III 5, 1114 III 8, a21–29, *epitimēseis* are more like reproaches and reproofs of one's behaviour and dispositions. Unlike exhortations, reproofs are associated with shame. In *EN* III 8, 1116a19–30 Aristotle argues that civic bravery is often motivated by legal penalties (*epitimiai*) and reproaches (*oneideis*). Reproaches inspire avoidance because they are shameful and not because they are painful like punishments (*EN* III 8, 1116a29). Reproofs and reproaches, presumably, are shameful and not painful because they point out that one's moral faults are worthy of reprobation. Hence, reproofs are shameful in themselves and

---

[40] At *Pol.* I 13, 1260a5–23 this idea is spelled out further. See also *EE* II 1, 1220a8–11 and *EE* II 2, 1220b5–6.

Aristotle's Peculiarly Human Psychology

they also discourage us from desiring certain things by characterising them as shameful.

Since they rely on the fine and the shameful, reproofs and exhortations are effective with well habituated non-rational desires. As Myles Burnyeat has argued,[41] in *EN* IV 9, 1128b15–20 shame is a semivirtue of learners. It prevents young people from acting on their feelings (*pathē*) even if they tend to live guided by feeling instead of reasoning. The recognition of shameful things brought about by reproofs has a preventative role similar to the role of shame. By characterising certain objects of desire as shameful, reproofs may lead one's non-rational part from being attracted to these pleasures to being disgusted by them. Similarly to reproofs, exhortations can generate correct non-rational desires because they encourage well habituated people to align their non-rational desires with their general pursuit of the fine.

The human rational part has the peculiar capacity to understand the fine and the shameful and to formulate effective commands on the basis of this understanding. These commands have a purchase on the non-rational part of the soul of an agent who has been trained to pursue the fine and to avoid the shameful. One may, nonetheless, think that these exhortations and reproofs are not the most suitable for the task. After all, non-rational desires and passions respond first and foremost to pleasure and pain (*EN* X 8, 1179b11–16). They require habituation in order to respond to the fine and the shameful. However, this objection loses force if we consider that the pleasures and the toils of a rational part are unlikely to have an effect on the non-rational part. The non-rational part, presumably, is unmoved by the prospect of the pleasure of intellectual contemplation or by the prospect of pleasure in virtuous action that gratifies the rational part.[42]

Clearly, the rational part can also exercise its ruling by bringing the agent's attention to prospective pains and pleasures, such as future rewards and punishments. However, since these are external incentives, they are likely to compel one's action without diverting one's desires. As we learn from *EN* III 8, 1116b29–1117a3, military commanders employ these external incentives to compel recalcitrant soldiers to withstand the pains of the battlefield for the sake of avoiding the pains of punishments. Presumably, a soldier threatened by her commander still desires to flee.

---

[41] Burnyeat (1980).

[42] *EN* X 7, 1177a22–27, *EN* IX 4, 1168b36, and *EN* IX 4, 1169a11–13. See *EN* IX 9, 1170a8–11 on the specific kind of rational pleasure that completes one's understanding and recognition of the fine. For discussion of rational pleasures of this sort, see Coope (2012, 155–60) and Warren (2014).

However, she does not act on her fear because of an even stronger aversion to punishment. For this reason, Aristotle might have thought exhortations and reproofs to be more appropriate persuasive measures for non-rational desires than external rewards and punishments.

Exhortations and reproofs persuade without arguing or explaining. However, it is plausible to think that reasoning too plays a role in the interaction between parts of the soul. The persuasive role of reasoning emerges in Aristotle's account of the appropriate use of admonition, i.e. the third kind of command suitable for the non-rational part. At *Pol.* I 13, 1260b2–7, unlike other kinds of commands, admonitions require some kind of explanation, or some kind of conversational rational engagement (*logos*).[43] This passage suggests that the admonitions of the rational part of a wise person are more persuasive than mere commands because they are accompanied by arguments and explanations (*logoi*). A related point is made in *EN* VII 7, 1150b22–25, where some people can control their non-rational affections (*pathē*) by awakening themselves and their rational calculation (*proegeirantes heatous kai ton logismon*). Aristotle does not tell us much about the nature of this awakening. However, we can suppose that it involves something like intellectual concentration and, perhaps, an appropriate narrow focus of our intellectual attention. By concentrating and by engaging in appropriate reasoning, we can prevent ourselves from boiling up in non-rational anger or from being blinded by appetitive desires. Aristotle's successors attributed a similar role to intellectual concentration. Simplicius, for example, discusses the ways in which awakening our attention helps us to control our emotions and desires.[44]

If this is right, human rational cognition is peculiar because it can be aided and hindered by non-rational cognition and desires. In addition, it has the peculiar ability to govern non-rational desires by means of exhortations and attention-directing arguments.

---

[43] Aristotle's view of admonition is embedded in a discussion of the correct interaction between masters and slaves. While it is clearly unacceptable as an account of human relationships, it can be used as an instructive analogy for the interaction between parts of the soul. On the connection between admonition, teaching and reasoning see *inter alia* Plato's *Apology* 26a3, *Phaedo* 94d5. For a case in which admonishing is contrasted to reasoning, see, however, *Sophist* 229e4–230a3. The reference to admonitions (*nouthetēseis*) and the analogy between parents/masters and children/slaves are clearly reminiscent of the description of the communication between parts of the soul in the *Nicomachean Ethics*.

[44] See Simplicius *Commentary on Epictetus' Handbook*, esp. 114.50 ff in the Dübner edition. See also Brittain and Brennan (2002, 92, comm. on ch. 33, lemma xliii). Cf. Epictetus *On Attention* (*Peri Prosochēs*) in his *Discourses*, 4.12 (Hard and Gill, 2014).

3 Conclusion

In *EN* I 13, 1102a14–24, Aristotle argues that ethicists, political scientists, and anyone who seeks to learn about the human good and human happiness should know something about the human soul. This means that the student of ethics should have a certain degree of familiarity with psychology and cognitive theory. Naturally, the student of ethics is not required to be familiar with these sciences as wholes, but only with some relevant topics (*EN* I 13, 1102a26–31).[45]

In order to determine which topics in psychology are relevant for ethics and political science, Aristotle employs a 'peculiarity criterion'. In *EN* I 13, 1102a33–*b*12 the nutritive part of the soul is not interesting for ethicists and political scientists because it is not peculiarly human, but shared between humans, plants, and non-human animals. Although it is required for the functioning of animal rational and non-rational cognition and desire, its operations are not in any way changed or affected by rational and non-rational cognition and desire (*DA* II 3, 414b28–415b8). According to some interpreters, the peculiarity criterion also suggests that the cognitive and desiderative faculties we share with non-human animals (e.g. perception) are not important for the study of ethics.[46] If this is right, however, our rational cognitive faculties (in particular theoretical thought) do not matter for ethics either. After all, they are shared between us and the gods.

On this view, the peculiarity criterion implies that neither rational cognition and desires nor non-rational cognition and desires are relevant for the study of ethics. This implication is, of course, implausible. Aristotle deals with perception and non-rational desires throughout the *Nicomachean Ethics*, for example in his account of *akrasia* and practical wisdom in book VI and VII. Similarly, he is concerned with an analysis of divine contemplation as the highest possible achievement for a human life at the very end of the *Nicomachean Ethics*. This suggests that we should either discard the peculiarity criterion, or show that human non-rational and rational cognition are peculiar in some sense.

In this chapter, I argued that humans are the only creatures in which the rational part of the soul and the non-rational part of the soul interact. By

---

[45] While it seems clear that a study of psychology can help us to elucidate Aristotle's ethics, it is hard to determine just how much psychology he expected a successful ethicist or political scientist to know. On this question, see e.g. Shields (2015) and Leunissen (2015).

[46] See further Fortenbaugh (1975, 26–31) and Fortenbaugh (2006, 122ff). My critique of this view follows Moss (2012, 72–74).

looking at this interaction, we can discover some peculiarities of the human cognitive and desiderative make-up. If my analysis is correct, these peculiarities include: an expanded perceptual, phantastic, and desiderative range; voluntary and synthesising deliberative *phantasia*; the cooperation between thought and *phantasia*; the rational ability to control desires by means of exhortations, reproofs, pleasure, pain, and intellectual concentration. Aristotle develops a peculiarly human psychology, even if he thinks that many aspects of human cognition are shared between humans and other beings. This is why human perception, thought, *phantasia*, and desire are distinctive enough to be relevant for the study of ethics.[47]

---

[47] This work benefitted greatly from the advice of Ursula Coope and Jessica Moss throughout my doctorate and beyond. I am very thankful to Katerina Ierodiakonou, Geert Keil, Nora Kreft, and Jessica Moss for their comments on the last draft. Thanks also to the members of the Thumos research group for their support and, in particular, to Tristram Oliver-Skuse for his careful proofreading.

CHAPTER 4

The Planetary Nature of Mankind
A Cosmological Perspective on Aristotle's Anthropology

Christof Rapp

In the following chapter I would like to draw the reader's attention to a passage in Aristotle's *De Caelo* that, to my mind, reveals some of Aristotle's deeply rooted presuppositions about the role and the standing of human beings within the cosmos. Strictly speaking, the passage, which is in book II, chapter 12 of *De Caelo*, is not meant to discuss anthropological questions; it rather unfolds a comparison between celestial bodies and living beings. In the course of this comparison it turns out, somewhat surprisingly, that out of all the kinds of celestial bodies, it is the planets whose nature is most akin to that of mankind. Since explanation, both in Aristotle and in real life, proceeds from what is better known and more fundamental to what is less known and in need of an explanation – in the given case from living beings, such as plants, animals, and humans, to celestial bodies – the very idea of this comparison presupposes that there are certain facts about human beings that are relatively uncontroversial and are not themselves in need of explanation. Owing to this general setting we can be confident that the characteristics of human beings that Aristotle adduces are thought to be general truths about the human condition – although he does not really engage with the details and the implications of these supposed truths.

By choosing this rather exotic approach to questions of Aristotelian anthropology, I do not want to imply that this passage offers something like 'the real key' to Aristotle's anthropology or another sort of privileged access to the set of questions that can be labelled 'anthropological'. I chose this cosmological context because it adds a different perspective on Aristotle's anthropological thinking (in addition to the more common perspectives), and because it adds an aspect that has often been neglected.[1]

---

[1] I originally came across this passage when working on a quite peculiar problem in Aristotle's astronomy. Some results of this occupation with astronomy have already been published elsewhere (see Rapp 2014). Since my overall understanding of Aristotle's solution to the cosmological puzzles is

78 CHRISTOF RAPP

1 A Problem Concerning the Movement of Heavenly Bodies

In book II,chapter 12 of *De Caelo*, Aristotle raises a question which, he says, is the strangest of all, and this is the question of why, in the case of celestial bodies, we find the greatest number and variety of movements 'in the intermediate bodies', i.e. the planets, and not – as one would expect – in the bodies farthest away from the primary motion, each body enjoying a number and variety of movements proportionate to its distance from primary motion.

In order to understand this problem, we have to recall that Aristotle is presupposing a geocentric model of the cosmos in which the earth is surrounded by concentric spheres, and that the outermost sphere is what Aristotle calls the 'first heaven' or the 'sphere of the fixed stars'. Whether this first heaven should be regarded as a genuine self-mover or whether it is moved by the unmoved mover is a matter of scholarly dispute; however, it is safe to say that it moves itself or is moved with one single, circular, uniform, and eternal movement. This first sphere is followed by the spheres of the five known planets, the wandering stars, which, as their name already indicates, carry out many, multifarious, and seemingly irregular movements.[2] The spheres of the planets are, in turn, followed by the spheres of the sun and the moon, and the two of them carry out significantly fewer movements than the planets. Concerning the sphere of the moon, Aristotle proudly reports that 'we have seen the moon, half-full, pass beneath the planet Mars, which vanished on its shaded side and came forth by the bright and shining part' (*DC* II 12, 292a3–6). Aristotle adds to this report that some of these relations are obvious from observation, thus implying that others or even most of the others are not. In any case, this is the cosmic order he takes for granted: the fixed star sphere first, then the spheres of the planets, followed by the sun and the moon and finally the earth, which does not move at all, in the centre of this system.

When Aristotle worries, then, about the movements of the 'intermediate bodies' he is obviously referring to the planets that are, indeed, in between the fixed stars on the outer side and the sun and the moon on the inner side of the system. And his worry is this: if the first heavenly sphere shows only one motion, we would expect that 'the body that is nearest to it

---

still the same, there will be a few passages in the earlier sections of this chapter that mostly summarise what I have already said in this other publication. The translations of sections of *DC* II.12 – initially based on Guthrie's, Leggat's and Jori's translations – are also taken from this previous publication.

[2] For the Greek ear the word for planets (from the Greek *planaō*, i.e. straying, wandering around) is inextricably connected with the association of wandering around.

The Planetary Nature of Mankind

should move with the fewest movements, say two, and the one next after with three, or in a similar arrangement' (291b33–35). Contrary to this expectation, however, it turns out that the bodies next to the first heaven carry out the greatest number of movements and display the greatest heterogeneity of movement, while the bodies that follow next to the planets, i.e. the sun and the moon, perform only a few types of movement, and significantly fewer movements than the planets. So, the cosmic reality as it appears to Aristotle disproves the expected order, which would have been *eulogon* – with good reason or reasonable[3] –, i.e. the expectation that, if the sphere of the fixed stars shows only one (kind of) movement, the number of movements of the other celestial bodies should proportionally increase with the distance from the outermost sphere.

Since the expected order does not apply, we are left, as it were, without any reason or cause, by which we could account for this remarkable phenomenon. And this is particularly worrying if the heaven, as a whole, is thought to be a paradigm of well-orderedness and regularity. Furthermore, if one explores the heaven, as Aristotle does, with the help of the teleological hypothesis that heavenly phenomena are as they are for the sake of something, it must seem disturbing that the movement of the planets apparently resists any good explanation.

2 A Thought Experiment

At one point it almost seems as if Aristotle was close to surrender in the face of this difficulty, because we have in these remote things, as he says, 'little to go upon and are placed at so great a distance from the facts in question' (*DC* II 12, 292a16–18). These severe difficulties notwithstanding, he braces himself for a somehow surprising, almost desperate new approach. It might be, he suggests (292a18–22), that the difficulties we are facing derive from the fact that we have so far considered the celestial entities in question only as three-dimensional bodies and units without soul. However, there is a chance of solving the problem if we think of these bodies as partaking in action and life, i.e. as animate and acting beings. As I said, this is a surprising move, and the exact status of this suggestion is unclear. On the one hand, the ancient Greeks certainly considered the stars divine entities; being divine, they might also be intelligent; and, being intelligent, they might be ensouled beings. On the other hand, Aristotle

---

[3] For a recent full discussion of the methodology corresponding to this notion see Falcon and Leunissen (2015).

does not explicitly say that they are animate, but suggests that we think of them as animate. And, while this could indicate that these celestial entities are in fact animate, it could instead introduce a counterfactual thought experiment, requiring only that as a part of an overall reasonable order the celestial bodies should be considered as though they were intentionally acting beings.[4]

We do not have to decide between these interpretative options, but can move on to the execution of this thought experiment.

> For it seems that to what is in the best condition the good belongs without any action; to what is closest to this (the good belongs) by means of a small and single action, to what is more remote (from it) by means of more actions ... (292a22–24)

The thought so far amounts to a three-level-scheme. (i) What is in the best condition, (ii) what can attain the good by means of a single action, and (iii) what is more remote from it. Obviously, whatever is in the best possible condition is not in need of further actions in order to attain this best condition and, hence, does not act at all. The background assumption is that whatever is done intentionally is done in order to attain a better condition and, ultimately, the best possible condition. Given this general picture, it is plausible to think that the more remote something is from this best condition, the more actions will be required to attain it.

3 A Vivid Illustration of the General Scheme

This nice little scheme is illustrated by an example from the domain of sports and their alleged contribution to bodily health:

> Just as in the case of the body one person is in good shape even without exercising, another by means of a little walking, while for another it takes running, wrestling and exercise in the dust. (*DC* II 12, 292a24–26)

(i) If the good bodily condition is the most desirable state (which is true of the domain of health), nobody who already has this best condition needs to exercise at all; (ii) For another person it only takes one kind of action which is not overwhelmingly exhausting, say taking a walk; and (iii) For still another person, it takes several kinds of action, involving greater

---

[4] The methodological status of the following discussion – i.e. whether it literally ascribes a soul to celestial bodies or whether it is more like a thought experiment (what would the celestial bodies do if they were rational agents?) – is clearly a matter of dispute. In Rapp (2014, n. 12), I compare some of the options represented in the current literature. For a more in-depth discussion see Falcon and Leunissen (2015, 234 ff).

The Planetary Nature of Mankind

effort, such as running, wrestling, and multiple exercises – even those that are performed in the dust. At this point Aristotle uses the sports example to introduce an additional level:

> While to yet another this good will still not belong, no matter what effort he makes, but something else (will belong to him). (292a27–28)

In this part of the example, Aristotle seems to be thinking of someone for whom the original end, i.e. the good, healthy bodily condition, is not attainable at all – no matter how many exercises of various kinds he or she undertakes. At the same time, however, there is some other good that is attainable for this latter kind of person. This leads to a fourfold scheme: (i) For those whose body is in good shape, no exercise is required, while (ii) for those who are already close to being in good shape, a little walking may suffice. (iii) For those who are more remote from being in good shape, a quite considerable variety of strenuous exercise is required, while (iv) for still others being in good shape turns out to be unattainable, so that no amount of exercise could bring them to this good. Notably, the agent at level (iv) is no longer aiming for the same good as the agents at the other levels. Once the agent is aware of the fact that no amount of exercise will ever lead him or her to the highest good, he or she will settle for a lower good, even though the original highest good remains somehow attractive to him or her. In a way, then, level (iv) is the level of resignation – though a reasonable kind of resignation, as the agent has good reasons for backing away from the originally pursued end.

Later in the chapter, Aristotle takes up the sports example again, in order to insert further differentiations into his general scheme.

> Thus, taking health as the end, there will be one thing that always possesses health, others that attain it, one by reducing weight, another by running and thus reducing weight, another by taking steps to enable himself to run, thus further increasing the number of movements, while another cannot attain health itself, but only running or reduction of weight, so that one or other of these is the end for such a being. (292b13–17)

Aristotle develops the idea of an increasing number of actions between level (i) and level (iii). This increase is explained by the remoteness of the desired end and the increasing number of intermediate steps we have to take in order to reach the good: perhaps we have to reduce weight in order to gain complete health – this seems to be still manageable; however, we might also have to run in order to lose weight in order to gain complete health, or even take yet further steps in order to prepare us for running in the first place, such as buying running shoes in the sports shop, acquiring the amount of money we need in order to buy running shoes, and so on. In this way the increasing distance from the good condition is mapped onto an increasing number of intermediate steps we have to perform in order to reach the best possible state. And this is also meant to give the rationale for the introduction of a fourth level and the phenomenon of 'reasonable resignation'. Once the rational agent comes to understand that he or she will never reach the best state, the best thing to do is to settle instead for one of the intermediate ends, for example, reduction of weight, which is thought to be closer and, hence, attainable. But, why is it desirable at all to lose weight for someone who knows that this will not bring him complete health? If we lose weight, one might speculate, this is likely to bring about intermediate ends, such as painlessness or absence of any sickness induced by obesity; these ends are not as good as health, but still better than the previous state. This is also Aristotle's explanation:

> For while it is clearly best for any being to attain the real end, yet, if that cannot be, the nearer it is to the best the better will be its state. (292b18–19)

Even though the highest good is not attainable for certain beings and is, hence, no *agathon prakton* – no good attainable or realisable through action – the highest good still serves as a standard for measuring suboptimal states that are attainable for those beings. In a way, this construal is reminiscent of what Aristotle says in *Eudemian Ethics* I 7, where he points out that none of the other animals that are naturally inferior to human beings have any claim to *eudaimonia* (happiness or the happy life); however, 'it is by some other mode of participating in things good that one of them has a better life and another a worse' (*EE* I 7, 1217a28–29, trans. Rackham). In this construal, *eudaimonia* would be a good that is not attainable for non-human animals, however hard they try; still, there is something else they desire, namely living well according to the standards of their species, which can be measured as a good against the standard of the highest good.

4 The General Scheme Applied to Sublunary Beings

Indeed, in the next step of the argument in this chapter, Aristotle inserts various species of sublunary living beings into his scheme:

> For on our earth it is man that has the greatest variety of actions – for there are many goods that man can secure; hence his actions are various and

The Planetary Nature of Mankind

directed to ends beyond them – while the perfectly conditioned has no need of action, since this is itself the end, and action always requires two terms, end and means. The other living beings have less variety of action than man; and plants have little action and perhaps only one kind. For either they have but one attainable good (as indeed man has), or, if several, each contributes directly to their ultimate good.

One thing then has and enjoys the best, other things acquire it – one immediately by a few steps, another by many – while yet another does not even attempt to secure it but is satisfied to reach a point not far removed from the ultimate [good]. (*DC* II 12, 292b2–13)

In the first part of this passage, Aristotle gives the brief and, as it were, anthropological sketch that provides one of the crucial links to the main topic of this chapter. We will return to it later. For the moment it suffices to grasp the general structure of this partly obscure passage. After the introduction of human beings, whose situation is highlighted because of the multitude and variety of actions they carry out, Aristotle quickly comments on other animals and on plants. This completes the picture of the situation 'on our earth', as he puts it, i.e. the situation in the sublunary world. What we actually learn about non-human animals is just that they perform fewer actions than human beings.[5] And what we learn about plants is that they have little action or, rather, activity; perhaps only one kind of activity.[6] Either there is, therefore, only one attainable good for plants or rather the one kind of thing they do is not the means to an attainable end,[7] but is itself the best for them. However that may be, it is clear that Aristotle aims to prove that plants engage in fewer actions or activities than non-human animals, and non-human animals in fewer than human beings. This still

---

[5] In ethical contexts, Aristotle usually denies that animals act or perform actions (*praxeis*) in the proper sense of the word (see *EE* II 6, 1222b18–20, *EN* VI 2, 1139a19–20), although in the biological writings '*praxeis*' can also be used for the activities of non-human animals (cf. *HA* VIII 1, 588a18). However, Aristotle clearly thinks that animals are able to perform intentional, goal-directed motions from one place to another – after all, this is the topic of his treatise *De Motu Animalium* (see Nussbaum, 1978). In this sense, Aristotle can allude to 'actions' performed by non-human animals.

[6] The case of plants is different because they lack the capacity to move themselves towards a desired goal. This is why Aristotle hesitates, for example, to regard stationary, sessile beings, such as sponges, as full-fledged animals (although they were reported to contract whenever one tries to detach them from their reef). According to *Historia animalium* VIII 1, 588b4ff., the transition from the inanimate to the animate and from plants to animals takes place in small steps and, thus, seems to be almost continuous.

[7] The idea that intentional actions can be analysed in accordance with the means-end-structure (or, more precisely, the difference between desired, intended ends and the things we do in order to attain such ends) pervades Aristotle's works; see e.g. the first sentence of Aristotle's *Nicomachean Ethics* (*EN* I 1, 1094a1–3). A similar idea was already promoted by Plato; see e.g. his *Gorgias* 467d: 'If a person does anything for the sake of something, he doesn't want this thing that he's doing, but the thing for the sake of which he's doing it?' (translated by Donald J. Zeyl, revised by John M. Cooper).

leaves doubts concerning the standing of each kind of living being in our general scheme. However, in the final third of the text just quoted, Aristotle abandons the restriction to the sublunary realm and alludes once again to the general scheme. This time he distinguishes between beings that already possess the best state and other things that try to attain it; among the latter group some are able to attain the best state immediately by a few steps, while others are said to need many steps. This is clearly meant to repeat the definition of levels (i), (ii), and (iii), and it is also clear that human beings that were characterised by the unusually high number of actions and activities cannot belong to either level (i) or level (ii). Thus, we can conclude that Aristotle wishes to assign human beings to level (iii), while the subhuman living beings that perform fewer actions can only belong to level (iv). All these relations can be summarised and illustrated in Table 4.1 (in which levels (iii) and (iv) represent the sublunary world).

If our reading of the passage is correct, the transition from human beings to the lower animals signifies the transition from the highest variety to a smaller variety of actions or activities and, thus, from an increasing to a decreasing number of actions or activities. This is the move to what we called the 'resigned' level (iv). Since our present passage indicates a significant difference between non-human animals and plants, we are entitled to insert a subdivision at level (iv). In a way this subdivision mirrors the criterion by which level (ii) and level (iii) were distinguished in the earlier stages of the argument, in that on level (ii) beings had to carry out only one kind of action to attain the best condition, while on level (iii) they had to carry out actions of several kinds.

Also, we now come to see that the domain of sports in the earlier stages of the argument was introduced just for the sake of illustration; the end of

Table 4.1

Level (i)	What is in the best condition?	
Level (ii)	What is closest to the best condition?	
Level (iii)	What is more remote from the best condition, but still struggles to reach it?	Human beings (perform many actions of various types)
Level (iv.a)	What cannot reach the best condition/few actions required?	Animals (perform fewer actions or activities of a few kinds)
Level (iv.b)	What cannot reach the best condition/no action or only one kind of action required?	Plants (perform a few activities of only one kind)

bodily health which can be attained by the means of athletic activities was especially suited for illustrating the different amounts of exercise, depending on the distance from the aspired end. Nonetheless, bodily health, however desirable it might be, does not provide the best possible state for human beings qua human beings. The sense of the highest good presupposed in this text must be somehow connected to the idea of living well, which, in the case of human beings, is regularly said to be equivalent with *eudaimonia*. Also, it is quite common both in Plato and Aristotle to use health as the bodily analogue to *eudaimonia*. Let us say then (in accordance with the *EE* I 7 passage quoted above) that *eudaimonia* is the kind of end that cannot be attained by living beings at levels (iv.a) and (iv.b). If *eudaimonia* consists, as we know from Aristotle's ethical and popular writings, in the activity of the rational part of soul, then non-human animals, which lack this part of the soul, cannot partake in this kind of activity. Why is it then that human beings are characterised by relative remoteness from the highest good? Well, possibly because, as bodily beings, they cannot partake in the full, unhindered activity of reasoning which is ascribed to the divine, incorporeal intellect. Hence, it seems to be this same divine intellect which is the best candidate for a level (i) being, since it would be true to say of the divine intellect, as conceived of by Aristotle, that it represents the best possible state and that, hence, there is nothing left for this intellect to strive for.

5   The General Scheme Applied to the Original Cosmological Puzzle

For the time being, let us leave the interpretation of the preliminary scheme at that. Before we raise more questions about the anthropological impact of all this, let us recall that all these manoeuvres were introduced only to provide a solution to the posed question of why it is that, with increasing distance from the sphere of the fixed stars, the number of movements does not always continue to increase, but from a certain point on even starts to decrease. The following piece of text is meant to drive the conclusion of the entire argument home:

> It is for this reason that the earth moves not at all and the bodies near to it exhibit few movements. For they do not attain the final end, but only come as close to it as their share in the divine principle permits. But the first heaven finds it immediately with a single movement, and the bodies intermediate between the first and last heavens attain it indeed, but at the cost of a multiplicity of movements. (*DC* II 12, 292b19–25)

86   CHRISTOF RAPP

According to Aristotle's geocentric world view, the earth is in the centre of the cosmos and remains there, being stable and unmoved. In chapters II 13–14, he takes pains to prove that the earth must be unmoved. What Aristotle takes to be a fact about the earth provides the basis for his concluding argument. The earth does not move at all, and the celestial bodies nearest to the earth, i.e. the moon and the sun, perform only a few movements. The reason for this phenomenon can now be taken from the analogical argument: just as plants and animals in the sublunary realm cannot attain the highest good, the earth and its immediate cosmic neighbours either do not move at all or perform only a few movements, because 'they do not attain the final end'. They, therefore, belong to what we called the level of 'reasonable resignation', namely level (iv) in our general scheme – the earth in particular corresponds to plants, i.e. level (iv. b), while the sun and moon correspond to animals, i.e. level (iv.a). In our current passage the highest good, which is unattainable for the earth, moon, and sun, is immediately identified as the 'divine principle'. This divine principle can be reached by the first heaven, the sphere of the fixed stars, with one single movement, the text says. The precise implication of this statement is not clear; however, we can speculate that the uniform, regular, eternal, circular movement of this sphere comes closest to the stable, uniform, necessary activity of the divine intellect or unmoved mover. In some contexts, Aristotle tends to flesh out this kind of kinship or proximity in terms of *mimēsis*, i.e. imitation in the sense that the first heaven with its regular, uniform, eternal movements aspires to imitate the life of the unmoved eternal realm; the idea seems to be that, for something that is moved, moving eternally and in a regular, circular and uniform way is as close as anything can get to the eternal unmoved mover. In a similar sense, Aristotle seems to assume that, to some extent, the sublunary realm (at least the elements therein) tries to imitate the regular movement of the eternal celestial bodies.[8] Be that as it may, it is clear that it is level (ii) that is designed to accommodate the first heaven.

What remains to be addressed is the level of the planets, which are between the first heaven, i.e. level (ii), on the one side and the sun and moon, i.e. level (iv.a), on the other. As a matter of fact, planets perform more movements, and less uniform ones, than the fixed stars; within the grand scheme, this fact is explained as an attempt to attain the highest good or to come close to the first divine principle, although, owing to their greater distance from the first heaven (and, thus, in a sense, from the first

---

[8] See e.g. *Met.* IX 8, 1050b28–30, *Gen. et Corr.* II 10, 337a1–7.

The Planetary Nature of Mankind

divine principle), this attempt requires more movements and movements of more kinds (i.e. movements along more heavenly spheres) than in the case of the fixed stars. This demarcates the planets from the fixed stars: the planets perform more movements in order to attain the more remote goal or end and they succeed in attaining this goal because, despite the complexity of their 'wandering' movements, they maintain a strict regularity. Compared to the situation of the earth and the sun and moon, on the other hand, the planets stand out in that they can attain the highest good in a sense in which earth, sun, and moon (allegedly) cannot; the latter, being unable to reach the best state (and hence belonging to the level of 'resignation'), perform significantly fewer movements. They can only seek comfort in Aristotle's previous dictum: 'the nearer it is to the best the better its state will be' (*DC* II 12, 192b19), but this cannot make up for their inability to attain, as it were, the highest good, i.e. the divine principle.

This completes Aristotle's admittedly speculative explanation through analogy. The different levels and the various analogical relations can be represented by Table 4.2.

As for the solution to the initially raised problem, the analogy between celestial bodies and living beings, as it is presented in the definitive scheme, provides an explanation, first, of why increasing distance from the best involves an increasing number of activities up to a point and, second, of why this pattern is reversed once we reach a level for which the best condition is unattainable. In other words, the solution presented draws on the idea that the intermediate beings, both in the celestial domain and in the domain of living organisms, still orient themselves towards the most ambitious goal, which is already remote, but, in a sense, still attainable to them, while the lower entities in both domains, being definitely unsuited

Table 4.2

			Earthly	*Celestial*
Level (i)	Best condition	No action	—	Divine principle
Level (ii)	Closest to the best condition	A few actions	—	First heaven
Level (iii)	More remote from the best condition	Many actions of many kinds	Human beings	Planets
Level (iv.a)	Unable to reach the best condition	Fewer actions	Animals	Sun, Moon
Level (iv.b)	Unable to reach the best condition	A few actions of a single kind/no action	Plants	Earth

88 CHRISTOF RAPP

for attaining the highest goal in any sense, settle for a more modest, easily reachable goal, which is still good for them to attain (due to a certain relation to the ultimate goal), but is distinct from the ultimate one.

In the definitive scheme[9] we finally see how and why planets and human beings occupy the same position – one among celestial beings and the other in the domain of living organisms. Both can attain what is best, but, due to their distance from it, the attempt to reach this level involves a considerable amount of effort.

6 The Divine Principle and the Limits of Analogy

The analogy seems to work quite smoothly for levels (iii), (iv.a), and (iv.b). Still, the empty slots in the 'Earthly' column for levels (i) and (ii) may indicate that Aristotle's grand analogy eventually reaches its limit; for, clearly, there cannot be a strictly speaking 'earthly' or sublunary counterpart to, e.g. the first heaven on level (ii), for, if there is anything closer than humans to the ultimate end of human beings, then surely it must be heavenly or superlunary. However, if there are certain celestial beings, say fixed stars, between level (i) and human beings, the involved celestial bodies will then play two different roles – an analogical and a non-analogical one: on the one hand different celestial bodies (including the earth) will be related to each other in a way analogous to the relation between human beings, non-human animals, and plants, on the other hand certain celestial bodies will be literally in a position that is located between the highest end (which, on this reading, would also be the highest end for human beings) and the level of human beings.

The same sort of problem becomes even more pressing with regard to level (i): planets and fixed stars, or so we are told, should be regarded as seeking to be like the first divine principle on level (i); and in a (limited) way even planets *succeed* in being like the first principle – through many movements on various spheres. Fair enough. But what about human beings? On a *non-analogical reading*, they try to imitate the same divine principle through the activation of the rational part of their soul, while on an *analogical reading* their highest good is defined by something that is only analogous to the divine principle in the cosmos. If we accept the non-analogical reading, we would face the same sort of infelicity that we already encountered in the previous paragraph: the same divine principle would

---

[9] For a previous statement of this analogy scheme see Leunissen (2010, 167, table 5.2). For a minor disagreement between Leunissen's and my reconstruction see Rapp (2014, n. 16).

The Planetary Nature of Mankind

figure in both columns, although these columns are meant to represent two different, only analogously related realms. On the other hand, we could try to defend an analogical reading by pointing out (and not unreasonably so) that the highest good for human beings is *eudaimonia*, and *eudaimonia* can only be analogous to the divine principle in the celestial column so that it is *eudaimonia* that is analogously related to the role of the divine principle in the celestial column. This sounds quite plausible. However, on closer examination, couldn't this kind of reasoning spoil the grand analogy that Aristotle wishes to suggest?

Let us look into the case of planets once more: what they do attain through their multifarious movements is being like the divine principle in a certain, limited, respect (this is, as it were, their criterion of success and what distinguishes the planets from the sun, moon, and earth), but not to become identical with this first divine principle or similar to it in all possible respects. If we want to construe the case of human beings as fully analogous to the planets, we would have to say something along the following lines: what human beings *can* attain through their multifarious movements is *eudaimonia* – the highest good for human beings (this is, as it were, their criterion of success and what distinguishes, as we have heard, human beings from non-human animals). However, just like the planets cannot become like the first divine principle in all respects, human beings, when they achieve a happy life, have a certain share in the highest form of life, but do not resemble the highest being in all possible respects. This means that human happiness, though being the highest good attainable for human beings, is not the highest good without qualification – for human beings are neither the best nor the highest beings in the universe (*EN* VI 7, 1141a21–22).

For the question of whether the divine principle from the celestial sphere plays a merely analogous role in human affairs or whether the best attainable state for human beings is directly (and non-analogously) determined by this divine principle, the following cautious answer seems to be plausible. Provided that Aristotle wants us to take the parallel between planets and human beings seriously, the point of comparison is not only that both have to perform many movements or actions in order to attain the good state; rather they are also similar in that it is not easy for either of them to attain the good state ('not easy' in the sense that it takes many movements and actions) and that this difficulty seems to be grounded in their specific natures, which are – in both cases – somehow inferior in comparison to a different entity, which by its own nature immediately manifests the good state.

90 CHRISTOF RAPP

For the planets this different entity is the unmoved mover which, by its nature, immediately displays the kind of uniform, necessary, eternal activity that the planets try to imitate by their regular, eternal movements (or the fixed stars sphere whose circular, uniform movement is considerably closer to the activity of the unmoved mover). For the human beings this different entity is god or the divine intellect, whose activity is eternally such as what human beings can enjoy only for a short period (see *Met.* XII 7, 1072b14–15). Commonly, 'unmoved mover' and 'divine intellect' are held to be just two different descriptions of one and the same entity.[10] If this is so, the divine principle that governs the cosmological realm as an unmoved mover is also relevant for human happiness – though under the different description of a 'divine intellect'. And, if this much is granted, the divine principle in our scheme plays both an analogical (as unmoved mover) and a non-analogical role (as divine intellect) for human happiness. According to its non-analogical role, the unhindered, eternal activity of the divine intellect measures and validates human *eudaimonia*; if human beings are active in theoretical thinking they activate what is the best and the most divine portion within them and, thus, attain a small and limited piece of the kind of life that the divine intellect enjoys without interruption and limits.

7 Anthropological Assumptions

Let us now step back from the immediate context of *DC* II 12, and take stock of the anthropological assumptions we encountered in the course of this discussion. In short, human beings are pictured as engaged in multifarious actions and activities. There is a thoroughly positive as well as a more forced dimension to this typically human 'hyperactivity': the good news is that human beings can indeed reach many good things, the bad news is that they have no choice but to engage in these activities – due to their nature, which seems somehow defective in comparison to the perfectly conditioned being. In addition, the number of actions required for human beings to attain the best possible state brings with it a risk of

---

[10] For a discussion that challenges the usual view, see Bordt (2011). However, Bordt's provoking title 'Why Aristotle's God is not the unmoved mover' boils down to the – thoroughly defensible – views that (a) the first *ousia* of *Metaphysics* XII is not identified with God in so far as it is an unmoved mover, but in so far as it is the actual activity of thinking and that (b) being an unmoved mover is not an essential feature of this first *ousia*. Hence, even Bordt could assent to saying that 'unmoved mover' and 'divine intellect' are different descriptions of the same entity (bracketing the problem of the number of unmoved movers in *Met.* XII 8).

The Planetary Nature of Mankind

failure, since the more we act the more we are vulnerable to mistakes or misfortunes. There seems to be an ultimate reason for why human beings are characterised by these, to some extent, conflicting tendencies: this is the so-called complex nature of human beings; they are partly akin to god, but partly just bodily, emotional, socially dependent and mortal beings. Owing to this complex or mixed nature people start asking themselves which part of them is more dignified or more authoritative – and one strategy of answering this question follows the *homoiōsis-theōi-*(assimilation to god)-scheme, which is better attested for Plato,[11] but also occurrent in Aristotle – though in a peculiar form.

7.1 The Optimistic Perspective

Comparing human beings and planets on the one side with the beings beneath the line of resignation – i.e. non-human animals and plants in the one column, sun, moon, and earth in the other – leads to a significantly optimistic perspective for both human beings and planets; after all, they are able to reach the best possible condition – though not in the fullest sense (as in the case of planetary motion) or not permanently (as in the case of human beings). For human beings in particular, Aristotle points out that they can secure many different goods, and that the multitude of goods reachable for human beings explains the variety of human actions. The fact that non-human animals and, all the more, plants perform fewer actions is taken as an indication of their standing in general, which is characterised by their inability to reach the best possible condition and, hence, the need to settle for an inferior good. According to this alleged difference, it is significant for the *condition humaine* that human beings have no reason for this kind of resignation, but, on the contrary, have reason for developing ambition and for longing for the best possible state – meaning that they long for *eudaimonia*, the best good attainable for them, which again manifests to some degree aspects of the best possible state *tout court*, i.e. the life of the divine intellect.

7.2 A Manifold of Actions

The emphasis on the manifold of human actions has two different implications: human beings perform a great number of actions and they perform actions of many kinds. Both aspects seem to be important for

---

[11] See, most notably, *Theaetetus* 176a–c, *Phaedo* 179d, *Phaedrus* 249a.

92 CHRISTOF RAPP

the comparison with planets, since planets not only exhibit more movements than other celestial bodies, but movements of different kinds – i.e. movements along various spheres. With respect to human beings, the variety of actions corresponds to the variety of goods that they can attain. What kind of variety is meant here? Possibly, Aristotle thinks of all the goods that ordinary human actions try to reach, e.g. health, wealth, beauty, bodily pleasures, friends, excellences of intellect and character, and so forth.[12] And, indeed, such a list of goods would make good sense in the comparison between human beings on the one hand and animals and plants on the other, since the latter do not choose between the same variety of goods, but are, by nature, disposed to realise one predominant good, namely their own survival and the reproduction of the species.[13]

7.3   The Need of Action

The section of *DC* II 12 we discussed rests on a straightforward and important assumption about the nature of (purposeful) action in general: 'For it seems that to what is in the best condition the good belongs without any action' (292a23–24), and 'the perfectly conditioned has no need of action' (292b5). Taken together, these two citations suggest that action is essentially an act of bridging the gap between a current, deficient, or, at least, not-yet-perfect state, and the envisaged better or (in the same respect) perfect state. To the extent that human beings in our passage are characterised by the need of many and various actions, this assumption also implies that human beings by their nature are in a situation that is somehow defective or non-optimal, but that they have the potential – through human effort and conduct – to bring themselves into a better condition. One might wonder, though, whether this definition of action is too narrow and whether it is compatible with Aristotle's well-known idea that there is a type of activity which has its end in itself. Are actions of this

---

[12] For an unbiased list of such goods see the list of goods in Aristotle's *Rhetoric* I 6 or the list of what he calls 'parts of happiness' in *Rhetoric* I 5.

[13] Indeed, this is also a way of partaking in the divine, as Aristotle famously remarks in *De Anima* II 4, 415a26–b1 (and elsewhere similarly): 'For the natural function of living beings ... consists in making another such as itself, an animal an animal and a plant a plant, so that it may, as far as this is possible, partake in the everlasting and divine'. If we want to bring this remark in line with the account in *DC* II 12, we should assume that this kind of participation in the divine represents the suboptimal goal for which non-human animals and plants have to settle because they are incapable of partaking in the activity that is most distinctive of the divine intellect, i.e. thinking. After all, this second-best goal is said to be 'not too far removed from the ultimate [good]' (*DC* II 12, 292b12–13).

The Planetary Nature of Mankind

latter type done just for the sake of escaping from the defective situation? This is not the place for going into this question; however, a quick response might be to say that, even in the case of activities that have their end in themselves, the agent will see an aspect within this activity that makes it desirable – e.g. that this activity promotes or is part of the agent's *eudaimonia* – and that performing this activity hence brings the agent from a worse to a better condition.

7.4   Risk of Failure

If the situation of human beings is such that they need to act and to be active in several ways in order to attain goods in general and the highest good in particular, they have no choice but to engage in these actions and activities. Within our chapter, *DC* II 12, the multitude of human actions seems to have two different aspects: the variety of goods they try to attain and the remoteness from the best possible condition, for the more remote a (still attainable) good is, the more intermediate steps are required. We do A for the sake of B, and B for the sake of C until we reach the desired state. It is remarkable that Aristotle immediately connects the remoteness from the desired end with the number of (intermediate) actions to be performed and the number of required actions with the increasing risk of failure:

> And again, whenever one has to do this for the sake of that, and that for the sake of something else, and this latter for the sake of something else, it is (relatively) easy to be successful when one or two steps are involved, but more difficult the more steps are involved. (292a28–b1)

The main thought of this passage seems to be clear: it is easy to succeed in one or two actions, but it gets increasingly difficult to succeed in many actions. The more actions, the greater the risk of failure. The reason why human beings are in a situation of having to perform many actions is their remoteness to the desired best state, plus the idea that this remoteness can only be bridged if they perform one step for the sake of the next step, and another step for the sake of still another step, and so on. One might wonder whether this idea is also meant to elucidate the situation of non-human animals and plants or of their celestial counterparts, the sun, moon, and earth. If they were rational agents who consider the number of steps they would have to perform to reach the grand end, they would come to see that this endeavour becomes impossible, so that they would have good reasons to settle for a more modest goal (in this sense their resignation would be reasonable).

94   CHRISTOF RAPP

However this might be, it is clear that this scenario has an impact for the situation of human agents. The immediate upshot of all this seems to be that human beings who need to perform many actions in order to reach the various goods they can attain and in order to make steps towards the highest good are bound to expose themselves to the risk of failure. In order to make use of their privileged situation within the universe, human beings have to perform many and many different actions, which involve major efforts and makes the outcome for the individual agent uncertain. Compared to animals who can aspire only to one end, say sexual reproduction, that is attainable by one sort of action, this situation makes the life of human beings stimulating, but also straining and difficult.

7.5   Complex Nature and Eudaimonia

The anthropological assumptions that we have extracted from the discussion in *DC* II 12 so far manifested two, to some extent, contrary tendencies. In contrast to non-human animals and plants, human beings are in the privileged position of being able to share, to some degree, in the highest good. This gives rise to ambition and hope. However, in contrast to the perfectly conditioned being, the condition of human beings is somehow forced, since they have to struggle and to engage in actions and efforts in order to make use of their privilege. From this perspective, the life of non-human animals and plants is significantly easier. Clearly, it is not the purpose of our passage from *DC* II 12 to elaborate on the reasons for this ambivalence of the human condition, but there are hints to the effect that human beings are characterised by what Aristotle elsewhere calls their 'complex', i.e. not simple, nature: they are sublunary beings, like non-human animals and plants, but having the capacity to reason they possess at least a spark of the best and most dignified being in the universe, the divine intellect. In a passage of the *Nicomachean Ethics*, the same idea is nicely captured by the formula that the nature of human beings – as opposed to the nature of god – is not simple:

> But in no case is one and the same thing always pleasant, because our nature is not simple, but also has in it an element of a different sort, in so far as we are mortal, with the consequence that if one of the two is active, this is contrary to nature for the other … Since if any being's nature were simple, it will follow that it would be always the same activity that is most pleasant to him. This is why god always enjoys a single, simple pleasure. (*EN* VII 14, 1154b20–26, transl. Broadie/Rowe)

The Planetary Nature of Mankind

Though the passage aims at a peculiar point – that for human beings different things might be pleasant at different times – the general contrast between simple, divine nature and complex, human nature seems clear enough. And it is also clear that, in this passage, Aristotle alludes to the difference between a mortal and a divine nature.[14]

In *Eudemian Ethics* II 8, 1224b26–36, Aristotle refers to reason and desire as two different parts or capacities of the soul, and emphasises that we possess both of them by nature – though not by the same nature. In *Nicomachean Ethics* X 6–9, the famous competition between the theoretical and the political form of life derives from the fact the excellent activities of both the rational part of the human soul and the non-rational part, i.e. character, seem to fulfil the general definition of *eudaimonia*. In spite of the notorious controversies about these chapters, there are two or three undisputed results. (a) The activity in accordance with intellectual virtue is ranked higher than the activity in accordance with virtue of character; accordingly, the theoretical life is ranked higher than the political one. (b) The superiority of the theoretical life is grounded in the superior status or value of the intellect (which is referred to as 'what is the best in us')[15] compared to character. (c) Complete happiness, consisting in continuous excellent activity of the intellect, is 'higher than the human plane; for it is not in so far as he is human that he will live like this, but in so far as there is something divine in him ...' (*EN* X 7, 1177b26–28). Again, these are unambivalent claims of the 'complex nature' of humans. Thesis (c) fully concurs with the peculiar situation of human beings as pictured in *DC* II 12: to some degree, they have access to the divine realm, but, owing to their complex nature they cannot, of course, catch up with god. Aristotle has a bundle of arguments for the superiority of the soul compared to the body, and of the intellect compared to other psychic capacities (that the appearance of the intellect defines the end and goal of ontogenetic development, that the intellect presents the true self, that the intellect is required for prudential and eudaimonistic reasons, etc.) – these arguments might be in the background of theses (a) and (b). However, in the argument of *EN* X 7 the superiority of the intellect and the theoretical life is associated several times with an axiology, according to which the divine intellect is the best in the universe, and human intellect accordingly the best within human beings. Many interpreters take this to be a

---

[14] See also Cagnoli Fiecconi in this volume (Chapter 3) on the (psychological) complexity of human beings.

[15] See e.g. *EN* X 7, 1177a13, a19, b34.

surprising move at the end of a treatise that was mostly dedicated to the life in accordance with virtues of character. The anthropological account presupposed in *DC* II 12 and, in general, Aristotle's ideas about the standing of human beings in the cosmos, seem to provide an appropriate background for this surprising shift.

PART II

Human Nature in the Light of Aristotle's Biology

CHAPTER 5

Is Reason Natural?
Aristotle's Zoology of Rational Animals

James G. Lennox

> If someone has considered the study of the other animals to lack value, he ought to think the same thing about himself as well; for it is impossible to look at the parts from which mankind has been constituted—blood, flesh, bones, blood vessels, and other such parts—without considerable disgust.
>
> (*PA* I 5, 645a25–30)[1]

1 Introduction

The Anthropology Department at my home institution consists of four major divisions: Archaeology, Social and Cultural Anthropology, Medical Anthropology, and Physical Anthropology. It would be a puzzling and ultimately fruitless enterprise to try and figure out whether any of Aristotle's many investigations of human beings would find a home in any of these categories. But that does not mean that Aristotle did not think of human beings as fitting objects for natural scientific investigation.[2]

Aristotle clearly thinks that human beings are one kind of animal among many, and, in his zoological works, we are among the many animals that are studied in comparison to all other animals. We are not the only bipeds, but our bipedalism is different from that of birds (*PA* I 3, 643a1–3), and is one reason why we don't belong to any of those kinds consisting of many

---

[1] All translations are my own, unless otherwise noted.

[2] Throughout this chapter the English term 'natural science' is a translation of *physikē epistēmē*, and refers to those investigations, including his zoological investigations, which Aristotle designates by that Greek expression. *Metaphysics* VI 1 argues that it is one of three 'theoretical' forms of knowledge, that is knowledge pursued for its own sake, the other two being mathematics and 'first philosophy' (i.e. metaphysics). The theoretical sciences are in contrast to practical and productive sciences, but there are interesting relationships among them: mathematics has many applications in the productive sciences, and I will argue in the last section of this chapter that the science of nature provides both substantive and methodological grounding for Aristotle's practical philosophy.

forms varying only by more and less.[3] We are the most upright, which means we are the only animal in which functionally defined 'up and down' aligns perfectly with cosmic up and down.[4] Human beings are possessed of the most hair on the head and the most moist brain (*PA* II 14, 658b2–10), and we have the largest brain relative to body mass (*PA* II 7, 653a27–30).

2 Soul and the Science of Nature

Like all living things, human beings are hylomorphic unities – we have dual natures, a fact intimately bound up with Aristotle's distinctive approach to causation, especially goal causation, as the following summative passage in *Physics* II 8 makes clear:

> And since the nature <of a thing> is double, the one <nature> as matter, the other as form, and this <formal nature> is an end, while the other things are for the sake of this end, this <formal nature> would be the cause in the sense of 'for the sake of which'. (*Phys.* II 8, 199a30–32)

The formal aspect of the nature of *living* things, however, is their soul, i.e. their capacities for nutrition, reproduction, perception, locomotion ... and reason.

> Therefore the soul must be substantial being in the sense of form (*ousia hōs eidos*) of a natural body having life potentially. But the substantial being is actuality (*hē d'ousia entelecheia*); hence soul is the actuality of such a body. (*DA* II 1, 412a20–22)

He goes on to distinguish two senses of actuality, illustrated by the distinction between the *possession* of knowledge and the activity of thinking, which leads him to refine his initial account of soul:

> If it necessary to state something common to all soul, it might be 'the first actuality of a natural, instrumental body'. (412b4–6)

On the basis of this outline of a theory of soul, there would seem to be a straightforward inference to the conclusion that an animal's soul

---

[3] On which, see Lennox (1987) and Lennox (2005). The only large kinds that bear live young are either aquatic (cetaceans) or quadrupeds. Aristotle is aware of our likeness to apes (*PA* IV 10, 689b32–33; *HA* II 1, 498b15–16; II. 8–9, 502a16–b24) and in the latter passage runs through many comparisons among the external parts of humans, apes, monkeys, and baboons, and concludes by saying that their internal parts are similar to those in mankind. This passage suggests a more extensive knowledge of primates than does the very brief mention of apes in *PA* IV 10, but it is unclear whether Aristotle would have considered creating a kind similar to our 'primate' order.

[4] *PA* II 7, 653a30–33; II 10, 656a11–13; IV 10, 689b10–12; *IA* 4, 706a24–26.

Is Reason Natural? Aristotle's Zoology of Rational Animals   101

constitutes a part, and the most important part, of its nature – in which case, it is clearly an object for the natural scientist to study.

(1)   Natural things are natural in virtue of two natures, their form and their matter, and nature as form is more nature than nature as matter.[5]

(2)   In the case of living things, their soul is their form, in the sense of first actuality of a living, instrumental body (412a19–20).

From which it follows that:

(3)   The souls of living things are their natures in the sense of their forms.

Aristotle would, thus, appear to be a naturalist when it comes to the study of the soul; it is a proper subject of investigation for the natural scientist. As Myles Burnyeat puts it: 'His psychology is designed to be the crowning achievement of his physics.'[6]

There are, however, a number of roadblocks in the way of endorsing that conclusion with respect to *human* nature and the *human* soul. Aristotle refers to the account of the soul provided in *DA* II 1 as a general or common account (412b5, b10), and concludes that chapter by explaining that he has simply sketched an outline (413a9–10). Nevertheless, just prior to this conclusion, he raises the possibility of an exception to the general account he has given:

> That the soul, *or some part of it*, is not separate from the body, if it by nature has parts, is not unclear; for the actuality of some parts is of the parts themselves. Nonetheless *nothing prevents some <parts of the soul> being separate, due to being the actuality of no body*. (413a4–8, emphasis added)

The 'part' of the soul he has in mind is reason (*nous*), and the possibility identified here is already hinted at in 403a3–10, 403a28–30, and flagged as more than a mere possibility in II 2, 413b25–29. Then, in III 4, we are

---

[5] *Phys.* II 1, 193a28–30; II 2, 194a12–13; II 8, 199a30–32.

[6] Burnyeat (2003, 36). Burnyeat cites the opening of *Meteorology* I 1 in defence of this claim, but, while the study of animals and plants is mentioned at least as the completion of the study of nature there outlined, a study of the soul is not mentioned. Compare: 'Aristotle introduces *De Anima* by suggesting that the study of the soul or psychology is part of the study of nature in general. Indeed, one of the reasons for studying the soul is that it contributes greatly to our understanding of nature. The reason for this is that the soul is like a principle of animals' (Johansen 1997, 7–8). In John McDowell's view, our rational soul poses no problem: 'In Aristotle's conception of human beings, rationality is integrally part of their animal nature ... What makes this possible is that Aristotle is innocent of the very idea that nature is the realm of law and therefore not the home of meaning' (McDowell 1994, 109).

102   JAMES G. LENNOX

told outright that reason has no organ and, therefore, cannot itself be the
actuality of a natural, instrumental body:

> Hence the capacity of the soul called reason (*nous*) is none of the things that
> are until it is thinking. Wherefore it is reasonable for it not to be mixed with
> the body; for it would then become qualified in some way, e.g. cold or hot,
> or there might be some organ for it, just as there is for the perceptive
> capacity; but in fact it has none. (429a24–26; cf. 429b5–6)

This concern about the ontological status of reason as a capacity of the
soul, in conjunction with Aristotle's hylomorphic conception of the proper
objects of natural science, provide the context for the following startling
passage in *PA* I 1:

> However, it is not the case that all soul is an origin of change, nor all its
> parts; rather, of growth the origin is the part which is present even in plants,
> of alteration the perceptive part, and of locomotion some other part, and
> not the rational (*to noētikon*); for locomotion is present in other animals
> too, but thought (*dianoia*) in none. So it is clear that one should not speak
> of all soul; for not all of the soul is a nature, but some part of it, one part or
> even more. (*PA* I 1, 641b5–10)

Just prior to this passage, Aristotle had raised an *aporia* about whether
natural science should investigate all soul or only part of it:

> In view of what was said just now, one might puzzle over whether it is up to
> natural science to speak about *all* soul, or some part, since if it speaks about
> all, no philosophy is left besides natural science. (641a34–b1)

This is sometimes referred to as 'the argument from correlatives,'[7] because
the grounds for the conclusion reached here, that if natural science studies
all soul it will be the only philosophy left, seems to turn on the idea that it
is up to the same science to study correlative phenomena; and since *nous*
and its objects are correlatives, if a single science studied *nous* and its
correlatives it would study everything.

There is general consensus that, as it stands, this is not a convincing
argument. The form of it is: If we were to accept the idea that all soul is
studied by natural science, then it would study *nous*; but if it studied *nous*,
natural science would study its objects as well. But the objects of *nous*
include not only natural objects, but mathematical abstractions and any
immaterial being there might be – i.e. it would study everything. So there
would be nothing left for another science to study. It is often treated as a

---

[7] Broadie (1996), Caston (1996a), Charlton (1987), Frey (2018), Segev (2017).

Is Reason Natural? Aristotle's Zoology of Rational Animals 103

reductio of some sort. But notice we're given no reason to reject this conclusion, and no reason to accept the *protasis* of the initial conditional. The role of this passage, in my view, is to raise a question or doubt about whether *nous* is a proper object of study for the natural scientist.

It is the passage quoted above, which follows the 'correlatives' argument, that presents Aristotle's positive argument against *nous* being an object for natural scientific investigations, and there is nothing conditional or aporetic about it – it is straightforward. It is arguing that rational soul is not a proper object for natural science because it is not 'a nature', that is, not an inherent source of *natural* change.

That conclusion appears to strike many readers as an impossible conclusion for Aristotle to accede to; surely human action is a kind of change, and surely it is the rational soul that is the inherent source of that change. I begin to address this skepticism by recalling a number of distinctions on which Aristotle insists.

First of all, there is the distinction between change (*kinesis*), activity (*energeia*), and fulfilment or actuality (*entelecheia*). Aristotle restricts the concept of *kinesis* to the three sorts of change mentioned in *PA* I 1 – quantitative change (growth/diminution), qualitative change (alteration), and change in place (locomotion).[8] Though he allows that *genesis* and its cognate verb can also be used to refer to changes in these categories as well[9] (something may be said to 'come to be' white, or tall), in its restricted, proper sense *genesis* refers to change in the category of substance – dogs and cats come to be without qualification, colours and sizes do not. The natural scientist studies these sorts of change and searches for their sources and causes. It seems clear that Aristotle does not think of human craftsmanship, moral and political action, or scientific thought as changes of this sort. And so it is plausible to think that, if natural science is restricted to investigating natural *kinesis*, *genesis*, and their sources and causes (including their final and formal causes, of course), then practical and theoretical reason and their associated activities will be the objects of *different* sciences, and not of natural science. Part of the purpose of this chapter is to explore this possibility and its implications for Aristotle's views about the constraints on a strictly naturalistic inquiry into human beings – in our language, an anthropology.

As noted above, Aristotle appears to think that at least some rational capacities are not the capacities of a specific organ; i.e. they are not the

---

[8] See the identical list of sorts of changes due to nature at *Phys.* II 1, 192b13–15.
[9] Cf. *Phys.* I 7, 189b32–190a13.

formal aspect of a hylomorphic part, in the way that, say, sight is the formal aspect of a living eye; so one might suppose that this would be his grounds for dismissing it as a proper subject of inquiry for natural science. As we saw above, if that were true, and the natural scientist were restricted to studying hylomorphic objects (as is clearly the case), then reason would be off limits for the natural scientist.[10]

Interestingly, Aristotle's argument in *PA* I 1 does *not* appeal to this issue of separability – at least not directly. So we need to begin by clarifying Aristotle's reasons for claiming that the investigation of reason and reasoning are not the subject of natural science before we proceed to draw out the implications of this claim, properly understood, for the zoological investigation of human beings.

3 Why *Nous* is Not Natural

It is important to recall that this passage in *PA* I 1 is not some obscure anomaly – the issue it raises is part of the discussion in *De Anima* from the very first chapter. In *PA* I 1, 403a27–28, Aristotle tells us that the study of the soul – *either all of it or of the sort being considered* (he has been discussing emotions)[11] – is within the domain of the natural scientist. He underscores the hesitation expressed here a few lines later:

> We said that the affections of the soul are inseparable from the natural matter of living things, *in so far as they are present in the way that anger and fear are*, rather than as line and plane are. (*DA* I 1, 403b17–19)

The contrast here seems to be between things than cannot even be conceptually separated from natural matter and mathematical properties, which, for Aristotle, can be studied in abstraction from matter, though they are ontologically inseparable.

The passage I looked at in *PA* I 1 is introduced with precisely the same disjunctive uncertainty (641a17–18, a23) as these passages at the beginning of the *De Anima*, but eventually concludes that the natural scientist

---

[10] Caston (1996a) argues that this needn't have a more general implication about soul as the formal aspect of a hylomorphic compound.

[11] Aquinas (cf. Pasnau 1999, 17) assumes Aristotle means 'ones attached to a body'; but it seems almost trivial, given Aristotle's starting position, to say that those aspects of the soul attached to the body are in the domain of the natural scientist. By 'of such a sort' I suppose he means the sort just discussed, any that are relevantly like the *pathē*, properly defined only by referring both to material changes undergone and a psychological state characterised teleologically – e.g. boiling of the blood due to a desire for revenge.

Is Reason Natural? Aristotle's Zoology of Rational Animals   105

should *not* speak of all soul, since not *all* of the soul is a nature, though one or more parts of it is (641b8–9).

Contrary to expectations from following the thread about the possible separability of reason in the *De Anima*, in *PA* I 1 the restriction on which parts of soul can be investigated by the science of nature is based primarily on an answer to the question, 'Are all of the soul's capacities sources or principles of natural change?'. In this passage he specifically denies that the rational capacity is a source of *locomotion*. The grounds of this denial initially seem weak, namely that many locomotive animals lack the capacity to think. That certainly shows that it is not a necessary condition for locomotion generally, but it does not rule out the possibility that it is a necessary condition of *human* locomotion.

William Charlton raises just this objection, and cites *DA* III 10, 433a9ff. as contradicting the conclusion in *PA* I 1.[12] Looking at that passage in the wider context of *DA* III 8–13 provides us with precisely the background we need to understand Aristotle's restriction on the study of the soul by natural science in *PA* I 1, and I turn to that discussion now.

If we begin with the passage cited by Charlton, the first thing to notice is that it restricts its claim that reason (*nous*) may be a source of locomotion to *practical* reason, and explicitly denies that theoretical reason could be – but even the restricted claim about practical reason is in the end called into question.[13] Here is the passage, with some important surrounding context.

> At least it appears that the moving source is one of these two things, desire (*orexis*) or reason (*nous*), *if one were to take imagination to be a sort of reasoning* (*noēsin tina*); for many people follow imagined things contrary to knowledge, and in other animals there is neither reason nor calculation (*logismos*), but there is imagination. Therefore both of these, that is, both reason and desire, are capable of moving things, *but by reason here I mean the one calculating for the sake of something, i.e. practical reason* (*ho praktikos*);

---

[12] Charlton (1987, 411). It should be noted, however, that Charlton concludes that Aristotle does not think that natural science should study reason (*nous*), and agrees that *PA* I 1 does not reach that conclusion on grounds of the immateriality of reason. Where we disagree is on how Aristotle reaches this conclusion.

[13] See Charlton (1987, 411), and Lennox (1999a, 4–5). Mary Louise Gill, in her comment on an early version of Lennox (2009), challenged me to look at these chapters, which resulted in that paper. She also felt there was conflict, and offered an ingenious reading of the *PA* I 1 passage on the hypothesis that it was an aporetic consideration of a view Aristotle in the end rejects. Her speculation appears to rest on Aristotle's remarks, following our passage, about order being more apparent in the cosmos than in animals – but this sentiment is also expressed in *De Caelo* II 8 (290a29–35) and *Physics* II 4. Gill has recently been followed by Frey (2018) and Segev (2017, 187–93). Both attempts seem motivated by the fact that taking *PA* I 1 at face value conflicts with prior interpretive commitments about the *De Anima*.

106   JAMES G. LENNOX

and it differs from theoretical reason in virtue of its end. And desire is always for the sake of something; for the object of desire (*hou hē orexis*) is *the starting point of practical reason*. (*DA* III 10, 433a9–16, emphasis added)

The central point here is picking up on a theme from III 9:

... neither is the mover the faculty of calculation (*to logistikon*) nor what is called reason (*nous*); for the theoretical faculty thinks nothing practical nor speaks about what is to be pursued and avoided, while [animate] motion is always in pursuit or avoidance of something. (432b26–29)

Later, in chapter 10, he reiterates that 'it is always the object of desire that causes motion' and, thus, 'it is this sort of capacity, that which is called desire, that moves' (433a29–30). The final summation of these two chapters on the cognitive faculties of soul involved in locomotion leaves out mention of reason altogether:

Since [animate] locomotion involves three things, first the mover, second that by which it moves, and third that which moves, while the mover is twofold one of which is unmoved while the other is both a mover and is moved—*the unmoved mover is the practical good, that which is moving and moved is the faculty of desire, and that which is moved is the animal.* (433b13–16, emphasis added)[14]

Aristotle's position, then, is tolerably clear and consistent. The mandate of the natural scientist is to explain natural change by searching for its sources and causes. In a highly qualified way, that *may* involve consideration of *practical* reasoning – but, even in that case, the search for the sources and causes of locomotion will point the natural scientist towards a study desire, imagination, and their objects, and away from a study of reason. In particular, it points to the sort of hylomorphic discussion one finds in *MA* 10–11, of the interactions that take place in the heart between desire, appetite, perception, and the inborn *pneuma*, which in the end produce movements in the limbs directed to the objects of desire. That discussion makes it clear that, while practical reason *may* be involved, it is neither necessary nor sufficient for the production of animal locomotion, including human locomotion.

These are surely the ideas in the background of our passage in *PA* I 1. Natures are sources of change (*kinēsis*) within the changing thing itself. Properly speaking, apart from substantial generation, there are only three categories of natural change, growth (quantitative change), alteration (qualitative change), and locomotion (change in place). He mentions all

---

[14] Compare *MA* 6, 701a4–6: 'For the animal moves and progresses by desire or choice, when some alteration has taken place in accordance with perception or imagination' (Cf. *MA* 8, 701b32–35).

Is Reason Natural? Aristotle's Zoology of Rational Animals   107

three here, pointing out that the part of soul that is a source of growth is shared even by plants, while the perceptive part, associated with alteration, and 'some other part' (*to orektikon?*), associated with locomotion, are shared by all animals.[15] He denies, however, that the part of the soul associated with locomotion is the rational part, and the passages from the later chapters of *De Anima* support, rather than conflict with, this very conclusion.

4   The Zoological Inquiry into Human Beings

The significance of what I have argued to this point for the zoological investigation of human beings is more minimal that might be expected. The systematic study of human beings plays a central role in zoological investigation, not only as a target of inquiry, but as a *standard of comparison* in a number of important respects, and I will focus the positive consideration of the place of human beings in Aristotle's zoology by considering three of these.

4.1   Mankind as the Standard for the Order of Zoological Inquiry

Having completed the methodological introduction to his *historia* of animals, Aristotle announces that, among the four fundamental differences[16] around which his inquiry is to be centred, he will begin with the parts from which the animals are constituted (*HA* I 1, 491a15). He explains:

> For it is first and foremost with respect to the parts that whole animals also differ – either by having or not having [a part] or by its position or arrangement, or with respect to the differences discussed previously, i.e. in form, by excess, by analogy, and by opposition of the affections.[17] And first we must take up the parts of mankind; for just as each people reckons currency in relation to what is most familiar to them, so also in other domains; and mankind is of necessity the most familiar of the animals to us. (*HA* I 1, 491a16–23)[18]

---

[15] The passage thus generally comports with the opening of *DA* II 3, that lists *threptikon, aisthētikon, orektikon, kinētikon kata topon,* and *dianoētikon* as the capacities of soul to be discussed (414a31–32). However, the capacity for movement in place is treated as related to, but distinct from, those of desire and perception.

[16] The first five chapters have illustrated how to investigate what Aristotle asserts in the first chapter to be the four fundamental ways in which animals differ: in their parts, their activities, their ways of life, and their characters (*HA* I 1, 487a10–15; b32–33; 488b12).

[17] These degrees of differentiation among parts are outlined in *HA* I 1, 486a15–487a1.

[18] Compare Leunissen 2018, 60–62. Her discussion of the normative role of human nature in Aristotle's zoology adds the important point that it is also rooted in our more perfect material nature.

108 JAMES G. LENNOX

This passage produces expectations about what is to follow that are not obviously born out. From the beginning of chapter 7 to the end of chapter 16, the external non-uniform parts are discussed in an order that reflects their position in humans, but what is distinctively human is not highlighted, and the discussion is often broadly comparative across the whole animal kingdom, with mankind being mentioned primarily when the organ in question is in some way unique in human beings: for example, only in humans is the front of the head referred to as a 'face' (491b9–10); human eye colour is more variable than in any other species (492a5–6); and our ears are especially immoveable (492a23–24). Aristotle concludes his survey of the external, non-uniform parts in mankind by reiterating the importance of discussing the parts in a certain order 'so that it is less likely that those parts arranged differently in other animals than in human beings escapes our notice' (494a25–26).

That requirement, however, poses a conundrum, since the bodies of other animals are not arranged like ours. And so, before moving on to the other animals, he discusses this very fact: our above and below are arranged in accordance with cosmic above and below (494a27–29); similarly our forward, backward, right, and left are, he claims, most 'in accordance with nature' (494a31), while in other animals things are not arranged in this way at all, or only in a somewhat confused way (494a31–34).

The arrangement of the external organs in mankind, then, is initially said to be appropriate as a standard of comparison because of its familiarity; but in this closing passage there are clear indications that it is also because Aristotle sees it as the most natural anatomical arrangement, in some sense of 'natural'.[19] However, as he turns to discuss the *internal* parts, Aristotle makes a remarkable claim:

> The parts that are visible externally are arranged in this manner, and as was said, are denominated and well known on account of familiarity – but regarding the internal parts the opposite is the case. The internal parts of mankind are for the most part unknown, so that it is necessary to focus attention on the parts of other animals, to which mankind is similar in nature. (494b19–24)

The order that Aristotle follows remains dictated by the arrangement of the internal parts in human beings – e.g. he begins with the brain. But, from

---

[19] In which sense? That is the topic for a paper unto itself, but for those interested in pursuing this question a good place to start is in Aristotle's discussion of the three pairs of directional dimensions in *IA* 2–6. There he notes that, of the three pairs, only above/below have both a definition established by reference to cosmic orientation and to function; forward/backward, and right/left are defined only functionally, by reference to perceptual orientation and initiation of locomotion.

this point in the text on, as Aristotle takes up the internal parts, his focus is primarily on the widest class to which the part belongs.[20] Immediately after stating that the brain is in the front of the head, for example, he notes:

> And [the brain] is similarly located in the other animals, *as many as* have this part; and *as many as* are blooded *all* have this part, and again the cephalopods[21]; in respect of magnitude, however, mankind has the largest and most moist brain. (494b26–29)

Apart from the problem referred to in note 21, the mention of cephalopods here is important for a reason more directly relevant to the topic at hand – it shows how widely Aristotle is surveying the animal world in trying to determine the full extension of each of the parts. Were he limiting his focus, as Peck's marginal note to this passage encourages readers to think, to the viviparous, blooded animals, cephalopods would not be on Aristotle's radar. Rather, his focus here is on all animals with brains and on what else they have in common: but he is starting with brains because he is starting at the top and working his way down, as determined by the animal with the most natural ordering of above and below – mankind.

The issue of the order in which to investigate the non-uniform parts is raised again when Aristotle makes the transition from explaining the differences in the uniform to the non-uniform parts in *PA* II 10. After an introduction in which parts related to functions shared with plants are discussed, he notes that animals with perceptual and locomotive capacities and even more human beings, who alone among animals have a share of the divine, have many more parts with much more variability (653a3–8). He goes on:

> So both because of this [partaking in the divine] and because the shape of the external parts of mankind is most familiar, one ought to speak about mankind first. For straight away the natural parts are disposed according to nature in this kind alone, that is, what is above for mankind accords with

---

[20] On this relentless focus on 'widest class generalizations' see Lennox (1991, 261–95) (repr. in Lennox 2001b, ch.2); and Gotthelf (2012, 307–42). In particular, Aristotle formulates the commensurate relationships among features with a double universal quantifier (*hosa ... panta*) as here: 'as many as have X all have Y'.

[21] This is one of many passages, noted by David Balme, in which the *HA* contradicts – and is more accurate than – *PA* (cf. Balme 1987, 13–16; and Balme's introduction to his edition of *HA*, 1991, 21–25). And it is an extremely important contradiction, since brains, according to PA, are primarily for cooling the blood (cf. *PA* II 7, 652b20–25, where he allows that the octopus has an analogue of a brain). That a whole class of bloodless organisms has a brain would appear to demand a fairly significant modification of theory on Aristotle's part. For further discussion of this issue, see Lennox (1996).

what is above in the whole cosmos; for mankind alone among animals is upright. (653a9–13)

As in *HA*, so here, familiarity with the external parts of mankind is one reason to take the parts systematically in the order we find them in our own kind. But, unlike *HA*, the fact that our above/below accords with cosmic above and below is also mentioned at the outset, as is some unexplained way in which we partake in the divine. It turns out, as we learn in *PA* IV 10, that these two claims about mankind are connected.

> Mankind, however, instead of forelimbs and forefeet has arms and what are called hands. For it alone of the animals is upright, on account of the fact that its nature and substantial being are divine; and it is a function of that which is most divine to reason and to think. (686a25–29)

Further on in the discussion Aristotle expands on his explanation for our upright posture by way of criticising Anaxagoras' understanding of our bipedalism.

> And being upright in nature, mankind has no use of forelimbs, and instead of these, nature provides arms and hands. Now Anaxagoras said it was because they have hands that human beings are the most intelligent of animals (*phronimōtaton tōn zōōn*); it is reasonable, however, that it is because they are most intelligent that human beings are given hands. For the hands are instruments and nature, like an intelligent human being (*kathaper anthrōpos phronimos*), always apportions each instrument to the one able to use it. (687a5–11)

He concludes by invoking his teleological axiom:

> So if it is better thus, and nature does, among the possibilities, what is best, it is not because they have hands that human beings are most intelligent (*phronimōtaton*), but because they are the most intelligent of animals (*dia to phronimōtaton einai tōn zōōn*) that they have hands. For the most intelligent animal would use the greatest number of instruments well, and the hand would seem to be not one instrument, but many; indeed it is, as it were, an instrument for instruments. Accordingly, to the one able to acquire the most arts, nature has provided the most useful of instruments, the hand. (687a15–22)

The vague reference to our divinity in *PA* II 10, as well as its connection to our upright posture, is now clear. As a consequence of our divine nature, we are rational,[22] capable of mastering many arts. We are, thus, in need of

---

[22] Though I'm not sure what to make of it, it is worth noting that Aristotle does not say that our divinity is rooted in our rationality, but the opposite – our being and nature is divine, and reason is a function of such a nature.

Is Reason Natural? Aristotle's Zoology of Rational Animals   111

forelimbs that can wield many instruments, that is, forelimbs with hands – that 'instrument of instruments'. And nature does what is best among the possibilities, in this case giving us an upright posture, freeing our hands for craftsmanship.

At this point it might seem that Aristotle is violating the very proscription discussed in the first part of this chapter – for do we not have, in this passage, the natural scientist studying reason and rational thought? I won't here rehearse the argument of my earlier paper on this topic,[23] but I stand by the conclusion I reached then. This discussion in no sense investigates reason as a possible source of natural change. There is a postulated *assumption* that human beings partake in the divine, and that reason and intelligence are functions of what is most divine – and this postulate serves as the basis of his account of two of our most distinctive *anatomical* features, our upright posture and our hands. An undefended aspect of this explanation is its assumption of a relationship between being 'the most intelligent of the animals' (687a16–17) and employing our hands instrumentally in a great many different crafts. For it is the fact that it is best for this instrumental use of our intelligence in craftsmanship that explains why our nature provides us with our upright posture and our hands. And an unexplored[24] implication of the constant use of the comparative form of the adjective *phronimos* in this chapter – that other animals are also *phronimos* – provides a fitting segue into yet another way in which mankind serves as a standard of comparison in another domain of Aristotle's zoology, his study of the activities, ways of life, and characters of animals.

4.2   Zoology and the Study of Cognition

HA VII begins by noting that animals differ not only in their parts and their modes of generation, the topics of the previous six books, but also in their activities (*praxeis*) and ways of life (*bioi*) – and indeed that these differ in accordance with their characters and nutrients (*kata ta ēthē kai tas trophas, HA* VIII, 588a16–19). Aristotle goes on:

> For even the other animals mostly possess traces of the characteristics to do with the soul, the differences of which are more apparent in the case of humans. For tameness and wildness, gentleness and roughness, courage and

---

[23] Lennox (1999a).
[24] By which I mean Aristotle does not pursue it in *PA* IV 10. This topic has been richly explored by Jean-Louis Labarrière (1984, 1990, 1993a, 2004).

cowardice, fears and boldnesses, temper and mischievousness are present in many of them together with intelligent reasoning (*tēs peri tēn dianoian syneseōs*), like the resemblances that we spoke of in the case of the bodily parts. For some characters differ by the more and less compared with mankind, as does mankind compared with the majority of the animals (for certain characters of this kind are present to a greater degree in mankind, certain others to a greater degree in the other animals), while others differ by analogy: for corresponding to art, wisdom and intelligence (*synesis*) in mankind, certain animals possess another natural capacity of a similar sort. (588a18–31; transl. Balme, slightly modified)

Similarly, when Aristotle focuses specifically on differences in character in Book VIII he notes that different animals have a certain natural capacity (*tina dynamin physikēn*) in relation to each of the affections of the soul, and explicitly mentions intelligence and stupidity (*phronesis kai euētheia*)[25] among them, noting that some animals partake in learning and teaching from each other and from humans. These texts provide an important background to Aristotle's discussion of the relationship between the character of the blood (and its analogue) and the character and intelligence of animals in *PA* II 4, 650b14–651a19.[26]

For our purposes, what is important to note is that, while mankind is treated as a standard of comparison in these texts, Aristotle insists that other animals having 'traces' of character traits and modes of reasoning found most clearly and obviously in human beings. And this sanctions him mobilising the categories of similarity and difference introduced at the very beginning of *HA* I: (i) sameness in form, (ii) sameness in kind with forms differing by more and less, and (iii) difference in kind, with attributes the same only by analogy. Do these uses of *nous* and *phronimos* in the later books of *HA* impact our conclusions about human reason and rationality as objects of natural scientific investigation?[27] I think not. Aristotle explicitly identifies the intelligence that we find in other animals as a certain natural capacity that is only an analogue 'corresponding to art, wisdom and

---

[25] At *HA* IX 3, 610b22, apparently picking up on this theme, he even refers to *nous* and *agnoia* in other animals. The following animals are said to be *phronimos*: deer (611a16), crane (614b18), and cuckoo (618a26); he also notes precision of thinking (*tēn tēs dianoias akribeian*) in the nest building of swallows (612b21; cf. 616b23–32); and skilfulness (*technikos*) in the nest building of wrens (615a19; cf. 616a5).

[26] And on the connections between these books and Aristotle's distinction between natural virtue and the ethical and cognitive virtues in his ethical works, see Lennox (1999b), reprinted in Henry and Nielsen (2015).

[27] And it is worth recalling that, in *Metaphysics* A 1, 980b22–26, Aristotle insists that animals with memory are more intelligent (*phronimōtera*) and better learners (*mathētikōtera*) than those without memory; And that bees, that lack hearing, are intelligent (*phronima*), but are incapable of learning.

Is Reason Natural? Aristotle's Zoology of Rational Animals   113

intelligence (*synesis*) in mankind'. There is no deliberation, formation of universals, or inductive or deductive reasoning here – they do skilful and clever things by nature, not due to thought.

These passages do, however, raise an interesting question about how Aristotle's willingness to include human beings as an integral part of his comparative study of all animals impacted his more focused study of human beings *qua* human. It is with this theme that I will conclude.

5   The Biological Character of Aristotle's *Politics*

The polis is, in Aristotle's view, a distinctively human outgrowth of a biological capacity we share with all organisms, the capacity to reproduce. This is not something we do deliberatively, but something we do 'like other animals and plants, because the urge to leave behind something such as ourselves is natural' (*Pol.* I 2, 1252a28–30). The distinction between ruler and ruled is also described as natural (1252a30–32), but it is clearly *human* nature that he is thinking about, for those are naturally rulers who have rational foresight (*tē dianoia prooran*). *Politics* I 2 traces the growth of the polis from these humble beginnings:

> A complete community constituted out of several villages, once it reaches the limit of total self-sufficiency, practically speaking, is a polis. It *comes to be* for the sake of living, but it *is* for the sake living well. Wherefore every polis exists by nature, since the first communities do. For the polis is their end, and nature is an end; for we say each thing's nature – for example, that of a human being, a horse, or a household – is the character it has when its generation has been completed.[28] Moreover, that for the sake of which and the end is best, and self-sufficiency is an end and best. (1252b28–1253a1; emphasis added)[29]

The development of the polis is, then, a natural, goal-directed process, with the achievement of a self-sufficient community as the goal. It is natural, I take it, because it is rooted, first in our natures as living things, and then in our natures as human beings, and its growth is not a process that is guided by a rational, deliberative process. A village arises by nature as families become extended families, with an elder as ruler; several villages, through various kinds of economic and cultural interactions, become self-sufficient, at which point a polis emerges. And, at that point,

---

[28] This is an application of the account of nature in *Phys.* II 1, 193b3–18.
[29] Transl. Reeve, with occasional minor revisions.

JAMES G. LENNOX

intelligence and deliberation can be applied, aimed not merely at living, but at living well.

That Aristotle is self-consciously embedding the investigation of the polis within his comparative study of living things seems clear from this discussion of the natural growth of the polis, and becomes even more clear in Aristotle's argument that human beings are 'by nature political animals' (*Pol.* 1253a2), a passage that rightly has been discussed in the context of a similar passage in *HA* I.[30] In this latter passage, Aristotle is providing examples of the sorts of differences he has in mind when he refers to animals having distinctive 'ways of life' (*bioi*). He divides animals into those that are gregarious and those that are solitary, and, within the former, gregarious group, we can distinguish between those that are 'political' and those that only group 'sporadically'. Political kinds of animals are those made up of distinctive subgroups, each of which makes a distinctive contribution to some one common function – examples of which are mankind, bees, wasps, ants, and cranes (*HA* I 1, 488a2–13).

Aristotle does not just claim we are by nature political animals, how-ever – he claims we are the *most* political of animals, because the possession of logos gives us the ability to distinguish good from bad and right from wrong (*Pol.* I 2, 1253a7–18).

That this biological conception of a 'way of life' provides the context for this argument that human beings are 'the most political of animals' is apparent from a passage a bit later in book I.

> But there are many forms of nutrition, for which reason there are also many ways of life (*bioi polloi*) for animals and for humans; for it is impossible to live without nutrition, so that differences in nutrients have produced differing ways of life for animals. For among wild animals some live in groups and some are solitary, whichever way of life is suited to their nutrition on account of their being carnivorous, graminivorous or omnivor-ous. So nature has defined their ways of life in order to facilitate their getting the food they desire. And since the same foods are not naturally pleasant for each but different foods are pleasant for different animals, even among the carnivores and the graminivores their ways of life are distinct from one another. And similarly for human beings, their ways of life are very different. (*Pol.* I 3, 1256a20–31)

It will be noted that the very division of ways of life featured in *HA* I is referred to here, and, as in the systematic discussion of ways of life in *HA*

---

[30] Cooper (1990); Depew (1995); Kullmann (1991); Miller (1995, 27–61); Mulgan (1974).

Is Reason Natural? Aristotle's Zoology of Rational Animals   115

VII, Aristotle here stresses the connection between nutrition and ways of life. The opening sentence of *HA* VII states:

> So, then, the nature of the animals in other respects and their generation has this character; but their activities and ways of life differ according to their characters and their nutrients.[31]

And, as one reads through the first book of the *Politics* we see that initially human ways of life are distinguished in terms of ways of acquiring food, until eventually trade, money, and specialisation of labour lead to ways of life not tied as directly to life's biological necessities – albeit ways of life that are ultimately still dependent on those that supply life's necessities.

Let us consider the claims Aristotle is making about the polis or 'city state' in these opening chapters. First, it is a *natural* development of less legally organised communities, which themselves are simply a natural development of family and tribal communities. Aristotle's teleological concept of nature allows him to argue that the constitutionally well ordered city state, as the natural *goal* of these less well organised communities, is their nature as well – they come into being *for the sake of* the polis, since it is the best form of social organisation there is.[32] This argument is likely in response to the so-called Sophistic movement, which had been arguing vigorously that laws (*nomoi*) are conventional and contrary to nature (*para physin*).[33] For Aristotle, being a political animal in the sense defined above is a broadly 'biological' category, and the propensity for human beings to make distinct yet complementary contributions towards the common life of the polis suits them well for this category. But we should not forget that the adjective coined for the category derives from the name of a uniquely Greek form of social organisation, and is being self-consciously broadened by Aristotle for biological purposes.[34]

That there is a wider, biological context for the *Politics* is clear in other ways as well. For example, book IV employs a method that is explicitly derived from his investigation of animals, as a means of bringing order into

---

[31] ... *hai de praxeis kai bioi kata ta ēthē kai tas trophas diapherousin.* The initial clause refers back to books I–VI; I–IV discussed the nature of animals with respect to their parts, and V–VI with respect to their modes of reproduction. In *HA* I 1, 487a10–13, Aristotle notes that the entire work will be organised around four kinds of differences: parts, activities, ways of life, and character traits.

[32] Cf. *Pol.* I 1 1252a1–7. For problems with the claim that the polis exists by nature, and a defence of the view, see Miller (1995, chapters 2 and 10, 336–46).

[33] For a valuable overview see Barney (2006, 77–97, esp. 82–87), in Gill and Pellegrin (2006).

[34] See Miller (1995, ch. 2).

116   JAMES G. LENNOX

the complexity of different human relationships, economic activities, laws, and form of rule – the method of multi-difference division[35]:

> Wherefore of the many political constitutions already discussed, we must say what they are (*tines*) and on account of what (*dia ti*), taking as our starting point one discussed previously. For we agree that every polis has not one part but many. So, then, it is just as if we were aiming to grasp the forms of animal – we would first determine what every animal must have ... and if there were just so many of these <features>, but of these there would be differences ..., then the number of combinations of these differences will from necessity make numerous kinds of animals ..., so that when all the possible combinations of these differences are grasped, they will produce forms of animal, and there will be as many forms of animals as combinations of necessary parts – <let us proceed> in the same way too with the political constitutions we have discussed. (*Pol.* IV 3 1290b21–38)[36]

Aristotle takes it as obvious from what he has already said that there are many different forms of political constitution, that each of them has many parts, and that we want to know, about each of them, what it is (knowledge of which will be in the form of a definition) and what accounts for its having the features that it has (which will provide us with demonstrative knowledge of it). Given the complexity of the objects we seek to understand and his views about scientific understanding, he argues that we need to proceed in precisely the ways defended in *Parts of Animals* I 2–3 – start by establishing the general differences shared by all constitutions, and then use simultaneous, multi-difference division (guided by a *historia* of differences of course; Aristotle is said to have gathered 158 constitutions for study) looking for correlations at each level of division in the search for causal definitions. For example, all have a form of rule: these come in three recognised forms, democracy, oligarchy, kingship – he later adds aristocracy as a fourth and a fifth, which is just termed *politeia*, but which combines elements of democracy and oligarchy; at the next level of determination there are four forms of democracy, four forms of oligarchy, while kingship comes in a proper form and in the corrupted form of tyranny.

Here it is not the fact that human beings are being viewed as animals of a distinctive kind that provides the zoological context for political inquiry, but the fact that human social organisation displays the same sort of

---

[35] I am omitting from this quote the running comparison with the necessary nutritive parts of animals.
[36] The wording here is closely parallel to that found in *PA* I 3, 643a7–23.

complexity that animals do, such that a distinctive kind of division is required in order to pursue an understanding of what these different kinds of social organisation are in the proper manner.

6 Conclusion

I began this chapter by noting that it would be a fruitless task to ask whether any of Aristotle's theoretical projects corresponded to something going on in Anthropology departments today. Instead, I asked a more tractable question: Does Aristotle see the study of human beings as an integral part of his natural investigations of animals, and, if so, how does that impact his investigation of human socio-political organisation in his *Politics*? One possible roadblock to offering positive answers to those questions is his claim in *PA* I 1 that the most distinctive features of human beings, our capacities to reason and deliberate, are not proper subjects for the science of nature. But, in fact, while Aristotle carefully honours that proscription, the investigation of human beings is a central feature of his zoology, and the results of that investigation provide an important foundation for his socio-political inquiries. One might identify these aspects of his thought as Aristotle's analogue to what we today refer to as Anthropology.

CHAPTER 6

Spot the Differences!
The Hidden Philosophical Anthropology in Aristotle's Biological Writings

Jörn Müller

The *Corpus Aristotelicum* contains several voluminous works which centre on animals, especially on their bodily parts, their behaviour, their generation, their movements, etc. These biological writings are a treasure trove for anyone looking for detailed information about human physiology and psychology, insofar as man is an animal (*zōon*).[1] But do the rich empirical observations in Aristotle's biology add up to a philosophically significant contribution to the question of what man really is?

In the following, I will delineate and evaluate the contribution of Aristotle's biological writing to the project of (re)constructing an overarching philosophical anthropology in Aristotle. First, I will balance the merits and possible drawbacks of taking into account the biological writings in general (Sections 1 and 2). I will raise three fundamental problems concerning the use of these works and their observations in the context of a philosophical anthropology. In addressing these challenges, I will show that there are no insurmountable obstacles to mining Aristotle's biological writings for anthropological purposes if we pay sufficient attention to his idea that the definition of a species has to be multi-layered (Section 3). Subsequently, I will argue that the best way to achieve this is to adopt a perspective of teleological essentialism, focusing on specific functions (*erga*) and the way in which they permeate a species' physical make-up as well as its way of life (*bios*) (Section 4). Finally, this approach can also be intertwined with Aristotle's practical anthropology (Section 5). The aim of my chapter is, thus, to establish a kind of structural framework for unearthing the hidden philosophical anthropology in Aristotle's biology and combining it with the anthropological observations from his ethico-political œuvre.

---

[1] By 'biological writings' I am referring mainly to Aristotle's *Historia Animalium*, *De Partibus Animalium*, *De Generatione Animalium*, *De Incessu Animalium*, and *De Motu Animalium*. I will also take into account *De Anima* and the *Parva Naturalia*, in particular *De Memoria et Reminiscentia*. For a recent analysis of Aristotle's biology see Meyer (2015, especially part 2).

1 'Man Is the Most Natural of All Beings': The Anthropocentric Background of Aristotle's Biology

The fact that Aristotle's biological writings contain a wealth of observations about human beings is largely due to the anthropocentric underpinning of his science of biology. This is evident on three levels:

(a) The study of animals is mainly motivated by our desire to know ourselves, as Aristotle argues in his famous defence of biological studies in *On The Parts Of Animals*. Since animals are 'closer to us and belong more to our nature [than imperishable beings, J. M.], they have their own compensations in comparison with the philosophy concerned with the divine things' (*PA* I 5, 645a3–4, transl. Balme). Biological studies are especially rewarding for scientific purposes: animals are easier to observe for us than the eternal beings, because they live nearby and thus provide a richness of empirical information which ought to be mined in our quest for (self-)knowledge.

(b) This natural proximity between humans and the other animals deeply influences the methodology of Aristotle's biological writings. The basic principles that organise the material are framed with a view to the human condition. This is signposted by Aristotle when he examines comparative morphology or anatomy, which comprise large parts of his biology:

> So first of all we must consider the parts of animals – the parts of which they are composed; for it is in respect of its parts first and foremost that any animal as a whole differs from another ... And first, we should consider the parts of the human body. Every nation reckons currency with reference to the standard most familiar to itself; and we must do the same in other fields: man is, of necessity, the animal most familiar to us. (*HA* I 6, 491a15–25, transl. Peck)

Aristotle maps his anatomical study of animal parts onto human physiology: this is his standard of reference and it serves as a basis for the whole enterprise of investigating animals.[2] This standard also applies to their behaviour, which is modelled on anthropocentric or even anthropomorphic standards: Aristotelian animal studies are based on physiological and psychological categories as well as on a vocabulary coined for human beings. The richness of information about the human condition in the

---

[2] Meyer (2006).

biological treatises is, therefore, a direct consequence of Aristotle's anthropocentric methodology in this area.

(c) This focus is also due to the special position that Aristotle assigns to mankind in the natural realm: man is the most natural and perfect of all living beings.[3] His divinity is stressed several times in the biological writings and accounts for the fact that, on the whole, man is the true measure and sample of physical nature (*PA* II 10, 656a6–14). By calling man the most natural and perfect animal, Aristotle mainly defies the prominent ancient and modern hypothesis that the natural equipment of human beings is fundamentally deficient and in need of compensation. Instead, Aristotle turns the table: all things considered, the other animals are, in important respects, inferior or deficient when compared to human beings.

This anthropocentric undercurrent of Aristotle's biology explains why humans appear time and again in these writings. Obviously, such a scientific program seems to be highly relevant for any attempt to construct an anthropology, because the methodological comparison with animals is bound to produce some insights into human nature, but it also has some pitfalls.

2 Aristotle's Biology as the Source of a Philosophical Anthropology? Three Possible Challenges

Are these observations on man in Aristotle's biological writings really suited for the purposes of a truly philosophical anthropology? The first and foremost task of philosophical anthropology is to tell us something about the nature of man – and not to collect random information on human physiology and psychology and to compare it with the rest of the animal world. Put in Aristotelian terms: we ought to look for a *logos tēs ousias*, a definition which describes the essence of the thing in question, i.e. mankind. If we follow the classificatory ideas that Aristotle develops in his *Organon*, this means combining the proximate genus with an ultimate difference, in order to establish the last or indivisible species that cannot be further subdivided (*Top.* I 8, 103b7–16; VI 6, 143a29–b10).

Now one might be inclined to think of Aristotle's biology as a taxonomic survey that catalogues and orders the whole animal world into well-defined genera and species. If this were the case, it would certainly support the essentialistic endeavours of philosophical anthropology. But the

---

[3] *IA* 4–5, 706a16–26 and 706b8–10; *HA* VII 1, 608b5–9.

general tendency in more recent scholarship, championed by Pierre Pellegrin,[4] points in the opposite direction: Aristotle's biology is not bent on demarcating razor-sharp boundaries in the animal world; in fact, the Aristotelian world is populated by many 'dualisers' that somehow occupy two opposing categories, thus undermining the picture of a neatly ordered animal world. Seals, e.g. are simultaneously water and land animals (*HA* VI 12, 566b27–31), apes dualise in their nature with man and the quadrupeds (*HA* III 8, 502a16–18; *PA* IV 10, 689b32–34), and man himself is no exception: he dualises, among other ways, by being both gregarious and solitary (*HA* II 1, 499b12–14), and with respect to the number of offspring, by having one, few, or many (*GA* I 18, 722a37–b3).

This 'messy' taxonomy is no accident: Aristotle does not so much intend to separate animal species, even though he discusses them in relation to the parts and features running through the whole animal world. It is rather these traits themselves that he wants to classify and compare. This descriptive and analytical focus does not lend itself naturally to a philosophical anthropology that is looking for the exact place of man in the world. Thus, the first problem with the biological writings, which seems to diminish or even undermine their contribution to philosophical anthropology, is their supposed *lack of essentialism*.

This issue is closely interwoven with another feature of Aristotle's biology, namely its apparent *gradualism*. Aristotle does not so much present the animal world, including man, as a saltatory staircase of nature (*scala naturae*), but as a biological continuum. He uses two types of differences in order to draw distinctions within this framework:

(Type 1)
Now generally speaking, differences exhibited in animals by most of the parts lie in contrasting oppositions of their secondary characteristics, e.g. of colour or shape: some exhibit the same characteristic, but to a greater or less degree; some differ in respect of possessing more or fewer of a particular feature; some in respect of its greater or smaller size, – i.e. generally, they differ by way of excess and defect. (*HA* I 1, 486a26–b8)

This difference, by 'more and less' (*to mallon kai hētton*), mainly serves to differentiate a larger genus, like birds or fish, into smaller species. It has to be distinguished from another mode of difference which serves to compare different genera:

---

[4] Pellegrin (1987).

(Type 2)
Some animals, however, have parts which are not specifically identical, nor differing merely by excess and defect: these parts correspond only 'by analogy': of which an example is the correspondence between ... feather and scale: in a fish, the scale is the corresponding thing to a feather in a bird. (*HA* I 1, 486b17–21)

For the purposes of philosophical anthropology, biological differences of type (1) are certainly much more informative than type (2) differences. The observation that gills in fish are analogously identical to lungs in human beings does not tell us much about the human essence. But do differences of type (1) really help us in building an adequate definition of the species 'human being'? It seems instead more likely that this biological differentiation, by 'more and less', marks a quantitative rather than a qualitative difference, thus blurring the categorical differences which are so cherished in logico-metaphysical taxonomies. This appears to muddy the waters for any essentialist anthropology.

Take, for example, the famous formula from *Politics*, book I, that man is by nature a political animal (*physei politikon zōon*). At first glance, this feature provides a categorical and species-establishing difference for mankind. But Aristotle immediately spices up his statement by adding that man is just 'more of a political animal (*mallon politikon*) than bees or other gregarious animals' (*Pol.* I 2, 1253a8). This remark obviously refers to the investigation of the social behaviour of animals in the *History of Animals*, according to which the cooperative fulfilment of a common task (*koinon ergon*) is the hallmark of the classification of an animal species as political (*HA* I 1, 488a7ff).[5] One might insist that, in *Politics*, Aristotle immediately adds another difference which appears to provide a better and seemingly clear-cut boundary, namely the possession of speech (*logos*) in humans, which enables him to engage in a different form of interaction in comparison with the pure voice of animals. But this attempt could be countered by many observations of bird dialects which sometimes come rather close to the semantic structure of human language (see Section 3). Instead, in the biological writings, the difference between human *logos* and animals sometimes appears to be of the type (1) distinction, and this also seems to hold for the treatment of *logos* as reason or intellect in Aristotle's biology: in fact, he offers many descriptions of quite intelligent behaviour in animals, and in certain places does not even refrain from talking about

---

[5] For a nuanced discussion of the different meanings of 'political', see Depew (1995).

Anthropology in Aristotle's Biological Writings   123

degrees of *nous* and *dianoia* in the animal kingdom (*HA* VIII 3, 610b20–22).[6]

This biological gradualism appears to challenge or even subvert the search for a qualitative, ultimate difference of man which sets him apart from all other animals. This is certainly in large part due to the anthropocentric methodological programme of Aristotle's biology as described above. In order to use man as a measure and guide in organising the animal world, the focus on comparable parts and features is self-evident – and this approach is simply not tailored to spotting the ultimate specific difference of man.

This predicament encapsulates the third problem: suppose that there truly is a categorical final difference of man which has no point of reference or comparison in the rest of the animal world, lifting man apart from the gradualist biological continuum. A suitable candidate in Aristotle is certainly mind (*nous*), which seems to occupy a special place in nature: in *On The Soul* and elsewhere it is attributed only to human souls (*DA* II 3, 414b16–19; *PA* I 1, 641b4–7), and even in the biological writings it is somehow mysteriously described as coming 'from outside' in the process of generation and of the embryo's growth out of the transmitted semen.[7] Furthermore, *nous* is at least partially separable from the body, which means that it falls outside the scope of a biological analysis fixed on embodied souls. Aristotle explicitly states that *nous* is no concern of the natural scientist (*PA* I 1, 641a17–b11),[8] and this obviously severely limits what can be said about it in the biological writings. But this appears to create another impasse for the relevance of biology in an Aristotelian anthropology: when it comes to such a vital part of this enterprise, the biological œuvre could only hint at this difference and would have to remain largely silent on it because it exceeds or transcends the limits of its own inquiry. Consequently, the biological writings can at least always be charged with a fundamental and inherent *incompleteness* in their outlook on matters of philosophical anthropology.

---

[6] For an overview of the relevant material see Coles (1997), who argues for more-and-less degrees of mind in Aristotle's biological *continuum*. A fervent critic of the idea that Aristotle attributes intelligence to animals is Sorabji (1993, 12–16).

[7] *GA* II 3, 736a24ff, esp. 736b29 (*nous thyrathen*).

[8] See also *Met.* VI 1, 1026a5–6 and *DA* I 1, 403a29–b16; for a thorough analysis of *nous* in its relation to nature and natural science see Charlton (1987). There is a growing tendency to reassess the 'separability' of the human mind in view of the bodily aspects of thinking which can be gathered from Aristotle's biological writings; see, e.g. van der Eijk (1997).

3 Meeting the Challenges: Essentialism, Gradualism, and Incompleteness Reconsidered

In order to address these challenges, one must first carefully disentangle some of the issues sketched above. A suitable starting-point is the first book of *De Partibus Animalium*. While the *History of Animals* provides a structured collection of biological data, *On the Parts of Animals* focuses on an aetiological analysis of this material, introduced by some general methodological reflections. In this passage, Aristotle is rather critical of the traditional idea that, in order to determine a species, one has to move down from the top of a single *arbor Porphyriana* until finally reaching one ultimate difference that singles out the last kind. Aristotle offers a poignant critique of the Academic method of *dihairesis* (*PA* I 2, 642b5–7), and draws from it an important conclusion: 'It is in fact clear from the following that none of the particular species can be obtained by dividing the genus dichotomously as some have thought. The particulars divided off cannot have just one difference, whether one takes them as simple or compounded' (*PA* I 3, 643b26–3).

Aristotle illustrates his critique using the standard example of 'footedness' as a basis for a dichotomous division that leads, in the case of humans, to the final differentia of 'biped' or 'toed' (echoing the famous Platonic definition of man as a featherless biped animal with broad toes[9]). He criticises this method for producing, underway, a number of distinctions that are ultimately somehow superfluous in light of the final difference. But the gist of his dissatisfaction is not a mere technicality. He thinks that such a definition is necessarily inadequate in an important respect:

> If man were merely a thing with toes, this method would have shown it to be his one differentia. But since in fact he is not, he must necessarily have many differences not under one division. Yet more than one cannot belong to the same object under one dichotomy, but one dichotomy must end with one at a time. So it is impossible to obtain any of the particular animals by dichotomous division. (*PA* I 3, 644a6–11)

There are two important conclusions which can be drawn from this critique:[10] First, according to Aristotle, the biological difference of a species does not consist in a single characteristic or trait, but in a number of them. What makes humans human in Aristotle's biology is a plurality of physiological as well as psychological features. And, second, these specific features

---

[9] Plato, *Definitions*, 121.   [10] Cho (2003, 189–90).

Anthropology in Aristotle's Biological Writings   125

do not follow vertically one upon another (as in dichotomous branching), but are instead situated on a horizontal level. Thus, the definition of a species is not established by naming just one of these ultimate differences, but by combining all of them on par with each other.

One might object that Aristotle probably uses a different understanding of 'difference' in his biology than in his logical and metaphysical works, thus mitigating the idea of a well-formed definition. But, in a telling passage in his *Posterior Analytics*, he confirms the idea of putting together a definition by adding several features. In order to have a valid definition of the number three, one has to say that it has three characteristics: it is odd, a prime number, and cannot be produced by the addition of other numbers (*APo* II 13, 96a24–b14).[11] Taken individually, all three characteristics are not unique to the number three; but together they form an unambiguous definition which describes no other number but three. This idea of a multi-layered definition of a species, where the difference is expressed by various differences, is also at the root of Aristotle's approach in his biology.

Furthermore, in his theoretical considerations, Aristotle leaves no doubt that the biological species is to be considered as a 'form in matter' (*eidos en tē hylē*), and that it is identical with the ultimate difference (*PA* I 3, 643a24–27).[12] And this enmattered form is also finally characterised as the substance (*ousia*) of the individual thing. This squares with some passages from *Metaphysics Zeta* and the *Posterior Analytics*;[13] therefore, it is not necessary to drive a wedge between the biological and the logico-metaphysical understanding of 'specific difference' and 'definition'. Aristotle certainly aims to give a substantial difference (*diaphora kat' ousian*), which is the final one, when he discusses the best way to pin down a species in *On the Parts of Animals*.[14] In pointing to the indispensability of several defining features, which also include bodily dispositions, Aristotle simply stresses that the members of biological kinds are hylomorphic beings which have to be understood in the complex interplay of psychology and physiology. There is no lack of interest in an essentialist understanding of animal species to be detected in Aristotle's biological writings; he just wards off anyone who presents an overly narrow and, thus, impoverished description that concentrates on just one of a species'

---

[11] See Kullmann (1974, 348–49). The last feature is based on the fact that 'one' is not regarded by Aristotle as a number (*arithmos*).

[12] For the different readings of this passage see Cho (2003, 184–93).

[13] *Met.* VII 12, 1038a9f and 25f, *APo* II 13, 97a12ff for the different uses of *diaphora*.

[14] In *PA* I 1, Aristotle unmistakably talks of the specific difference as *atomos* (643a8–9), *eschatē* (643a18–19, 644a2), and *teleutaia* (644a3).

126   JÖRN MÜLLER

formal features. Thus, the overall charge of a lack of essentialism in Aristotle's biology seems to be misguided.[15]

But what about gradualism? This challenge may be met by a closer look at the way in which Aristotle handles features unique to man. One prominent example of this is even presented within a biological context, namely at the beginning of the *History of Animals*:

> The only animal which is deliberative (*bouleutikon*) is man. Many animals have the power of memory (*mnēmē*) and can be trained; but the only one which is capable of recollecting (*anamimēskesthai*) is man. (*HA* I 1, 488b24–26, transl. Peck, altered)

In this passage, Aristotle appears to draw a clear-cut line between man and all other animals, thus offering a differentialist (and undermining a gradualist) account of man. Thus, if one is looking for a categorical, qualitative, anthropological difference, this seems to be a highly suitable candidate. But, in order to evaluate such a claim, it is necessary to determine the scope of this difference as exactly as possible.

First of all, one has to identify the *tertium comparationis* between deliberation and recollection that is implicitly presupposed in the passage above. Aristotle provides the link himself in his treatise *On Memory*:

> The explanation is that recollecting is, as it were, a sort of reasoning (*syllogismos*). For in recollecting, a man reasons that he formerly saw, or heard, or had some such experience, and recollecting is, as it were a sort of search. And this kind of search is an attribute only of those animals which also have the deliberating part (*bouleutikon*). For indeed deliberation is a sort of reasoning. (*Mem.* 2, 453a9–14, transl. Sorabji)

The basic link between deliberation and recollection is the ability of inferential thinking (*syllogizesthai*): for deliberation this basically means that one is capable of forming, out of several propositions, a practical syllogism that triggers the ensuing action; for recollection it designates the ability of running mentally from a starting point through a series of interconnected images towards the item one is searching for. Now both of these processes presuppose the 'ability to combine several images (*phantasmata*) into one' (*DA* III 11, 434a9–10, transl. Hett).[16] Aristotle explains the importance of this ability to combine different mental contents with regard to practical deliberation as follows: 'For to decide whether one shall do this or that calls at once for calculation (*logismos*), and one must measure by a single

---

[15] See also Granger (1985).
[16] Cagnoli Fiecconi (ch. 3, 61–69) gives a detailed analysis of this passage on deliberative *phantasia*.

Anthropology in Aristotle's Biological Writings 127

standard; for one pursues the greater good.' Put in modern terms: in order to form an 'all things considered judgment' (D. Davidson) which arrives at the conclusion that this is the best thing to do with regard to all available options, we need a unifying principle in the soul of the agent, a special psychic power. This is identified by Aristotle straightforwardly as the deliberative imagination (*phantasia bouleutikē*), which is alternately called rational imagination (*phantasia logistikē*; *DA* III 11, 434a7) because it relies on the kind of inferential reasoning sketched above that is also present in recollection. Therefore, summarising this specific difference, man is the only calculating animal because he possesses inferential thinking.

The anthropological gist of this idea becomes even clearer in light of an underlying faculty psychology. Instead of reserving imagination completely for human beings, Aristotle explicitly extends it to animals.[17] The possession of imagination is the basis of memory, because *mnēmē* calls for a mental representation of sensual impressions that outlasts the end of the actual perceptual process: the images stay in the imagination. But Aristotle thinks that the imagination of animals is limited to sensual experiences; it is a purely sensual imagination (*phantasia aisthētikē*) which sticks to particular items and does not allow for the complex combination of them, as in inferential thinking.[18] This does not bar animals from learning or even acquiring a certain sort of experience, but it precludes them from higher cognitive functions like opinion, science, etc., which are only available to human beings.

There are at least two areas which are profoundly influenced by this difference between sensual and rational imagination:

(1) *Movement and action*: Aristotle elaborates his idea of the practical syllogism as a cause of self-movement in his *On The Motion of Animals*.[19] Imagination plays a significant causal role in producing movements because it prepares the desire (*orexis*), which in turn prepares the bodily affections and the organic parts that actually carry out the physical action. But *phantasia* itself has two distinct sources: it may 'come about either through thought (*noēsis*) or through sense-perception' (*MA* 8, 702a17–19). This ties in nicely with the distinction between the two sorts of imagination (*DA* III 10, 433b27–30) and with Aristotle's remark in *De Anima*

---

[17] *DA* III 3, 428a9–11, where Aristotle only excludes particular animals, like the ant, the bee, or the grub, from the possession of *phantasia*. See also *Met.* I 1, 980b25–26. For the role of this faculty in the mental life of animals according to Aristotle, see Osborne (2007, 79–94).

[18] For the relationship between human and animal imagination see Labarrière (1984; 2005b, ch. 4).

[19] For detailed discussion see Nussbaum (1978, essays 4–5).

128   JÖRN MÜLLER

about an 'imagination from inference' (*phantasia ek syllogismou*).[20] It also
explains why Aristotle sometimes equates thinking and imagination when
explaining animal self-movement. The causation of action can be
described in syllogistic terms as combining a major proposition expressing
desire ('I have to drink') and a minor proposition ('Here's drink') delivered
by cognition. The conclusion is the action itself, in this case: drinking (*MA*
7, 701a32–33). But this certainly does not mean that Aristotle ascribes to
all animals the formulation of inferential syllogisms as a kind of explicit
event in the psyche.

Nevertheless, one should note that Aristotle is keenly interested in the
structural parallelism of human and animal behaviour that allows for an
overarching 'common explanation'[21] of both of them. The practical syllogism is basically an explanatory device used to describe how self-movement
is causally triggered, focusing on the required psychological components of
desire and cognitive content. This is another instance of the anthropocentric orientation of his biology: in applying the notion of the syllogism to
animal behaviour, he once again models animals in comparison with man.
There are also concrete instances in the biological works where Aristotle
ascribes to animals a kind of intelligent behaviour that seems to come close
to human inferential reasoning: before dolphins follow their prey down to
the depths of the sea, 'they restrain their breath as though from calculation
(*hōsper analogisamenoi*)' (*HA* VIII 48, 631a26–27).[22] The swallow shows
considerable ingenuity in providing and combining nesting material,
which prompts Aristotle to remark that she builds her nest 'just as men
(*kathaper hoi anthrōpoi*)' do (*HA* VIII 7, 612b25). Especially in book VIII
(IX) of his *History of Animals*, Aristotle describes many forms of intelligent
behaviour resembling human planning and foresight.

But one has to note that the two examples given above with their 'as if'-
character (*hōsper, kathaper*) rather point to a type (2) difference, namely a
mere analogy of inferential reasoning. Aristotle phrases this connection
carefully as follows: 'In general, with regard to their lives, one may observe
many imitations (*mimēmata*) of human life in the other animals' (*HA* VIII
7, 612b18–19, followed by the example of the swallow's nest-building
quoted above). This echoes his rather cautious attribution to animals of

---

[20] *DA* III 11, 434a11. As constructed by Hicks; see Nussbaum (1978, 264).
[21] Nussbaum (1983).
[22] Sorabji (1993, 13) stresses the 'as if'-character of such statements and sees them rather as 'casual
everyday descriptions' and not as serious attributions of intelligence to animals.

Anthropology in Aristotle's Biological Writings 129

intellectual understanding that differs not by degree – type (1) – but 'by analogy: for corresponding to art, wisdom, and intelligence in man, certain animals possess another natural capacity of a similar sort' (*HA* VIII 1, 588a28–31). Despite their possession of sensual imagination and memory, even more highly developed animals share very little experience, which in humans is the source of technical skill and science. The lack of deliberative or rational imagination in animals lurks in the background again, since technical skill arises when, out of many thoughts provided by experience, one general assumption about the similar is formed.[23] The ability to transform several pieces of mental content into one seems to be the specific capability of human beings. It is somehow only 'imitated' by animals, and not truly instantiated in them because their imagination is bound to singular sense perceptions.

(2) *Language*: As Jean-Louis Labarrière has convincingly argued, the distinction between sensual imagination and rational/deliberative imagination is also highly relevant for the question of whether animals possess language.[24] This has been a hotly contested issue in recent scholarship on Aristotle's biology.[25] At first glance, it appears to be flogging a dead horse, because the distinction between animal voice (*phonē*) and human speech (*logos* or *dialektos*) is made quite unambiguously by Aristotle himself in his *Politics* and in *De Anima*.[26] On the other hand, the account which Aristotle provides in his *History of Animals* on the different dialects of birds seems to come very close to attributing to them human-like speech.[27]

It is worthwhile probing a bit further into this problem, in order to find out how deep the distinction between animal and human imagination really is. First of all, it has to be noted how Aristotle describes 'voice' (*phonē*), which is shared by humans and animals. It is not enough to have a tongue to produce a sound, 'but that which even causes the impact must have a soul and use some imagination; for the voice is a sound which means something, and it is not merely indicative of air inhaled, as a cough is' (*DA* II 9, 420b31–33). The voice has a semantic content which is

---

[23] See *Met.* I 1, 980b25–981a7 (quotation: a5–7) and *APo* II 19, 100a1–10.
[24] See Labarrière (1984; 1993b; 2005b, chapters 4 and 8).
[25] For an instructive overview of the evidence and the contested positions see Cho (2012).
[26] *Pol.* I 2, 1253a7–18, and *GA* V 7, 786b16ff. For the involved linguistic concepts see Ax (1978) and Zirin (1980).
[27] See especially *HA* II 12, 504b1–3: 'More than any other animals and second only to man, certain kinds of bird can utter articulate sound (*grammata*)'. See also the discussion of bird dialects (*dialektoi*) in *HA* IV 9, 536b8–18.

obviously due to the use of imagination, and in his discussion of birds Aristotle provides some instructive examples of the advanced kind of communication which is allowed by this feature.[28] But this ability of significative communication is obviously completely due to and to be explained by the presence of sensual imagination in the animals in question. This faculty allows for a kind of natural representation relying on signs (*semeia*) that can be produced as well as understood by animals.[29] On the other hand, Aristotle's account of human language ultimately relies on the use of symbols (*symbola*) that require more complex articulation, composition, and convention.[30] This calls for a more advanced form of representation that can be traced back to the use of rational imagination.

The two forms of imagination thus form the basis for the distinction between animal voice and human language. But, in the biological writings, this difference is not so categorically put. In fact, this difference once more turns out to be of type (2), which at least maintains an analogy between human speech and animal language, with the latter being measured by the former. Therefore, animal voice is no mere mimicking of human speech, as in the reproduction of words or sentences by parrots – it is instead a true form of mutual communication, although obviously limited in its scope.

The overall relevance of the distinction between animal imagination and human imagination for the purposes of philosophical anthropology is as follows: by investigating how Aristotle treats the analogous faculty of sensual imagination and the scope of its functions, it is possible to obtain a much clearer understanding of where exactly the higher capacities of human cognition (like deliberation, concept-formation, science, etc.) start and how they operate on a basic level. This comparison presupposes a certain continuity between the two concepts of imagination, without simply turning their relationship into a type (1) difference of more and less. Aristotle's gradualist approach is, thus, capable of establishing an important qualitative difference in human psychology without losing track of the idea of a biological continuum.

When handled in this refined manner, gradualism does not defy the purposes of philosophical anthropology, but rather deepens its understanding of man's special place in the natural world. At the same time, it paves the way for a better grasp of man's higher intellectual capabilities (*nous*), which ultimately fall outside the domain of natural philosophy. The final charge of *incompleteness* tends to obscure the biological writings'

---

[28] See, e.g. the communication between cranes, as described in *HA* VIII 10, 614b22–26.
[29] *HA* VIII 1, 608a17–21 and *Resp.* 11, 476a19 (*pros tēn hermeneian*). [30] Labarrière (1984, 39).

Anthropology in Aristotle's Biological Writings 131

contribution to an Aristotelian philosophy of mind: it is much more informative to reflect on the relationship between sensual and deliberative imagination than to just state that man has an exclusive claim to *logos* or *nous* and to immediately turn one's back on analogous phenomena in other animals, because those phenomena might help us to clarify the abilities in which the specific intellectual differences of mankind are ultimately grounded. Therefore, the charge of a fundamental incompleteness of the biological perspective seems to be alleviated.

4 Teleological Essentialism and Philosophical Anthropology in Aristotle

After this apologetic tour de force, let us return to the basic idea of a multilayered description defining the essence of man. Although Aristotle does not explicitly accomplish this himself, it seems to be a project that can be reconstructed out of his biological writings. One straightforward approach would be to collect a comprehensive sample of special features by which man somehow stands out in the animal world. Such a list would include, among other things, the following items, randomly selected from the *History of Animals*:[31]

- Humans have the most extensive variety of eye colours of all animals.
- Of all animals that possess ears, humans are the only ones unable to move them.
- Humans are the only animal that can actually become ambidextrous.

One could considerably expand this list by adding other unique features mentioned in the biological writings. But such a naive add-on approach would certainly miss what we are looking for, because it misses the difference between the accidental and essential, that is, between the merely peculiar and the truly characteristic features. At the very least we need some overarching structural principles in order to organise such data into a more informative account and to gain a better understanding of man's essence. In other words: we need a kind of definitional frame within which to proceed.

Aristotle provides us with a clue about how this could be achieved for humans as well as for other animal species. After having broached the general distinction between biological type (1) and type (2) differences, he continues: 'Further differences exhibited by animals are those which relate

---

[31] *HA* I 10–11, 492a1–6, a22–23, 497b31–32.

132   JÖRN MÜLLER

to their ways of life (*bioi*), their activities (*praxeis*), their characters (*ēthē*), as well as their parts (*moria*). Let us describe these first in general outline, and then we will go on to speak of the various kinds, giving special attention to each' (*HA* I 1, 487a11–14). At first glance, this is simply the structural outline used by Aristotle to organise his empirical material in the *History of Animals*: in the first four books he compares the parts of animals, thus delivering a kind of zoological anatomy; from book V onwards he turns to ethology, combining considerations on animals' different characters, activities, and ways of life, all of which admit of type (1) as well as of type (2) differences.[32] But there is a deeper rationale at work here. These three ethological layers are not simply presented in a parallel fashion. Instead, as James Lennox argues, they prove to be tightly interwoven concepts: 'Character traits are to be understood as dispositions to perform activities in certain ways, e.g. timidly, ferociously . . . The characteristic way that an animal performs its activities is regularly related to the animal's overall way of life.'[33]

Thus, a *bios* is a kind of basic explanatory concept in biology that safeguards the unity of the whole ethological account, because it integrates the various traits and the activities enabled by them. The traits aim at the realisation of activities, which in turn build up a certain way of life characteristic of the animal kind.[34] There is certainly a strong teleological undercurrent at work here that is reflected throughout all of the biological treatises: the fundamental importance of the final cause, which establishes the 'for the sake of which' (*to hou heneka*) of a certain natural arrangement, is stressed explicitly by Aristotle in his methodological considerations in *PA* (see especially: I 1, 642a1ff). Furthermore, the biological works offer abundant examples of Aristotle's repeated claim that nature does nothing in vain, but is always goal-oriented towards the better or best.[35] To understand why something happens or is constituted in the way that it is, one has to look at the natural end to which it somehow contributes.

Aristotle does not restrict this teleological idea to the ordered interplay of the three ethological layers, but instead also takes into consideration the physiological parts: they are formed in a certain way in order to support, in the best possible manner, the various psycho-physical activities with which

---

[32] See *HA* VII 1, 588a17–18: 'Their activities and lives differ according to their characters and nutrition.'

[33] Lennox (2010b, 245).

[34] Depew (1995, 166): 'The array of traits distributed to an animal kind enables it to express and utilize its essential capacities as fully and effectively as possible'.

[35] See Lennox (2001b, 205–23).

Anthropology in Aristotle's Biological Writings 133

they are involved. The body is ultimately a kind of instrument for the soul (*PA* I 5, 645b14–20). Some of the bodily organs even have a kind of double causal function: they contribute not only to what is necessary for the survival of the individual, but also to other purposes. Aristotle repeatedly emphasises 'nature's habit of using an organ for secondary purposes' (*PA* IV 10, 690a1–4),[36] and this idea of a double function (*ergon*) is regularly and especially applied to human physiology, e.g. in Aristotle's aetiological account of the human lips and tongue: the lips are not only useful in protecting the teeth (as in other animals), but also serve the good purpose (*to eu*) of making the use of speech possible (*PA* I 5, 645b20–28).

Especially in humans, the material constitution of the organs, basically revolving around the necessary, is often additionally ordered towards another 'good' form of use (*chrēsis*) or function (*ergon*), in which man somehow differs from the other animals. This ties in nicely with the distinction of three kinds of activities that Aristotle introduces in order to structure his ethological account. One has to distinguish between:

(a) common activities (*praxeis konai*) that are present in all animals, e.g. nutrition;
(b) generic activities (*praxeis kata genos*) of certain larger groups, like birds; and
(c) specific activities (*praxeis kat'eidos*) on the level of ultimate kinds, like man (*PA* I 5, 645b20–28).

An animal's entire way of life (*bios*) is composed of activities of all these kinds. A comprehensive survey of human life will include all these kinds of activities; and, in turn, these activities account for the presence and shape of all the bodily organs engaged in them. But, if we hold fast to the essentialist conception of philosophical anthropology, we have to dig deeper, especially when it comes to everything that is somehow related to level (c). The ethological framework established in the biological writings, which causally traces physiological features back to psychological activities, is very useful here. It allows Aristotle to view empirical details in the light of their goal-directed function, thus creating a complex interplay of the material and final causes, an interplay that comprises the core of a 'teleological essentialism' at work in his biology.[37] 'Teleological essentialism' means that the essential form of a thing is to be understood in terms of the function(s) that it is structured to perform. What an animal is can be gathered from its activities in their goal-directedness. With regard to this

---

[36] See also *Resp.* 11, 476a18–22. [37] For teleological essentialism see Lennox (2001b, 173–78).

function, the formal and the material nature of the animal go hand in hand; form and matter constitute a functional unity. This teleological essentialism, which focuses on an animal's way of life and its various activities, does not defy the purposes of a biological classification in genus and kinds, but instead tackles it in a sophisticated manner: 'To see the unity that *integrates* these many parts with their many different activities, one must understand that they are *coordinated* contributions to a single way of life.'[38] The functions (*erga*) and the way in which they permeate the physical make-up, as well as the ordered life activities of a species, are of vital importance in understanding what it is to be a member of this kind. Therefore, any multi-layered definition of a species has to pay particular attention to these teleological functions, which also structure the interplay between the physical (material) and the psychological (formal) nature of hylomorphic beings.

What are the implications of this teleological essentialism for the (re)construction of a philosophical anthropology out of Aristotle's biological writings? First and foremost, it is necessary to evaluate the material about man with a special view to the functions introduced for purposes of explanation. Special emphasis has to be placed on the aforementioned dual functions, which often already point the way towards the specific activities essential to human life. On closer inspection, it will certainly turn out that not all human peculiarities documented by Aristotle really contribute to an understanding of a specifically human *bios*. Teleological essentialism actually forces us to distinguish between idiosyncratic and accidental features, which can be neglected in our anthropological picture, and vital and essential characteristics, which definitely have to be taken into account for the purposes of defining man. It also calls for a penetrating analysis of these more important features, which might contribute to an essentialist account of mankind. The general approach would be bottom-up, looking at the material and behavioural features with a view to their functional contributions to activities characteristic of human life.

It is beyond the scope of this chapter to chart all the specific activities, functions, and corresponding organs that essentially enable and constitute a human life. I will offer only two examples:

(i) Aristotle names several physiological conditions that are needed for articulated human speech.[39] As already mentioned above, the characteristics of the lips and tongue play a significant part in this:

---

[38] Lennox (2010b, 254).   [39] For further details see the instructive discussion in Meyer (2011).

Anthropology in Aristotle's Biological Writings 135

> The human tongue is the freest, the broadest, and the softest of all: this is to enable it to fulfil both its functions ... It has, also [in addition to tasting; J.M.], to articulate the various sounds and to produce speech, and for this a tongue which is soft and broad is admirably suited, because it can roll back and dart forward in all directions; and herein too its freedom and looseness assists it. (*PA* II 17, 660a17–25)

The suitable physiological conditions of the human tongue mark an anthropological difference of the type (1) category (of more and less), especially when compared to the tongues of certain birds that are credited with similar – albeit still inferior – flexibility.[40] But birds have no teeth, and these also play a significant part in the articulation of human speech. According to Aristotle, the different human teeth are not only perfectly adapted for biting off and chewing food, but also mostly (*malista*) suited for the purposes of speech, because of their significant contribution to the formation of sound (*PA* III 1, 661b6–15). The function of articulated speech is, therefore, a considerable explanatory resource for the account of special human features. But this also goes the other way round: if we regard speaking as an essential activity of human beings, contributing massively to their specific way of life, the description of its physiological presuppositions will certainly enter into any informative philosophical anthropology.

(ii) Aristotle discusses in several places the upright posture of human beings (see especially *PA* IV 10).[41] This seems to be a truly unique human characteristic (although Aristotle also speaks of degrees of uprightness in the animal world; *PA* III 6, 669b4–6). The upshot of these discussions is that the comparative weight of the upper body in humans is very favourable to the function of thinking, because too much upper body weighs down the motion of the intellect. Aristotle repeatedly points out that the human body in its internal structure and posture is the most 'natural' one, because it ultimately corresponds to the superior part of the universe.[42] Human's uprightness, in turn, explains many anatomical features, e.g. why their legs are fleshy, and why they have buttocks and no tail, why they have the largest feet of all animals, etc.[43] But these are rather necessary conditions and not essential prerequisites of the function optimally supported by human posture, namely thinking. Another, more important consequence of upright posture is that humans have no need for front legs, where

---

[40] See *PA* II 17, 660a28–30, and *HA* II 12, 504a35–b3, where Aristotle points out that the articulation of birds with their tongue is 'second only to man'.
[41] For the anthropological importance of upright posture, see Bayertz (2012, 49–59).
[42] *IA* 6, 706b8–10; *HA* I 15, 494a26–b1; *PA* II 9, 656a10–13.
[43] *PA* IV 10, 689b1–31, 690a27–28.

136   JÖRN MÜLLER

instead they possess arms and hands. The possession of hands is an especially important sign of their intelligence: hands are not instruments with a single function, but can, instead, be used for multiple purposes between which humans can choose. Hands are 'instruments for many instruments', and their use involves deliberation and facilitates a wide variety of activities and functions (*PA* IV 10, 687a2ff).

This anthropological short-list is certainly incomplete and needs deeper analysis of its content. But if we wish to avoid the trap of a simple add-on anthropology, it is necessary to further specify teleological essentialism.

5 Biological and Ethical Functions: Towards an Outline (*typos*) of Aristotle's Philosophical Anthropology

In his *De Anima*, Aristotle offers a kind of hierarchical *scala naturae*, revolving around the different functions (*erga*) of living things.[44] The basic functions of nutrition, growth, and producing offspring are attributed to all kinds of souls (including plants), while the higher functions of sensual perception and local movement belong only to animal souls. The obvious pinnacle of this pyramid of functions, reached via the important link of imagination (see Section 3), is thinking; and thinking is ascribed solely to rational souls. This *scala naturae* of functions provides not just a hierarchy of value for ensouled beings in cosmological terms. It also describes, at the level of the individual soul, an ordered functional whole in which the lower psychic functions are ultimately in place for the sake of the higher ones. Thinking is the final and essential function of man that structures his entire way of life.[45] This squares with the famous statement that 'man is the only animal that stands upright, and this is because his nature and essence is divine. Now the function of that which is most divine is to think and to be intelligent (*noein kai phronein*)' (*PA* IV 10, 686a27–29). The supreme human function, therefore, comprehends theoretical (*noein*) as well as practical (*phronein*) thinking, and it is around these activities that human life is specifically structured.

A final criterion for our anthropological foray into Aristotle's biological writings emerges from this perspective. That criterion will be focused on the contribution of bodily parts, character traits, and activities towards a form of life that is structured by the different functions of thought and intelligence. This is certainly the point where the anthropological

---

[44] *DA* II 2, 413a20–414a4; *HA* VIII 1, 588b22–589a2.   [45] See Kullmann (1974, 314–15).

Anthropology in Aristotle's Biological Writings

enterprise in Aristotle has to be broadened with a view to his other writings, especially his *Ethics* and *Politics*. Insofar as the final end (and thus the *ergon*) of human beings is not just to live, but to live well and to realise their potential for *eudaimonia*, Aristotle's practical philosophy truly is 'the philosophy of human affairs' (*EN* X 9, 1181b15).[46] Tellingly, the teleological essentialism of the biological works interlocks in several places with the account given in his practical philosophy. In particular, the notion of human function (*ergon*) plays a central role in Aristotle's ethics and marks a kind of transition from natural to practical philosophy. The ethical account of human function in Aristotle is ultimately not justified by recourse to biology, although at least in some essential elements it is rooted in it.[47]

Where does ethical consideration enter this biological framework? Aristotle emphasises that, in many respects, humans seem to be the most complex and versatile of all animals.[48] Although as an ultimate and simple kind they shows no further differentiation into other kinds, they are seemingly more various within their own kind than any other species of animal.[49] This certainly allows for a wide variety of activities and for different ways of life, as Aristotle suggests in the beginning of his *Ethics* (*EN* I 5, 1095b14–19). While animals naturally follow their function, it is ultimately part of man's pivotal function of thinking to decide on his own way of life: 'Man's *ergon* lies in his capacity for choice and action so that his nature is not wholly determinate. To live well, being human, we must do our own living.'[50] While animals do not share in choice (*prohairesis*) and are not the principle of action (*praxis*) in the way human beings are,[51] humans not only need to choose their actions and their way of life from several possible alternatives, but they are also finely equipped to tackle this task: human choice mainly presupposes rational calculation (*bouleusis*), measuring different alternatives by a single standard, and finally coming to a judgement about what is best. And this is exactly what is safeguarded by man's unique possession of deliberative/rational imagination (see Section 3).

My final point is, thus, as follows: especially in view of their heightened biological status at the top of many natural functions, which they have to integrate into a single way of life, humans virtually have to be a deliberating animal bent on thinking about the good life (and thus sharing in a kind

---

[46] See Frede (ch. 13) for further discussion.   [47] See Müller (2006; 2016).
[48] *PA* II 10, 656a3–8; IV 10, 687a23–b5.   [49] See Clark (1975, 17) and Depew (1995, 181).
[50] Clark (1975, ix).   [51] *EE* II 6, 1222b18–20; *EN* III 2, 1111b9–10.

138   JÖRN MÜLLER

of ethical inquiry).[52] And this is an important consequence to be drawn directly from the description of the versatile and complex nature of human beings given in Aristotle's biology.

To conclude and summarise my argument: any attempt to construct a fully-fledged account of Aristotle's philosophical anthropology will have to take into account what the biological writings teach us about the teleological structure of human bodily parts, character traits, and activities, as well as about the way of life they support. Instead of looking for the one big anthropological difference, we have to be keenly aware of spotting several differences in their functional and teleologically ordered interplay, all of them contributing on different levels to human flourishing and living well. Providing an adequate essential definition of man in Aristotle means approaching the human soul in its bodily-realised activities (thus taking into account the formal as well as the material nature of man) and combining that approach with interlocking ethico-political considerations, especially with regard to the central notion of man's 'function' (*ergon*).[53]

Therefore, it is neither necessary nor helpful to suppose – as is sometimes done – that Aristotle has unknowingly provided us with two rather contradictory approaches to philosophical anthropology: a 'differentialist' picture of man in his practical philosophy on the one hand, and a 'gradualist' conception in his biological writings on the other. This dichotomy is not fine-grained enough to capture the underlying spirit of Aristotle's analyses: in the biological writings, gradual differences between humans and animals – which still allow for comparisons and a unified terminology, as in the case of *phantasia* (see Section 3) – can ultimately also amount to qualitatively specific features when viewed in the light of the different functions of the species. Therefore, a multi-layered philosophical anthropology, held together by an overarching teleological essentialism, might be gathered from the *Corpus Aristotelicum*, with the biological writings being a natural starting-point for such an approach. In constructing it, there needn't be a fierce rivalry between Aristotle's biology and his practical philosophy; it could rather be a fortunate joint venture. The intention of this article was to defend such a project as well as

---

[52] This is also mirrored by the fact that 'man is the only animal that has hope and expectation of the future' (*PA* III 4, 669a19–21).

[53] See Kietzmann (ch. 1) for an opposing view: Kietzmann denies the possibility of an essential definition of human beings in Aristotle.

to provide a structural framework for it. As it stands, it is certainly only an 'outline' (*typos*) in the Aristotelian sense, which basically means that many details still have to be filled in to get the whole picture. But, as Aristotle used to point out, such a philosophical outline is always useful, serving as a target in order to hit the mark.[54]

[54] I would like to thank Therese Cory, Sabine Föllinger, and Dag Nikolaus Hasse for helpful comments on this chapter.

CHAPTER 7

Aristotle on the Anthropological Difference and Animal Minds

Hans-Johann Glock

... contradictions by scholars, [are] the penalty for attributions to Aristotle.
(Quine)[1]

1 Aristotle and Anthropology

Aristotle did not deal with anthropological topics under that name. Small wonder, since that label was only coined in the sixteenth century. Nor did he devote a specific treatise to what we would nowadays call philosophical anthropology. But the impact of his writings on biology and the philosophy of mind have been second to none. At a methodological level, Aristotle's essentialist metaphysics and the ensuing doctrines of definition and taxonomy ('Porphyrian tree') have provided the most important paradigm for anthropology's endeavour to determine the nature of human beings. This quest immediately leads on to the two central problems of anthropology down the ages. On the one hand, there is the question of

anthropological constants or universals: Are there features shared by all ('normal') human beings, irrespective of their social and historical context.

On the other hand, there is the question of

the human–animal or anthropological difference: Are there features that are unique to humans, i.e. set them apart from all non-human animals (henceforth simply 'animals')?

Now, it is not beyond the wit of man to specify unique features of human beings. As the comedian Loriot observed. 'Man is the only creature that can partake of a hot meal in flight'. In their search for the anthropological

---

[1] Quine (1960, 199).

140

Aristotle on the Anthropological Difference and Animal Minds 141

difference, however, philosophical anthropologists are looking for a difference with a difference. They are looking for features of homo sapiens that

(a)   are essential to being human;
(b)   set us apart categorically or qualitatively from all animals;
(c)   are fundamental, in that other relevant differences derive from them but not vice versa; and
(d)   are important to our self-image.

Elsewhere I have argued that there is no single anthropological difference satisfying these conditions, one that separates all individual humans from all individual animals. Instead, what sets humans apart is a type of social organisation characterised and underpinned by a unique combination of features possessed to a unique degree.[2]

This chapter deals with Aristotle's second seminal contribution to anthropology, namely his claims about human-animal differences. For one thing, he explicitly though briefly discussed the nature of the divide (see Section 5). For another, his corpus maintains of several features that they are unique to humans.

Two of these concern physical endowments, namely upright posture and the free use of hands. Both of them fail on several counts. First, Aristotle *PA* IV 10, 686a27–29 notwithstanding, we share upright posture with other bipeds, notably certain birds. Second, the alleged *loci classici* for manual dexterity as an anthropological difference do not express such a straightforward view.

> This instrument of all instruments . . . has been given by nature to man, the animal of all animals the most capable of acquiring the most varied arts. (*PA* IV 10, 687a22–24, transl. Ogle)
>
> Of all animals man alone can learn to make equal use of both hands. (*HA* II 1, 497b31, transl. Thompson)

Furthermore, both passages are erroneous. Other animals possess the 'instrument of all instruments', i.e. hands. Second, many of them, especially the Great Apes, make 'equal use of both hands'. Third, *HA* 497b13 presupposes that humans are equally proficient with both hands. This is mistaken. Only 1% of humans are naturally ambidextrous. Ironically, handedness, i.e. a preference for either the right or left hand, is a more plausible candidate for being unique to us. But recent findings indicate

---

[2] See Glock (2012).

that handedness is present at least in some primates as well.[3] Finally, while recognising the uniqueness of our use of hands, Aristotle himself characterises it as a fallout from our singular cognitive capacities.

> Anaxagoras anyway says humans are the smartest animals due to having hands, but it's reasonable instead to say that we get hold of hands due to being the smartest. (*PA* IV 10, 687a8–14)

This is in line with one of the few claims on which most philosophical anthropologists converge. If there is such a thing as the anthropological difference, it must concern our mental properties and capacities.[4] This disqualifies the physiological feature of hands with opposable fingers. Indeed, for better or worse, *HA* 497b13 implies that even the manual dexterity such hands enable does not pass the test of (c), since it is derivative of our loosely speaking technical intelligence.

Other claims to uniqueness by Aristotle are contentious; this holds of agency (*EE* II 6, 1222b18–20), deliberate recollection (*HA* I 1, 488b), and anticipating the future (*PA* III 6, 669a19).[5] Yet others are not fundamental: the ability to laugh may be important to the self-image, at least of certain cultures, thereby meeting condition (d); yet it is derived in a complex way from physiological, emotional, and cognitive capacities, thereby failing condition (c). And, at least as regards evolutionary origins, our ability to discriminate right and wrong, such as it is anyway, derives from cognitive, emotional, and social capacities prerequisite to human communities.[6]

In the sequel I shall only consider candidates for an anthropological difference which satisfy two conditions: first, they are of a mental kind; second, they are prima facie plausible, not just from a philosophical point of view or in the light of evidence available to an observational naturalist like Aristotle, but even by the standards of contemporary biology and ethology. These are: rationality, language, and a special kind of sociality (see Section 9).

2 Aristotle and the Philosophy of Animal Minds

This restriction requires focusing on proposals for an anthropological difference that are interwoven with the Aristotelian contribution to a field

---

[3] See McGrew et al. (2013).   [4] e.g. Hacker (2007, 2).

[5] For philosophical animadversions to the contention that animals cannot act, see Glock (2009) (but contrast Keil, 2012); for ethological refutations of the claims about recollection and anticipation see, respectively, Clayton, Griffiths, and Dickinson (2000) and Mulcahy and Call (2006).

[6] See van Schaik (2016, 351–62).

Aristotle on the Anthropological Difference and Animal Minds 143

known as 'the philosophy of animal minds'.[7] Its central problem is, predictably, the *question of animal minds*:

Do some animals have minds / mental properties / mental powers?

Regarding that question, there are two basic stances. *Differentialists* maintain that there are categorical differences separating us from animals; *assimilationists* hold that the differences are merely quantitative and gradual.

Aristotle left a tremendously influential legacy to the philosophy of animal minds. First, as the founder of biology, he set in train the development of the scientific disciplines without which the question of animal minds cannot be tackled. Second, as a philosopher he pioneered a 'capacity approach' to the mind. Third, regarding the contrast between assimilationism and differentialism, his stance is Janus-faced.

As a biologist, Aristotle painted a picture of gradual differences between types of organisms – the model of the 'great chain of being' as it came to be known (e.g. *PA* IV 5, 681a9ff). But, as a philosopher of mind, he detected sharper divides. While Aristotle credited animals with emotions and portrayed the differences concerning temperament as a matter of degree, he regarded those concerning the intellect as qualitative rather than quantitative.[8]

Aristotle's legacy is also ambivalent as regards merit, or so I shall argue. On the *positive* side:

- Aristotle recognised that humans are animals, biologically speaking;
- an Aristotelian capacity approach is a prerequisite for understanding the minds of humans and animals alike; and
- Aristotle was alive to the special character of human societies.

On the *negative* side, Aristotelianism:

- Aristotelianism confines the mind proper to the intellect;
- Aristotle separated perception and belief, crediting animals with the former but not the latter;
- he encouraged a 'transformative theory' according to which our rational faculties alter the very nature of our other mental capacities, thereby undermining the idea that we share the latter with (higher) animals; and
- he mishandled the importance of language.

---

[7] See Lurz (2009).
[8] e.g. *HA* IX 1, 608a11–21 vs. *DA* III 3, 428; see Sorabji (1993, 13–14) and Section 6.

3 The Aristotelian Hierarchy

Aristotle introduced a threefold hierarchy among living things. All living creatures possess a *psychē*. That term is commonly translated as 'soul', yet in fact it expresses a notion that is more biological than psychological. The psyche is the life force of every individual organism, the source of its distinctive activities; at the same time, it makes that individual the kind of being that it is. Plants, animals, and humans differ in the kind of psyche they possess. Plants have *threptikon* and *gennētikon*, that is, the capacities for nourishment, growth, and reproduction. Animals have *aisthētikon* and *orektikon*, that is, the capacities for perception and sensation on the one hand, desire on the other. This means that they possess *aisthēsis* – sensation (*DA* II 2, 413b1–24). Higher animals, in addition, possess *phantastikon* and *kinētikon*, that is, the capacities for imagination and movement.

Simplifying somewhat, plants have a 'vegetative soul', animals a 'perceptive' or 'sensitive' and a 'locomotive soul', and humans a 'rational soul'. Each higher type of soul encompasses the capacities of the lower types, as well as additional distinctive powers. Humans are living things because they have the capacity for nourishment, growth, and reproduction. Humans are animals because they also have the capacity for perception and movement. We are a species of animal – *zōon* (*Cat.* 1a 8–10), though of a very special kind, because of our rational faculties.

4 The Contours of 'Mind'

In philosophy, three delineations of the scope of 'mind' and 'mental' boast of a significant following to this day, namely those associated with, respectively, Aristotle, Descartes, and Brentano. According to Cartesianism, the mind is co-extensive with the realm of consciousness (sentience, experience), the things we are immediately and infallibly aware of. For Brentano and his followers, intentionality – being directed or about something – rather than consciousness is the distinguishing feature of the mental.[9]

A distinctively Aristotelian delineation counts only the intellect (*nous*), i.e. the higher faculties of reason and rational will, as part of the mind proper. It consigns perception and other forms of sentience to lower forms of *psychē*, such as Aquinas' sensitive soul (*anima sensitiva*). On the assumption that the adjective 'mental' goes with the noun 'mind', this implies that

---

[9] Brentano (1874, I.2.i.5).

only intellectual or rational capacities count as mental. Thus, Kenny confines the mind to the intellect and ties the latter to language. This allows him 'to do justice both to my admiration for Descartes and my affection for my dog. I can agree with the former that animals do not have minds while according to the latter a full measure of non-mechanical consciousness'[10]. Indeed, some Aristotelians hold or imply that it is *partly constitutive* of the term 'mind' that it cannot or ought not to be applied to animals. According to Hacker, another leading neo-Aristotelian – 'Aristotelians conceived of the mind as the array of powers that distinguish humanity from the rest of animate nature'.[11]

Setting us apart from animals may have been a prime motive behind Aristotle's distinction between *nous* and *psychē*. Irrespective of the employment of terms like '*nous*' or '*mens*' at the time he and subsequent disciples were writing, however, being the preserve of humans is *not* part of the *current* meaning of 'mind'. To insist that mental phenomena are *by definition* absent in animals is at best a stipulation, and an unproductive one at that. For it simply passes the buck to the question of what precisely should be *deemed mental*. It also begets quaint follow-up questions like 'Should belief, desire, intelligence, or even simple types of reasoning no longer count as mental traits, if it turns out that certain animals share them with us?'

This holds *mutatis mutandis* for an Aristotelian differentialism that sets out from the term 'animal' rather than 'mind'. Thus, Rödl maintains that there is a 'pure notion of an animal'[12] according to which animals perceive, yet do not think. Admittedly, there are labels that imply a lack of mental faculties, notably 'brute'. Furthermore, there is an established use of 'animal' and its cognates that carries the connotation of a lack of rational self-control – as in 'animal instinct'. But there is also a non-committal use of 'animal'; it predominates in philosophy and science, and is part of everyday discourse as well. An understanding of 'animal' that excludes the capacity for thought *ab initio* is 'purer' than this non-committal use, only in the sense of being more restrictive. It once again merely transfers the crux of the debate between differentialists and assimilationists, this time to the question of which creatures should *count as animals* in this narrow sense.

It is far less confusing to conduct this debate without linguistic stipulations, regimentations, and subterfuges, in terms recognisable to philosophers, scientists, lawyers, politicians, artists, and laypeople alike. This is

---

[10] Kenny (1975, 5).   [11] Hacker (2013, 11).   [12] Rödl (2007, 72).

achieved by posing the question of animal minds. If that question is to have any point, neither the notion of an animal nor that of the mental should be explained *ab initio* so as to prejudge either a negative or a positive answer. Rather, biological and mental notions should be construed in ways that are plausible or fruitful *on independent grounds*. Perhaps ascribing some or all mental properties (in the established sense) to animals (in the established sense) is indeed nonsensical. That will have to be a consequence of other features of these concepts, however, and one to transpire from painstaking analysis of specific mental notions.

A weaker version of Aristotelianism does not define 'mind' and its cognates *ab initio* as exclusive to humans. Instead, it maintains that these terms signify only the 'higher' echelons of the overall psychic domain, namely intellect and rational will. This raises the bar animals have to clear to qualify for mental powers, without simply stipulating it to be out of reach. In this vein, Kenny defines the mind as a 'second-order capacity' to acquire the first-order symbolic capacities that he regards as prerequisite for the intellect.[13] His aim is to preserve the mind as a distinguishing feature of humans. On the one hand, even pre-linguistic humans have the capacity to acquire language; on the other, Kenny regards it as a matter of empirical fact that animals lack that capacity.

Kenny contends that such a definition captures 'the ordinary concept of a mind'.[14] However, the exalted Aristotelian equation of the mind or the mental with reason and rational will is out of step with our established use of the term 'mental' and its cognates, both in the behavioural and cognitive sciences, and in everyday parlance. Even in philosophy, the equation is confined to Aristotelians and rationalists. It is not for nothing that Mill already inveighed against 'a popular perversion' by which 'the word Mind is withdrawn from its rightful generality of signification, and restricted to the intellect'.[15] At the same time, it is in line with our established notion of the mental to draw the line at creatures lacking *sentience*. Prince Charles and certain botanists hankering for publicity notwithstanding, therefore, plants lack mental powers.

---

[13] Kenny (1989, 20, 24–25).

[14] Kenny (1975, 2). My portrait of Aristotelianism as confining mind to intellect is not an artifice of translating *nous* as 'mind' rather than 'intellect', therefore. The equation has explicitly been advocated in Aristotle's name, and for noteworthy reasons. In contrast, regarding 'animal' and 'human' as mutually exclusive is out of step with Aristotle, since the latter recognised that humans are animals.

[15] Mill (1843, 1.3.3).

Aristotle on the Anthropological Difference and Animal Minds 147

Measured against the standard of established use, all three extant demarcations of mental phenomena founder, principally because they are *unduly restrictive*.[16] Current parlance in everyday life and science tends to accept as mental not just the phenomena acknowledged by any single one of them, but the whole lot. Mental concepts comprise at least those referring to powers of reason and rational will (as Aristotelianism has it), those referring to phenomena about which the subject cannot be mistaken (as the Cartesian criterion glossed in Wittgensteinian fashion suggests), and/or those connected to intentionality (as conceived by Brentano). So each one of these features is *individually sufficient* for qualifying as mental; however, none of them is *individually necessary*. Accordingly, none of our venerable positions furnishes a definition that captures the meaning of 'mind', or even its extension.

One might try to capture that extension through a disjunctive definition: a phenomenon is mental if it is intellectual or displays first-/third-person asymmetry or intentionality. But there is no guarantee that this disjunction exhaustively captures everything we are prepared to call 'mental' in everyday parlance, science, and philosophy. Even if there were, such a disjunctive definition does not capture our understanding of 'mental' and its cognates, since it does not guide their use by competent speakers.

A more promising approach to the contours of mental notions relinquishes Aristotelian essentialism in favour of Wittgensteinian anti-essentialism. As currently employed, 'mind', 'mental', and its cognates are *family-resemblance concepts* à la Wittgenstein. The phenomena they signify are united not by a single common feature, but by a complex network of overlapping and criss-crossing similarities. What holds the family together and gives it its unity is not a 'single thread' running through all cases, but an overlapping of different fibres, as in a rope.[17]

5 What Abilities Can Do for the Philosophy of Mind

While Aristotelianism fails to provide a convincing analytic definition of 'mind', its approach to mental concepts is sound. In the wake of Descartes, the mainstream of Western philosophy has treated 'mind', its equivalents, and cognates as the label of a special kind of thing, whether it be a separate mental substance, as in dualism, or the brain, as in materialist monism.

---

[16] For the shortcomings of Cartesian and Brentanist demarcations see Hacker (2013, 11–58).
[17] Wittgenstein (1953, 66–67); see Glock (1996, 120–24).

This contrasts with an Aristotelian-*cum*-Thomist tradition revived unwittingly by Wittgenstein and knowingly by Ryle. Having been sidelined by a materialist mainstream since the 1960s, their perspective is currently rehabilitated, partly through a renaissance of expressivism[18] and the rediscovery of the central role of cognitive and conative capacities.

According to what I call a 'capacity' approach, the mind is not a bona fide thing of any kind.

> 'Mind' is no more the name of a thing than 'space', 'time', 'habit' or 'influence'. The words descriptive of the mind are not to be taken literally: a person's mind is not literally shallow, deep, sharp, dirty, brilliant; I don't literally have an idea at the back of my mind as I have my socks at the back of my drawer, any more than I have the name of an artist literally on my tongue.[19]

Nor is the mind a kind of stuff or matter like water or gold: 'mind' is a count-noun, and hence unsuitable as the name of a stuff.

The capacity approach offers an alternative by regarding the mind as a kind of *potentiality* or *power*. The distinction between actual and potential properties was one of Aristotle's greatest contributions to philosophy.[20] Potential properties are *bona fide* attributes possessed by particulars and substances, contrary to various forms of reductionism. At the same time, a potentiality must not be reified, treated as a thing of a peculiar kind that somehow coexists with the particular or substance that possesses it – contrary to what has been called 'transcendentalism'.[21] A power is neither a fiction, nor a flimsy actuality, nor an ethereal substance.

In this Aristotelian spirit, Kenny defines the mind as the capacity for behaviour of a sophisticated and symbolic kind, the ability to speak a language. Later that definition is modified, in order to include prelinguistic human infants. The mind is 'a second order capacity: an ability to acquire or possess abilities', namely of the aforementioned symbolic kind.[22] Even leaving aside its contentious restriction of mental capacities to subjects with language, this definition does not cover all aspects of our ordinary use of the term 'mind', as is obvious with respect to uses like 'I've changed my mind' or 'It's all in your mind'. Yet this is not Kenny's ambition. He seeks an account of what it is for a creature to *possess* a mind, i.e. mental properties. Whether a creature has mental properties depends not on his or her actual behaviour, but on what he or she is capable of doing. Most importantly, Kenny's definition is roughly in line

---

[18] Bar-On (2004). [19] White (1972, 464–65). [20] Kenny (2010); Hacker (2007, 90–121).
[21] Ayers (1968). [22] Kenny (1989, 7; 20).

Aristotle on the Anthropological Difference and Animal Minds 149

with the ordinary use of 'having a mind', allowing for exceptions like 'Our daughters have a mind of their own', where it signifies a first rather than second order capacity.

According to the capacity approach, to have a mind is to have a range of cognitive, volitional, and affective powers. These powers must not be confused with

(1) their exercise (in bringing about or undergoing change, either physically or mentally);
(2) the conditions that must hold for manifesting or exercising the ability:
    • opportunity conditions: I may be able to dissect an angle with compass and ruler, yet lack the necessary equipment.
    • enabling conditions: I may possess that ability and have the prerequisites, but be impeded by disease (high fever) or injury (broken hands), just as I do not lose my linguistic competence under general anaesthetics.
(3) their possessor (the individual animal or person); or
(4) the vehicle of the ability, i.e. the physical ingredient or structure of the possessor that causally sustains the ability, i.e. causally enables the possessor to exercise it (subject to opportunity and enabling conditions).

The capacity approach does not furnish a causal explanation of the phylo- or ontogenesis of mental phenomena, or of the proximal (neurophysiological) mechanisms that constitute their vehicle. In that capacity, capacities are out of their depth. The appeal to capacities or powers instead promises a *conceptual* explanation of *what mental phenomena amount to*. Appealing to capacities or potentialities is often bad science, yet can nonetheless constitute good philosophy.

In particular, an Aristotelian capacity approach avoids the Cartesian riddle about how two utterly distinct substances like mind and body (or brain) can causally interact, since it recognises that the former is not a substance to begin with. Contrary to some advocates,[23] however, it would be hasty to conclude that it thereby dispatches the mind–body problem *tout court*. For one thing, capacities require a causal substratum, implementation, or vehicle. This poses a *scientific* challenge – facing cognitive neuroscience and information theory – of explaining precisely *how* the vehicle or organ of mental powers – the brain – causally sustains the

---

[23] Maslin (2001, 209–19).

power. For another, capacities are defined by reference to how they are exercised. These exercises in turn are episodes, loosely speaking. Therefore, the question remains of what role causation plays for the *episodic* behavioural, mental, and neurophysiological phenomena through which mental capacities are actualised or implemented. It won't do to claim, for instance, that feeling a pain is simply the actualisation of the (passive) mental capacity for sentience. That answer is unexplanatory, not just in a factual-*cum*-scientific, but also in a conceptual-*cum*-philosophical capacity.

Nevertheless, as a conceptual elucidation, the capacity approach also offers distinctive advantages as regards the philosophy of *animal minds*. Unlike the presence of a Cartesian soul-substance, the possession of capacities is neither an *all-or-nothing* affair nor reducible to isolated parameters. Capacities can come in *different combinations*. More importantly still, their possession is standardly a *matter of degree*. This helps to make the question of animal minds more tractable. The focus shifts to questions such as

- What mental phenomena require what types of capacities?
- How are the latter distributed within the animal kingdom?
- What capacities are prerequisite for higher ('intellectual') faculties like intentional states, conceptual judgement, reasoning, and language?

6 Perception and Belief

While Aristotle laid the foundations for recasting the question of animal minds in these fruitful terms, his own answer goes astray in at least one crucial respect. In contrast to many pre-Socratics and to the predominant strand in Plato, Aristotle reserved to humans not just reason (*logos*), intellect (*nous*), and thought (*dianoia*), but also belief (*doxa*).[24] Initiating a differentialist strand reaching down to Davidson, McDowell, and Brandom, he denied that animals can have thoughts or beliefs, either true ones or false ones.

Sorabji has pointed out that Aristotle's denial of belief to animals precipitated a 'wholesale re-analysis', also known as redefinition, of a broad spectrum of mental concepts, including 'perception', 'memory', 'intention', and 'emotion'.[25] If animals are to be deprived of belief, while being granted perception, the latter must be conceived as substantial enough to explain their complex behaviours. According to Sorabji, Aristotle was

---

[24] *DA* I 2, 404b-4–6; II 3, 428a and 433a–437a; *PA* I 1, 641b7.   [25] Sorabji (1993, 3).

Aristotle on the Anthropological Difference and Animal Minds 151

unable to carry through this reconceptualisation consistently. In my view, the Aristotelian stance on animal belief is simply untenable.

It would be absurd to deny *tout court* that higher animals endowed with sense-organs are capable of perception, a cognitive capacity that transcends the kind of information-processing plants engage in. However, Aristotelian differentialists contest the assumption that animals can perceive that *p*. Animal perception, they insist, is confined to perceiving *x*, i.e. to perceiving objects or events; it does not include perceiving that *p*. Animal perceptions have correctness conditions, i.e. can be accurate or inaccurate. But it is confined to object-oriented intentionality, without encompassing that-ish intentionality and, hence, truth conditions. In terms made popular by Dretske, animals might be barred from 'epistemic seeing' or 'seeing facts'. Against this position, I argue that animals are capable not just of perceiving 'things' (including organisms and events), but also *that* things are thus-and-so.[26] Animal experience is not restricted to *object perception*.

(PO) A perceives x (the snake, the explosion, etc.).

It also includes that-ish perception.

(PT) A perceives that p (there is a snake ahead, there is an explosion, etc.).

This is demonstrated by the connection between perception and complex animal behaviour. The perceptually informed reactions of intelligent animals to their environment can only be explained by a capacity for (PT).

Consider a dog who has been taught not to grab anything when it is lying on the table, but only when it is lying in its bowl. This dog now sees a bone on the table, but refrains from grabbing it and instead looks on, panting. Yet, as soon as the bone is placed in the bowl, the dog goes for it. This mundane sequence of events is not explained by the dog simply perceiving discrete objects – the bone, the table, and the bowl. It can only be explained in terms of the following opposition:

(1) The dog sees at time $t1$ that the bone is on the table; and
(2) The dog sees at time $t2$ that the bone is in the bowl.

Why? Because at both $t1$ and $t2$ the dog can see all three objects: bone, table, and bowl. So, perception of the conglomeration formed by bone, table, and bowl cannot explain the difference in its behaviour at $t1$ and $t2$.

It might be objected that this behaviour can be explained in a less demanding fashion. We only need to posit

---

[26] Cp. Dretske (2004); Künne (1995).

(1') stimulus at *t1*: 'bone on the table' – reaction at *t1*: 'do not take', and
(2') stimulus at *t2*: 'bone in the bowl' – reaction at *t2*: 'take'.

But what sort of stimulus? Is it purely proximal and physiological, like the pain stimulus to which even an oyster will react? This behaviourist fairy tale ignores the distinction between lower animals and higher ones like dogs, dolphins, or primates, which possess a range of different sense organs and corresponding sensory centres in the brain. Primates, at least, score well in the standard tests for object permanence and object identification in line with Piaget,[27] and, thereby, satisfy precondition (b) of perception. They not only perceive the same distal object x in spite of altering proximal stimuli, they can also keep track of x, even as x moves in space and changes some of its properties. In short, higher animals do not experience the world as a 'blooming, buzzing confusion', in the striking phrase that James[28] used with regard to babies. Nor are they barred from perceiving an objective world, as Pittsburgh dualism would have it.

The alternative to the behaviourist tale is to admit that the dog's reaction is not just to a proximal stimulus, but to information about distal objects acquired through vision. But how can this information be specified if not as that the bone is, respectively, on the table and in the bowl? An apparent way out of this dilemma for the differentialists might be as follows: what the dog perceives is not that the bone is on the table or in the bowl; what he perceives is 'bone on the table' or 'bone in the bowl'. However, this is not really a way out. For either the determinants 'on table' and 'in bowl' are used *restrictively*, to indicate which bone the dog perceives; but this would not explain the divergent behaviour of the dog, who perceives the *same* bone at *t1* and *t2*. Or, alternatively, they are used as *ellipses* for 'lying on the table' and 'lying in the bowl'. This would explain the dog's divergent behaviour. But to perceive *the bone as lying in the bowl* is nothing more nor less than to perceive – albeit by another name – *that the bone is lying in the bowl*. One way or another the dog's behaviour can only be explained on the assumption of factual perception, perception that p.

As a last ditch attempt, differentialists could insist that the kind of perception we ascribe to the dog to explain its behaviour is *sui generis*. Accordingly,

(1*) The dog sees the bone on the table at *t1*, and
(2*) The dog sees the bone in the bowl at *t2*

---

[27] Seed and Tomasello (2010, 409).   [28] James (1890, 488).

Aristotle on the Anthropological Difference and Animal Minds   153

can neither be reduced to (1') and (2'), nor inflated to the that-ish idiom of (1) and (2).

However, an adult human could also engage in the behaviour described. What possible rationales are there for regarding

(1") A sees the bone on the table at *t1*, and
(2") A sees the bone in the bowl at *t2*

as permitting and indeed demanding a that-ish analysis when A is human, while precluding such an analysis when A is an animal? One possibility is this. Unlike most of the individuals – objects and events involved in them – facts themselves are *abstract* entities without a location in space and time (see Strawson, 1971, 195–99; Glock, 2003, 128–31). But recognising the abstract status of facts militates against the idea of 'perceiving facts' in both the animal *and* the human case. For what we can see, hear, touch, etc., is located in space and time. On the other hand, we say of both humans and animals that they perceive that *p*; and since it is a fact that *p*, one is then driven to the idea that they perceive facts. This conclusion is misleading, however. Facts are not items of ontological furniture within the physical realm. Speaking of facts is a way of characterising the world at a more abstract and sophisticated level, namely *with a view to the cognitive capacities of subjects*. The crucial point in our context: complications concerning the perception of facts apply to animals *no more and no less* than to humans. Moreover, the claim that animals can perceive *that* something is the case no more depends on the misguided or at least misleading idiom of 'perceiving facts' than the idea that we can. Both humans and animals can see that *p*. If it is a fact that *p*, one can say that both perceive a fact, keeping in mind what facts are.

The only other rationale I can think of for diagnosing a disparity between (1") and (2") as applied, respectively, to humans and animals, is the assumption that belief is *ab initio* tied to language: crediting *A* with perceiving that *p* requires that *A* be able to state that *p* in some language or other. But that assumption runs counter to established parlance, which brooks applying that-ish constructions to non-linguistic subjects, as in (1) and (2). Second, it is obviously question-begging. Third, it not only fails to vindicate the differentialist stance, it does not even afford any surplus illumination of its content. It purports to explain the alleged fact that animals do not perceive that *p*, by reference to their lack of language. But, under probing, the explanation boils down to a tendentious way of restating that animals lack language.

7 Seeing is Believing!

Having established that animals can perceive that something is the case, the second step in my argument simply pays deference to the English proverb 'Seeing is believing'. From the proposition 'A sees that p' (the sun is shining, etc.), we may conclude either 'A knows that p' (where 'seeing' is used factively) or 'A believes that p' (where this is not the case). But both 'knowing that p' and 'believing that p' are cases of 'thinking that p' in the sense that is relevant here.

Due deference to the proverb requires acknowledging its limitations. Starting with the obvious, the concept of seeing (or of perceiving) is distinct from that of believing. Next, even the inference from A sees (perceives) that p to A believes that p is not universally valid. There is perception falling short of belief in subjects in whom there is no decoupling of conative and cognitive factors, e.g. a leopard frog capable only of what Millikan calls 'pushmi-pullyu representations'. But obviously this does not hold of clever beasts like our dog, who is capable of ignoring the bone's change of location when it is completely satiated or more interested in other things, e.g. mating or playing. The second exception is trickier. A subject who knows herself to be suffering from an optical illusion might 'see' that p in a non-factive sense, namely of it *seeming to her just as if p*, without believing that p. Conversely, she might factively see that p, while erroneously mistrusting her senses and withholding belief, judgement, or acceptance on spurious grounds.

This qualification does not undermine the argument from animal perception-that to animal belief. To be sure, there is some evidence that certain animals are susceptible to perceptual illusions similar to ours.[29] However, my inference ticket fails only for subjects who are not just prone to perceptual illusions, but capable of *recognising* their illusory character and, hence, of *questioning their own perceptual beliefs*. The same holds for subjects mistakenly refusing to trust their senses. By trivial implication, both exceptions are confined to subjects who *have* beliefs to begin with. For animals with meta-cognition who might fall into that category, there is no need, therefore, to establish their capacity for belief by appeal to the inference. Furthermore, the inference from *factive perception* to *knowledge* is unaffected by these exceptions. And animals no less than humans perceive accurately in standard cases, without misfirings like illusions and

---

[29] Kelley and Kelley (2014).

Aristotle on the Anthropological Difference and Animal Minds 155

hallucinations or mistakes due to distraction. What is more, they can alter behaviour based on a casual glance as a result of more careful examination.

8 Additive vs. Transformative Theories

At this juncture, a more general aspect of Aristotelian differentialism needs to be confronted. It maintains that, even if attributing that-ish perception to animals is legitimate, it amounts to something different to attributing that-ish perception to humans. There are two interpretations of Aristotle's hierarchical model.[30]

Additive: humans possess the vegetative, sensitive, and locomotive capacities of animals, plus rational capacities.

Transformative: humans realise animal capacities in a rational way that fundamentally alters their vegetative, sensitive, and locomotive capacities.

The transformative model implies that we do not (strictly speaking) share a capacity for perception and locomotion with animals. It thereby lends succour to a very pronounced, though diffuse form of differentialism. The transformative picture is not the dominant strand in Aristotle's oeuvre. But it is intimated, even in a passage where the main emphasis is on qualitative differences, and which is thereby congenial to assimilationism.

> Some of these qualities in man, as compared with the corresponding qualities in animals, differ only quantitatively: that is to say, a man has more of this quality, and an animal has more of some other; other qualities in man are represented by analogous qualities: for instance, just as in man we find knowledge, wisdom, and sagacity, so in certain animals there exist some other natural capacity akin to these. (*HA* VIII 1, 588a25–31)

And

> ... so that one is quite justified in saying that, as regards man and animals, certain psychical qualities are identical with one another, whilst others resemble, and others are analogous to, each other. (608a11–21)

Pittsburgh philosophers have pursued the transformative approach by reference to both Aristotle and Aquinas. McDowell has drawn a sustained and influential contrast between the ways in which humans and animals, respectively, experience the world. While animals display 'perceptual sensitivity to features of the environment', only we enjoy 'experience of

---

[30] See Section 4.

objective reality'. For the latter requires concepts. Our sensory 'transactions' with the world are 'already conceptual' through and through; our conceptual capacities do not operate 'on non-conceptual deliverances of sensibility'. For, in the cooperation between 'receptivity' and 'spontaneity' which enables *bona fide* experience, the former 'does not make an even notionally separable contribution'.[31] McDowell's dualism concerning types of perception is part of a wider trend initiated by Sellars. Because of their (actual or presumed) lack of concepts, animals cannot perceive the world in a sense of 'perception' that applies univocally to humans as well. All perceptual experience is 'conceptually structured'. As a result, animals only perceive in an attenuated 'second class' sense rather than literally speaking.[32]

In short, 'objective experience, i.e. genuine perception', depends on concept-possession and, hence, on rational/linguistic faculties. Because of their (actual or presumed) lack of concepts, animals cannot perceive the world in a sense of 'perception' that applies univocally to humans as well.[33]

Intriguing though the transformative model is, it does not stand up to closer scrutiny. Even if there is a difference in the 'way of perceiving' between conceptual and non-conceptual perception, it does not follow that creatures without concepts cannot perceive what creatures with concepts can perceive – the same objects and facts. It only follows that they cannot *understand or characterise* what they see in conceptual terms.

Nor does it follow that animals only perceive in an attenuated sense rather than literally speaking. 'Perception' is not equivocal between a kind of sentience that is mere information processing and what Pittsburgh differentialists deign to call real 'perception' or 'experience'. Perceiving *amounts* to something different in conceptual and non-conceptual subjects. It has different preconditions and implications, since it enables the former to do a lot more. But this does not imply that 'perception' *linguistically* means something different in the two cases. In both it means roughly: the capacity to gather information about the proximal and distal environment with the aid of sense-organs – organs dedicated to this purpose, information that is subject to a distinction between being correct and incorrect, and, in the case of that-ish perception, of the more demanding distinction between true and false. Irrespective of whether that analysis is accurate, 'perception' is a univocal term, even if it covers conceptually distinct sub-classes.

---

[31] McDowell (1996, xx, 9, 39, 69).   [32] Brandom (1994, 150; 2002, 93).
[33] e.g. Boyle (2017); Rödl (2007).

Aristotle on the Anthropological Difference and Animal Minds 157

Transformative differentialism is ultimately fuelled by an extreme holism, according to which *any* significant difference in the context of a phenomenon per se *constitutes a distinct phenomenon*. But such holism reduces to absurdity, at least in the case of animal perception. This was brought out by Plutarch in his criticism of the radical differentialism of the stoics.

> As for those [stoics] who foolishly say of animals that they do not feel pleasure, nor anger, nor fear, nor do they make preparations, nor remember, but the bee only 'as-if' remembers, and the swallow 'as-if' makes preparations, and the lion is 'as-if' angry, and the deer 'as-if' afraid: – I do not know how they will treat someone who says that they do not see nor hear either, but 'as-if' see and 'as-if' hear, and do not give voice, but 'as-if' give voice, and, in general, do not live, but 'as-if' live. For these last statements, I believe, are no more contrary to plain evidence than their own.[34]

However, why should holistic as-ifness about perception or emotion imply as-ifness about form of behaviour like acoustic signalling or about life? Because, by the holists' own lights, it is partly constitutive of the concept of perception that the information perception provides can guide activities like signalling, running, swimming, etc. Similarly, it is partly constitutive of that concept that such information can be put in the service of biological functions, and, hence, roughly speaking, of life. By the same token, it is partly constitutive of those behavioural and biological concepts that the activities and functions they express are capable of being guided by perception. But now, if what is partly constitutive – of running, for example – differs between humans and animals, then what is constituted must differ as well. The moral for the moderns is manifest: all capacities interact, in the behavioural repertoire of a subject that possesses them, not just in causal but also in conceptual ways. Therefore, if lack of rational powers barred animals from anything other than as-if perception, it would also bar them from anything other than as-if running, as-if digestion, as-if life, etc. Anyone willing to bite that bullet incurs the consequence of lead-poisoning.

9 Reason, Language, and Community

Returning to the anthropological difference, it is neither knowledge nor belief. But let us assume, for the sake of argument, that Aristotle is correct

---

[34] Plutarch (1957).

in diagnosing that the intellect is the *differentia* of humans. What does that *differentia* amount to? Aristotle offers two answers through its definitions of humans (*Pol.* I 2, 1253a3–4, 9–18; 1332b3–8):

> Human Being = 1: *zōon logikon* or *zōon logon echon*, i.e. the rational animal (1253a9).
>
> Human Being = 2: *zōon politikon*, i.e. the political or communal animal

Definition 2 connects being human to a communal social organisation, definition 1 to language. By *logos*, Aristotle means a capacity – reason – notably when he distinguishes parts of the soul according to whether they involve logos. In other contexts he means sentence, speech, or language. It seems true to the spirit – if not the rather disparate letter – of Aristotle's writings to assume that reason is a capacity for linguistically structured reasoning and that speech or language – as opposed to the sounds emitted in animal communication – is rationally controlled. In consequence, Aristotle propounds both a *lingualist conception of rationality* and a *rationalist conception of language*.

On the one hand, my reading deliberately avoids a reduction of logos to an independently defined linguistic capacity. On the other hand, in line with a mainstream in Aristotle scholarship it recognises the importance of language to reason. However, in a highly interesting contribution to this volume, McCready-Flora challenges that mainstream. He rejects the widespread assumption that for Aristotle rationality as a distinguishing mark of humans is connected to language: 'nothing about speech constitutes human rationality according to Aristotle'. He pithily summarises his argument as follows:

(1) If something is a means deployed to serve rational cognition, then it is not the rational-making feature. (*a fortiori* from close reading of *On the Parts of Animals* IV 10.)

(2) Speech – including symbolic prowess – is a means deployed to serve rational cognition. (Close reading of *On Sophistical Refutations*)

Therefore, (3) Speech is not the rational-making feature. (Chapter 2, 46)

I shall not engage with McCready-Flora's exegesis of *PA* IV 10 and *SE* 1, 7. For it makes copious use of learned interpretations of other difficult passages, thereby quickly leading a non-Graeculus like myself out of his depth. My animadversions run as follows: (i) *if* (1) is indeed the import of *PA* IV 10, then this passage is mistaken; (ii) *if* (2) is indeed the import of *SE* 1 & 7, then these passages are at least contentious; (iii) the conclusion (3) stands in *palpable tension* with other passages in Aristotle's corpus.

Aristotle on the Anthropological Difference and Animal Minds 159

(Ad i) By the same token, conceptual thought cannot be a rational making feature. For it definitely is a means deployed to serve rational cognition. What McCready-Flora seems to have in mind is that a means externally related to what it is a means for cannot be constitutive of what it is a means for. That is a truism, but assumes rather than establishes that speech is extrinsically related to rationality (see ii). Furthermore, not every phenomenon X that can legitimately be characterised as a *means* for achieving Y is externally related to Y. Hammers are a means of hammering, yet the connection between the latter and the former is not extrinsic. A fixed pivotal point is a means of initiating rotation. But the notion of rotation cannot be understood without reference to that of a pivotal point.

(Ad ii) Those Aristotelians who stress the linguistic dimension of logos (e.g. Kenny and Hacker) would precisely deny that language is a mere means for communicating thoughts that are entirely non- or prelinguistic. The connection between language and thought is not just that of an extrinsic instrument to its purpose. They are right in at least one respect: it is only by reference to its linguistic expression that it makes sense to attribute to thought the kind of articulation logic detects in it (see Glock, 2013).

(Ad iii) First, *Pol.* I 2, 1253a characterises *logos* as a distinguishing feature of humans. What is more, in this context Aristotle clearly means *speech* by *logos*, since he contrasts the latter with 'mere voice'. Second, he also regards rationality as a distinguishing feature of humans. Third, in doing so he uses the term logos. Fourth, he does not explicitly state that logos in this context is not to be associated with language. In view of these four points, lumbering him with a complete separation of rationality and speech on account of the unsound line of reasoning McCready-Flora ascribes to him is uncharitable.

Even if I am right in pleading for charity on this score, Aristotle's position on the role language plays to the anthropological difference was ambivalent. On the one hand, he described animal vocalisations *as phone semantikē* (meaningful sounds). Animal vocalisations also qualify as *deloun*.[35] He also granted that bird-song possesses articulation, a kind of grammatical structure. In this respect he anticipated recent discoveries of syntactic structure in bird-song.[36] On the other hand, Aristotle maintained that the absence of speech (*logos*) accounts for the 'inability to form a civic society' that sets animals apart unfavourably from humans. Genuine words (*onomata*) require convention (*synthēkē*). And animals cannot enter into such conventions.

---

[35] *Pol.* I 2, 1253a9–18; *DA* II 8, 420b32–32; *DI* 16a26–29.   [36] See Fitch (2010).

Prima facie, this combination is circular. Animals lack speech because they lack conventions; at the same time animals cannot enter into conventions because they lack speech. At second sight, circularity is avoided if these claims are interpreted as follows. The first is *constitutive-cum-conceptual* in the spirit of Peirce's famous tripartite conception of signs: the vocalisations of animals do not qualify as speech (what Peirce calls 'symbols'), since they are not subject to conventions. In contrast, the second claim is causal: animals are prevented from developing conventional systems of communication because of their lack of speech.

Alas, a third look reveals a profound problem. The combination of Aristotle's two claims renders the emergence of language entirely mysterious. If only communication subject to *conventions* counts as language, and if *linguistic* communication is a prerequisite for the creation of convention, neither conventions nor language could have arisen.

At the same time, Aristotle's account of the difference between human language and animal communication, in combination with his definition of humans as political animals, rightly emphasises that what makes human speech unique is not primarily syntax, but the cooperative nature of the communication that it serves. But to spell out that profound insight must be left to another occasion.[37]

---

[37] See Glock (2012); Tomasello (2014).

PART III

Aristotle's Moral Anthropology

CHAPTER 8

Why Human Virtue Is the Measure of All Virtue
Kathi Beier

When Aristotle analyses the essence of human virtue (*aretē anthrōpinē*) in *Nicomachean Ethics*, book II, he states that

> every *aretē*, whatever it is an *aretē* of, both gives that thing the finish of a good condition and makes it perform its *ergon* well, as for example the eye's *aretē* makes both it and its *ergon* excellent; for it is through the *aretē* of the eye that we see well. Similarly, the *aretē* of the horse makes it an excellent horse and good at running, carrying its rider and facing the enemy. If, then, this is so in all cases, the *aretē* of a human being too will be the disposition (*hexis*) whereby he becomes a good human being and from which he will perform his own *ergon* well. (*EN* II 6, 1106a15–24, transl. Rowe/Broadie)[1]

Aristotle establishes in this passage a strong link between a substance's *ergon* and its *aretē*.[2] *Ergon* is commonly translated as 'function'.[3] In many cases, it is even conceived of as something's function or purpose in the literal sense. At least this is how Socrates appears to define the term at the end of the *Republic*, book I, claiming that a substance's *ergon* refers to the work for which the substance is the sole or best instrument (352e and 353a). Socrates' reference to the pruning knife to cut vines is the paradigm case. While their shoots could also be cut with a carving knife, or a chisel, or many other tools, Socrates explains how no tool does it better than the pruning knife, which is made for the purpose. Thus, according to him, we are entitled to define the *ergon* or function of the pruning knife to be the act of pruning. As Socrates further states (353b), everything that has an *ergon* also has a distinct virtue (*aretē*) or vice (*kakia*). While it is through its virtue that it performs its *ergon* well, the opposed vice makes it perform its

---

[1] In *EE* II 1, 1218b36–1219a5, Aristotle takes the cloak, the boat, and the house as examples.
[2] Due to the diverse translations, I will use the Greek term *ergon* in both text and citations, and use 'virtue' as the translation of *aretē* in the text, but stick to the Greek term in citations.
[3] Cf. the respective translations by Broadie and Rowe (2002), Irwin (1999), Rackham (1934), and Ross (1984).

163

ergon poorly (353c). Socrates claims this model holds not only for artefacts such as the pruning knife, but more generally: In the same way it is attributed to the knife, it is also attributed to the eye, the horse, and the human being. Since artefacts are considered paradigmatic, we may call the Socratic model the *functionalist conception of virtue*. Virtue here means a substance's fitness to serve a distinct purpose that is assigned to it; it means aptitude, serviceability, or even instrumentality.[4]

The functionalist reading of virtue is often also taken to be Aristotelian. The aim of this chapter, however, is to show that this is a misreading. My claim will be that Aristotle presents a non-functionalist, *psychological* rather than a *functionalist* conception of virtue, and that he reverses the Socratic line of argumentation. As I will argue, there is reason to believe that Aristotle defines virtue with respect to human virtue, and that he takes the so-called virtues of other things, the virtues of the horse, for example, to be virtues merely by analogy. Therefore, this chapter will (i) reject the functionalist reading of Aristotelian virtue, and (ii) reflect on the question whether, for Aristotle, human virtue is the measure of all virtue. In doing so, I shall refer to those passages inside and outside Aristotle's ethical writings that suggest both a non-functionalist and an analogous conception of virtue (Section 2). I shall then give a more detailed account of what human virtue is – the kind of virtue I take to be magisterial (Section 3). Before turning to Aristotle himself, however, I shall set the stage for the debate by looking at some contemporary neo-Aristotelian approaches to virtue ethics that define human virtue in functionalist terms (Section 1). This will help to see, first, how popular the functionalist understanding of human virtue still is, second, that it is taken to be Aristotelian, and, third, that the claim that Aristotle does *not* have a functionalist conception of human virtue goes beyond pure exegetical issues, since it sets him apart from both his predecessor Plato and some of his successors in modern virtue ethics.

1 The Functionalist Conception of Human Virtue in Modern Ethics

The functionalist understanding of human virtue can be found in both anti-Aristotelian and neo-Aristotelian approaches to modern ethics. That

---

[4] Cf. Barney (2008, 299): 'This conception of function as instrumentality—that is, as necessarily connected to *use* and a *user*—is evidently an important point for Plato.' Barney reminds us of *Republic* X, 601d, where Plato rhetorically asks: 'Then aren't the virtue or excellence, the beauty and correctness of each manufactured item, living creature, and action related to nothing but the use (*chreia*) for which each is made or naturally adapted?'

Why Human Virtue Is the Measure of All Virtue 165

is, for some it serves as a reason to reject Aristotle's ethics, whereas others take it to be an important reason for its renaissance. In contemporary anti-Aristotelianism, a common line of argumentation runs like this: The heart of Aristotle's ethics is the so-called *ergon* argument in *EN* I 7; in this argument, Aristotle assimilates the way human beings can be called (morally) good to the way things having a particular function are called good; as, for example, a good shoemaker is one who is good in shoemaking, or as a good pair of scissors is one which is good in cutting, so a human being is good if it is good in fulfilling its function. Being able to fulfil one's function means being virtuous. However, human beings, as such, have no function in this sense, since they are neither products made for specific purposes, nor can they be reduced to specific roles. Therefore, what it means to be good as a human being needs to be elucidated in a non-Aristotelian way. This argumentation assumes that there is no essential difference between Aristotle's *ergon* argument and the *ergon* argument we find in Plato's *Republic*; both Aristotle and Plato are taken to endorse a functionalist reading of human virtue, and it is because of this functionalism that their ethics is denied any plausibility. However, if it can be shown that Aristotle does *not* have a functionalist understanding of human virtue, his approach to ethics might well be seen as worth considering.

Yet the very same functionalist reading of virtue also plays a significant role in many neo-Aristotelian approaches to modern virtue ethics, both in its naturalistic and in its culturalistic version. As the following gloss of a critique will reveal, this causes problems for their respective interpretation of Aristotle's texts. So, if it can be shown that Aristotle does *not* have a functionalist understanding of human virtue, this might help to reformulate these approaches in order to make a stronger case for neo-Aristotelianism in modern ethics.

Neo-Aristotelian *ethical naturalists* concentrate on what culturalists call 'first nature', claiming that the *ergon* or function of human beings is basically biologically determined. For them, being good as a human being primarily amounts to being good as a living being, as a member of a specific life form. Accordingly, the good human life is taken to be some sort of 'flourishing'. In this vein, Philippa Foot, for example, describes her own, allegedly neo-Aristotelian meta-ethical project as one of 'likening the basis of moral evaluation to that of the evaluation of behaviour in animals', or to the vital operations of plants.[5] She believes the way an individual living being ought to be is determined by the inbuilt natural teleology of

---

[5] Foot (2001, 16).

166   KATHI BEIER

living things, i.e. by what is needed for development, self-maintenance, and reproduction.[6] Alluding to Peter Geach, she holds 'that virtues play a necessary part in the life of human beings as do stings in the life of bees'.[7] This is a functionalist reading of virtue, for it takes virtue to be a living being's fitness to serve the purposes given to it by nature, including development, self-maintenance, and reproduction. However, in over-emphasising the similarity between human and non-human living beings, ethical naturalists tend to have difficulties integrating reason and intellect (*nous*) into the overall picture of a good human life. Unlike Aristotle, they would, e.g. have to say that a person who voluntarily refrains from reproduction in order to dedicate her life to contemplation exhibits a natural defect, and is, thus, vicious rather than virtuous.[8] As a last resort, some of them even put into question whether the claim that *nous* is divine and the most excellent element in human beings can be attributed to Aristotle at all.[9]

In contrast, neo-Aristotelian *ethical culturalists* concentrate on what they call 'second nature', claiming that the *ergon* or function of human beings is basically determined by the social and cultural circumstances the individ-ual human being is subject to. Hence, being good as a human being primarily amounts to being good as a social being, i.e. as a member of a certain culture or community. Alasdair MacIntyre, for example, quite explicitly calls this a functional concept of 'man' that he thinks was prevalent in the classical tradition, in Homer's, Plato's, and Aristotle's time.[10] Ethical culturalists take the good human life to be some sort of 'cultural functioning', and regard virtues as those capacities that allow human beings to fulfil what is socially demanded. It is on the basis of this assumption that MacIntyre raises the following question: 'If a good deal of the detail of Aristotle's account of the virtues presupposes the now-long-vanished context of the social relationships of the ancient city-state, how can Aristotelianism be formulated so as to be a moral presence in a world in which there are no city-states?'[11] MacIntyre's answer to this question is to link virtue to the concept of practice, defining virtue as a kind of quality

---

[6] Foot (2001, 33). For a naturalistic approach to modern virtue ethics, cf. also Hursthouse (1999, 2004).

[7] Foot (2001, 35). Cf. Geach (1977, 17, p. vii).

[8] For a naturalistic solution of this point, cf. Hursthouse (1999, 216) and Annas (2005, 16). For a broader discussion of problems in neo-Aristotelian ethical naturalism, cf. also Frede (2015), Hacker-Wright (2009), Hursthouse (2013), McDowell (1995), Reader (2000), and Sturgeon (2006).

[9] Cf. Nussbaum (2001, 376), who thinks that 'the text of *EN* X seems to be oddly composed, giving rise to suspicion that chapters 6–8 are not originally parts of the same whole.'

[10] Cf. MacIntyre (2007, 58f).   [11] MacIntyre (2007, 163).

Why Human Virtue Is the Measure of All Virtue   167

that helps its owner to achieve the goods that are inherent to practices.[12] Because the existence of a given practice depends on the cultural circumstances of a specific community, practices have their own history and tradition – hence so do the virtues. For MacIntyre, the historical dimension is crucial, since it reveals the sense in which teleology applies to virtue. By establishing a 'socially teleological account' of virtue, MacIntyre wishes to overcome the 'biologically teleological account' which he also ascribes to Aristotle, but which he rejects.[13] According to MacIntyre, what is worth being saved in modern ethics is the culture-dependent functionalist concept of virtue he takes Aristotle and other ancient thinkers to advocate.

Hence, both neo-Aristotelian ethical naturalists and neo-Aristotelian ethical culturalists assume that Aristotle himself conceives of virtue as a functional term, and they try to revive Aristotle's ethical thinking by considering virtue either as a biologically determined functional concept or as a culture-dependent functional concept. However, if it is true that Aristotle does *not* think of human virtue in functionalist terms at all, there is reason to look for versions of neo-Aristotelian virtue ethics that avoid the notoriously problematic polarity between ethical naturalism and ethical culturalism.

Having, thus, shown what is at stake regarding modern ethics, we can now turn to Aristotle himself.

2   Aristotle's Non-Functionalist Conception of Virtue

In ancient Greek, *aretē* – usually translated as 'virtue' or 'excellence' – applies to many things. Since the term was used as the noun corresponding to the adjective *agathos*, which means 'good' in the attributive sense,[14] the Greeks could either say 'This is a good X' or 'This has the virtues typical of X'. Accordingly, it was just as natural for them to speak of a knife's or a horse's virtue as it was to call a human being virtuous. Grammatically speaking, the use of the term *aretē* was neither confined to human beings nor to the now so-called moral qualities of a person. As we have already seen, Socrates attaches *aretē* to 'anything that has an *ergon*' (*Rep.* I, 353b), be it an artefact like the pruning knife, an animal like the horse, a sense organ like the eye or the ear, or the human being as a whole. According to what I have called the functionalist conception of virtue, *aretē* is a generic

[12] Cf. MacIntyre (2007, 191).   [13] Cf. MacIntyre (2007, 197).

[14] The main reference for the distinction between the attributive and the predicative meaning of an adjective is still Geach (1956).

168 KATHI BEIER

term. There are as many kinds of virtue as there are things that possess an *ergon*. Human virtue, then, is supposed to be nothing other than a special kind of virtue. It is the kind of virtue that human beings can have and that makes them realise their *ergon*. The virtues of non-human living beings are of a different kind, encompassing different species of virtues such as the horse's or the dog's virtues. The virtues of artefacts belong to yet other kinds of virtue.

When Aristotle introduces the term *aretē* in *EN* I 7, it seems as if he is taking virtue to be a generic functional concept. In the *ergon* argument, he links human *aretē* to the peculiar human *ergon*. He states, first, that 'a human being's *ergon* we posit as being a kind of life, and this life as being activity (*energeia*) of soul and actions accompanied by reason (*logos*)', second, that 'it belongs to a good man (*spoudaiou de andros*) to perform these well and finely (*kalos*)', and, third, that 'each thing is completed well when it possesses its proper *aretē*' (*EN* I 7, 1098a12–16). Throughout the argument, Aristotle insinuates that human virtue allows human beings to actualise their *ergon* in the same way that the virtue of the flute player allows the flute player to actualise her *ergon*, and the virtue of the eyes allows the eyes to actualise theirs. In the passage cited at the beginning of this chapter, Aristotle seems to highlight this similarity.

To conceive of virtue as a genus-concept implies that the different kinds of virtue are predicated univocally. Thus, a knife is supposed to be virtuous in the same sense in which a horse, an eye, or a human being is virtuous – although this sense needs to be explicated on a more abstract level on which 'being virtuous' means something like 'works as it should'; this is fully compatible with its attributive use.

Such a reading of Aristotle's concept of virtue as a generic term predicated univocally is shared by many scholars. We find it, for example, in Sarah Broadie's *Ethics with Aristotle*. Broadie states that 'an excellence or virtue, as Plato and Aristotle understand that concept, is nothing but a characteristic which makes the difference between functioning and functioning well'.[15] Likewise, Michael Pakaluk refers to what he calls the 'interdefinability of goodness, function, and virtue' and claims that, for Aristotle, 'a good thing of a certain kind is that which has the virtues that enable it to carry out its function well'.[16] In line with this, David Bostock uses the term univocally when he claims that what Aristotle calls *aretē* is not confined to moral virtues alone, and that we, therefore, 'can say, for

---

[15] Broadie (1991, 37).   [16] Pakaluk (2005, 6).

Why Human Virtue Is the Measure of All Virtue 169

example, that the virtue of a knife is to cut well, the virtue of an eye is to see well, and the virtue of the reasoning part is to reason well'.[17]

In challenging the widespread interpretation of Aristotelian virtue as a generic functional concept, I do not wish to deny that Aristotle establishes a close connection between *ergon* and *aretē*. He does so quite explicitly.[18] However, I do wish to deny that he uses *aretē* univocally for different kinds of things that have an *ergon*. Just as *ergon* is to be understood differently when applied to different kinds of things, so is *aretē*. Ultimately, this means that, according to my reading, Aristotle's concept of virtue is not a generic but a specific concept; it is defined exclusively with respect to human beings. To say that a horse or a knife is virtuous, then, is to speak metaphorically. In other words, my claim will be that Aristotle uses 'virtue' in the broad sense not univocally (synonymously) but equivocally (homonymously) and sometimes analogously. This claim will become clearer as we proceed.

Samuel H. Baker has recently shown how Aristotle seeks a general meaning of *ergon* but allows different kinds of *erga*.[19] Baker believes the general meaning is indicated in the *Eudemian Ethics*. There Aristotle holds that 'the end (*telos*) of each [thing] is its *ergon*', explaining that 'the end is the best in the sense of the last [thing] for the sake of which everything else [is *or* is done]' (*EE* II 1, 1219a8–11). According to Baker, we can say that the *ergon* of X is 'the end for the sake of which an X, *qua* X, has being'.[20] This account of what an *ergon* is fits nicely with *EN* I 1, 1094a3–6, where Aristotle takes *ergon* to be an activity (*energeia*) in some cases, but a product in others, depending on what X is. As Aristotle holds, the eye's *ergon* is seeing, and the horse's is running, carrying the rider, and facing the enemy, whereas the shipbuilder's *ergon* is the ship, and the sculptor's the sculpture. This gives rise to the assumption that, since the things that have an *ergon* are different, so are the corresponding *erga*. And, similarly, the virtues must be different, too, due to their close connection with *erga*.

This is a fine point. However, it still does not settle whether *ergon* has a univocal meaning in Aristotle. For this, I think we need to consider the concept of *ergon* with reference to both natural substances and artefacts. This will help us to see that Aristotle does not use *ergon* univocally. For Aristotle makes clear that these are two species of things that do not have a

---

[17] Bostock (2000, 20).

[18] Cf. Barney (2008). Note, however, that what I have called the *functionalist conception of virtue* is not the same as what Barney calls the 'function thesis' (294), i.e. Aristotle's claim that human beings have a function or, as I would prefer to say, a distinct work.

[19] Cf. Baker (2015).   [20] Cf. Baker (2015, 248).

common genus. Although artefacts belong to the kind of things whose *ergon* consists in an activity, i.e. a use, Aristotle insists that the *ergon* and, thereby, the virtue of an artefact is *categorically different* from the *ergon* and the virtue of natural substances, e.g. of horses, eyes, or human beings. As far as I can see, there are three main arguments for this claim.

The first concerns the difference in nature between artefacts and natural substances. According to Aristotle, it is with respect to artefacts alone that *ergon* means 'function' in the strict sense of the term, since artefacts are produced to serve a specific purpose and are designed accordingly, i.e. to be functional in relation to that purpose. The purpose of an artefact is defined with reference to human needs, which the artefact is supposed to help satisfy. This functional conception of a substance's *ergon* can by no means be transferred, however, to natural substances such as human beings, for artefacts and natural substances, according to the *Physics*, are ontologically different: while natural substances are self-contained entities that contain the principle of their existence and change in themselves, the very existence of artefacts depends entirely on external purposes (*Phys.* II 1, 192b12–34).[21] Accordingly, the respective *telē* and *erga* are categorically different. While an artefact's *telos* is defined with reference to purposes external to it, i.e. to human needs and desires, the *telos* of a natural substance is internally defined. According to Aristotle, its *telos* consists in the preservation of its life form and the full development of itself as the thing it is (*Phys.* II 8, 199a26–30 and 199b).[22] Since artefacts cannot be substances in the same sense natural substances are, their *ergon* must be of a different nature, too.

The second argument has to do with the idea of a functional equivalent, which is applicable only to artefacts. As Plato's Socrates points out, the shoot of a vine can also be cut with a carving knife, or a chisel, or any other tool, if it does the same work as the pruning knife. Hence artefacts are to a certain extent interchangeable. And so is their matter, Aristotle adds. To be sure, one cannot make a saw blade out of paper, but it can be made of iron or of any other matter that has similar qualities (*Phys.* II 9, 200a10–15). None of this applies to natural substances. Neither can the *ergon* of one natural substance be actualised by another natural substance, nor can a natural substance be made of arbitrary kinds of material. A dog that is made of bronze is not a dog, but a sculpture.

---

[21] The fact that artefacts are not substances in the same sense as natural substances is expressed in Aristotle's claim that 'art (*technē*) imitates nature (*physis*)' (*Phys.* II 2, 194a21).

[22] Therefore, artefacts and not natural substances can become out of fashion.

Why Human Virtue Is the Measure of All Virtue 171

The third argument considers the different ways of making something fit to fulfil its *ergon*. If an artefact is not yet functional, or if it ceases to be functional, that is, if it is not 'virtuous' but 'vicious', as Plato would say, it needs to be completed or repaired. That means that *an artisan* has to make it fit (again) to serve its purpose. And artisans do so by (re-)arranging its matter, by whetting the blade of a knife, for example. This is nothing but an external treatment that the specific artefact undergoes. A human being, in contrast, does not acquire a virtue via external treatment or material readjustment. According to Aristotle, human beings acquire virtues only through practice; they acquire intellectual virtues mostly by learning, he says, and ethical virtues by habituating oneself to acting virtuously (*EN* II 1, 1103a15–18). Hence, for a human being to acquire virtue is to partake in the process of virtue acquisition, which is an activity of the human soul. The result is a certain way of being – a *hexis*, Aristotle says – that indicates a change in the soul, that is, in the human being's form rather than in its matter. The same holds, *mutatis mutandis*, for the acquisition of virtues in animals.

In light of these arguments, we have good reason to conclude that *ergon* is not a generic term with a single sense. Because natural substances and artefacts are ontologically different and cannot be called substances in the same sense, their *erga* too must be different – a difference Plato seems to have ignored. *Ergon* means function only when it is applied to artefacts. Due to the strong link Aristotle establishes between a substance's *ergon* and its virtue, we can conclude that the conception of virtue in terms of function is not applicable to living things. Put conversely, the term 'virtue', when applied to artefacts, has a special meaning: their aptitude or service-ability, i.e. their fitness in serving external purposes. Moreover, unlike Plato, Aristotle never even speaks of an artefact's virtue. This lends support to my general claim that Aristotle develops a psychological, non-functional account of virtue, hence that artefacts, for him, can only metaphorically be said to be 'virtuous' or 'vicious'.[23] If this is so, then Aristotle's use of

---

[23] Baker identifies another difference between Plato's and Aristotle's accounts of what an *ergon* is. For Plato, as we have seen, the *ergon* of X is what X can achieve best (cf. *Rep.* I, 353a1–8), where, according to Baker, 'the notion of "best" is with respect to a comparison class of things that can achieve similar *erga*'; for Aristotle, however, the *ergon* of X is the end that is best in the sense of being the last thing for the sake of which everything else is or is done (cf. *EE* II 1, 1219a10–11), where, according to Baker, 'the notion of "best" is with respect to a comparison class of other things that an X, qua X, can achieve, and the way that one of these things is best is by being the last thing for the sake of which' (Baker 2015, 242). It is for this reason that I think that, for Plato, the *ergon* argument is indeed a function argument, while for Aristotle it is not. Though for different reasons, Baker only believes the latter, i.e. that in Aristotle 'the *ergon* argument is not a "function" argument' (ibid., 253).

'virtue' deviates not only from Plato's use, but from the general usage of this term in ancient Greece.

Now, according to Aristotle, living things differ likewise in kind. We learn from books II and III of *De Anima* that plants, animals, and human beings are ontologically different from one another insofar as their souls have different parts that give rise to different capacities.[24] Aristotle mentions the distinction in *EN* I 7, 1098a1–8; he claims that the life of plants exhibits merely the nutritive capacity (*threptikon*), whereas the life of animals also exhibits the perceptual capacity (*aisthētikon*) and the capacity for locomotion (*kinētikon*); human beings, in contrast, have all these capacities plus the capacity for thinking (*dianoētikon*).[25] Moreover, the capacity for thinking differs radically from vegetative and animal capacities, in that the former does not have a bodily organ whereas the latter do have organs. This suggests that the concept of virtue, though basically psychologically defined, is not a generic term used univocally if it is applied to both human beings and animals. Does this mean that Aristotle uses the concept of virtue equivocally? Given the ontological proximity of human beings, animals and plants (they all belong to the genus of living substances), this does not seem entirely credible. However, in order to find a middle way between strict univocity and pure equivocation, one has to argue that Aristotle uses the term 'virtue' *analogically* when he compares the virtues of human beings with those of other living beings, based on some analogy between human nature and the nature of non-human living substances.

One promising way to do so is to show that the different kinds of virtue Aristotle mentions are related to one another such that one of them is authoritative or magisterial. My suggestion is that, by 'virtue', Aristotle first and foremost means human virtue. For Aristotle, human virtue is prior to any other kind of virtue. Animals and sense organs can be said to be virtuous only insofar as they relate to human virtue. If human virtue is the exemplary of virtue and the basis for understanding the other forms of virtue, then, according to Aristotle, human beings alone can have virtues in the proper sense of the term; other things are virtuous only by analogy or, as in the case of artefacts, in a loose and metaphorical sense. Three reasons speak in favour of this conclusion. The first concerns the definition of virtue as *hexis* and *diathesis*, the second animal virtues, and the third the virtues of bodily organs.

---

[24] Cf. Whiting (2002) and Corcilius and Gregoric (2010) for helpful discussions of how Aristotle relates the soul's capabilities to the parts of soul he distinguishes.

[25] Cf. also *Met.* I 1, 980a27–981a15, i.e. Aristotle's distinction between the kinds of *phronēsis* that animals and humans have.

Why Human Virtue Is the Measure of All Virtue   173

(i) When Aristotle talks about virtue in his non-ethical writings, he links it to the concept of *hexis*. In *Categories* 8, 8b32, he claims that virtues such as justice and temperance are *hexeis*, i.e. acquired stable and long-lasting habits that do not change easily. Together with *diatheseis* in the narrow sense, i.e. dispositions such as being either hot or cold, which do change easily, *hexeis* constitute the first species of quality. According to the *Categories*, virtues are neither capacities nor affections, nor do they have anything to do with a substance's shape – these being the other three species of quality Aristotle is eager to discern.[26] Now in *Categories* 8, as well as in *Metaphysics* V 20, *hexis*, in turn, is defined as *diathesis* in the broad sense – that is, every habit is defined as a disposition. And, according to *Metaphysics* V 19, 'we call a disposition the arrangement of that which has parts, in respect either of place or of capacity or of kind; for there must be a certain position, as the word "disposition" shows' (*Met.* V 19, 1022b1–3).

This leads us to two considerations. The first and rather obvious one is that proper Aristotelian virtues can be possessed only by a living substance whose soul is composed of different parts in the relevant sense. That is, among the parts of the soul, there must be one that is oriented towards the good rather than the bad; according to Aristotle, this is either the part of the soul by which the living being can listen to reason or the part of the soul that has reason itself. Put conversely, living things that are either not made up of different parts, or that have parts but not in the relevant sense, cannot have virtues. Thus, God, for example, cannot be virtuous, for God as the first mover 'cannot have any magnitude, but is without parts and indivisible' (*Met.* XII 7, 1073a6). In *EN* X 8, 1178b8–24, Aristotle therefore refuses to ascribe ethical virtues to Gods.[27] Of course, this does not mean that gods are vicious. According to Aristotle, they are essentially good. Their goodness, however, does not come into existence by an arrangement of their parts, that is, by acquiring virtues. Plants, too, cannot be virtuous, but for contrary reasons: the soul of plants has no part in the relevant sense, since it lacks both the part that is able to listen to reason and the part that has reason as such. Aristotle, therefore, never ascribes virtues to plants. This corresponds to his claim in *EN* I 13, 1102b12 that, in

---

[26] It is worth noting that Aristotle only lists two human virtues, but no animal virtue here. While this certainly does not prove anything, it nevertheless speaks in favour of the claim that the focal meaning of virtue, for Aristotle, is human virtue.

[27] We may safely add that gods do not have intellectual virtues either, because they do not have to learn anything.

174 KATHI BEIER

human beings, the plant-like, nutritive capacity (*threptikon*) 'has no share in human virtue at all'.

A second, rather tentative, consideration is that virtue in the proper sense of the term does not just require heterogeneous parts but, more specifically, heterogeneity in the formal parts of a living being, i.e. in its soul. As we have already seen, this holds for human beings. Human beings are not only composed of body and soul; the soul itself, Aristotle claims, comprises different, highly heterogeneous parts that give rise to very different kinds of capacities. While some of these capacities constitute us as living beings in virtue of being tied to bodily organs and, hence, can be found in plants and animals, too, others constitute us as rational beings and make us god-like, as Aristotle stresses in *EN* X 6–8. In contrast, the soul of animals does not exhibit such a complex composition. Like humans, their soul comprises the part that is responsible for the growth and maintenance of the body (*threptikon*) as well as the parts that are connected to sense organs (*aisthē-tikon*) and cause motion (*kinētikon*); but, unlike humans, they lack the immaterial, non-organic part that gives rise to the capacity for thinking (*dianoētikon*). That is, in vegetative and animal souls, every part of the soul is tightly connected to bodily organs and bodily functions, whereas only some parts of the human soul are organic in this sense. The most important part of the human soul is not organic. Nevertheless, Aristotle explicitly mentions animal virtues, the horse's virtues, for example. In order to explain this usage of 'virtue', we need a second consideration.

(ii) According to *EN* II 6, 'the *aretē* of the horse makes it an excellent horse and good at running, carrying its rider and facing the enemy' (1106a18–21). How are we to explain this, given that it is human beings alone that are genuine possessors of virtue? First of all, it is worth noting that two of the horse's *erga* mentioned here are defined with respect to human needs. The horse's quality of carrying its rider, as well as its quality of facing the enemy, both relate to human practices. They are, therefore, not animal virtues in the strict sense of the term, but have a human imprint. The *aretē* of the horse that makes it good at running, in contrast, seems to be a genuine animal virtue. In *HA*, Aristotle mentions further animal virtues that have no relation to human practices (*HA* I 1, 488b12–23 and IX 3, 610b20). However, in *HA* VIII 1 he declares how these virtues are to be understood by making the following distinction:

> Some of these qualities in man, as compared with the corresponding qualities in animals, differ only quantitatively: that is to say, a man has more or less of this quality, and an animal has more or less of some other;

Why Human Virtue Is the Measure of All Virtue 175

other qualities in man are represented by analogous and not identical qualities: for instance, just as in man we find knowledge (*technē*), wisdom (*sophia*), and sagacity (*synesis*), so in certain animals there exists some other natural potentiality akin to these. (*HA* VIII 1, 588a24–30, transl. Thompson)[28]

What seems to be a genuine animal virtue, Aristotle claims here, turns out to be a virtue by analogy, that is, a virtue that is transferred from its original context to a different context, from human beings to animals. The kind of analogy Aristotle seems to have in mind is the identity of proportion, i.e. a quadripartite equation of the form 'A relates to B as C relates to D'. Just as, for example, we can find in some human beings a quality which we call the virtue of wisdom, so we can find in some animals a quality that resembles wisdom in the human domain, and that we therefore call wisdom, knowing that animals cannot have virtues such as wisdom in the strict sense of the term. As a shorthand, we say, for instance, that foxes are clever, or that Indian elephants are meek. This is a metaphor which is based on a proportional analogy.[29]

(iii) Similar to how Aristotle explains the meaning of the term 'animal virtue' in *HA* VIII 1, he also explains what it means to ascribe virtues to bodily organs in *Met.* V 20. Eyes, for example, can be called virtuous, he claims, insofar as they are parts of the human body; for, according to *Met.* V 20, 'parts of the substance that is able to acquire *hexeis* can have *hexeis* too' (1022b12–14). Again, it is with respect to the whole human being that its living, bodily parts can be called virtuous, i.e. they are virtuous by analogy.

If the conclusion I draw from the above considerations is correct, then there is reason to believe that Aristotle considers human virtue to be the measure of all virtue, for it is in comparison with human virtue that other, non-human virtues can be said to exist. In other words, non-human virtues are virtues by analogy. To develop this thought a bit further, I will now turn to elucidating the nature of human virtue, i.e. the kind of virtue I take to be the standard of virtue.

3   The Nature of Human Virtue

According to Aristotle, the *ergon* of a human being as such is an 'activity of the soul in accord with reason or requiring reason' (*EN* I 7, 1098a8). The

---

[28] For a useful discussion of this passage, cf. Lennox (1980).
[29] For analogy-based metaphors, cf. *Poet.* 1457b15–20.

176   KATHI BEIER

human soul, however, has two parts that possess reason. The one part, the desiring part (*orektikon*), participates in reason 'in so far as it is capable of listening to it and obeying it' in the way 'one is reasonable when one takes account of advice from one's father or loved ones' (*EN* I 13, 1102b32–34), the other part has it 'in the proper sense and in itself' (1103a3). It is for this reason that human virtue is the genus of two kinds of virtue, ethical and intellectual.[30] Whereas ethical virtue enables the desiring part to achieve its *ergon*, thereby enabling the human being to feel, decide, and act rationally, intellectual virtue enables the part of the soul that has reason as such to achieve its *ergon*, thereby enabling human beings to think rationally. As they are different in kind, the way of acquiring the respective virtues is different, too. According to Aristotle, intellectual virtue 'mostly both comes into existence and increases as a result of teaching (*didaskalia*)', while ethical virtue 'results from habituation (*ex ethous*)' (*EN* II 1, 1103a16–17). Since Aristotle does not explain the different ways of acquiring virtue in more detail, one may assume the explanation stems from his account of the human soul. He seems to have the following in mind: Since the desiring part of the soul comprises the affections and feelings (*pathē*), and since these are originally non-rational, they have to be disposed such as to obey reason, and they are adapted to what reason demands through the process of habituation. Because there are no affections in the rational part of the soul, there is no need for habituation, but merely learning and teaching. This explanation fits nicely with what Aristotle says about the difference between what he calls 'natural virtue' (*physikē aretē*) and virtue proper. In *EN* VI 13 he seems to hold that some of the ethical virtues, for example, justice, temperance, and courage, belong to us by nature since some of us are courageous or just from the moment we are born rather than through a process of habituation. But, without reason and intelligence (*nous*), Aristotle says, they are harmful. He, therefore, concludes that 'if a person acquires intelligence, it makes a difference to his actions, and the disposition which was merely similar to *aretē* in the primary sense will then be that *aretē*' (*EN* VI 13, 1144b12–14).[31] This implies that natural virtues are not full-blown ethical virtues because, in the case of natural virtues, the affection is not yet habituated to reason and intellect.

---

[30] This is the primary sense of Aristotle's principle that the 'part of the substance that is able to acquire *hexeis* can have *hexeis* too' (*Met.* V 20, 1022b12–14).

[31] Cf. Müller (2004) and Vogler (2013) for useful comments on Aristotle's concept of natural virtue.

Why Human Virtue Is the Measure of All Virtue 177

One should note, however, that Aristotle subsumes very different virtues under the common genus 'ethical virtue', depending on the different affections that are in play, and that he takes 'intellectual virtue' to be itself a genus term that encompasses two species of intellectual virtues. As it turns out in *EN* VI 1, there is one part by means of which we reflect upon things whose principles cannot be otherwise, which Aristotle calls the scientific (*epistēmonikon*) part of the rational part of the soul. And there is another one by which we reflect upon things that can be otherwise; this is the calculative (*logistikon*) part of the rational part of the soul. As the *erga* of these parts are different, so are their virtues. Hence, Aristotle claims: 'It holds, then, of both intelligent parts that their *ergon* is truth; so the *aretai* of both will be the dispositions in accordance with which each of them will grasp truth to the highest degree' (*EN* VI 2, 1139b11–14). The *ergon* of the calculative part is the truth with respect to practical matters; with the calculative part we deliberate about what truly needs to be done in a given situation and what that situation is truly like. Aristotle calls the corresponding virtue, i.e. the *hexis* that allows its possessor to deliberate well (*eu*), practical wisdom or prudence (*phronēsis*). The *ergon* of the scientific part, in contrast, is theoretical truth; the corresponding virtue, i.e. the *hexis* that allows its possessor to think well with respect to those matters, that is, neither practically nor productively, as Aristotle says, is wisdom (*sophia*).[32]

However, instead of discussing the inner complexities of the table of virtues Aristotle provides us with, I would like to stress the fact that Aristotle defines every single human virtue, ethical and intellectual alike, as a *hexis*. Why does he do that and what does this mean? Aristotle's definition of human virtue in *EN* II 5 starts by identifying its genus term. He does so by way of elimination:

> Now since the things that occur in the soul fall into three kinds, i.e. affections (*pathē*), capacities (*dynameis*), and *hexeis*, excellence will be one of these . . . If, then the excellences are neither affections nor capacities, the only thing left for them to be is *hexis*. We have said, then, what the genus of excellence is. (*EN* II 5, 1105b20–1106a13, transl. Rowe and Broadie)

Scholars disagree about how the conclusion, most particularly its first premise, is to be understood. Is Aristotle tacitly referring to what he stated in the *Categories*? Or does he confine himself to the definition of ethical

---

[32] For a more detailed account of what it means for each of these soul-parts to be rational and, hence, to achieve its *ergon*, cf. Moss (2017).

178   KATHI BEIER

virtue? Here is an argument in favour of the latter position. It is from
David Bostock:

> There is evidently a premise that he [i.e. Aristotle] has failed to state: these
> are the things that occur in *that part* of the soul which has feelings, i.e. the
> part that can listen to reason but does not have reason 'in itself'. Of course,
> in other parts of the soul there are other things that occur ... But Aristotle,
> without saying so, has already narrowed his attention to that part of the soul
> which he has earlier said (in I.13) is the part with which virtues of character
> are concerned.[33]

Michael Pakaluk presents a similar argument.[34] This might or might not
be a correct interpretation of *EN* II 5. I do not think, however, that this
means that *only* ethical virtues are *hexeis*. For as it turns out in *EN* VI, not
only every single ethical virtue, but also every single intellectual virtue is a
hexis. Besides textual evidence, there is also an independent systematic
consideration in favour of this claim: If human virtue is a generic term that
encompasses different species of virtue, the meaning of 'virtue' must be the
same across the different species. Aristotle's definition of virtue for the one
species, say ethical virtue, must also hold for other species of virtue.

Moreover, there are striking similarities between *EN* II 5 and *Categories*
8. Thus, as it seems to me, when Aristotle identifies the genus of virtue in
EN II 5, he is relying on what he has said in the *Categories*. Given that
virtue terms denominate a person's qualities, and given that there are four
kinds of quality, virtue must be one of these. Since we already know that
virtue makes the human being realise its *ergon*, and that the human *ergon* is
an activity of the soul, we can exclude shape and external form from the list
of possible genus terms. What we are left with are affections, natural
capacities, and *hexeis*. Now, according to Aristotle, neither virtues nor
vices can be affections or feelings. Whereas affections arise involuntarily,
virtues and vices do not. Furthermore, we are praised for virtues and
blamed for vices, but we are neither praised nor blamed for having an
affection. For much the same reasons, virtues are not capacities either. We
are born neither as virtuous nor vicious, but instead with certain natural
capacities such as sense perception and natural desires. If something arises
in us by nature, Aristotle explains, we first have the capacity for it, and later
learn to perform the activity. We are not born with virtues because they
need to be acquired, and they can only be acquired by having learned to
perform virtuous acts (*EN* II 1, 1103a26–b3). What is more, capacities are

---

[33] Bostock (2000, 36).   [34] Cf. Pakaluk (2005, 105).

Why Human Virtue Is the Measure of All Virtue   179

ethically neutral, i.e. we can use them either for good or bad ends; virtues, in contrast, are not. If Aristotle concludes that virtue is neither an affection nor a capacity, then it must be a *hexis*, which means *hexis* is the genus term for both ethical and intellectual virtues.

Now what does it mean to say that human virtues are *hexeis*? Three aspects are worth mentioning. First, insofar as *hexis* belongs to the broad genus of *diathesis*, i.e. insofar as every *hexis* is a disposition, the virtues bring order into what is not yet ordered or arranged. In acquiring the virtues, the different parts of the human soul are arranged such as to be oriented towards reason, the most specific of the human capacities. The acquisition of virtues changes a person's way of being by transforming her soul to the effect that reason assumes the leading role. Consequently, virtues dispose us to live in accord with our specific rational nature, i.e. to perform rational acts. Second, designating virtues as *hexeis* means they are stable and long-lasting qualities. They dispose us so profoundly that we cannot easily lose them. Rather, we have them as a kind of permanent possession or, as some would say, as a 'second nature'. Third, as something like a 'second nature', we can see that virtues are something actual in one sense and something potential in another. As *acquired* habits, the virtues are actualisations of our potential to acquire them. In this respect, Aristotle holds that 'the *aretai* develop in us neither by nature nor contrary to nature, but because we are naturally able to receive them' (*EN* II 1, 1103a24–25). However, once we have received them, we have received stable *dispositions*, i.e. potencies, in this case potencies to act well. This also implies that the acquisition of virtues is not an end in itself; we do not acquire virtues merely for the sake of possessing them; rather, we acquire them in order to be able to *act* virtuously.[35]

4   Conclusion: Human Beings Alone Can Be Virtuous in the Proper Sense of the Term

A prevalent view in the scholarly work on Aristotle's ethics and in neo-Aristotelian approaches to virtue ethics treats virtue as a univocal, generic term. According to this reading, virtue is nothing but a substance's fitness or aptitude to perfectly perform its *ergon*. Virtues, therefore, can be possessed by anything that has an *ergon*, whether by human beings, non-rational living beings such as animals, or non-living entities such as knives.

---

[35] Cf. the explanation of virtue as a firm grip, a possession, and a kind of persistent orientation in Pakaluk (2005, 107–8).

I have called this reading the *functionalist conception of Aristotelian virtue*. According to this conception, having an *ergon* is both necessary and sufficient for being able to have virtues. Since there are many things that have an *ergon*, human virtue is but one species of virtue.

In this chapter, my aim has been to show that Aristotle does not have a functionalist conception of virtue. For Aristotle, *ergon* means function only when applied to artefacts. Yet artefacts are ontologically different from living substances, and the *erga* of living things are not to be understood in functional terms. On the basis of the close connection Aristotle establishes between a substance's *ergon* and its *aretē*, one may conclude that the virtues of living substances too are not to be understood in functional terms. Moreover, the kinds of living substances Aristotle distinguishes, i.e. plants, animals, and humans, are ontologically different, too, which means the concept of virtue cannot be used in a fully univocal sense here. Nor can it be merely equivocal. As I have shown, there is reason to believe that, for Aristotle, virtue is an analogous concept for which human virtue is the measure of all other virtues. This is because Aristotle defines virtue as *hexis*, i.e. as a stable arrangement or disposition. Virtue, thus, presupposes something that is composed of heterogeneous parts or elements that can be arranged in different ways. According to Aristotle, it is primarily human beings that have such a complex nature, since they are not just composed of form and matter, but have a highly complex and heterogeneous form, i.e. a soul that consists of both organic and non-organic parts. On the one hand, a human being is a *zōon*, i.e. an animal or living being endowed with animal powers such as sense-perception and passion. On the other hand, it is a *zōon logon echon*, an animal endowed with rational capacities such as reason (*logos*) and intellect (*nous*). Aristotle even refers to *nous* as 'something divine, or the divinest of the things in us' (*EN* X 7, 1177a17). No other living creatures, let alone non-living entities, have such a complex composition and, hence, can have virtues in the proper sense of the term. Thus, the virtues of organs and the virtues of animals, which Aristotle mentions, are virtues by analogy. They are qualities that are called virtues because they resemble human virtues in one way or another.

If Aristotle does not maintain a functionalist reading of human virtue, then neither ethical naturalism nor ethical culturalism are fully convincing as interpretations of Aristotelian ethics. In fact, human beings are living substances, and *qua* living substance they have a specific *ergon*, i.e. to preserve their life form and to develop fully as the things they are. This is what speaks in favour of ethical naturalism. However, Aristotle is eager to emphasise that what is most specific to humans is intellect (*nous*), the divine element, which is why he believes contemplation is the best life for human beings.[36] It is precisely this aspect of Aristotelian ethics that neo-Aristotelian naturalism finds most difficult to accommodate. Ethical culturalists, in contrast, base their reading on those passages in which Aristotle speaks of certain human beings as having functions in the proper sense of the term. For example, the function of the house-builder is to build houses, and the function of the ship-builder to build ships. However, what makes the house-builder able to perform his or her function is not a virtue, but a skill or competence, for competences are ethically neutral, while virtues are not.[37]

In light of the arguments presented in this chapter, we may conclude that, given the essence of virtue, it is due to the special nature of human beings – of their being simultaneously animal-like and god-like – that Aristotle believes human beings alone can be virtuous in the proper sense of the term. From his various writings we know that Aristotle characterises humans as the only animal that possesses speech (*Pol.* I 2, 1253a10), is capable of deliberation (*HA* I 1, 488b24), originates actions (*EE* II 6, 1222b19), and stands erect (*PA* IV 10, 686a26). Although Aristotle may not state this explicitly, I think that we can add that, for Aristotle, of all the animals, humans alone are capable of being virtuous in the strict sense of the term.

---

[36] Cf. also *PA* IV 10, 68a26–29, where Aristotle claims that a human being's 'nature and substantial being are divine; and it is an *ergon* of that which is most divine to reason and to think'.

[37] It is true, however, that Aristotle defines some ethical virtues, for example, courage or pride (*megalopsychia*), in social terms; yet they are not defined in terms of a social function.

CHAPTER 9

Aristotle on Friendship and Being Human

Nora Kreft

1 Introduction

Human beings are not the only social animals, according to Aristotle. He doesn't even think they are the only political animals. And in the beginning of book 8 of the *Nicomachean Ethics*, he suggests that non-human animals can also be friends with each other: most of them entertain friendships with their young, as well as with other members of their own species.[1] So, is friendship not uniquely human either?

In this paper, I argue that what Aristotle considers to be *proper* friendship is indeed a uniquely human type of relationship, meaning: for Aristotle, only human beings are able to have friends in the proper sense of the term. The intimate relationships between non-human animals that Aristotle initially refers to as 'friendships' share some features of proper friendship, but they also lack some central features that are available only among humans.

Further, I argue that being able to have proper friendship is not just a uniquely human feature, but an essential one. This is because being friends with others in this proper sense is part of what it means to be fully, or rather actually, human (in Aristotle's sense of 'actually human', where this refers to the actualisation of the human form). Human beings are rational animals for Aristotle. They have a share in divinity insofar as they have *nous*, that is (roughly) the mental faculty of reason. In short, they are animals with *nous*. On the reading I propose, part of what it means for *nous* to be actualised in humans is that it is shared with others – more precisely, that the activities that constitute its actualisation are shared with others. And it turns out that, according to Aristotle, these activities are shared in the relevant sense among and only among friends.

---

[1] 'And the affection of parent for offspring and of offspring for parent seems to be a natural instinct, not only in man but also in birds and in most animals; as also is friendship between members of the same species', *EN* VIII 1, 1155a16–19 (transl. Rackham).

Aristotle on Friendship and Being Human 183

I start with Aristotle's conception of friendship and the questions it raises in Section 2. I focus on his account of virtue friendship in particular because virtue friendship is more puzzling than the other forms of friendship he identifies. I propose an account of virtue friendship in Section 3. I then trace Aristotle's reasons for thinking of virtue friendship as the only proper friendship in Section 4, and argue that only human animals can have this form of friendship. From there, I move on to the role proper friendship plays in what Aristotle considers the actualised human life. In Section 5, I discuss potential problems with Aristotle's arguments in *EN* IX 9 and propose a reading of the so-called argument from nature that comes to the conclusion mentioned above.

2 A Difficulty with Virtue Friendship

Aristotle characterises friendship as a relationship of mutual goodwill between two or more individuals: they each desire that the respective other may fare well, and they know this of each other (*EN* VIII 2, 1155b34–1156a5). A few passages later, he adds that they also typically live with each other. In fact, 'there is nothing so characteristic of friends as living together' (VIII 6, 1157b19, transl. Rackham).

Further, two or more individuals enter and continue such relationships and desire each other's good in this way, because they appear to be good *for* each other, in contrast to simply good *simpliciter*.

> Then, do men like what is really good, or what is good for them? For sometimes the two may be at variance . . . Now it appears that each person loves what is good for himself, and that while what is really good is lovable absolutely, what is good for a particular person is lovable for that person. Further, each person loves not what is really good for himself, but what appears to him to be so; however, this will not affect our argument, for 'lovable' will mean 'what appears lovable'. (*EN* VIII 2, 1155b22–28)

Being good for someone and being good *simpliciter* in the sense of 'a good person in general' (or 'really good' in Rackham's translation) can come apart at times: someone can be good for another person without being a good person in general, or in a way that is unrelated to being good in general. At other times, they come together and someone is good for another person because they are a good person in general. But in each of these cases, what explains the friendship is that each friend is good for the respective other – or rather, *appears* to the respective other to be good for them. At least, that seems to be what Aristotle is suggesting here. Even though the good *simpliciter* are 'lovable absolutely' (I come back to this), individual persons love what they perceive to be good for them, and this perception seems to be both necessary and sufficient to explain the (continued) existence of a friendship.[2]

Aristotle then distinguishes between three ways in which someone can be good for us: they can be useful for us, or pleasurable, or *agathos*, i.e. virtuous. Correspondingly, he distinguishes between three types of friendship, namely utility-, pleasure- and virtue friendship (*EN* VIII 2, 1155b21 and VIII 3, 1156a6–12). It seems plausible that being useful and being pleasurable are ways in which someone can be good for us. Roughly, X is useful for Y iff X has properties that are helpful in producing one of Y's ends. And X is pleasurable for Y iff X has properties that produce some kind of pleasure in Y. Insofar as reaching their ends and feeling pleasure are good things for Y, if X is either useful or pleasurable for Y, then X is good for Y. But in what sense is being *virtuous* a way of being good for someone else?

It is natural to say that someone is useful or pleasurable for us, but not so natural to say that someone is virtuous for us (if we don't just mean 'appears virtuous to us'). Of course, a virtuous person can be useful or pleasurable for us on account of their virtue. In fact, virtuous persons will be useful and pleasurable to most people around them, given that they are kind, generous, just, and so on – virtuous behaviour is generally beneficial to its recipients in these ways. But, if this is what Aristotle has in mind, i.e. if this is the way in which virtuous persons can be good for us, namely by being useful and/or pleasurable on account of their virtue, then why isn't virtue friendship just subsumed under and a special case of utility- and/or pleasure friendship?

On the face of it, being virtuous is just Aristotle's term for being good *simpliciter*, rather than a genuinely third way of being good for someone, next to and on the same level as being useful and pleasurable. So, is Aristotle saying that virtue friendship comes about because the friends perceive each other to be good *simpliciter* instead of good for each other? Or at least in addition to also being good for each other?[3] Either would be in tension with the earlier claim. For as soon as we think of being good *simpliciter* as an independent ground for virtue friendship, and not just a possible explanation for why friends are good for each other, we have to

---

[2] 'Necessary' because he seems to be saying that there couldn't be a friendship without perceiving the friend as being good for oneself. And 'sufficient' because he is suggesting here that some friendships are based on this perception alone (for example, in cases where the friend only appears to be good for oneself but not good *simpliciter*).

[3] Whiting (2006, 280) proposes this reading, for instance.

Aristotle on Friendship and Being Human

give up the claim that friendship (*any* friendship) exists only because and insofar as the friends perceive each other to be good for each other in some way.

So, the problem seems to be that either virtue friendship collapses into utility- and/or pleasure friendship, or Aristotle is not really serious about the earlier claim, at least not when applied to virtue friendship. We might be tempted to embrace the second horn of this dilemma and argue that Aristotle isn't necessarily endorsing the earlier claim anyway. After all, the passage starts with 'it appears that' (*dokei*), and perhaps Aristotle is just reporting some *legomena* about friendship at this point. But that wouldn't be convincing, in part because he quite clearly endorses similar claims in other passages. For example, in the sections on friendship in the *Eudemian Ethics* he writes:

> It is debatable whether what is good merely for oneself is dear (*philos*) or what is absolutely good . . .; for things not absolutely good but possibly evil are to be avoided, and also a thing not good for oneself is no concern of oneself, but what is sought for is that things absolutely good shall be good for oneself. For the absolutely good is absolutely desirable, but what is good for oneself is desirable for oneself. (*EE* VII 5, 1236b34–40, transl. Rackham)

Unlike people who are good for us, people who aren't good for us are of 'no concern' to us, he says. They don't move and attract us. In order to love the good *simpliciter* and to love them on account of being good *simpliciter*, we first have to learn to see their general goodness as being good specifically for us then. So far, this would still be compatible with an account where virtue friendship is based on both the perception of the friend being good for us (call this condition A) *and* the perception of the friend being good *simpliciter* (B). However, Aristotle goes on to point out that (1) the good *simpliciter* are in fact good for us, in contrast to the 'not absolutely good but possibly evil', and (2) individuals always love what is good for them, rather than what is good *simpliciter* (the 'but' (*de*) is contrastive). The combination of (1) and (2) suggests that Aristotle does not think of B as an independent ground of virtue friendship, in addition to A. Instead, if everything goes well, B is the explanation for A. In other words, ideally, we are only friends with the good *simpliciter*, but this is just because they turn out to be the only ones who are in fact good for us (this would also explain why Aristotle calls the good *simpliciter* 'absolutely lovable' in the earlier *EN* passage – it just means something along the lines of 'truly good for us', for example in the sense of 'truly useful' or 'truly pleasurable').

186 NORA KREFT

Should we embrace the first horn instead? That seems unattractive, too, given how much time Aristotle devotes to spelling out the differences between virtue friendship on the one hand, and utility- and pleasure friendship on the other. As mentioned, in later sections, he calls virtue friendship 'proper' or 'actual' friendship, in contrast to both utility- and pleasure friendship (*EN* VIII 5, 1157a25–32).[4] It would be odd if proper friendship turned out to be a sub-category of an improper type of friendship.

3 Taking Pleasure in Virtue as Such

To make progress, we need to think more about why the good *simpliciter*, i.e. the virtuous, turn out to be the ones that are in fact good for us. I already mentioned that they are likely to be useful and pleasurable to many people in various contexts. For example, given that they will be reliable and trustworthy, they will make great babysitters; so, if I need a good babysitter, a virtuous person would be useful to me. Or, given that they will be kind and attentive, they will be pleasing to be around, at least if I am the kind of person who enjoys being attended to in that way. And, given that they are emotionally stable, they might have a calming and a soothing effect on me if I happen to be a nervous and unstable person. Such examples are easy to come by.

But they can be pleasing in another way, too: to some, the mere perception of another person's virtue as virtue is *itself* pleasurable. In these cases, it is not just a particular effect of their virtue that is pleasing, but their virtue as such. The people for whom perceiving another person's virtue is in itself pleasurable are of course the virtuous themselves. Aristotle already mentions this in *EN* book 1: it is a sign of being virtuous that one takes pleasure in virtue as such – not just in acting and thinking virtuously oneself, but also in perceiving and contemplating virtuous acting and thinking quite generally, whenever one comes across it. A virtuous person relates to virtue just as a lover of horses relates to horses in that respect: the genuine horse lover finds horses pleasing and exciting to watch, study, and be around in general, and not just when it comes to their own horse (*EN* I 9, 1099a7 ff).

I propose, then, that we understand virtue friendship as a relationship between two or more people who take pleasure in perceiving and contemplating each other's virtue as such. In utility- and 'normal' pleasure friendship, by contrast, it is not the perception of virtue itself that is useful

---

[4] I come back to this in Section 4.

Aristotle on Friendship and Being Human

or pleasurable, but at most some further consequence of this virtue. I say 'at most', because utility- and pleasure friendships might also be completely unrelated to the friend being virtuous: lots of these kinds of friendships come about because of (what can appear to be) useful properties such as wealth, or pleasurable properties such as good looks. But the point is that, even in cases where they *are* related to the friend's virtue, they are related to it in a different way than in virtue friendship. We might say that virtue friends value each other's virtue for its own sake, given that the mere perception of each other's virtue gives them pleasure and makes them want to be with each other. Utility- and pleasure friends, however, value their friend's virtue instrumentally. To the extent that they care about the friend's virtue at all, they are concerned with the useful and pleasurable effects of it (makes for good babysitting, makes one feel special, calm, and so on).[5]

Note that being valued for its own sake does not mean being valued disinterestedly here. On this picture, virtue friendship still exists because and only because the friends perceive each other to be good for each other – namely, pleasing in this special way. It is just that who the friends are as persons, that is, the way they act and think, is in itself pleasing to one another, so there is no need to refer to any further goods and pleasures to explain their friendship. When Aristotle says that they wish each other well 'for their own sakes' (for instance at *EN* VIII 4, 1156b9), it doesn't necessarily imply any disinterested concern either. It just means that they wish well for each other because they take pleasure merely in who the respective other is as a person.[6]

Yet isn't this a way of subsuming virtue friendship under pleasure friendship? It can look that way, since virtue friendship is explained by a particular kind of pleasure here. I don't think this is right, however. The reason is that *all* three types of friendship must, in some sense, be explained by pleasure, so what distinguishes pleasure friendship from utility- and virtue friendship can't simply be that it is explained by pleasure, and it was a mistake to think of it that way. Or so I want to argue.

---

[5] In utility- and pleasure friendship, 'the friend is not loved for being what he is, but as affording some benefit or pleasure as the case may be', EN VIII 3, 1156a18–19.

[6] Annas (1977) thinks that Aristotle's account of virtue friendship breaks with what is sometimes called the 'ethical egoism' of the earlier books in *EN*, and introduces the idea of a genuinely disinterested concern for others. I agree that it is important to him to make space for a type of friendship that goes beyond a merely instrumental relationship. But I don't think we have to attribute a notion of disinterested concern to him to make sense of this. Besides, apart from the passages already cited above, there are others in the books on friendship that invoke the moral psychology of the earlier books. See *EN* IX 8, 1169a16, for example: '*nous* [here in the sense of "every instance of *nous*"] always chooses that which is best for itself, and the good man obeys *nous*'.

As mentioned, in *EN* book 1, Aristotle says that it is characteristic of the lovers of virtue (i.e. the virtuous) that they take pleasure in virtue, meaning: they find acting and thinking virtuously pleasing, both when they do it themselves and when they perceive it in others. The same goes for lovers of horses, lovers of plays, and so on (*EN* I 9, 1099a7–23). The principle seems to be that loving something or someone comes along with taking pleasure in doing and/or perceiving it. Now, we might ask whether this pleasure *explains* the love for these things, or the other way around. Let's think about this with regard to the virtuous first. Does the pleasure they get from virtue explain why they want to perceive virtue in others and to act and think virtuously themselves?

At first sight, the answer seems to be no. As Aristotle points out several times, they love virtue because virtue is good (in the sense of good *simpliciter*); i.e. they want to act and think virtuously, and to perceive virtuous acting and thinking, because acting and thinking in this way is good (see *EN* IV 2, 1120a23, for instance).[7] They will always and inevitably get pleasure from virtue, but that doesn't seem to be why they seek it. On further reflection, however, the answer is more complicated. For it turns out that virtue is in some sense *made* good by being pleasant in this particular way.

In *EN* X 4, Aristotle talks about what makes an act of perceiving perfect, and he distinguishes between two things in this context: (a) perception is made perfect by the interaction between a well-functioning sense organ and an object that is most worthwhile for this sense (does he mean 'most worthwhile' in the sense of most suitable to it?); and (b) it is perfected by the pleasure the perceiving subject takes in perceiving in this manner (*EN* X 4, 1174b21–24). Further, he says that the difference between (a) and (b) concerning the way in which they relate to perfect perception is analogous to the difference between the way in which a doctor and health relate to being healthy, respectively (1174b24–26).[8]

What does he mean by this? Both the doctor and health explain the state of being healthy, but in different senses of 'explain'. The doctor explains

---

[7] See Frede (2006, 259–60).

[8] Harte (2014, 304) points out that all Aristotle might be saying here is that (a) and (b) contain different senses of 'perfecting', just as a doctor and health cause being healthy in different senses of 'causing'. I agree that the passage allows for this weaker reading. Still, I think the stronger reading is more plausible. After all, 'perfecting' or 'making perfect' is a way of *causing* perfect perception, so it doesn't seem random that Aristotle chooses this particular analogy. According to the weaker reading, it seems that he could have chosen any term that can be used in different senses as an example.

Aristotle on Friendship and Being Human

this state in the sense that they bring it about. Whereas health explains it in the sense that it is the good-making feature of this state (at least this seems to be a plausible reading): if someone were to ask us what is good about this state, we would point to health. Now, surely, the pleasure we get from perceiving the most worthwhile object with properly functioning senses is not what brings it about that we perceive perfectly, at least not in the same sense a doctor brings about health. It is more fitting to say that the interaction between the object and the organ brings it about. Pleasure does not play the part of the doctor, then – the interaction does. So, pleasure must play the part of health: pleasure makes perception perfect in the way health makes the state of being healthy good, namely in the sense of being the good-making feature of this state. If someone were to ask us what is so great about the kind of perception that comes about as a result of a well-functioning sense organ being directed at a suitable object, we should point to the pleasure it gives us.[9]

What Aristotle says about perfect perception can be extended to virtuous (i.e. perfect) thinking in general, as well as to virtuous (i.e. perfect) acting (*EN* X 4, 1174b20–22 and 33–35). The pleasure a virtuous person gets from virtuous activities is in fact the good-making feature of these activities.[10] If that is correct, then we shouldn't contrast the goodness of virtue with its pleasantness in the way we did when we were asking whether the former *or* the latter explains why virtuous persons act virtuously (in a contrastive sense of 'or'). It seems that the correct answer should be 'both', since they are not really separate.

This also fits with what Aristotle writes a few paragraphs later, where he himself wonders whether we choose (the virtuous) life because of the pleasure it brings or the other way around. His answer is that we don't need to ask this question, because 'they appear to be inseparably united' (X 5, 1175a18–21). So, in some sense, virtuous persons *do* choose and love virtue because it gives them pleasure.

---

[9] Aristotle's distinction between the different types of causes comes to mind here. The doctor plays the role of the efficient cause, but it is not clear whether health is supposed to be the formal or the final cause. Likewise, we might ask whether pleasure plays the role of the formal or the final cause. I will not go into this here, however. See Gosling and Taylor (1982, ch. 13) and Shields (2011) for more discussion.

[10] If this means that virtue is that which the virtuous take pleasure in, it might sound dangerously circular. But the claim is that virtue is made good by the pleasure the virtuous take in it; and if we disentangle 'virtuous' and 'good' so that they don't mean the same thing, the danger goes away. 'Being virtuous' refers to the state of actualising the human form, whereas 'being good (*simpliciter*)' arguably refers to something that is worthwhile attaining. Then the claim would be that virtue is worthwhile attaining on account of the pleasure the virtuous take in it. This is a difficult issue, however, and I can't go into it in detail here.

190   NORA KREFT

And this is also plausible given that Aristotle thinks of the life devoted to virtuous activity as *eudaimonia*. Aristotle characterises *eudaimonia* as a state in which we are not only not lacking anything important, but in which life is experienced as deeply worthwhile living (I 5, 1097b14–20). It is a pleasurable state, in other words. In fact, it seems to be the most pleasurable state possible. To identify the virtuous life with *eudaimonia* is to identify the virtuous life with this profound and highest pleasure. And so, asking whether we choose virtue because of pleasure or the other way around is just as futile as asking whether we choose virtue because of *eudaimonia* or the other way around. In both cases, the answer should be 'both', since they turn out to be the same thing.[11]

What is true of the lovers of virtue seems to be true of other lovers, too. Aristotle says that every activity comes along with its own distinctive pleasure, including bad activities (X 5, 1175b24–29). Or rather, as he qualifies a little later: bad activities can *feel* pleasurable for some people, and in distinctive ways, even though they are not in fact pleasurable, i.e. not pleasant *simpliciter*. What is pleasant *simpliciter* is what is pleasant for virtuous persons, because the virtuous experience the kind of pleasure that is specifically human and the phenomenal 'fabric' of human *eudaimonia*. Other kinds of pleasures only feel pleasurable in a certain context and for a particular person (1176a15–29).[12] In any case, it is plausible that lovers of non-virtuous activities nevertheless love them for the distinctive pleasures they get from them.

Back to the three types of friendship. I have argued that virtue friendship is explained by the pleasure the friends receive from perceiving each other's virtue as such. And I have defended the more general principle that the love for X is explained by the pleasure one takes in doing and perceiving X. If that is right, then utility- and pleasure friendship are also explained by pleasure, but pleasure in different things. In utility-friendship, the friends take pleasure not in each other, but in the respective ends they achieve with each other's help. They don't actually love each other, but these ends. By contrast, in pleasure friendship, the friends do take pleasure in each other, but in things other than each other's virtue as such – further qualities that are or are not related to each other's character. They do love each other in some sense, or rather: they love something

---

[11] See also Sauvé Meyer (2016, 58): 'This [the *ergon*-argument, *EN* I 7] is to identify happiness with virtuous activity, not to claim the latter is instrumental to the former ... Acting for the sake of the *kalon* counts as acting for the sake of happiness'.

[12] See Harte (2014, 313–14) for further discussion.

about each other. But they don't love each other as the persons they are. Pleasure friendship, therefore, comes closer to virtue friendship than utility friendship, as Aristotle also mentions several times (VIII 5, 1157a10–15, and VIII 7, 1158a17–20).

Why is pleasure friendship called 'pleasure friendship' then? Why single out pleasure in this case when it has the same explanatory force in all three? A possible answer would be that paradigmatic examples of pleasure friendship are about what people commonly (though often mistakenly) think of as pleasures: the pleasure one takes in good looks, say, or in certain entertaining qualities, or, more generally, the pleasures that Aristotle has in mind when he refers to the 'life of pleasure' in *EN* I 3, 1095b15–21. There, he rejects the 'life of pleasure' as a candidate for *eudaimonia*. Given what we heard about pleasure and the virtuous life, this can't be a rejection of pleasure as such, but only of certain kinds of pleasures – the kinds he thinks are sought by someone like Sardanapal of Ninive (who allegedly said that we should just eat, drink, and make love as much as possible, since nothing else is of any worth, see 1095b21).

4 Proper Friendship and Relationships between Non-Human Animals

If we understand virtue friendship as based on the pleasure the friends take in perceiving each other's virtue as such, we can explain the characteristics Aristotle ascribes to virtue friendship. First, since taking pleasure in virtue as such is a sign of being virtuous oneself, both friends must be virtuous here, so only the virtuous can be virtue friends.[13] By contrast, anyone can have utility- and pleasure friendships: bad people, the 'neither good nor bad', as well as couples of virtuous and bad, or virtuous and 'neither good nor bad' persons (*EN* VIII 5, 1157a16–20). Aristotle doesn't discuss whether two virtuous persons could also have a mere utility- or pleasure friendship, but I don't think they could: given that they will each find the respective other's virtue pleasing as such, they will 'fall into' virtue friendship as soon as they start spending some more time with each other (I come back to this in the last section).

---

[13] In the paradigmatic case of virtue friendship, the friends are equally virtuous. However, Aristotle does allow for virtue friendships between persons who are unequal in virtue: between children and parents, for instance. As long as they still take pleasure in each other's virtue as such, they still qualify as virtue friendship, even though the parents are more virtuous than the child (*EN* VIII 8, 1158b12–29).

Second, adding to this that virtue is lasting and not easily lost, virtue friendships are stable relationships (*EN* VIII 4, 1156b12–13). If they are not separated by external misfortunes, the friendship will last a lifetime. Utility- and pleasure friendships are more volatile (1156a21–b5), both because the useful or pleasurable properties at issue might be less stable than virtue (unless they are also related to virtue, of course), and because they might cease to be useful or pleasurable to the friend: ends and preferences can easily change throughout a person's life, if they are not the ends and preferences of a virtuous person *qua* being virtuous. It is somewhat accidental if a utility- or a pleasure friendship lasts a long time, then.

Third, virtue friendship is a lot more intimate: since virtue friends take pleasure in perceiving each other's virtue as such, and since being virtuous means actualising the human form, i.e. actualising *nous*, virtue friends take pleasure in perceiving the way one another thinks, reasons, feels, and acts. They get to know each other very well, as the persons they are, and they develop together as persons too. This is also what living together means for virtue friends (remember that living together is what all friends typically do): virtue friends think, reason, feel, and act together (IX 9, 1170b11–14). Another way of describing this would be to say that they are actualising *nous* together. Their form of togetherness is an essentially human kind of togetherness then. We might say that they enjoy being human together.

It is not surprising that Aristotle thinks of utility- and pleasure friendship as imperfect compared to virtue friendship (VIII 4, 1156b6). A little later, he goes even further and denies that they are proper friendships at all, reserving that spot for virtue friendship alone.[14] In other words, utility- and pleasure friendship are not only less good than virtue friendship, they are not actually real friendships. We call them 'friendships' because they have a few things in common with virtue friendship, such as wishing the friend well because they are good for us in some way and sharing at least some parts of one's life with them (VIII 8, 1158b1–11). So, it is not accidental that they have the same name. But, in the end, the differences between them mean they are an altogether distinct sort of relationship. (It is strange to say that something is both an imperfect P and not a real P – it seems that, if something isn't a real P, then the standards of perfection that are relevant to P do not apply to it. But perhaps we can say this: utility- and pleasure friendship are not real friendship, and they are also less valuable types of relationship than friendship. So, they are not imperfect *as* friendships, but imperfect in the looser sense of 'less good' than real friendship.)

---

[14] *EN* VIII 5, 1157a25–32; 6, 1157b3–4, and 8, 1158b1–11.

Aristotle on Friendship and Being Human 193

It is not easy to see what criteria are in play to determine whether something is a distinct subgroup of a type, or a different type altogether, and Aristotle doesn't make these criteria explicit here. But, if virtue friendship is an essentially human kind of relationship in the above sense, whereas utility- and pleasure friendship are not, then perhaps this explains why the differences between them are greater than differences between various subtypes of friendship would be. As we have seen, virtue friends love each other as the persons they are, whereas utility- and pleasure friends only love certain, often accidental features of each other. So, there is a sense in which utility- and pleasure friends are not really friends with *each other.*

Let us now turn to the relationships between non-human animals: can they have friendship or not, according to Aristotle? We should divide this into two questions: can they have proper, i.e. virtue friendship? And can they have utility- and pleasure friendship? We might think that they can't have virtue friendship, simply because they can't do the things virtue friends typically do together, namely actualising *nous* together. This would be too quick, however. Of course, they can't do these things because they don't have *nous* – that is why they are non-human rather than human animals; but that doesn't mean that they couldn't share the kinds of activities that make them the sort of animals they are. Birds could sing together, for example, and horses could run through the fields together, and generally every species could share the sorts of things that would be their equivalent of actualising *nous*. And if they did this together, why wouldn't this be their equivalent of virtue friendship?

I think the reason they indeed cannot have virtue friendships is that they cannot value each other for their own sakes in the above sense, i.e. they cannot enjoy their non-human equivalent of goodness *as* goodness. And this is simply because non-human animals, according to Aristotle, cannot perceive things *as* good. In several passages, and explicitly in *Pol.* I 2, 1253a16, Aristotle says that a 'sense of good and evil, just and unjust, and the like' is something only humans have. There is a reason for that: perceiving things as good means perceiving them as actualising their form, but, in order to perceive them as such, one needs to have an understanding of this form. Understanding forms is the ability that sets human cognition apart from non-human cognition: in *DA*, Aristotle says that what it means to have *nous* is to be able to understand what things really are, i.e. their forms (*DA* III 4, 429a10–18). So, without *nous*, one cannot perceive things as being of a certain form, and, consequently, one cannot perceive them *as* good.

The pleasure in seeing something as good is a peculiarly human pleasure then. I have argued that this is the mark of virtue friendship, and what explains why Aristotle thinks of it as proper friendship, in contrast to utility- and pleasure friendship. So, if I am correct, then non-human animals can't have (an equivalent of) virtue friendship because they can't take pleasure in each other's goodness as such. Virtue friendship is not only an essentially human relationship in the sense that it consists in the most human form of togetherness, but also in the sense that it is peculiarly human. In fact, since god doesn't have friends, according to Aristotle, it is indeed a uniquely human form of relationship (*EE* VII, 1245b17). I briefly come back to this in the last section.

It seems that being able to perceive something as good is not required for utility- and pleasure friendship, however. One could react to or even perceive something as being useful and experience its effects as pleasurable without perceiving it as good in Aristotle's sense of the term – even if it is in fact good and this goodness is the source of the utility or the pleasure. So, nothing seems to rule out that non-human animals can have utility- or pleasure friendship.[15] When Aristotle writes that animals can be friends with their young as well as with other members of their species, I suggest we read him as saying that they can have utility- and pleasure friendships with each other.[16] They can wish each other well and care for each other, share parts of their lives together, but they can't value each other for their own sakes.

5 Why We Need Friendship to Actualise *Nous*

From the fact that virtue friendship is an essentially human kind of relationship it doesn't yet follow that it is also an essential relationship for human beings, i.e. it doesn't follow that humans need to have this sort of relationship in order to be fully human and to actualise *nous*. However, as I have mentioned, Aristotle also holds this further claim.

---

[15] Defenders of the so-called transformation thesis who hold that the presence of *nous* substantially changes the nature of other human capacities such as perception might want to extend their claim to the capacity to have friendship, even in the case of utility- and pleasure friendship. They might argue that just as *nous* transforms human perception, it turns utility- and pleasure friendships between humans into something substantially different from the utility- and pleasure friendships between other animals. I stay neutral on this issue here. All I want to argue is that non-human animals cannot have virtue friendship (or a genuine equivalent thereof). For discussions (or applications) of the transformation thesis, see Geert Keil's *Introduction* (Section 3) as well as Cagnoli Fiecconi (Chapter 3) and Glock (Chapter 7).

[16] Compare also to *EE* VII, 1236a5–8: 'This friendship [virtue friendship], therefore, only occurs in man, for he alone perceives purpose (*prohairesis*); but the other forms occur also in the lower animals. Indeed, mutual utility manifestly exists to some small extent between the domestic animals and man, and between animals themselves, for instance Herodotus's account of the friendship between the crocodile and the sandpiper . . .'.

Aristotle on Friendship and Being Human

In *EN* XI 9, 1169b2–10, he says it would be strange to think of a person without friends as *eudaimōn*: intuitively, even if they have all the other goods, they wouldn't be *eudaimōn* if they didn't also have friends.[17] The reason cannot be that friendship is instrumental in attaining any of these other goods, since by stipulation the person in question already has all the goods friendship could possibly be a means to. If they are still missing something when they have all the other 'ingredients' of *eudaimonia*, it seems that friendship is a constitutive part of being *eudaimōn*, not just a means to it. For the same reason, Aristotle cannot be talking about utility- or pleasure friendship here. The only potential candidate for being a part of *eudaimonia* is virtue friendship (henceforth just 'friendship').

Now, given that *eudaimonia* is the fully human life – the life in which we actualise what is specifically human – it would seem that, if friendship is a part of *eudaimonia*, it is also a part of the state humans are in when they are actualising *nous*.[18] In other words: Aristotle doesn't only think that friendship is essentially and peculiarly human, but also essential in order to actualise *nous*.

Why does friendship play this central role for human beings? Why couldn't we actualise *nous* without having friends? Doesn't Aristotle hold that the contemplative life (the best possible human life) is also the most self-sufficient life? (*EN* X 7, 1177a27–35) If it is true, however, that humans need friends in order to be *eudaimōn* and to actualise *nous*, then even the self-sufficient contemplators would need friends. And we can read him as saying as much: even for them, he writes, it is better to contemplate together with others than alone (1177a34). Since the *eudaimōn* always need what is best (IX 9, 1170b17–19), this means that they need others for joint contemplation. By 'others' here, Aristotle must mean other similarly devoted and virtuous contemplators. Given that two virtuous persons who spend some time doing the things they love together will become friends,[19]

---

[17] Kosman (2004) argues that Aristotle doesn't mean to say that we need friends in order to be *eudaimōn* here, but wants to explain why the *eudaimōn* would find friends desirable. However, given that whatever the *eudaimōn* find desirable is also what they need (see *EN* IX 9, 1170b17–19 for instance), and 'what they need' is short for what they need in order to be *eudaimōn*, it seems that the second reading collapses into the first.

[18] *Eudaimonia* consists in virtuous activity and is the actualised human life, but Aristotle also points out that we need certain external goods to be *eudaimōn* (health, a certain amount of money, etc., see *EN* I 9, 1099a31ff). However, they are external goods for a reason: we should think of them as enabling conditions, rather than as constituents of *eudaimonia*.

[19] See the beginning of Section 4 above (and remember that when I say 'friends' here I always mean 'virtue friends' from now on).

saying that contemplators need other contemplators for joint contemplation effectively means that they need friends. But why?

Note that, by giving an account of why friends are good for each other – namely, because they take pleasure in each other's virtue as such – we haven't already answered this question. For things can be good for us even if they are not constitutive parts of *eudaimonia*. True, as we heard, taking pleasure in virtue is a central part of being virtuous and, thus, of being *eudaimōn* and of actualising *nous*. But it might be enough to take pleasure in one's own virtue. The pleasure of perceiving the virtue of others could just be an ultimately superfluous bonus. So, in order to show that friendship is a constitutive part of *eudaimonia*, Aristotle still has to explain why we need this specific pleasure of perceiving *other* people's virtue to actualise *nous*.

There has been quite a lot of discussion about the series of arguments he presents to show this in *EN* IX 9.[20] It is not easy to make sense of them, for several reasons. First of all, it is not clear how they relate to each other: are they separate arguments, or part of one (or more) 'overarching' argument(s)? Second, on the face of it, none of them is fully convincing (at least not on their own). There is the argument that we need friends in order to act well. In short, the idea is that virtuous people act well in the sense of doing good deeds; they need recipients for this; and it is better if these recipients are friends instead of strangers; so, since virtuous people always need what is best, as we have seen above, they need friends (IX 9, 1169b10–13). But, even if we accept all the (occasionally questionable) premises of this argument, it doesn't really explain why we need friendship even in the contemplative life, where virtuous action in the sense of actively benefitting others isn't central. If the contemplator's life consists mainly of thinking, and thought doesn't have (or, at least, doesn't need) recipients in the way virtuous actions do, then these considerations do not cover the contemplator.

The second argument looks more promising. In short, it says that virtuous persons need to perceive and contemplate virtue; we can either perceive and contemplate our own or a friend's virtue, but it is easier to perceive and contemplate a friend's virtue; hence, virtuous persons need friends (1169b30–1170a4).[21] The problem is that we don't really get an explanation for why it is easier to perceive and contemplate our friend's virtue. Besides, the fact that it is more difficult doesn't yet show that

---

[20] See Cooper (1977), Smith Pangle (2003), Kosman (2004), Liu (2010), Hitz (2011), et al.

[21] There are various ways of spelling out this argument. I am just presenting a short version here. See Liu (2010) for more discussion.

Aristotle on Friendship and Being Human

perceiving and contemplating our own virtue is impossible. In fact, a few paragraphs later, Aristotle asserts quite explicitly that it *is* possible when he describes the pleasure of perceiving oneself perceiving and contemplating well. This implies that human beings are able to perceive their own virtuous activity, at least insofar as it takes place in the mind: we perceive our own perceiving and thinking (1170a25–34). The second argument isn't immediately convincing either, then.[22]

Finally, the longest, so-called argument from nature at the end of IX 9 seems to suffer from a problem first pointed out by Cooper: the main idea is that just as we take pleasure in perceiving ourselves perceiving and contemplating virtue, we take pleasure in perceiving our friend perceiving and contemplating virtue, because just as we like to know that we are doing well ourselves, we like to know that our friend is doing well, and perceiving and contemplating virtue is a sign of faring well and of being (at least close to) *eudaimōn* (1170a12–b19).[23] Put this way, Cooper is right when he complains that this doesn't show why we need friends to be *eudaimōn* – but only why, once we have friends, we want them to fare well and enjoy perceiving their *eudaimonia*.[24]

However, I suggest that we read this last argument a little differently, and take into account the very end of the passage. The argument culminates in the observation that, since friends take pleasure in perceiving each other's virtue and *eudaimonia*, they will live together and share the activities that constitute the actualisation of *nous*:

> And this [perceiving the respective other's goodness] is attained by their living together and by conversing and communicating their thoughts to each other; for this is the meaning of living together as applied to human beings, it does not mean merely feeding in the same place, as it does when applied to cattle. (1170a12–b19)

---

[22] Liu (2010) argues that, in perceiving the friend, we are also perceiving them perceiving us. In particular, we perceive that they perceive us as good, and this is both an important piece of information and pleasurable for us: it further confirms to us that we are virtuous ourselves, and it allows us to enjoy our own virtue more. I find this convincing. But again, I am not sure if it really shows that virtuous persons *need* friends and that it is impossible to perceive one's own virtue without the friend's confirmation. As mentioned, it seems that Aristotle says that it *is* possible to perceive one's own virtue when one perceives oneself perceiving and thinking (*EN* IX 9, 1170a25–34).

[23] Strictly speaking, Aristotle doesn't say that we need to perceive and contemplate virtue in particular here. He doesn't specify the object. However, since he is talking about the *eudaimōn* here, it seems legitimate to assume that we are talking about virtuous perception and contemplation – and that is perception and contemplation of virtue (or, more generally, of forms, i.e. the actuality of things which is also the state in which they are good).

[24] See Cooper (1977, 292). See also Hitz (2011) for a more extensive discussion of this argument.

This is often taken to be an afterthought, but if we read it as the actual conclusion of the argument, we might be able to escape Cooper's critique. The point of the passage would then be that, *because* friends are such that they find perceiving and contemplating each other's virtue in itself pleasurable, they share their life in the encompassing sense mentioned before. And this is why human beings need friends: because with them, and only with them, can they share the activities that constitute the actualisation of *nous*. In short: only with friends can they share *nous*. If this is the argument, then what Aristotle is telling us is that human beings need friends because they need to share *nous* in order to actualise *nous*.

Before we can think about this any further, I need to defend the claim that friends are the only ones with whom we can share *nous*. Why couldn't we share *nous* with people who are not our friends? Here is the argument: (i) people who are not virtuous can't share *nous* with others, both because they are not interested and because they don't go about it in the right way (they don't direct their attitudes according to reasons in the right way – this is what explains why they are not virtuous); (ii) people who are (sufficiently) virtuous can share *nous* with others; so (iii) only (sufficiently) virtuous people can share *nous* with others. Further, (iv) sharing *nous* takes some time, because it involves getting to know and understanding one another's attitudes as well as actively exchanging reasons; (v) (sufficiently) virtuous people who spend this amount of time together will form a friendship (as I suggested in the beginning of Section 4); so, (vi) if people share *nous*, they will form a friendship. In other words, friends don't only share *nous*, but people who share *nous* are also friends.

But, even if what I proposed is the correct reading of Aristotle's last argument, and even if we need friends in order to share *nous* – *why* is this the reason we need friends? *Why* does Aristotle think we need to share *nous* in order to actualise *nous*? I am going to leave this question open here, and end with two further observations. First, the claim that humans need to share *nous* in order to actualise *nous* and to be fully human is further supported in *Pol.* I 2, when Aristotle writes that nature 'makes nothing in vain', so humans haven't been given speech in vain either. They have been given speech to communicate about 'the expedient and inexpedient' and 'likewise the just and the unjust' (*Pol.* I 2, 1253a8–18), and if they don't ever communicate about these things – if they don't share *nous*, in other words – they either turn into a god or a strange creature, not really recognisably human (1253a1–6).

Second, according to Aristotle, the other bearer of *nous* – god – doesn't need any friends.[25] Is this a problem for my proposal? No, because the claim is not that friends are needed in order to actualise *nous* at all, but only that they are needed for humans to actualise *nous*. And Aristotle seems to think that the way humans actualise *nous* is different from god's in various ways anyway (they need imagination, for example, and their thinking is directed at things other than themselves).[26] The need for friends is just one more difference among many.

6 Conclusion

I have argued that virtue friendship – that is, *proper* friendship – is uniquely human because non-human animals cannot take pleasure in each other's virtue as such. Taking pleasure in the friend's virtue as such sets virtue friendship apart from utility- and pleasure friendship: it explains in what sense virtue friends value each other for their own sakes, instead of (merely) instrumentally. This is not in tension with Aristotle's claim that friendship exists because (and only because) the friends perceive each other to be good for each other. Nor does it subsume virtue friendship under pleasure friendship.

Further, I argued that the ability to have virtue friendship is not only unique to humans, but that having virtue friends is also essential for being fully human, according to Aristotle. He thinks that being fully human means actualising *nous*, and that, in order for humans to actualise *nous*, they must share it with others. Since virtue friends and only virtue friends can share *nous*, humans need virtue friends to be fully human.[27]

---

[25] See, for example, *EE* VII, 1245b17: 'God is not of such a nature as to need a friend'.

[26] For the need for imagination, see *DA* III 3; see also Cagnoli Fiecconi (Chapter 3). For the need to contemplate things besides ourselves, see *EE* VII, 1245b15–20.

[27] I would like to thank Jonathan Beere, Joseph Bjelde, Geert Keil, Christian Kietzmann, and Andrew Stephenson for their helpful comments on earlier drafts. I am also grateful to the audience of the Ancient Philosophy Section at the DGPhil Congress in 2017 and the members of Geert Keil's research colloquium for their thought-provoking questions.

CHAPTER 10

Aristotle on the Possibility of Moral Perfection
Christoph Horn

An important question regarding Aristotle's moral anthropology is whether or not human beings can become perfectly good. Should we consider Aristotle's paradigmatically virtuous agent (who appears under the different names of *spoudaios*, *phronimos*, *agathos*, *epainetos*, *epieikēs*, or *kalos kagathos*) as an ideal figure, i.e. as someone who permanently and infallibly executes morally correct actions? Is his character irreversibly transformed into a state of perfection? Might we describe his inner condition as that of perfect psychic harmony? Or is it true, as some interpreters claimed, notably Shane Drefcinski and Howard Curzer,[1] that the virtuous man (Aristotle never mentions female candidates) can act badly? Does he perform, at least to some extent or from time to time, slightly suboptimal actions, or perhaps even more: evil deeds? If Aristotle's moral anthropology allowed for some imperfection or even considered imperfection as an unavoidable part of the human condition, it would be close to the view of the *philosophos* held by Plato. If, on the other hand, Aristotle defended an ideal of absolute perfection, he would be somewhere contiguous to the Stoic concept of the sage (*sophos*).

On my reading, the Aristotelian texts ultimately point to the Stoic direction, not the Platonic one. This is certainly a surprising result and hard to accept for those scholars who, like Martha Nussbaum in her important work *The Fragility of Goodness*[2] – consider Aristotle as a 'tragic' moral philosopher, i.e. as rejecting the idea of personal detachedness or immunity. But I think we should be cautious in ascribing to him such views as the tragic shortness and fragility of human life or a less ambitious concept of practical rationality. As we will see at the end of this paper, Aristotle immediately connects his moral anthropology with his metaphysical idea of perfection.

---

[1] Drefcinski (1996); Curzer (2005).   [2] Nussbaum (2001).

Concerning moral anthropology in antiquity, the paradigmatically virtuous agent (who appears under different names in all of the schools) is a highly significant topic. On a careful reading of the relevant passages in Aristotle's ethical writings we will see that he develops a strong idea of the moral excellence of his paradigmatic agent. One should, however, keep in mind that Aristotle's use of the various expressions *spoudaios, phronimos, agathos, epainetos, epieikēs*, or *kalos kagathos* is not an unambiguous, let alone a terminological one.[3] It will be an important outcome of my reading that Aristotle allows for *different degrees* of eminently possessing the virtues. He sometimes admits a sort of usage of these expressions for people who are good in a quite conventional sense. Nevertheless, we can identify an Aristotelian idea of absolute personal goodness which is absent in Plato.

1 The Virtuous Person According to the 'Idealisation Reading'

As we learn from Plato's remarks on moral anthropology, absolute perfection is impossible in this world – at least in a pure and invariant form: according to Plato, human beings are weak, corrupt, and susceptible, even the best among them (see e.g. *Laws* IX 875a-c). This might seem astonishing for a philosopher who bases his concept of infallible rational insight on a theory of intelligible forms and who develops a political idea of expertocratic philosopher-kings on this fundament. But, for Plato, even philosophers who received an optimal moral and intellectual education according to the curriculum of the *kallipolis* have a permanent tendency of falling back into suboptimal cognitive and ethical conditions, e.g. by miscalculating the 'marriage number' for the next generation (*Rep.* VIII 546b) or by losing their good character under the misleading influence of poetry (X 605c-607a). The sensible, alterable world is too unstable to allow for intellectual permanence. An important part of this Platonic claim, which reminded twentieth century readers strongly of Freud's theory of 'subconscious' desires, is his account of 'repressed' wishes which emerge in nightly dreams (IX 571c).[4] As Plato seems to think, human beings living under earthly conditions can never fully pacify their souls; they fail to

---

[3] Important questions are: Why does Aristotle use so many different expressions? Are they equivalents? Do they differ only regarding the context of usage, or is there also a deeper semantic difference? An explicit identification of the expressions *epieikēs* and *phronimos* is given at *EN* VI 11, 1143a25–35. In several texts, we find the words *epieikēs* and *spoudaios* used more or less interchangeably: e.g. *EN* IX 4, 1166a10–23 and X 5, 1175b24–28. In what follows, I take them as rough equivalents. On this point, see Hoffmann (2010, 165–72).
[4] In Werner Jaeger's *Paideia* (1947, 74) we even find the remark that Plato is 'the father of psychoanalysis'.

transform them into invariably rational entities. Even in the higher world, the soul can turn in a bad direction by 'losing its wings', as Plato famously says in the *Phaedrus* (246c–d).

But what about Aristotle? Since most interpreters think that he has a somewhat less demanding idea of reason and of rational life than Plato, they believe analogously that his concept of a paradigmatically virtuous individual should be weaker. Aristotle, however, describes, in several passages of the *Nicomachean Ethics* and the *Eudemian Ethics*, a fully virtuous person – perfect without any restriction. To be sure, what he presents to us is not an ideal of omniscience, infallibility, and political expertocracy. But it is a view that apparently amounts to an ideal of unrestricted moral perfection.

A first, an albeit rough list of features to be attributed to this figure in Aristotle should contain the following points:

(1)   The *spoudaios, phronimos,* etc. is a man who is characterised as permanently doing what is noble and morally required and who never voluntarily acts in a wrong way (*EN* IV 15(9), 1128b22–32, *EE* II 11, 1228a5–7). He acts for the sake of the moral good (*EN* IX 8, 1168a33–35).

(2)   By always performing correctly, he is the personal criterion or standard of appropriate action (*EN* II 6, 1106b36–1107a2; *kanōn kai metron*: III 6(4), 1113a33).

(3)   He continuously has the appropriate sort of emotions and, therefore, permanently acts on the basis of an adequate motivation: he feels pleasure when acting nobly (*EN* III 6, 1113a31–34 and X 5, 1176a15–18).

(4)   The virtuous man has practical reason by which he always possesses full truth and is never deceived (*EN* VI 6(4), 1141a3–4).

(5)   He can always make the best out of a given non-ideal situation (I 11, 1101a2–3).

(6)   His habit of being virtuous is considered as irreversible; once having arrived at the excellent level, he cannot lose it again.

(7)   Furthermore, Aristotle tells us that, since the *epieikēs* is uninterruptedly capable of acting correctly, he has no reason to be ashamed of his conduct (IV 9(15), 1128b21).

(8)   Aristotle additionally describes the *epieikēs* as entirely committed to the truth (IV 7(13), 1127b3).

(9)   He feels self-love in its highest and most appropriate form, i.e. as love for his own intellect (IX 8, 1169a16).

Aristotle on the Possibility of Moral Perfection   203

(10) The virtuous person is in harmony with himself (*houtos gar homo-gnōmonei heautōi*; IX 4, 1166a13) while his counterpart, the *kakos*, suffers from inner conflict and disruption; IX 4, 1166b19–22).[5]

(11) The life of the virtuous is more pleasurable than that of other people (VII 14(13), 1154a5–7).

(12) The *epieikēs* is friendly, lenient, and benevolent towards all people with whom he interacts, including those unknown to him. He tends to take less of a good that is in high demand than he is entitled to, especially if this relinquishment leads him to the possession of a higher-order good.

From this impressive material, we can draw the conclusion that Aristotle wishes to describe an *unambiguously ideal person*. Let us call this interpretation, following Howard Curzer, the 'idealisation reading' of the Aristotelian *spoudaios*, *phronimos*, etc.[6] A probative passage that can be adduced in favour of the idealisation reading is *EN* III 6(4), 1113a22–33, where Aristotle describes the *spoudaios* as a person having the right sort of wish or will (*boulēsis*), namely the desire for the good 'in the true and unqualified sense' (*haplōs men kai kat'alētheian boulēton einai tagathon*):

> ... perhaps we should say that what is wished for in the true and unqualified sense is the good, but that what appears good to each person is wished for by him; and accordingly that the good man wishes for what is truly wished for, the bad man for anything as it may happen (just as in the case of our bodies, a man of sound constitution finds really healthy food best for his health, but some other diet may be healthy for one who is delicate; and so with things bitter and sweet, hot, heavy, etc.). (III 6(4), 1113a22–29, transl. Rackham)

The relativistic principle according to which each person has his or her own good to strive for doesn't hold for the virtuous figure. As Aristotle emphatically claims, the *spoudaios* is the person who identifies the good appropriately, whereas the bad person (the *phaulos*) goes for seeming goods which are deviations from the true value. Aristotle then describes the good man as a perfect standard and as a normative ideal:

> For the good man judges everything correctly; what things truly are, that they seem to him to be, in every department for the noble and the pleasant have a special form corresponding to each of the faculties of our nature, and perhaps what chiefly distinguishes the good man is that he sees the truth in

---

[5] The inner disruption of the bad individual is, e.g. the topic of *EN* IX 4, 1166b19–22. As the text makes plausible, the opposite figure, the virtuous individual, must be completely free of this sort of tension.

[6] Curzer (2005).

each kind, being himself as it were the standard and measure of the noble and pleasant. (1113a29–33)

If we simply accept what the quoted passage says, the *spoudaios* is someone 'who judges correctly on everything' and to whom 'everything appears as it is (in its truth)' (*ho spoudaios gar hekasta krinei orthōs, kai en hekastois talēthes autōi phainetai*). Aristotle's claim is that we should not ascribe to the *spoudaios* any deviation from a fully adequate desire. It is he who grasps the true good, and, hence, whatever he goes for is truly good. This is why the *spoudaios* 'is, as it were, the criterion and standard of these (i.e. good) things' (*hōsper kanōn kai metron autōn ōn*).

We find another relevant passage in *Eudemian Ethics* VIII 3, 1248b40–1249a18. Here too the paradigmatically virtuous individual is the personal standard of right axiology. What is especially interesting about this text is its differentiation between 'natural goodness' (*ta physei agatha*) and 'nobility of character' (*kalokagathia*). This distinction is made in the first part of the text:

> There are those who think that one ought, it is true, to possess goodness, but for the sake of the things that are naturally good; hence though they are good men (for the things naturally good are good for them), yet they have not nobility of character (*kalokagathian de ouk echousin*), for it is not the case with them that they possess fine things for their own sake and that they purpose fine actions, and not only this, but also that things not fine by nature but good by nature are fine for them. For things are fine when that for which men do them and choose them is fine. (*EE* VIII 3, 1248b40–1249a8; transl. Rackham)

Following the text, it would be a mistake to exploit virtue (*aretē*) as a means for the end of natural goods. The possession of *kalokagathia* is precisely what prevents someone from committing this mistake. Aristotle then proceeds by describing the *kalos kagathos* as the personal standard of what is valuable:

> Therefore to the noble man the things good by nature are fine; for what is just is fine, and what is according to worth is just, and he is worthy of these things; and what is befitting is fine, and these things befit him – wealth, birth, power. Hence for the noble man the same things are both advantageous and fine; but for the multitude these things do not coincide, for things absolutely good are not also good for them, whereas they are good for the good man; and to the noble man they are also fine, for he performs many fine actions because of them. But he who thinks that one ought to possess the virtues for the sake of external goods does fine things only by accident. Nobility of character then is perfect goodness. (*ibid.*, 1249a8–18)

Aristotle on the Possibility of Moral Perfection   205

The *kalos kagathos* does not consider the 'natural goods', such as wealth, birth, or power, as ultimate ends, and exactly thereby they become real, if only instrumental goods to him (*dioti tōi kalōi kagathōi kala esti ta physei agatha*).[7] While the merely good individual uses the virtues to gain these natural goods, the *kalos kagathos* uses these goods for noble or fine purposes which he considers as ends-in-themselves. For this reason, Aristotle tells us, nobility of character should be seen as perfect virtue (*estin oun kalokagathia aretē teleios*) (*EE* VIII 3, 1249a18).

The view that the good individual is to be regarded as the personal standard of right axiological judgement is confirmed by the famous passage where Aristotle defines ethical virtue as a mean and brings in the *phronimos* as the normative figure (*EN* II 6). As he says, virtue is 'a mean relative to us, this being determined by a rational principle, and by that principle by which the man of practical wisdom would determine it' (*en mesotēti ousa tēi pros hēmas ōrismenēi logōi kai hōi an ho phronimos horiseien*) (1106b36–1107a2). A clear implication of these lines is that the determination of the right mean by the *phronimos* is a full equivalent of its determination by the *logos*, i.e. by right reason. The *phronimos* is a personified version of practical reason.

The idea of practical infallibility is further formulated by Aristotle with regard to the intellectual virtue of wisdom (*sophia*). In *EN* VI 6, we find the claim that true and infallible knowledge cannot be gained only about invariable objects, but also about the changing world:

> If then the qualities whereby we attain truth, and are never led into falsehood, whether about things invariable or things variable, are scientific knowledge, prudence, wisdom, and intelligence, and if the quality which enables us to apprehend first principles cannot be any one among three of these, namely scientific knowledge, prudence, and wisdom, it remains that first principles must be apprehended by intelligence. (*EN* VI 6, 1141a2–7)

This point sounds very un-Platonic: Aristotle apparently accepts the idea that we can gain infallible knowledge of things which are unstable (*ei dē hois ... alētheuomen kai mēdepote diapseudometha peri ta mē endechomena ē kai endechomena allōs echein*) (1141a2–4). I take that point to be the basic difference in moral epistemology between Aristotle and Plato. It allows him to claim the stability of moral insight.

Another conclusive piece of evidence to be found in the *EN* concerns the question of moral emotions. In *EN* IV 15(9), 1128b21–29 we learn

---

[7] The axiology of the *Eudemian Ethics* is extensively discussed in Buddensiek (1999).

206 CHRISTOPH HORN

that the virtuous man never feels shame, since he never has any reason to be ashamed:

> For indeed the virtuous man does not feel shame (*oude gar epieikous estin hē aischynē*), if shame is the feeling caused by base actions; since one ought not to do base actions (the distinction between acts really shameful and those reputed to be so is immaterial, since one ought not to do either), and so one never ought to feel shame. Shame is a mark of a base man, and springs from a character capable of doing a shameful act. And it is absurd that, because a man is of such a nature that he is ashamed if he does a shameful act, he should therefore think himself virtuous, since actions to cause shame must be voluntary, but a virtuous man will never voluntarily do a base action (*hekōn d'ho epieikēs oudepote praxei ta phaula*).

The good individual will *never (oudepote)* act shamefully. This strict exclusion of even the possibility of wrongdoing by the virtuous person is corroborated in subsequent lines by the counter-factual thought experiment that the *epieikēs* might (*per impossibile*) feel ashamed:

> A sense of shame will indeed be hypothetically something decent – *if* one did such-and-such, one would be ashamed; but this is not a feature of the excellences (*ouk esti de touto peri tas aretas*). If shamelessness is something bad, and so is not being ashamed at doing shameful things, that doesn't make it decent to do such things and be ashamed. Self-control is not an excellence either, but a sort of excellence that's mixed with something else (*ouk esti d'oud' hē egkrateia aretē, alla tis miktē*). (1128b29–34, transl. Broadie/Rowe)

As far as I can see, the quotation permits no other reading than that according to the idealisation interpretation. The virtue of the most excellent person must be seen as stable. In the *EN*, Aristotle also claims that the stability (*bebaiotēs*) of moral virtue is invariable. The presence in its bearer even exceeds the permanence of knowledge:

> For no function of man has so much permanence as virtuous activities (*peri ouden gar houtōs huparchei tōn anthrōpinōn ergōn bebaiotēs hōs peri tas energeias tas kat'aretēn*) (these are thought to be more durable even than knowledge of the sciences), and of these themselves the most valuable are more durable because those who are happy spend their life most readily and most continuously in these; for this seems to be the reason why we do not forget them. The attribute in question, then, will belong to the happy man, and he will be happy throughout his life; for always, or by preference to everything else, he will be engaged in virtuous action and contemplation, and he will bear the chances of life most nobly and altogether decorously, if he is 'truly good' and 'foursquare beyond reproach'. (I.11(10), 1100b12–22, transl. Rackham)

Aristotle on the Possibility of Moral Perfection 207

The passage again provides a clear basis for the idealisation reading: Among the human functions (*tōn anthrōpinōn ergōn*), the virtuous activity is the most stable; it is even more permanent than knowledge, since it is not threatened by forgetfulness. Hence, virtue and happiness will be with the ideal person under consideration 'throughout his life' (*estai dia biou toioutos*).

There is, however, one element in the last quotation that might seem to endanger my reading: I mean the words *aei gar ē malista pantōn praxei kai theōrēsei ta kat' aretēn* (1100b19–20). In the Revised Oxford Translation, quoted above, these words are rendered as 'for always, or by preference to everything else, he will be engaged in virtuous action and contemplation'. Broadie and Rowe translate the phrase as 'for he will always, or most of all people, do and reflect what is in accordance with excellence'. Regardless of whether the text implies a temporal or personal meaning, it suggests a certain relativisation of the Aristotelian ideal. Similarly, in *EE* VIII 3, 1248b11–16, we are told that the possession of *kalokagathia* presupposes the possession of particular virtues in the same way as having a healthy body implies that all parts – or most of them or the most important ones – are healthy:

> Now it is manifest that one who is to obtain this appellation truly must possess the particular virtues; for it is impossible for it to be otherwise in the case of any other matter either – for instance, no one is healthy in his whole body but not in any part of it, but all the parts, or most of them and the most important, must necessarily be in the same condition as the whole (*outheis gar holon men to sōma hugiainei, meros d'outhen, all' anagkaion panta ē ta pleista kai kuriōtata ton auton echein tropon tōi holōi*).

We should, hence, wonder whether this phrase might imply the possibility of a deviation from moral perfection, even if only a slight one. Does Aristotle allow for exceptions from the ideal of absolute perfection? Is he perhaps ultimately on Plato's side regarding the thesis that perfection is impossible in this world?

2 Objections to the 'Idealisation Interpretation'

A number of scholars still prefer a realistic rather than an idealised interpretation of the paradigmatically virtuous person. One might highlight the following three pieces of *prima facie* evidence in favour of such a relativisation: (i) Aristotle thinks that practical philosophy does not allow for strict generality; generalisations are valid only 'for most of the cases' (*ōs epi to polu*)[8]. Hence it seems impossible that the *spoudaios* possesses a sort of practical knowledge which always provides a virtuous person with insight into the best possible way of acting. (ii) Aristotle claims that happiness depends, at least to some extent, on external factors. It seems, therefore, excluded that someone can reach an invariant state of virtue and happiness. (iii) For Aristotle, the most perfect human *ergon*, namely theoretical activity according to virtue, is possible only in certain moments of a human life: rational contemplation can be realised only under favourable conditions, such as being a cognitively outstanding, free, male, well-situated, and well-educated individual having sufficient leisure (*EN* X 8, 1178b7–32). Given that happiness is mainly the result of virtuous activity under these precarious circumstances, it seems unlikely that one can have it uninterruptedly.

I find none of these objections convincing. (i) The lack of generality, as Aristotle puts it, is precisely filled by the idea that there is a person who can supplement the gap whenever this is necessary: the *epieikēs*. In *EN* V 10 (14), the competence signified as 'the equitable' (*to epieikes*) is described as the capacity which enables its bearer to improve written law if it is in need of correction or to complete written law if it is incomplete. Thus, the virtuous is not seen as defective, but rather as the compensation of defects.[9] (ii) In *EN* I 8–10, the discussion on the contributive relevance of external goods shows that their deficiency cannot ultimately destroy the happiness of the virtuous individual, e.g. that of Priam; all their lack can do is to reduce the happiness of someone from being *makarios* to being *eudaimōn*.[10] (iii) In *Metaphysics* Lambda 7, 1072b14–15, we learn that, while the life of the God is always the best, we can have it only for a little while. But this is not meant as an equivalent of Plato's view that the sensible world can never be fully accorded to reason. Aristotle's view seems to be that, even if human life is suboptimal compared to that of God, and even if it is mixed of dianoetic and ethical virtuous activities, it can be perfect according to human standards.

But could it not be that Aristotle's paradigmatically virtuous figure as we know it from the passages quoted above sometimes takes wrong or at least suboptimal actions? In my view, this is excluded for two reasons: the first is that, in this case, Aristotle's distinction between full virtue (*aretē*) and mere

---

[8] *EN* I 1(3), 1094b12–27; I 7, 1098a25–34.

[9] I have argued elsewhere that the personal form of the expression *epieikēs* is sometimes (but of course not always) used for the bearer of the competence called *epieikeia*: see Horn (2006).

[10] I follow in this view the classical study of Irwin (1985).

Aristotle on the Possibility of Moral Perfection   209

continence (*enkrateia*) would lose its meaning. *Enkrateia* signifies the self-mastery of someone who overcomes his bad impulses and inappropriate desires; but, according to all of Aristotle's descriptions, the possessor of *aretē* does not have to fight against temptations. The temptations are simply absent; while the *enkratēs* feels pain in doing enforced good actions, the good person feels pleasure while effortlessly realising the absolute good (*haplōs*) (*EN* II 2 and VII 13). The second reason is that the paradigmatic figure can even less be said to sometimes surrender to inappropriate desires, as the incontinent person (*akratēs*) does – namely against his better insight. If we had to ascribe wrong behaviour to the virtuous person, then he would resemble the *akratēs*, being different from the incontinent person perhaps only statistically or extensionally: he would then commit misdeeds only less often and to a lesser degree.

Drefcinski and Curzer, however, defend the view that the Aristotelian *spoudaios* actually is far from being an ideal and perfect agent.[11] Curzer distinguishes four different cases: (a) the virtuous person might do vicious acts involuntarily, (b) he might commit excusable vicious acts, (c) he could perform untypical acts, and (d) he could do, in some rare cases, even vicious acts. Let us regard some of the passages brought up by Curzer in defence of his realistic interpretation.

One important text discussed by Curzer in favour of his reading is Aristotle's analysis of concrete practical motivation in *EN* V 6(10), 1134a17–23. According to the passage, it is perfectly possible that some-one commits an unjust act without being unjust. Aristotle's examples are the following: 'a man may have intercourse with a woman knowing who she is, yet not from the motive of deliberate choice (*prohairesis*), but under the influence of passion'. Aristotle continues: 'in such a case, though he has committed injustice, he is not an unjust man: for instance, he is not a thief, though guilty of theft, not an adulterer, though he has committed adul-tery' (transl. Rackham). Now, Curzer believes that what is at stake here is that someone can – in the rare situation of a sudden affect – be ravished to do something wrong without being unjust in general. But this reading is incorrect. Curzer's position has rightly been criticised by Magdalena Hoffmann, who indicates that Aristotle does not mean that affective adultery or theft are compatible with having full virtue.[12] What Aristotle claims is that someone can show up as a partially suboptimal person without being completely bad.

---

[11] Drefcinski (1996); Curzer (2005).   [12] Hoffmann (2010, 210).

210 CHRISTOPH HORN

Another relevant passage which has been adduced by Curzer is *EN* IX 3, 1165b13–20. There Aristotle says that, when a seemingly good person turns into a bad one, there is no need to remain his friend:

> Again, supposing we have admitted a person to our friendship as a good man, and he becomes, or we think he has become, a bad man: are we still bound to love him? Perhaps it is impossible to do so, since only what is good is lovable; and also wrong, for we ought not to be lovers of evil, nor let ourselves become like what is worthless; and, as has been said above, like is the friend of like. Should we therefore break off the friendship at once? Perhaps not in every case, but only when our friends have become incurably bad; for so long as they are capable of reform we are even more bound to help them morally than we should be to assist them financially, since character is a more valuable thing than wealth and has more to do with friendship.

In my eyes, it would be a serious misreading of the passage to take the goodness of the person under consideration – the one I regarded so far as my friend – as an objective fact. What Aristotle instead says is that I *erroneously* considered him to be a good individual; I falsely accepted him as an excellent person (*ean d'apodechētai ōs agathon*) (*EN* IX 3, 1065b13). So the passage does not imply the possibility of a change from goodness to vice.

Likewise, in the next case, I don't believe that Curzer has a valid example for the so-called misdeeds of the virtuous individual. In *EN* IV 2(1), 1121a1–7, Aristotle seems to say that the virtuous person feels pain when having spent money inappropriately:

> If the liberal man should happen to spend in a manner contrary to what is right and noble, he will feel pain, though in a moderate degree and in the right manner; for it is a mark of virtue to feel both pleasure and pain on the right occasions and in the right manner. Also the liberal man is an easy person to deal with in money matters; he can be cheated, because he does not value money, and is more distressed if he has paid less than he ought than he is annoyed if he has paid more: he does not agree with the saying of Simonides.

On my reading, all Aristotle wants to tell us in this text is that the generous man (*ho eleutherios*) will never commit the mistake of Simonides, namely to become a miser when growing older. The only thing that might happen is that he mistakenly spends too much money for someone who does not deserve it. But this is an error concerning the facts, not the axiology. In the passage immediately before this quotation, in 1120b27–1121a1, the *eleutherios* is described as someone who always knows the right mean

Aristotle on the Possibility of Moral Perfection

between excess and defect when giving or receiving money (provided that he knows the facts), who does that both in small and in big cases, and who executes his virtue with pleasure. As this implies, the mistake 'contrary to what is right and noble' merely *happens* to him, as the formulation *ean de para to deon kai to kalōs echon symbainēi autōi analiskein* shows. I therefore think that the text does not contradict the passage *EN* IV 9(15) quoted above, in which Aristotle told us that the virtuous man never feels shame, since he never has any reason to be ashamed. Even if the defenders of the idealisation reading thus have to admit, in this case, that the Aristotelian *eleutherios* makes a mistake, it is not described as a morally relevant one. On the contrary, by giving too much, the *eleutherios* still avoids the failure of becoming a miser.

A final pertinent text is *EN* V 4(7), 1132a2–4, where it is said that the decent individual is punished by the law when he commits evil actions in the same way as the bad person is penalised:

> For it makes no difference whether a good man has defrauded a bad man or a bad one a good one, nor whether it is a good or a bad man that has committed adultery; the law looks only at the nature of damage, treating the parties as equal, and merely asking whether one has done and the other suffered injustice, whether one inflicted and the other has sustained damage.

This text seems highly peculiar with regard to everything we have seen so far. Does Aristotle really believe that a good man can defraud a bad man in the same sense as *vice versa*, and that it makes no difference if a good or a bad person commits adultery (*ouden gar diapherei, ei epieikēs phaulon apesterēsen ē phaulos epieikē, oud' ei emoicheusen epieikēs ē phaulos*)? *Prima facie*, this sounds very strange. How might it be possible to resolve this riddle?

3 A Possible Defence of the 'Idealisation Interpretation'

How can we find a sufficient explanation of what is going on in the last quotation? Are the 'ideal' features of the virtuous person (as mentioned above) rhetorically exaggerated, while in fact being much weaker? There are three possible explanations, namely: The ideal of the paradigmatically virtuous individual might be restricted to (a) *fallible perfection in the assessment of facts*, (b) *fallible perfection in morality*, (c) *statistical perfection in morality*, or a combination of these.

(a) *Fallible perfection in the assessment of facts*: Even the perfectly virtuous person can be mistaken in assessing a situation, as in the case that he spends too much money for someone who does not deserve it.

(b) *Fallible perfection in morality*: The paradigmatic figure can be mistaken in his moral judgement, even in cases in which he has a fully adequate picture of a given situation.

(c) *Statistical perfection in morality*: The ideally virtuous person acts appropriately only in most of the given situations, not in all. His perfection is only a statistical one. If someone who normally is a brave soldier once flees from a dangerous situation while he courageously fought in dozens of others, we should still describe him as perfectly virtuous.

To my mind, (a) holds true, but it is not very helpful, while (b) and (c) can be excluded. Regarding (a), we must clearly concede this point. Otherwise the Aristotelian *spoudaios* could not even be defrauded or deceived by a hallucination. It might be that this is a Stoic claim concerning the *sophos*. Given that Aristotle defends an epistemology that is founded on less demanding assumptions than those of the Stoics, one should admit that cognitive infallibility is not part of the Aristotelian ideal. The sort of perfection and stability Aristotle has in mind does not require this type of insight. But I think it does require a sort of infallibility and permanence which are incompatible with (b) and (c). What then might be an appropriate reading of the last quotation from Section 2?

The most plausible interpretation of what happens in *EN* V 4(7), 1132a2–4 is based on the observation that Aristotle sometimes uses his vocabulary on the paradigmatic individual, i.e. *spoudaios*, *phronimos*, *epieikēs*, etc., to designate a quite ordinary type of excellent individual. We learn, e.g. that he regards Pericles as an historical example of a *phronimos*.[13] Aristotle certainly does not take Pericles as an example of ideal morality. Apparently, there must be an ambiguity in his usage of the term *phronimos* if it can apply both to the fully virtuous man and to someone like Pericles. We find a similar ambiguity in Aristotle's use of the word *epieikēs*: in the *Politics*, the expression *hoi epieikeis* is sometimes used simply to signify citizens of relatively noble character (e.g. in *Pol.* III 10, 1281a28). A government guided by these decent people would rule without making mistakes and, hence, would be highly desirable (VI 4, 1318b32–1319a4).

There is an interestingly weak use of '*spoudaios*' in the famous accumulation argument in *Pol.* III 11, 1281a40–b10 (transl. Jowett and Barnes):

---

[13] *EN* VI 5, 1140b8; while, in the same context, he describes Anaxagoras and Thales as '*sophoi*', not as *phronimoi*': 1141b3–4.

Aristotle on the Possibility of Moral Perfection 213

> The principle that the multitude ought to be in power rather than the few best can be maintained, and it might contain some difficulty, but perhaps also some truth. For the many, of whom each individual is not a good man, when they meet together may be better than the few good, if regarded not individually but collectively, just as a feast to which many contribute is better than a dinner provided out of a single purse. For each individual among the many has a share of excellence and practical wisdom, and when they meet together, just as they become in a manner one man, who has many feet, and hands, and senses, so too with regard to their character and thought. Hence the many are better judges than a single man of works of music and poetry; for some understand one part, and some another, and all of them together understand the whole.

How can Aristotle claim that the members of a multitude possess each a 'part' of *aretē* and *phronēsis*? And how can they be collectively better than an excellent person, although, individually, each is not a *spoudaios anēr* (*tous gar pollous, hōn hekastos estin ou spoudaios anēr, homōs endechetai synelthontas einai beltious ekeinōn*)? If we take seriously what we saw about Aristotle's view of the paradigmatic figure, it makes no sense that a combination of shares of virtue outweigh the competence of a *spoudaios* – provided that this expression designates an ideally virtuous person. Here again, there is an ambiguity in Aristotle's reference to the excellent man. One wonders if he thinks, in *Pol.* III 11, of an absolutely best person or only the relatively best individual. In the first case he would have in mind that a multitude, living under good constitutional circumstances, can outweigh even the absolutely ideal person. In the second case, the central message would be that there are cognitively excellent people who are, nevertheless, weaker than a multitude in its joint judgement. Aristotle repeats this point in *Pol.* III 11, 1281b10–15:

> There is a similar combination of qualities in good men, who differ from any individual of the many, as the beautiful are said to differ from those who are not beautiful, and works of art from realities, because in them the scattered elements are combined, although, if taken separately, the eye of the person or some other feature in another person would be fairer than in the picture.

The *spoudaios* under consideration in this text represents a level of excellence which compares to an appropriate combination of good qualities: *alla toutôi diapherousin hoi sopudaioi tōn andrōn hekastou tōn pollōn, hōsper kai tōn mē kalōn tous kalous phasi.* We know such combinations from works of art, Aristotle tells us, where beautiful individual features are combined and connected into some unity. This *spoudaios* can of course be cognitively less perfect than a multitude. But it is impossible to see in this *spoudaios* the absolutely best person. This is obvious when we continue to read *Pol.* book III and finally arrive at III 17–18. Already in III 13, 1284a3–11, we find the following unambiguous statement:

> If, however, there be some one person, or more than one, although not enough to make up the full complement of the state, whose excellence is so pre-eminent that the excellence or the political capacity of all the rest admit of no comparison with his or theirs, he or they can be no longer regarded a part of the state; for justice will not be done to the superior, if he is reckoned only as the equal of those who are so far inferior to him in excellence and in political capacity. Such a man may truly be deemed a God among men (*hōsper gar theon en anthrōpois*).

If the absolutely perfect individual is 'like a God among human beings' then, I think, we can conclude that the *spoudaios* of *Pol.* III 11 is not identical with him. The person who is characterised as such a quasi-divine being is seen by Aristotle as incommensurable with all of his fellow-citizens, a characterisation that certainly does not fit the description of the *spoudaios* in *Pol.* III 11. We can infer that the use of *spoudaios* in *Pol.* III 11 is simply a somewhat exaggerated way of labelling a relatively good person. Those whose judgement can be overridden by the multitude are not perfectly virtuous people *sensu stricto*. But the person who is said to be godlike is different from these merely virtuous individuals.[14]

As Aristotle claims, complete political power should be transferred to such a person.[15] In *Pol.* III 17, 1288a15–29, we are told that an excellent person in this strict sense (or even a family of them) should be the king, and that he must never be a victim of ostracism:

> But when a whole family or some individual, happens to be so pre-eminent in virtue as to surpass all others, then it is just that they should be the royal family and supreme over all, or that this one citizen should be the only king of the whole. For surely it would not be right to kill, or ostracize, or exile such a person, or require that he should take his turn in being governed. The whole is naturally superior to the part, and he who has this pre-eminence is in the relation of a whole to a part. But if so, the only alternative is that he should have the supreme power, and that mankind should obey him, not in turn, but always.

---

[14] For a more detailed view on *Pol.* III 11 see Horn (2016).
[15] Curzer 2005, 241. It is indicated that in *Pol.* III 16, 1287a31–32 each seems to be characterised as affective and hence as non-ideal. But this passage is located shortly before Aristotle's description of the divinely perfect king.

The person who is described in this quote from *Pol.* III 17 is so pre-eminently good that he deserves to be the king without qualification, while the citizens simply have to obey. I don't think that there is any irony or reservation in this text: the quasi-divine figure – even if he might be extremely rare – should have supreme power: *hōste leipetai monon to peithesthai tōi toioutōi kai kurion einai mē kata meros touton all all' haplōs.*

What is said at the end of *Pol.* III on absolute kingship has its fundament in the Aristotelian distinction between moral virtue and exceptional moral virtue, as we find it in *EN* VII 1 (this is different from the dichotomy of natural and proper virtue in *EN* VI 13). At the beginning of *EN* VII, Aristotle briefly explains some basic concepts of his moral psychology, namely vice (*kakia*) and virtue (*aretē*), incontinence (*akrasia*) and self-mastery (*enkrateia*), and, finally, 'bestiality' or 'brutality' (*theriotēs*), and contrasts virtue with a divine type of perfect virtue. He then claims that 'divine goodness is something more exalted than virtue, and bestial badness is different in kind from vice' (1145a25–27). We are told that the bearer of such a virtue, the *theios anēr* according to a Lacedaemonian expression, is extremely rare and unusual (1145a27–30). Aristotle develops this point as follows:

> And inasmuch as it is rare for a man to be divine, in the sense in which that word is commonly used by the Lacedaemonians as a term of extreme admiration – 'Yon mon's divine,' they say –, so a bestial character is rare among human beings; it is found most frequently among barbarians, and some cases also occur as a result of disease or arrested development. We sometimes also use 'bestial' as a term of opprobrium for a surpassing degree of human vice. (1145a25–31)

As the passage tells us, we should accept a conceptual opposition between a very rare bestiality – which can be found, according to Aristotle, 'among barbarians' – and a perfect virtue that can be ascribed to very few people. Curzer in his article interprets this 'heroically virtuous person', as he calls it, in the sense of a stronger and smarter individual, i.e. as someone who can bear a higher degree of challenges.[16] But this is clearly not what Aristotle means here; what he has in mind is a small group of individuals possessing a divine perfection in being virtuous. The opposition required by the Aristotelian concept of bestiality cannot be provided by Curzer's figure of a high-capacity *spoudaios*; what is in question is an extraordinarily good person.

---

[16] Curzer (2005, 236).

We find Aristotle making a similar point in *EN* V 10(14), where *epieikeia* is discussed. There, too, he assumes the existence of a perfect moral competence which overrides even justice. *Epieikeia*, we are told, is itself a form of justice, but at the same time it goes beyond justice, since it enables the person who possesses it to improve or supplement written law. As Curzer rightly observes, Aristotelian virtue can come in degrees.[17] The decisive point, however, is not the possession of virtue in continuous grades, but the fact that the expressions *phronimos*, *spoudaios*, *epieikēs*, etc. can be used both for a relatively good person and for the absolutely excellent level. Aristotle already describes as *spoudaios* a person with merely very good moral and cognitive attributes. But this does not at all relativise his ideal.

The moral ideal of the perfect agent is ultimately rooted in the idea of a contemplative life by which a human being leads a quasi-divine life. In *EE* VIII 3, 1249b14–25, this thought is explained as follows:

> For God is not a ruler in the sense of issuing commands, but is the end as a means to which wisdom gives commands . . .; since clearly God is in need of nothing. Therefore whatever mode of choosing and of acquiring things good by nature – whether goods of body or wealth or friends or the other goods – will best promote the contemplation of God, that is the best mode, and that standard is the finest; and any mode of choice and acquisition that either through deficiency or excess hinders us from serving and from contemplating God – that is a bad one. This is how it is for the spirit, and this is the best spiritual standard – to be as far as possible unconscious of the irrational part of the spirit, as such. Let this, then, be our statement of what is the standard of nobility and what is the aim of things absolutely good.

As Aristotle says in this text, the best state a human being can reach is that of divine contemplation, the *bios theōrētikos*. It consists in regarding God not as the commander of the universe, but as the ultimate end towards which all goods should be directed. In the last sentence of this quotation, this state of human perfection is explicitly called *kalokagathia*: *tis men oun horos tēs kalokagathias, kai tis ho skopos tōn haplōs agathōn, estō eirēmenon*. But *kalokagathia* is what the ideally virtuous person possesses. He is, hence, perfect by his realisation of a theoretical or philosophical life.

---

[17] Moral perfection can be owned on different levels as we are told, e.g. in the *EN* X 3, 1173a18–22: 'the same will be true of justice and the other excellences in respect of which we plainly say that people of a certain character are so more or less in accordance with these excellences; for people may be more just or brave, and it is possible to act justly or temperately more or less'.

I argued in this section that the most persuasive explanation for the seeming attenuation of the paradigmatic agent is that Aristotle, when he uses the expressions *spoudaios*, *phronimos*, *epieikēs*, etc., need not speak about the ideally paradigmatic individual. This has to do with the Aristotelian distinction between moral virtue and exceptional moral virtue. Aristotelian virtue comes in degrees. The decisive point, however, is not the possession of virtue in continuous grades, but the fact that there is a single excellent level. Aristotle can already describe as *spoudaios* a person with merely very good moral and cognitive attributes.

At first glance, my reading seems to be paradoxical: Aristotle is defending a more ambitious and more idealistic view of the paradigmatic figure than Plato does. But there is an explanation for this surprising fact: while Plato defends a dualistic position, distancing the intelligible forms from the sensible world and, thus, interpreting the latter as unstable and non-ideal, Aristotle sees the forms as working within the objects of the sensible world and regulating their development. And, whereas Plato leaves room for moral improvement in a post-mortal life and within several reincarnations, the idea of personal immortality is absent in Aristotle (as well as in the Stoics). So, the full Aristotelian ideal must be realisable on earth, or it is not realisable at all. Aristotle argues for a weaker position than the Stoics, insofar he is not defending the idea of a general cognitive infallibility of the *spoudaios*.

Nevertheless, he is speaking of real perfection. In *Physics* VII 3, we can identify its metaphysical background. Aristotle tells us that 'excellence (*aretē*) is perfection (*teleiōsis*) for, when anything acquires its proper excellence, we call it perfect, since it is then if ever that we have a thing in its natural state (*kata physin*)'. Even if human beings are finite and weak, they can be perfect when they attain their proper nature.[18]

---

[18] An additional argument can be made based on the complicated phenomenology of bad people in Aristotle. On this see Mulhern (2008), Curzer (2012), Fermani (2014), and Kontos (2014). The point is that there is, for Aristotle, only one way of getting it right, but a great number of possible deviations from the best personal state.

PART IV

Aristotle's Political Anthropology

CHAPTER 11

Political Animals and Human Nature
in Aristotle's Politics

Joseph Karbowski

The claim that human beings are by nature political animals is one of the most fundamental of Aristotle's *Politics*, and, understandably, it has received a lot of attention.[1] One very interesting, and fruitful, trend has appealed to the biological works to illuminate this famous thesis.[2] This strategy has brought to light a broad conception of politicality which is exhibited by humans and other gregarious animals, including bees, wasps, ants, and cranes.[3] As scholars have rightly emphasised, political animals in the broad sense collectively pursue a common end via a differentiation of roles or tasks. Different broadly political species have different common ends. Bees promote the good of the hive, wasps that of the nest, and so on. Nonetheless, every broadly political species has a shared end – really, a shared way of life – that all of its members promote in different ways. This is true of humans, although their way of life specifically involves forming and sustaining poleis, which makes them political in another, narrower, sense as well.[4]

In this chapter, I continue to mine the biological works for useful insights into the *Politics* and the conception of human nature contained therein. I shall articulate some important implications of Aristotle's broad conception of politicality. Specifically, I identify two structural features of broadly political animal kinds that have been overlooked in the literature.[5]

---

[1] See Cooper (1990); Depew (1995); Keyt (1991, 123–26); Kraut (2002, 247–53); Kullmann (1991); Miller (1995, 30–37); and Mulgan (1974).

[2] See Cooper (1990); Depew (1995); and Kullmann (1991).

[3] In distinguishing between 'broad' and 'narrow' political ways of life I follow Miller (1995, 30–32).

[4] Compare the apt remarks of Cooper: 'Human beings, then, like bees or cranes, are political animals in what is from the point of view of zoology (though not of course etymology) the fundamental sense of having a work or function that the members of a human group all do together; but because in this case the common work involves maintaining the structure and organization of a city, they are political in the further, more literal, sense of being naturally suited to life in cities' (Cooper 1990, 225).

[5] Up to this point, scholars only emphasise that the members of broad political kinds have a common goal and divide the labour in working towards it, see Cooper (1990, 226–27) and Depew (1995, 171).

First, broad political species naturally divide into functionally distinct subgroups, e.g. bees naturally divide into kings, workers, and drones. Second, the members of these subgroups exhibit natural morphological and psychological differences coordinate with their distinct roles in the community, e.g. king bees are larger than workers in virtue of their reproductive role. These two features are well attested in the biological works, and there is strong evidence that they informed Aristotle's conception of the structure of human nature in the *Politics*. A major benefit of this interpretation is that it renders intelligible Aristotle's postulation of psychological differences between human beings, and illuminates the place of natural slaves and women in his view of human nature. If the current interpretation is correct, Aristotle's endorsement of the existence of natural slaves and women and his views about their rational abilities do not threaten the coherence of his conception of human nature. Instead, they betray his acceptance of a rather complex, hierarchical anthropological theory.

I   Two Structural Features of Broad Political Animals

I shall begin by exploring Aristotle's view of broad political animals and their way of life. This topic receives its most extensive treatment in the biological works, but it also appears in the *Politics* and informs its conception of human nature (cf. *Pol.* I 2, 1253a7–18 discussed below). In this section, I draw attention to two overlooked features of broadly political species. The next section examines the particular way in which mankind exhibits them.

In *Historia Animalium*, Aristotle distinguishes the ways of life (*bioi*) of animals[6]:

> Some are gregarious, some are solitary ... And of the gregarious ... some are political, while others are scattered. Gregarious creatures are, among birds, such as the pigeon, the crane, and the swan ... Political creatures are those among which there is some one and common function [*to ergon*] for all; and this property is not common to all creatures that are gregarious. Such political creatures are man, the bee, the ant, and the crane. Again, of these political creatures some submit to a ruler, others are subject to no rule: as for instance, the crane and the several sorts of bee submit to a ruler, whereas ants and numbers of other creatures are subject to no rule. (*HA* I 1, 487b33–488a13, transl. Thompson)

They do not point out that the individuals that carry out these different jobs must themselves form distinct natural subkinds and differ accordingly in their morphological and psychological orientations, as I point out below.

[6] This passage has textual issues, which are ably discussed in Cooper (1990, 222–24, n.5).

Political Animals and Human Nature in Aristotle's Politics 223

By 'way of life' (*bios*) Aristotle means a specific pattern of activity by which animals of a certain kind exploit a given environment.[7] In this passage he initially distinguishes animals that exhibit a gregarious way of life from those that are solitary. The former are zoological kinds whose members form groups in order to survive, and the latter are those whose members do not. Aristotle then proceeds to divide gregarious animals into those that exhibit political and those that exhibit scattered ways of life.

Aristotle describes political animals as 'those among which there is some one and common function [*to ergon*] for all'. From this description it is clear that the pursuit of a single, shared goal or end is central to a political way of life. What is not so clear, however, is that it, more specifically, involves the pursuit of a common goal by way of a distribution of individual tasks among the members of the species.[8] In some sense, cows grazing together in a field have an end in common, but Aristotle nonetheless wants to distinguish their 'scattered' activity from the coordinated role-division exhibited by bees and other similar animals.[9] All bees, for instance, promote the good of the hive, but they do not do so in the same way; kings, workers, and drones by nature make different contributions to their shared way of life.[10] The same holds for other political animals with respect to their peculiar communities.[11] This feature of the political way of life explains why

---

[7] Compare Depew (1995, 167). For further discussion of the roles that the notion of a way of life plays in Aristotle's biology, see Lennox (2010b).

[8] See Cooper (1990, 226–27); and Depew (1995, 171).

[9] On this interpretation the contrast between scattered and political activity is a contrast between different types of group activity. That is what makes both of them divisions of gregariousness. Gregarious animals essentially live in groups. Cows, for instance, live in herds, just as bees live in swarms. However, their group activities differ. In particular, those of cows and other scattered animals are not differentiated and coordinated in the way that those of bees and other political animals are. On this reading, a differentiation of roles is essential to a broadly political way of life; it is not a feature that all political animals just happen to share. I thank the editors for pressing me to clarify this point.

[10] Aristotle explicitly says of bees that 'their functions are differentiated' (*diērēntai de ta erga*) (*HA* IX 40, 627a20). King bees exclusively have a reproductive role in the hive; they hermaphroditically generate kings and workers (*GA* III 10, 760a2–4; b7–10, transl. Peck). Workers too have a reproductive function; they hermaphroditically generate drones (*GA* III 10, 760a29–30). However, they also tend to the hive and its food supply (*HA* IX 40, 627a20–24). Aristotle is reticent about what role, he thinks, the drones play in the hive. He believes that they somehow increase the industry of the workers (*HA* IX 40, 627b8–11), but precisely how they do so is left unsaid.

[11] Wasps naturally divide into mothers and workers (*HA* IX 41, 627b31–33, 628a1–3). Like king bees, mother wasps play a primarily reproductive role in the nest (*HA* IX 41, 628a10–21). However, unlike king bees, they reproduce both the mothers and workers via copulation (*GA* III 10, 761a6–8). Worker wasps tend to the nest and provide nourishment to the mothers when they are resting (*HA* IX 41, 628a21–23). Cranes fall into leaders, heralds, and the (unnamed) rest (*HA* IX 10, 613b21–23). Leader cranes fly at the head of the flock and keep lookout while the others are

224 JOSEPH KARBOWSKI

political animals are more intelligent and have greater attachment to their young than the rest.[12] Since the members of political animal kinds promote a common goal by coordinated division of roles, they need more sophisticated communication skills and patterns of attachment than the members of zoological kinds who do not coordinate their activities.

David Depew captures these features of political animals in the following four conditions, which he considers to be jointly necessary and sufficient for being political in the broad sense:

(i) Exhibit associative behaviour of some kind.
(ii) Have a common or shared work (*koinon ergon*) beyond reproductive activity.
(iii) Exhibit a division of roles in contributing to that work.
(iv) Possess dispositional emotional and cognitive traits that facilitate the achievement of a *koinon ergon*.[13]

The first condition (i) ensures that the animal kind in question is gregarious, while the next two, (ii) and (iii), locate it within the political subdivision of the gregarious way of life. The fourth feature (iv) guarantees that the members of broadly political species are emotionally and cognitively equipped to meet the demands of a way of life that essentially involves a coordinated division of roles.

This is currently where the discussion stands. I would like to take it further by pointing out two overlooked structural features of broadly political zoological kinds. First, broadly political species exhibit what I shall call *functional division*: they naturally divide into subkinds with distinct roles or functions in their respective communities. For instance, the division of bees into kings, workers, and drones is not something that bees conventionally impose upon themselves or that we impose upon them; those are objective, mind-independent subkinds (*genē*) into which nature herself sorts bees.[14] The same is equally true of the functionally distinct subkinds into which other broadly political zoological kinds divide; they too constitute genuine joints in nature.

Broadly, political zoological kinds exhibit a functional division because it optimally promotes their way of life. Such kinds naturally negotiate their environments by forming complex communities, like hives, nests, etc.; and,

---

asleep (*HA* IX 10, 613b23–26). Heralds fly on the boundaries of the flock and alert the others of potential dangers by making a hissing sound (*HA* IX 10, 613b22–23).

[12] *HA* VIII 1, 588b30–589a4; cf. *PA* II 4, 650b24–27; *GA* III 2, 753a7–17. The classic discussion of Aristotle's attribution of intelligence to animals is Labarrière (1990).

[13] Depew (1995, 171).   [14] Cf. *HA* V 22, 553b7; *GA* III 10, 759a17, 760a28.

Political Animals and Human Nature in Aristotle's Politics   225

while it would have been possible for nature to make each member of these species multifunctional, Aristotle believes that the requisite roles in these communities are likely to be performed best if they are distributed to different individuals.[15] Since nature aims at the best for each species relative to its substantial nature,[16] a natural division into functionally distinct subkinds is built into the structure of each broadly political species.

Another important structural feature of broad political kinds is what I shall call *coordinated diversity*. Not only do broadly political species differ emotionally and cognitively from non-political species – see feature (iv) above – the members within a single broad political species also differ morphologically and psychologically from one another in principled ways. The reason for this second structural feature of broadly political animals is simple. Different roles within a community require different physical, emotional, and cognitive aptitudes; and, since the members of a broadly political species naturally fall into subgroups with different roles in their community, they will have to differ from one another morphologically and psychologically in ways that promote the performance of their specific functions. Consider Aristotle's explanation of why king bees are larger than workers:

> Besides, it is well that the kings, who have, as it were, been made with a view to producing young [*hōsper pepoiēmenous epi teknōsin*], should stay within … and that they should be large, since their body has been constituted as it were for procreation [*hōsper epi teknopoiian sustantos tou sōmatos autōn*] … but the [worker] bees are intermediate between the two other kinds, for this is useful for their work [*chrēsimoi gar houtō pros tēn ergasian*]. (*GA* III 10, 760b7–14, transl. Peck)

In this passage Aristotle explicitly gives a teleological explanation of the different sizes of bees. King bees are larger than worker bees, he says, because their bodies are 'constituted with a view to bearing young'. In contrast, worker bees must be smaller because that size is 'useful for their work'. The underlying teleological principle here is perfectly general and is voiced repeatedly in Aristotle's natural works: 'nature makes the instruments to fit the function, not the function to fit the instruments'.[17] This principle guarantees that nature does not assign a function to an item 'in vain', and explains why the members of different subgroups of a broad political kind will naturally differ from one another.

---

[15] *Pol.* I 2, 1252b1–5; cf. *PA* IV 6, 683a20–26.
[16] *IA* 2, 704b12–18; 8, 708a9–12; 12, 711a18–29.
[17] *PA* IV 12, 694b13–14, transl. Lennox; cf. *PA* I 5, 645b14–20; 4.10, 687a10–14; *GA* I 3, 716b17–27.

226 JOSEPH KARBOWSKI

Aristotle is explicit in *HA* I 1, 488a9, that mankind (*anthrōpos*) is a broadly political animal. In fact, in *Pol.* I 2 he goes so far as to say that man is 'more political' than bees and the other broadly political species mentioned in *HA* I 1:

> It is also clear why a human being is more political than a bee or any other gregarious animal. Nature makes nothing in vain, as we say, and no animal has speech except a human being ... But speech is for making clear what is beneficial or harmful, and hence also what is just or unjust. For it is peculiar to human beings, in comparison to other animals, that they alone have perception of what is good or bad, just or unjust, and the rest. And it is community in these that makes a household or polis. (*Pol.* I 2, 1253a7–19)[18]

Humans are more political than other gregarious species, Aristotle explains, because they alone have speech (*logos*), whose purpose is to 'make clear' their perceptions of moral values. These capacities enable humans to form households and poleis, functional communities whose complexity surpasses that of beehives, ant hills, or wasp nests.

This argument is telling for our purposes because it not only reveals that Aristotle carried the notion of a broadly political way of life into the *Politics*; it confirms that it influences his conception of human nature in that treatise. In particular, the previous argument presents proof that, at the very least, humans possess the four features articulated by Depew (i–iv). For, it depicts mankind as a broadly political species whose distinctive intelligence (perception of good and evil, etc.) enables its members to coordinate their activities far better than bees, wasps, ants, and cranes.[19] But what about the two structural features of broadly political species that were recently identified, functional division and coordinated diversity? Is there evidence for thinking that they informed Aristotle's conception of humanity in the *Politics*? To answer this question, we must examine mankind's distinctive suitability for life in a polis, and what implications it has for the structure of human nature.

2 The Functional Division and Coordinated Diversity of Mankind

The previous section explored a political way of life which was broad in the sense that it is exemplified by a number of zoological kinds. Humans exhibit

---

[18] For translations of the *Politics*, I follow Reeve, sometimes with slight revisions.
[19] The passage does not say anything about our attachment to our young, but Aristotle comments upon this in the *Nicomachean Ethics* (*EN*) VIII 12, 1161b24–27.

Political Animals and Human Nature in Aristotle's Politics   227

this way of life, but they are also political in another way in which other zoological species are not: they alone are naturally constituted to live in poleis. This 'narrow' conception of politicality is most prominent in the ethico-political works,[20] and within the framework of Aristotle's natural teleology it implies that human nature exhibits the two features identified in the previous section, albeit in a manner specifically tailored to life in a polis.

A polis is a multitude of citizens that share a constitution and aim collectively at happiness or wellbeing (*eudaimonia*).[21] The requirement for citizenship vacillates throughout the *Politics*, but that does not change the fact that a polis is essentially a complex whole (*holon*) whose existence – and flourishing – depends upon the performance of a vast array of necessary and noble tasks (*erga*).[22] Like Plato, Aristotle believes that these tasks will be best performed if they are distributed to different individuals. This presumption has implications for the statesman or lawgiver: he must not assign the same jobs to the same citizens in the polis.[23] However, it also has implications for the structure of human nature (see *Pol.* I 2, 1252b1–5). For, humans are by nature constituted to live in poleis – that is one of the upshots of the famous argument at the beginning of *Pol.* 1.2 (see 1253a1–4); and, since a polis has the best chance at success if its tasks are distributed to different individuals,[24] and nature does nothing in vain, nature must distribute different tasks in the polis and household to different individuals. This implies that mankind (*anthrōpos*) will naturally divide into subkinds with different roles in the household and polis, just as bees fall into natural subcategories with distinct roles in the hive.

This functional division of human nature is well attested in the ethico-political works. Throughout the *EN* and *Pol.* Aristotle distinguishes subclasses of humans with different roles in the household and polis. Some passages distinguish natural rulers from natural slaves (*Pol.* I 2, 1252a30–34); others argue for a distinction between natural slaves and women (1252a34–b6) or between (male) natural rulers and their female subordinates.[25] In each of these passages, Aristotle is clear that these divisions are *natural* (*kata physin* or *physei*), as opposed to purely

---

[20] *EN* I 7, 1097b8–11; VIII 12, 1162a17–19; 9.9, 1169b17–19; *EE* VII 10, 1242a22–27; *Pol.* I 2, 1253a1–3; III 6, 1278b17–21.
[21] *Pol.* I 2, 1252b27–30; III 1, 1274b41; III 3, 1276b1–2; III 9, 1280b40–1281a2.
[22] *Pol.* I 1, 1252a18–20; I 2, 1253a18–26; III 1, 1274b38–41; IV 4, 1290b38–1291b13; VII 8, 1328b5–15.
[23] *Pol.* II 11, 1273b9–10; VII 9, 1328b33–1329a2.
[24] For further defence of this claim see pp. 233–4 below.
[25] *Pol.* I 5, 1254b13–14; I 12 1259b1–2; cf. *EN* VIII 13, 1162a22–24.

228   JOSEPH KARBOWSKI

conventional, and in many of them he also explicitly indicates that the members of these different subclasses have different functions (*erga*).[26] Perhaps the most striking – and explicit – assertion of the functional division of human nature appears in *Pol.* 1.5:

> For whenever a number of constituents, whether continuous with one another or discontinuous, are combined into one common thing, a ruling element and a subject element appear. These are present in living things, because this belongs to living things from nature as a whole (*ek tēs hapasēs physeōs*) ... First of all, an animal is constituted of soul and body: the soul is the natural ruler; the body the natural subject ... For the soul rules the body with the rule of a master, whereas understanding rules desire with the rule of a statesman or a king ... The same applies again in the case of human beings with respect to other animals ... Moreover, the relation of male to female is that of natural superior to natural inferior, and that of ruler to ruled. But, in fact, the same holds true of all human beings. (*Pol.* I 5, 1254a28–b16)

According to Aristotle, natural hierarchies are present throughout nature, wherever a multitude of elements are combined into a unified, non-aggregative whole. A natural distinction between ruling and subject elements, he thinks, can be found within animals (soul/body), the soul itself (reason/desire), the sublunary sphere (human beings/other animals), and, most importantly, natural human communities. It follows that some humans will be natural rulers while others are natural subjects, and they will all have different functions or tasks (*erga*) (cf. *Pol.* I 5, 1254a27–28). Included among the latter for Aristotle are natural slaves and women, and their peculiar functions are manual labour (I 2, 1252a32–33; I 6, 1254b17–19) and the preservation of property (III 4, 1277b24–25), respectively.

Since humans naturally divide into subkinds with different roles in the polis and household, they will naturally differ in body type, emotional disposition, and even cognitive ability. Such morphological and psychological differences are necessary because different jobs in the household and polis require different skills or aptitudes. Evidence for this coordinated diversity of human nature is peppered throughout the ethico-political works. Consider first the following passage[27]:

---

[26] *Pol.* I 2, 1252a34–b4; I 5, 1254a25–28; cf. *EN* VIII 13, 1162a22–24.

[27] In the sequel to this passage, Aristotle goes on to admit that nature sometimes fails to coordinate the bodies and souls of these individuals (*Pol.* I 5, 1254b32–34). (The Greek here is a bit difficult. For the most plausible reading, see Schütrumpf (1991, 268–70).) This is not necessarily problematic; it is consistent with his well-known dictum that nature achieves its aims only 'for the most part', cf. Schofield (1990, 14–15).

Political Animals and Human Nature in Aristotle's Politics   229

> Nature tends, then, to make the bodies of slaves and free people different too, the former strong enough to be used for the necessities [*pros tēn anagkaian chrēsin*], the latter useless for that sort of work, but upright in posture and possessing all the other qualities useful for the political life [*chrēsima pros politikon bion*] – qualities divided into those needed for war and peace. (*Pol.* I 5, 1254b27–32)

In this passage, Aristotle explains why naturally free individuals have different bodies from those of natural slaves in terms of their distinctive functions in society. Nature, he says, tends to make the bodies of slaves 'strong enough to be used for the necessities' (*ischura pros tēn angkaia chrēsin*), and those of the naturally free upright in posture and generally unfit for manual labour. Aristotle also adds that nature bestows upon naturally free individuals all of the other qualities 'useful for the political life' (*chrēsima pros politikon bion*).[28] These qualities, which are needed for war and peace, include character traits, like temperance, courage, and endurance (see *Pol.* VII 15, 1334a19–20). Thus, in addition to implying that humans exhibit bodily differences which coordinate with their peculiar roles in society, this passage attests to the existence of functionally coordinated character or emotional differences between humans as well.

Given their distinct roles in the household and polis, humans will also have to differ in their cognitive or rational abilities. Aristotle is most explicit about those differences in a well-known passage of *Pol.* I 13, 1260a9–14:

> For free rule slaves, male rules female, and man rules child in different ways, because, the parts of the soul belong to all these people, but they *belong* in different ways. The deliberative part of the soul is entirely missing from a slave; a woman has it but it lacks authority; a child has it but it is incompletely developed.

These rational differences can be traced to differences in the natural functions assigned to these individuals. Natural slaves do not need a functioning (practical) deliberative part of the soul, because their job is manual labour, not any sort of practical decision-making endeavour.[29]

---

[28] Note that the '*chrēsimos + pros*' construction here is also found in Aristotle's teleological explanation of the different sizes of bees at *GA* III 10, 760b7–14 (quoted on p. 225 above). This is just what we should expect, on the current interpretation.

[29] Natural slaves do not need to be capable of practical deliberation, but other remarks made by Aristotle (*Pol.* VII 7 1327b27–28 with *Pol.* I 2 1252b6–9; I 6 1255a28–b2) suggest that at least some of them should be capable of technical or productive deliberation, see Heath (2008, 244–53); Kraut (2002, 283–94); and Schofield (1990, 14). It is unclear whether natural slaves are capable of craft knowledge (*technē*), but that issue need not detain us here.

Women, in contrast, need at least a partly functioning deliberative faculty, because their job is to preserve the property and manage the indoor affairs. However, since they do not have ultimate ruling authority in the household or polis, their deliberative faculty must itself 'lack authority'.[30] The 'incomplete' status of a child's deliberative faculty reflects his status as an incompletely developed human (cf. *Pol.* I 13, 1260a31–33), and, similarly, a freeman's architectonic rational capacities are coordinate with his architectonic function (*ergon*) in the household and polis.[31]

3 The Status of Natural Slaves and Women

On the current interpretation, the existence of rational differences between human beings is neither puzzling nor problematic. Indeed, they are quite necessary, from a teleological point of view, for the flourishing of our species in its natural setting, viz. a polis. For, as I have been arguing, Aristotle thinks that our species will be optimally suited for life in a political community if its necessary tasks are distributed by nature to different people; and this natural distribution of functions, in turn, engenders the need for rational, emotional, and physical differences between the members of the various subgroups. A virtue of this interpretation is that it demystifies the place of women and natural slaves in Aristotle's conception of human nature.

Perhaps the first thing to stress about natural slaves and women is that Aristotle duly recognises that their existence is no less necessary than that of natural rulers. He explicitly acknowledges that there needs to be human beings naturally fit to perform subordinate tasks in the household and polis. Just as not every sailor can be a captain (*Pol.* III 4, 1276b20–29), nor every bee a king,[32] not every human can be a natural ruler (1276b35–1277a12). In fact, the passage quoted above in which Aristotle describes the existence of hierarchies as a natural feature of non-aggregative communities appears in his defence of the existence of natural slaves

[30] What it means for a woman's deliberative faculty to be 'without authority' (*akuron*) is subject to debate. The standard view, defended by Fortenbaugh (1977) and, more recently, in Miller (2013, 50), is that a woman's deliberative faculty is naturally unable to control her emotions (perhaps because of their lack of spirit and consequent submissiveness). For a different interpretation, which instead construes that qualification as a natural inability to exert authority over men, see Deslauriers (2003, 229); Kraut (2002, 286–87 n.22); and Scott (2010, 112–13). I develop a nuanced alternative to these two views in Karbowski (2014).

[31] *Pol.* I 13, 1260a18–19; cf. *Pol.* I 2, 1252a34–b4; III 4, 1277b21–30.

[32] Aristotle explicitly rejects the view that kings only generate their own kind on the grounds that 'the whole class [of bees] would then be leaders' (*GA* 3.10, 760a17–18). This comes a few lines before he comments upon how beautifully nature has designed the generation of bees so that the entire kind remains continually in existence (*GA* III 10, 760a35–b2).

Political Animals and Human Nature in Aristotle's *Politics* 231

(I 5, 1254a28–b16); it effectively confirms that nature has made a place for them within the species. To be sure, Aristotle is explicit that natural slaves have a *subordinate* place in the hierarchy of human nature; they are essentially 'living tools' to be used by their masters for the sake of action (I 4, 1254a8, a13–17). But, he is no less clear that they have a natural niche within the species, just as the body has a natural, albeit subordinate, place in a living organism and desire has a natural, albeit subordinate, place in the soul (I 5, 1254a34–b16). The same holds for women too: they constitute a natural, albeit subordinate, class of human beings (I 5, 1254b13–14; I 12, 1259b1–2). However, unlike natural slaves, Aristotle maintains that they are naturally free (I 12, 1259a39–40; I 13, 1260b18–19), and even have authority over certain domestic affairs (*EN* VIII 10, 1160b32–1161a1).

The foregoing implies that we must resist the temptation to compare natural slaves and women with maimed or deformed, e.g. congenitally blind, humans.[33] There is a superficial similarity between natural slaves and women, on the one hand, and deformed humans, on the other. For, both groups are deficient relative to other members of the species in certain ways. However, it must not be overlooked that the rational deficiencies exhibited by women and slaves are *natural* or in accordance with nature (*physei* or *kata physin*),[34] whereas those of congenitally maimed or deformed individuals are contrary to nature (*para physin*). Blind humans, for instance, do not constitute a natural subclass of humans; they represent a failure on the part of nature to achieve one of its natural goals.[35] For this reason, there are no virtues or excellences (*aretai*) or even functions (*erga*) of maimed or deformed classes (cf. *Phys.* VII 3, 246a13–17). In contrast, natural slaves and women do constitute *natural* subclasses of humans whose members are amenable to genuine character virtues like temperance, courage, etc., which are relative to their specific functions (*Pol.* I 13, 1260a2–5, a14–24). According to Aristotle, the generation of a natural slave or a woman is not a failure, because these individuals fulfil necessary, albeit subordinate, roles in society (*Pol.* I 5, 1254a28–b16).[36] Because of

---

[33] Cf. Gallagher (2011, 383–84).

[34] It is clear that he thinks these rational differences are natural because Aristotle appeals to them as part of an explanation for why 'the various forms of ruling and being ruled are natural (*physei*)' (*Pol.* I 13, 1260a8–9).

[35] *Phys.* II 8, 199b1–4; *GA* IV 4, 770b9–13.

[36] For further defence of this conclusion see Karbowski (2012). I do not have the space to address the remarks in the *GA* that lend credence to the view that female animals result from failed teleological processes. Suffice it to say that I think the remarks do not support any such reading. Henry (2007) and Gelber (2017) develop the discussion along the lines that I find most promising.

232   JOSEPH KARBOWSKI

their naturally subordinate roles and inferior rational abilities, Aristotle maintains that natural slaves and women are inferior (*cheiron*) to the natural rulers.[37] But that does not compromise their status as a natural subcategory of humans any more than the fact that drones are incapable of generation compromises their status as a natural kind of bee. Aristotle never calls drones deformed or defective bees.

Scholars have sometimes been puzzled by whether, and if so how, Aristotle's attribution of deficient rational abilities to slaves and women is consistent with his claim that rationality is the peculiar human function (*ergon*).[38] But Aristotle himself suggests an answer to this issue with his defence of the humanity of natural slaves in *Pol.* 1.13.[39] In motivating the first half of the dilemma that structures the chapter, he claims 'If they [slaves] do not [sc. have character virtues], absurdity results, since they are human and have a share in reason' (*ontōn anthrōpōn kai logou koinōnountōn*) (*Pol.* I 13, 1259b27–28).[40] This remark suggests that, in order to be human it suffices to be capable of rational activity in a broad sense, which is satisfied by the ability to perceive the rational injunctions of others (cf. *Pol.* I 5, 1254b22–24) no less than the ability to deliberate about the good oneself; the human *ergon* is not narrowly restricted to practical deliberation.[41] To be

[37] *Pol.* I 5, 1254b13–14; cf. *Met* XII 10, 1075a14–15.
[38] Different versions of this puzzle can be found in Adkins (1991, 91); Johnson (2005, 238, 243); Modrak (1994, 207); Mulgan (1977, 42); Shields (2007, 372); Ward (2009, 75–77); and Witt (1998, 124).
[39] Cf. Heath (2008, 258–59).
[40] Aristotle's assertion of the humanity of natural slaves in *Pol.* I 13 is not a one-off remark. In his earlier definition of the natural slave, Aristotle reiterates twice that natural slaves are humans, and he never qualifies that status: 'For anyone who, while being human [*anthrōpos ōn*], is by nature not his own but someone else's is a natural slave. And he is someone else's when, while being human [*anthrōpos ōn*] he is a piece of property' (*Pol.* I 4, 1254a14–16).
[41] See Fortenbaugh (1977, 136); Deslauriers (2003, 214–21); and Karbowski (2012, 345–46). This broad interpretation of rationality is supported by Aristotle's description of the human function as 'activity of soul in accordance with or not without reason' (*psychēs energeia kata logon ē mē aneu logou*) (*EN* I 7, 1098a7–8). The 'not without reason' likely refers to the activity of the motivational part capable of obeying *logos*, see Broadie and Rowe (2002, 277). Some scholars construe the *praktikē* at 1098a3 as evidence that Aristotle restricts the human function to practical deliberation. However, it is doubtful that that adjective is used to single out practical as opposed to theoretical reasoning in this context. For one thing, that distinction has not yet been articulated at this point in the treatise, nor will it be until the further division of reason in book six. Second, *praktikē* is sometimes used in a sense which encompasses both practical and theoretical reasoning (see *Pol.* VII 3, 1325b16–21), and it could very well be used in that inclusive sense in *EN* I 7; cf. Broadie and Rowe (2002, 276). Third, in the function argument of *EE* II 1, Aristotle explicitly describes a *praktikē* life as *chrestikē*, i.e. one which is oriented towards an activity, use, or employment (*chrēsis*) (1219b3–4). This suggests that the human *ergon* involves the use or employment of one's rational faculties (where these include the motivational part of the soul which is capable of obeying reason, cf. *EN* I 7, 1098a4–5); there is no good reason to think that it is restricted so narrowly to practical deliberation.

Political Animals and Human Nature in Aristotle's Politics   233

sure, only the individuals capable of the latter are able to achieve happiness (*eudaimonia*), because only they are able to acquire and exercise practical wisdom (*phronēsis*) in a complete life.[42] However, according to standard Aristotelian doctrine, in order to be a genuine member of a kind one only needs to be capable of performing the relevant function to some extent; one need not be able to perform it well or in the best possible way.[43] Therefore, there is no inconsistency between Aristotle claiming that natural slaves and women are humans genuinely, or non-homonymously, and denying them the rational abilities necessary for achieving happiness.

Admittedly, one might still feel uncomfortable with the fact that it is a presupposition of Aristotle's conception of human nature that not all humans are capable of achieving happiness. Wouldn't it be better for him to maintain that all humans are capable of happiness? Certainly, from our contemporary standpoint, the answer to this question should be affirmative. However, Aristotle's own philosophical commitments entail a negative answer to that question. According to Aristotle, nature is not omnipotent; its design for a species is subject to certain constraints set by the species' essence.[44] This explains why, in his view, snakes are not scurrying around on countless legs like large centipedes. Their status as blooded animals implies that they can at most move about on four limbs, but, because that design is suboptimal, nature omitted limbs from them altogether (*IA* 8, 708a9–20). The optimisation principle that governs Aristotle's treatment of the limbs of snakes is found throughout the *Politics*.[45] Therefore, we should also expect nature to operate in the same constrained manner with respect to the structure of the human species.[46] If that is right, then the configuration in which every human is capable of

---

[42] Aristotle denies that natural slaves are capable of achieving happiness at *Pol.* III 9, 1280a32–34. He is less clear about a woman's prospect for happiness; at least, he never directly comments on the matter in the extant treatises. However, in *Pol.* III 4 he is quite clear that he believes practical wisdom is a virtue peculiar to the ruler; true belief is the virtue of the subordinates (1277b28–30). Therefore, it stands to reason that happiness is out of reach for women as well. Emphatically, this denial of happiness to natural slaves and women does not preclude them from leading good or flourishing lives *quā* natural slaves or women. It is worth remembering that Aristotle views happiness or *eudaimonia* as a quasi-divine status which pertains to someone's life when it appropriately approximates that of the gods (*EN* X 8, 1178b25; cf. *EE* I 7, 1217a22–29). The details of his view of the perfectly happy human life (or lives) are notoriously controversial, but suffice it to say that he believes that the best life of a slave or even a woman does not qualify as a close enough approximation to that of the gods to count as happy or *eudaimōn* in any robust sense.

[43] *Meteor.* IV 12, 390a10; *PA* I 1, 640b34–641a5.

[44] Cf. *IA* 2, 704b12–18; 8, 708a9–12; 12, 711a18–29.

[45] *Pol.* I 2, 1253a9; I 8, 1256b20–21; II 5, 1263a41–b1. For further discussion of Aristotle's 'optimality' principle see Henry (2013); Lennox (2001a); and Leunissen (2010, 124–35).

[46] See Karbowski (2012, 339–45).

performing the highest types of rational activity and achieving happiness is *not* a possible configuration for the human species. The reason is that humans are not simply rational animals. Rationality is described as our characteristic function (*ergon*) in *EN* 1.7, but it is not our only essential feature. In addition to being rational animals humans are essentially polis-dwelling animals, and the latter feature sets constraints upon the distribution of rationality throughout the species.[47]

As I have been stressing above, in order for human nature to be adequate to meet the demands of life in a polis, Aristotle thinks that different rational, morphological, and emotional aptitudes must be distributed to different members of the species. If all human beings had the same aptitudes and were naturally assigned the same role in the polis – even ruling – they would not be capable of flourishing in the context of a polis.[48] In that case, the natural rulers would themselves have to trade off in performing the necessary jobs, which would severely hinder the quality of their rule,[49] or else a number of them would have to band together and unjustly coerce a large number of their equals to do manual labour for which they are not naturally suited.[50] In either case, if all humans were naturally assigned the same specific tasks, their survival would come at the cost of their flourishing. Nature's efforts would, then, be in vain. Since that consequence runs contrary to the entire thrust of the teleological framework in the background of the *Politics*, different humans must have different aptitudes which coordinate with their different roles in the polis. This implies that some human beings must sacrifice the ability to perform the best kinds of rational activity and achieve happiness, but Aristotle duly accepts that implication when he acknowledges that a polis constituted solely by the 'best men' cannot flourish any more than a chorus full of leaders (*Pol.* III 4, 1276b35–1277a12).

4 Conclusion

A general picture of Aristotle's conception of the structure of human nature has begun to emerge. This picture, which draws upon material

---

[47] Aristotle does not explicitly say that the suitability for life in a polis is an essential feature of human beings, but that is implied by the fact that it is a description of our peculiar way of life (*bios*). For, as Lennox has persuasively argued, a species' way of life is an essential feature of it, see Lennox (2010b).

[48] This is arguably the point of the argument in *Pol.* III 4, 1276b35–1277a12, see Frede (2005, 172–76).

[49] *Pol.* II 11, 1273a32–35; VII 9, 1328b33–1329a2.

[50] For an illuminating discussion of Aristotle's 'non-coercive' conception of rule, see Keyt (1993).

Political Animals and Human Nature in Aristotle's Politics   235

from the biology and *Politics*, is more complex and interesting than what we can ascertain solely by focusing upon the *Nicomachean Ethics* and, in particular, its fundamental thesis that rationality is the characteristic human *ergon*. Emphatically, this is not to downplay the importance of the latter for an understanding of Aristotle's ethico-political anthropology. However, the fact that it appears near the very beginning of a treatise that Aristotle describes as the first of a two-part 'philosophy of human affairs' (*EN* X 9, 1181b12–23) suggests that it is not the whole story and that a complete understanding of his view of human nature requires an integration of the material contained both in the *Nicomachean Ethics* and in the *Politics*. Admittedly, a full integration of the lessons of these two treatises would require a book-length treatment. The current chapter has simply started the ball rolling. Let me conclude with a synoptic sketch of our preliminary findings and what they tell us about Aristotle's view of the relationship between the rational and political facets of human nature.

Our brief detour into the biological works highlights that Aristotle believes that mankind (*anthrōpos*) exhibits not just one, but actually *two* layers of functionality. At the highest level of generality, i.e. the level of the species, there is a single, shared function (*ergon*) for all humans. Anything that is to count as a human being non-homonymously must be capable of performing this function. In *EN* 1.7 Aristotle describes it as rational activity, and so, any human, as such, must be capable of performing rational activity in some way or to some extent. This much we know from the *Nicomachean Ethics*. The *Politics*, or rather the *Politics* by way of the biology, brings more clearly into view that Aristotle also acknowledges a natural differentiation of functions *below* the species level. Mankind divides by nature into various subgroups with distinct functions in the household and polis: natural rulers, natural slaves, women, etc. A peculiar psychological, including rational, and bodily makeup, which facilitates the performance of its function, is naturally associated with each human subgroup (*Pol.* I 5, 1254b27–32; I 13, 1260a9–14). However, insofar as all of these subgroups are natural subclasses of humans, they will exhibit some general morphological and psychological similarities, e.g. they will all be bipedal, capable of articulate speech (*logos*), capable of feeling emotions like anger and fear, and, most importantly, capable of some degree of rationality and virtue.

In addition to exhibiting different functional levels, Aristotle's conception of human nature is also hierarchical: some subgroups are naturally

236   JOSEPH KARBOWSKI

better than or superior to others (*Pol.* I 5, 1254b13–14).[51] Natural rulers, for instance, are superior to natural slaves and women, both because their architectonic function is more noble than the subordinate functions of the latter, and also because the rational activities that they can perform are better than those of the latter. Since natural slaves and women lack certain desirable faculties or abilities possessed by the natural rulers, they can be considered 'less perfect' (*atelestera*) than their ruling superiors. But it should be stressed that we lose much of the richness and complexity of Aristotle's conception of human nature if we solely or exclusively view natural slaves and women as departures from a single norm set by freeborn male natural rulers. Undoubtedly, in Aristotle's view natural slaves and women do fall short from natural rulers in certain respects; but they, nonetheless, constitute their own natural, and hence normative, kinds, with their own peculiar standards of virtue and goodness determined by their specific roles in the polis.

This is by no means an exhaustive or complete treatment of Aristotle's view of human nature. Many important topics from the *Nicomachean Ethics* and *Politics* have been intentionally omitted from this discussion. But, at the very least, the current chapter suggests that Aristotle does not simply view our political nature as the gravy on top of our rational nature: the two are intimately connected and mutually informing. The influence of our rationality on our political nature is clear from the beginning of the *Politics*. Aristotle's explanation of why the polis is a natural community and one for which we are naturally constituted crucially depends upon its status as the community that best enables us to achieve happiness (*Pol.* I 2, 1252b27–1253a4), which, as we know from the *Nicomachean Ethics*, is a rational perfection. Consequently, the nature of the rational perfection that constitutes happiness will have an important influence upon the structure of the polis or at least its ultimate end. The foregoing, however, has brought to light that the arrow of influence does not only run in this one direction. As we saw above, our political nature impacts the way that rationality is distributed throughout the species. If we were solely rational animals, not rational animals constituted for life in a polis, then nothing would prevent every human from possessing the rational faculties necessary

---

[51] Compare Schofield's (1990, 21) astute observation that the notion of a natural hierarchy informs Aristotle's conception of natural rule in the *Politics*. My interpretation is consistent with his claim that Aristotle recognises distinct forms of natural rule because 'there is a great variety of deliberative capacities among human beings' (Schofield 1990, 21). In fact, the current chapter essentially develops that proposal by explaining why, according to Aristotle, there are natural rational differences among human beings.

Political Animals and Human Nature in Aristotle's Politics 237

for achieving happiness; but, since we are essentially rational, political animals, a diverse array of rational abilities is necessary. Although there is much in Aristotle's conception of human nature that we cannot nowadays accept, e.g. his defence of natural slavery, the subjection of women, and the restriction of happiness to a select few, we can still marvel at the complexity, ingenuity, and internal consistency of his theory.

CHAPTER 12

Political Animals and the Genealogy of the Polis: Aristotle's Politics and Plato's Statesman

David J. Depew

1 From *Statesman* to *Politics*

In *Politics* I 2, Aristotle claims that *anthropos* is a political animal (*zōon politikon*) and that indeed human beings are 'more political animals than any kind of bee or any herd animal' (*Pol.* I 2, 1253a2–9).[1] These propositions serve as premises in his genealogy of the *polis* as natural in the same chapter. Accordingly, an appropriate test of what Aristotle means by *zōon politikon* is afforded by whether from a proposed definition his genealogy of the *polis* can be derived. The question is not about this or that *polis* or constitutional form, but about the *polis qua* form of association or community (*koinōnia*). We know this because, in *Pol.* I.2, Aristotle portrays the *polis* as the *terminus ad quem* of a natural process of social complexification, differentiation, and integration from less complete but intuitively natural forms of association: households and villages (*Pol.* I 2, 1253b15–28). But why not end up with a more cosmopolitan form of association than the Greek *polis*? Why not a nation state? Why not a world state? To determine what makes the *polis* the most authoritative, comprehensive, and complete association, as Aristotle calls it (*Pol.* I 1, 1252a4–6), it seems we need a contextually relevant conception not only of *zōon politikon*, but also of *polis*. A deficient definition of either is likely to lead to defective conceptions of the other, leaving it even more doubtful whether Aristotle's conclusion can be shown to follow from his premises. Valid and sound inference is hostage to semantics in just this way.

It is easy to go wrong on both counts. We might, for example, imagine the *polis* to be a form of association whose *raison d'être* depends on chipping in something of one's own in order to meet shared economic and military needs, and whose stability over time is ensured by fairly distributing offices whose powers would otherwise be abused. This is not

---

[1] Translations from *Politics* are from Lord (1984), sometimes with minor variations.

238

Aristotle's Politics and *Plato's* Statesman 239

an odd notion. In fact, it is our own idea of the state *qua* commonwealth. However, it fails as an interpretation of *Pol.* I 2. For one thing, Aristotle explicitly repudiates it. The *polis*, he writes, 'is not a partnership in a location and for the sake of not committing injustice against each other and of transacting business' (*Pol.* III 9, 1280b29–32). For another, this interpretation defines 'political animal' in terms of an accessible capacity for rational choice it is assumed individuals already possess, whether they enter into political association or not. Even when it is evoked or propelled by a natural inclination (*hormē*) (*Pol.* I 2, 1253a30), taking *zōon politikon* to refer to a preexisting psychological capacity for deliberative choice turns humans into the only political animals, reducing the modes of communication and role division among bees and other species (to which Aristotle alludes in 1253a9; *HA* I.1.488a8) to metaphorical projections of what properly belongs to rational deliberators alone.[2]

The line of interpretation under consideration also makes the *polis* look suspiciously like forms of political organisation that we ourselves often take to be as unsurpassable as Aristotle judged the *polis* to be. The approach correctly portrays the *polis* as differing from an alliance by its permanence and subjection to law, but it also paints it as more contractual and artificial than Aristotle allows, and insufficiently distinguishes its formation from constitution giving. In its openness to inalienable rights and enforceable laws, it calls on justice more than friendship to form lasting bonds between citizens.[3] Thomas Hobbes was a good enough interpreter of Aristotle to realise that a contractual state can more surely be derived by regarding humans as naturally solitary than naturally political.[4] Still, Hobbes may not have realised that the *polis* is not a state, a post-Mediaeval concept of which he was an early theorist.

It also matters what we mean by 'derive'. In the contractual model familiar from early modern political theory, a genealogy of the state depends on psychologically recapitulating and evaluating the reasoning by which an ideal deliberator decides to enter into political affiliation. Aristotle's method is not at all like this. It depends on conceptual clarification of key terms by dialectical ascent (*epagōgē*) to essential definitions and,

---

[2] See Depew (1995).
[3] Miller (1995) is a heroic attempt to make Aristotle into a theorist of the modern state *avant le lettre*. The concept of rights is central. Miller usefully distinguishes between rights as claims on others that arise in and through relationships from the abstract duty-free 'natural' rights that in modern political theory belong to individuals prior to any relationships into which they enter. If Aristotle has a theory of rights it will certainly be the former kind.
[4] Hobbes, *Leviathan*, 1651, Ch. XIII.

if they survive scrutiny by putative counter-examples, using these definitions to resolve questions proper to a field of inquiry (*apodeixis*). In this respect, Aristotle both follows and departs from Plato. In the late dialogues, which reflect discussions in the Academy when Aristotle was making his bones there, Plato relies on dichotomous division to arrive at definitions. Aristotle does not do away with the method of division, but he does reform it in accord with his most distinctive contribution to Academic debates: testing proposed definitions by means of rules set down in *Topics*.[5] By using these rules, propositions purporting to be definitional can often be shown to be either predicates of a subject or biconditionals that are only incidentally universal – *idia*, such as *anthropos* as laughing animal – rather than essential and so fruitful of explanation.

Aristotle subjects Plato's dialogues to severe criticism by use of this weapon. In doing so he habitually excises claims from their dramatic context and ignores the fact that the interlocutors in Plato's dialogues frequently revise or abandon defective definitions as a dialogue proceeds. The bloodless way in which Aristotle does this may leave an impression that his approach is unfair to Plato, and not dialectical at all. The first accusation is fair, but the second is a misconception. In the first books of many of Aristotle's treatises we are treated to an ascent towards essential definitions by mapping the controversies of predecessors. Even when these are missing, a keen interpretive ear will sense a thick intertextual dialogue, permeating not only the ascent towards definitions, but also demonstrations from them, which Aristotle insists must make sense of common sense sayings and the opinions of the reputedly wise (*endoxa*) if airy hypothesising is to be avoided.

Politics is a case in point. In its first chapter, Aristotle criticises the inadequacy of the successive dichotomous divisions in Plato's *Statesman* for distinguishing between, and hence defining, slave master (*despotēs*), household manager (*oikonomikos*), statesman (*politikos*), and king (*basileus*).[6] This is a theme-setting text, to be sure, but it is not the only passage from *Statesman* to which he nods. At *Pol.* I.2, 1252a7–9 he refers to Plato's characterisation of humans as herd animals at *Statesman* 261D and, alluding to his own differentiation between political and (merely) herdlike behaviour at *Historia Animalium* I.1, 488a8, says that *anthropos*

---

[5] This method is the only contribution to Academic inquiry about which Aristotle overtly brags (*SE* 34, 184b1–10).

[6] *Pol.* I 1, 1252a9–11; *Statesman* 258e. I address whether Aristotle misconstrues Plato's claim, which is restricted to whether these four sorts of rulers possess the same *science*, in the final section.

Aristotle's Politics and *Plato's* Statesman 241

is a political animal, a *zōon politikon*. This difference, I will show, supports Aristotle's claim in *Pol.* I.2 and in *Pol.* I as a whole that economic role-division within households, not exchange between them, as in Plato, is the locus of the division, differentiation, and definition that leads to and culminates in the *polis*. The shadowy presence of Aristotle's critical encounter with *Statesman* is also at work in his treatment of citizenship and kingship in *Pol.* III, 7, in the six-fold model of constitutions he commandeers from his former mentor (*Statesman* 302c–d), and in other passages.

In this chapter I will reconstruct key arguments of Aristotle's political theory as a dialogue with *Statesman* more basically than with *Republic* or *Laws*. I do so in part to suggest that, even if it incorporates texts from various periods and was assembled by an editor, *Politics* is more argumentatively integrated than is sometimes alleged. More importantly, I hope to show that viewing *Politics* in this light clarifies why Aristotle takes the *polis* to be the most authoritative, comprehensive, and complete of all human forms of association (*Pol.* I 1, 1252a4; b28). His reason lies in the naturally end-like character of shared leisure-time activities (*Pol.* VIII 3, 1338a23–31). Only in the *polis*, Aristotle thinks, can religious festivals, artistic performances, practices of reflective criticism, and all forms of systematic inquiry appear as 'the very purpose and flower of associated life'.[7] Even if we didn't have to in order to survive, we would take delight in associating with one another for these purposes. 'It was on this account', Aristotle writes, 'that marriage connections arose in *poleis*, as well as clans, festivals, and the pastimes of living together' (*diagōgē en tē scholē*).[8] His argument is that the *polis* alone, for detailed reasons I will review, can make the enjoyment of leisure not only possible for all citizens, but by ensuring economic self-sufficiency makes leisure the very point of *polis* life. Accordingly, he concludes that 'the *polis* does not exist only for the sake of living (*zēn*), but living well (*eu zēn*)' or, happily, the most endlike of ends (*Pol.* III 9, 1280a30–32). After reviewing why he does not believe Plato's political theorising adequately captures these points, I will reflect on the extent to which forms of political association that have arisen since Aristotle's time are capable of endorsing and supporting the hierarchy of lived values he finds in the *polis*. I end by raising objections to my interpretation and saying something about Aristotle's philosophical anthropology.

---

[7] *Pol.* VII 3, 1338a23–31, quoting *Odyssey* IX 5–6.
[8] *Pol.* III 9, 1280b36–37; VII 14, 1333a35–36; VII 15, 1334a37–38.

242   DAVID J. DEPEW

2 Political and Herd Animals

At *Statesman* 260c, Plato identifies the art of governing human beings (indiscriminately called kingship, statesmanship, or the royal art) as acting by giving orders. Discussion thereupon turns to those to whom orders are given. The inquiry proceeds by way of successive dichotomous division. The beings governed are, as a first pass, said to be living rather than inanimate (261b–c). Ruling over animate beings is identified with the art of animal husbandry, which in turn is divided into husbandry over single animals and animals in herds (261d). The royal art is aligned with governance over herds. Herd animals having been divided into tame and the wild, the art is then identified with governance over herds of tame animals. Since herd animals, both domesticated and wild, can also be divided into land, water, and air-dwelling species by reference to means of locomotion – land animals have feet, water animals fins, birds feathered wings – the art of governing converges on tame land-dwelling and, hence, footed herd animals. These are then divided into four- and two-footed kinds. Domesticated or tame species of four-footed animals are said to have horns while those with two legs are hornless (267c). We are hornless and two-footed. Some two-footed species have cloven feet, and some are whole-footed. We are whole-footed. To ensure that the wielder of the royal art does not govern whole footed hornless bipedal domesticated animals that forage in flocks – some birds – it is at last determined that the king or statesman rules over featherless two-footed whole-toed hornless tame herd animals that graze on land (267d).

   Aristotle is not the only philosopher to protest that this procedure is rife with mistakes of the sort against which he warns in *Topics*. Diogenes the Cynic famously, if characteristically performatively, refuted Plato's definition of man by tossing a plucked chicken over the wall of the Academy. Many Academics addressed the issue, among them Plato's nephew (and by nepotistic succession the Academy's second director) Speusippus. Aristotle's own solution is most fully worked out in relation to the task he set himself in the *Historia Animalium* and in the *Progression of Animals* of describing the variety of animal traits and explaining their distribution to animal kinds by reference to what is needed to conduct their distinctive forms of life. His appreciation of zoological complexity leads him to see that successive dichotomous division is prone to confusing predication with definition, making too much of correlations that are at best incidental, encouraging cross-classifying practices that break up natural groups, and identifying final differentiae that are often of subordinate importance

Aristotle's Politics and Plato's Statesman 243

with the essence of a kind.[9] Aristotle's biological realism also makes it obvious to him that you cannot treat the absence of a trait, such as wing*less* or horn*less*, as a trait. You can't divide through nothing and call it something.[10]

The proper procedure, Aristotle says, is first to conduct an exhaustive survey of all animal traits and sort them into types: morphological (*moria*), characterological (*ethē*), behavioural (*praxeis*), and ways of making a living (*bioi*) in terrestrial, aquatic, and aerial environments (as well as 'dualising' combinations of them, such as the eponomously amphibious *bios*) (*HA* I 1, 486b5–487a28). Each type may then be divided into subtypes, sometimes dichotomously. Footed animals, for example, may be cloven or whole footed. But, traits of various types cannot be ordered into a concerted line of successive divisions, whether dichotomous or not, without running a large risk of violating *Topics*'s rules of predication. 'The tame or the white is not a differentiation of feathered', writes Aristotle, 'but begins another line of differentiation and is incidental here' (*PA* I 3, 643b22–24). To see how and why fine-grained traits from all four types are distributed to and combined in each animal kind, you must determine from field experience the role each trait plays in sustaining the distinctive life form of each kind.[11] Aristotle is a biological teleologist because he is a biological functionalist. His reform of division enables him to avoid the fallacies that inevitably creep into long repetitive dichotomous divisions and to focus on what is truly distinctive of and so essential to a kind. To this end he stipulates that traits are to be given functional explanations at the highest level at which they are convertibly shared. Eagles have wings because they are birds, not because they are eagles. By the same token, it is not because they are eagles that they have clawed feet and sharp eyes, but because they are birds of prey.[12]

The doctrine of *HA* and *PA* bears directly on *Pol.* I.2. In *HA.* 1.1, Aristotle divides modes of animal activity (*praxeis*) into solitary (*monadikos*), scattered (*sporadikos*: disbursed into small isolated families or clans), living in herds (*agelaios*), and political (*politikos*) (*HA* I 1, 487b32–488a4). Political activity is a differentia of herd behaviour (488a2). In contrast to patterns in which members of a herd, flock, or school of fish all do the same things in close proximity to one another, political behaviour is

---

[9] *PA* I 2, 642b10; 643b10–16; 3, 643b13–16; 644b2–8.   [10] *PA* I 2, 642b22, 643a6.
[11] *PA* I 5, 645b2–46a4, echoed at *Pol.* IV 4, 1290b25–36 with respect to types of political constitution.
[12] See Lennox (2001b, 39–71) for an informed analysis of these procedures.

244   DAVID J. DEPEW

predicated of kinds whose subgroup and individual behaviours contribute different things to a work (*ergon*) that is, nonetheless, 'one and common' (*hen kai koinon*) (488a7). Aristotle goes on to divide political animals into leaderless or anarchic (ants, for example) and those that require governing (bees, for example, who in Aristotle's [and Plato's] quaintly sexist view live under a king) (*HA* I 1, 488a10–13; *Statesman* 301e). Humans are political animals of a governed sort. All (and perhaps only) political animals possess means of communication to facilitate and coordinate their cooperative role-division. What is distinctive about *anthropos* is communicating through articulate discourse (*logos*) rather than mere sound (*phonē*) (or scent, as we now know to be true of ants) (*Pol.* I 2, 1253a11–15). Upright bipedal posture, among other features, is functionally derived by hypo-thetical necessity from this difference-making, reference-establishing trait (*PA* IV 10, 686a27–31).

In the light of this division, Aristotle regards Plato's claim that human beings are herd animals as a mistake. The mistake is set afoot by the notion that, before the present age, humans were under the direct care of gods who governed them as shepherds govern sheep. 'A god tended them, taking charge of them himself, just as now human beings, themselves living creatures, but different and more divine, pasture other kinds of living creatures more lowly than themselves' (*Statesman* 271d). It is acknowledged at a later point in the dialogue that, now that the gods have fled, humans are in charge of their own affairs and, hence, that governance rests on the willing assent of the ruled (274d, 276e). True enough. But Plato's way of deriving this important proposition is insufficiently self-corrective to lead the interlocutors in *Statesman* to call into question their earlier decision to treat humans as herd animals when they hit upon human freedom, which requires that we cooperate in our own governance. Plato's weakness for treating myths as starting points, which Aristotle does not share, is part of the problem. But more fatal is having antecedently failed to survey and subdivide all the *differentiae* of animal activity. According to Aristotle, not having done so leads Plato's characters to move too quickly from herded to governed. They miss role-divided political behaviour as a distinct differentia. As a result, citizens are treated as herd animals to which other properties, some quite accidental, have merely been added. Sheep-like beings who agree, or by threats can be made to agree, to follow a shepherd-like ruler are still sheep-like. Shepherd-like rulers who govern them are still shepherd-like. The mistake is akin to Aristotle's complaint in *Pol.* I.1 that Plato's *Statesman* underdifferentiates masters of slaves, heads of household, statesmen, and kings by his merely quantitative

Aristotle's Politics and *Plato's* Statesman

measure of how many people they govern (1252a12–13). Since the art of the *politikos* is the very thing for which the interlocutors in *Statesmen* profess to be looking, these mistakes are not trivial.

It is true that from Plato's *Republic* to Cicero's *De Re Publica* the standard remedy for treating the *polis* too contractually (as Glaucon treats it in *Rep.* I, for example) has been to characterise human beings as naturally gregarious.[13] For Aristotle that is not enough. In *Nicomachean Ethics*, he pointedly remarks that, 'In the case of human beings what seems to count as living together (*suzein*) is community in speech and thought, not sharing the same pasture, as in the case of grazing animals' (*EN* IX 9, 1170b10–14). He expresses contempt for the many as 'slavishly preferring a life fit for grazing animals' (*EN* I 5, 1095b16–20). His complaint is predicated on his claim that humans are naturally political, not naturally herd animals. The implications are many.

3 The Natural History of the *Polis*

It is impossible not to see Aristotle's so-called zoological definition of political animals at work in *Pol.* I 2. In recounting the genealogy of the *polis*, he begins with two behavioural traits (*praxeis*): permanent monogamous mating – solitary animals, in contrast, have a hit-and-run approach to reproduction – and securing a stable food supply for oneself, one's mate, and one's offspring by using domesticated animals and slaves. (Aristotle quotes an *endoxon* in which Hesiod remarks that, for poor but free people, an ox takes the place of a slave (*Pol.* II 2, 1252b10–11). Both relationships involve cooperative role division, but fusing them intensifies it. By saying that the household is the first (*prōtē*) community that comes to be when the first communities (*prōtē koinōniai*: man–wife, master–slave) are permanently combined, and by stating explicitly that something is what it is (and can be seen *as* what it is) 'only when its full state of development has been reached' (*Pol.* I 2, 1252b30–34), Aristotle signals that the household can be adequately differentiated from other associations only when it has reached a condition in which man–domestic animal, master–slave, husband–wife, and parent–child relationships have come to be distinguished from each other by the assignment of functional roles, distinctive

---

[13] Schofield (1999, 184). I avoid translating *agelaios* as 'gregarious' because it gives an impression that flocking, schooling, or congregating is an animal disposition (*ethē*) like fierce or timid rather than a behavioural pattern (*praxis*). By the time of Cicero that is what it had become and has largely remained.

246 DAVID J. DEPEW

communicative abilities, and various kinds and degrees of moral and intellectual virtue to each relationship and partner (*Pol.* I 13, 1260a1–19). Role-dividing developments within the household not only mark off the household, but the *polis* as well.[14] Only when heads of households cease to be confused with slave masters can they appear in public as free and equal citizens who are capable of deliberating about the common advantage (*koinon sympheron*) for the constituent households that make the *polis* a self-governing transgenerationally linked community (*Pol.* III 6, 1279a17–22).

Aristotle makes these seminal points by comparing the *polis* to the often much larger and superficially more powerful social structures of the Middle East. There, he says, 'The woman holds the same rank (*taxis*) as the slave' (*Pol.* I 2, 1252b4–9). This is telling insofar as a lack of role differentiation within the household means a lack of role division beyond it. There are no citizens in barbarian kingdoms, because they are all slaves of despotic rulers. There are no heads of households or rulers of *poleis* either. The two have not been sufficiently differentiated to have distinctive functions. Aristotle thinks that the difference between *poleis* and the large urban agglomerations of Asia implies that the differences between slave and master, head of household, statesman, and king must rest on something more than numbers ruled. For Plato even to have suggested this weak criterion casts doubt on his ability to give a satisfactory genealogy and, hence, definition of the *polis*. His quantitative definition blurs the qualitative difference between 'a large household and a small *polis*', rendering suspect his judgements about both (*Pol.* I 1, 1252a12–13).

We should suspend our ideological objections to Aristotle's views about women and slaves and his culturally biased ethnography just long enough to appreciate the conceptual sophistication of this analysis. In their haste to laud the freedom and personal distinction available in the public sphere, readers of Aristotle as insightful as Hannah Arendt are too quick to construe the household as a realm of despotism and violence.[15] In fact, Aristotle makes women deliberative partners in raising children to be citizens and wives of citizens (*Pol.* I 13, 1260a15), just as in *Generation of Animals* (*GA*) they play a greater role in reproduction than feminist critics often assume.[16] Similarly, he insists that slaves are not like dumb beasts, who respond only to blows and commands, but in the household context possess a modicum of moral virtue, because they share in

---

[14] See Karbowski (Chapter 11, 226–34) for further discussion of role divisions in the *polis*.
[15] Arendt (1958).   [16] See Connell (2016) for a correction.

Aristotle's Politics and Plato's Statesman 247

discursive speech, to the extent of being able to hear and heed it (*Pol.* I 5, 1254b21–24). *Logos* permeates communicative activity in the household as much as in the public sphere. If it didn't, there would never be a *polis*.

Aristotle's analysis makes clear the efficient and final causes that lead to the *polis*. The process of role differentiation and integration is driven by an all-too-real quest for economic self-sufficiency (*autarkeia*). Appreciating this imperative might be thought to unleash an impulse for associations larger, more economically diversified, and more militarily powerful than the *polis*.[17] But to think this way is to ignore a key claim of *Politics*: Economic self-sufficiency is reliably achieved only through public deliberation of the sort conspicuously missing in cancerously self-replicating but politically primitive aggregations like Babylon, which Herodotus tells us was endemically open to subversion, attack, and conquest because of its lack of public-spiritedness.[18] Aristotle contends that in the sorts of households that are constituent parts of the *polis*, the extremes of hand-to-mouth provisioning and luxurious consumption are replaced with a supply of consumables reliable enough, abundant enough, widely enough shared, *and limited enough* to shift the point of association from the compulsive pursuit of 'bare life' (*zēn*) to the cultivation of virtues, both ethical and intellectual, that enable citizens to 'live well' (*eu zēn*) in leisure.[19] These norms can appear clearly only in the discursively free space of rational deliberation by assembled citizens whose power to conceptually grasp and discursively use the means-end distinction leads them to tailor wealth to whatever mean quantity facilitates the choice of peace over war and leisure over labour (*Pol.* VII 14, 1333a30–b4). 'People consider any amount of virtue to be enough, but wealth, commodities, power, reputation, and all such [external goods] they seek to excess without limit', Aristotle writes. '[But contrary to what the many may think] ... humans do not acquire and safeguard the virtues by means of external things, but the latter by means of the former' (*Pol.* VII 1, 1323a35–b1). In *Pol.* VII–VIII, he argues

---

[17] We should not overly identify the *polis* with urbanisation. In the ancient world, production was overwhelmingly agricultural and *poleis* included their hinterlands as a well as their urban centres. Many families had homes in both *chora* and *astu*. Athens had an exceptionally, even suspiciously, large urban population, but the eight or nine hundred distinct *poleis* that we can identify typically had populations of no more than two or three hundred families (Nagle, 2006). Aristotle mentions rural Arcadia as an *ethnos* (nation) composed of reproductively linked villages that may or may not be in the process of becoming a *polis*, with Megalopolis as an emerging centre (*Pol.* II 2, 1262a27–29).

[18] *Pol.* III 3, 1276a29–30; VII 7, 1327b27–28; Herodotus, *Histories* I 181, 191. Aristotle's jaundiced fourth-century eye would doubtless have fastened on Herodotus' mention of dancing and feasting while their city was being attacked as evidence of the preoccupation of Asian barbarians with the life of enjoyment. A society that conceives leisure only as pleasure seeking cannot really be a *polis*.

[19] *Pol.* I 2, 1252b27–30; 8, 1256b30–32; III 6, 1278b17–26; 9, 1280a31–33; VII 2, 1325a7–10.

248   DAVID J. DEPEW

that legislators should take as their highest priority devising shared forms of education that lead the young to internalise this hierarchy of values (VII 14, 1333b3–4; VIII 3, 1338a23–31). What makes fully role-differentiated households – what Brendan Nagle has called '*polis*-households'[20] – the constituent elements of the *polis* are that values adopted in the public sphere feed back into the process of *logos*-mediated role differentiation already at work within households. Before the end state of social differentiation has been reached, *polis* and *oikos* are too indistinctly differentiated to be defined. That is what happens in barbarian cities.[21] The *polis* is by definition prior to the household because only when role-differentiated social development has become proximate matter of the *polis* are households really households (*Pol.* I 2, 1253a19–25).

These insights lead Aristotle to locate the origin of the *polis* in the interactive emergence of the household and public sphere, not in exchange of goods and services. This is not to say that economics is ignored. In fact, Aristotle devotes a considerable amount of argumentation in *Pol.* I 8–11 to determining what forms of the art of provisioning (*chrēmatistikē*) are parts of household management (*oikonomikē*), what forms are auxiliary to it, and what forms are at odds with the ends of both *polis* and *oikos*. These questions are raised and answered, however, from definitions of *oikos* and *polis* that are prior to and, therefore, explanatory of them.

In *Pol.* II, Aristotle finds Plato's ideal states wanting by these standards. In *Republic*, Plato attempts, like Aristotle, to find the nature of the *polis* by 'observing from the beginning how something comes into being' (*Pol.* I 2, 1252a24–26). The difference is that, in *Rep.* II, Plato locates the dynamic of *polis* formation in exchange between craftsmen rather than role differentiation within households. Social complexification is set afoot when Socrates's preference for a simple *polis* consisting of a farmer, a weaver, a builder, a cobbler, and perhaps a few other craftsmen cannot withstand Glaucon's objection that more craft specialisations, and hence a larger population, are licensed on demand by the principle that each citizen

---

[20] Nagle (2006).

[21] Aristotle thinks things will stay this way because, in his Hippocratic-sounding approach to ethnography, the Asian climate, which he assumes to be fixed, does not generate social matter capable of *polis* formation. Unlike the barbarians of cold northern Europe, whose excess of spiritedness (*thymos*) prevents them from founding *poleis*, the barbarians of Asia are intelligent, but not spirited enough to act in accord with virtue (*Pol.* VII 7, 1327b23–30). Garver (2011) ascribes the natural slavishness Aristotle imputes to them to this deficiency, which affects how they use their intelligence. There lurks an implicit argument that, if true *poleis* have not already arisen in a geographical area, they are unlikely to do so. Aristotle's anthropology is limited in this and similar ways and feeds into what has been called 'Orientalism'.

should do only what he is good at, which all parties to the discussion adopt (*Rep.* 369d–70b; 372a–d). The same principle guides the transformation of what Glaucon invidiously calls a '*polis* of pigs' into a *polis* devoted to luxurious living, replete with beauticians, physicians, gourmet cooks, musicians, actors, and other purveyors of the entertainments that are presumed by default to be the only way of using leisure time (372e–73d). The resulting rise in population sets afoot a demand for more land, and hence for an offensive army to get it (372b3–74b). At this point, Socrates senses a glimmer of salvation. The principle of 'one person one job' requires the military to know how to recognise friend from foe, protecting the first and aggressively attacking the second (375b–e). Protecting fellow citizens means protecting them from their own desires as well as declining to offer a rich target to external enemies. Forthwith, the fevered city begins to reverse its expansionist dynamic and comes to resemble something closer to its initial condition. Consumption is trimmed back. Behaviour is controlled. Art is censored and turned from mere entertainment to moral ends. Eventually, these norms are inculcated and enforced by assigning rotational rule to a subclass of guardians trained in philosophy (473d–e). One may doubt, however, whether prescribed forms of leisure activity possess the reverence, spontaneity, and shared pleasure that Socrates praises in his first, simple *polis* (372a–c).

Aristotle was probably not the only Academic to suggest that Plato's would-be Kallipolis – beautiful *polis* – is not beautiful at all. The craftsmen are left wondering whether they are citizens or not. The guardians live in a barracks and are forbidden to own property, but, unlike philosophers, have no inclination to give it up. The philosophers must leave their life of study to rule over fellow citizens whom they disdain (*Pol.* II 5, 1264b15–25). The objection that this is not a happy *polis* is raised in *Republic* itself by Adeimantus (*Rep.* IV 419). Socrates' protestation that it was never his aim to make any class especially happy, but the *polis* as a whole, is blunted by Aristotle's remark that a *polis* cannot be happy if its citizens are uniformly unhappy (*Pol.* II 5, 1264b15–19).

It may have been in response to this and other objections recited in *Pol.* II that Plato's second best *polis*, the Cretan *polis* of *Laws*, was put forward as a 'second sailing'.[22] In the *polis* portrayed in *Laws* (and implicitly in

---

[22] A second sailing is proverbially a second-best alternative. It refers to the use of oars when wind is not available. Plato himself calls *Laws* a second sailing in this sense at *Statesman* 300c; Aristotle uses it the same way at *Pol.* III 13, 1284b19. In these passages there may be an allusion to Plato's ill-conceived and ill-fated second sea voyage to Sicily, with a view to imposing the regime of *Republic* on the Syracusans.

250 DAVID J. DEPEW

Statesman 300c) citizens rule themselves – an essential condition for personal happiness – but only under conditions of geographical isolation, relegation of long-distance traders to a port located away from the *polis* proper, confinement of retail merchants to a special *agora*, and, above all, the inculcation into the citizens of a seemingly timeless and unchangeable myth about the origin of the laws they are scrupulously to obey. These impersonal laws take the place of the guardians and philosopher kings of *Republic*, who are no longer targets of anyone's envy, wrath, or ridicule. Still, Aristotle rightly complains that constraint is the dominant *ethos* of Magnesia, the *polis* of *Laws*. Activity in accord with virtue, he says, is collapsed into the single, rather passive virtue of self-control (*sōphrosynē*) (*Pol.* II 6, 1265a27–36). Since for Aristotle happiness is dependent on, indeed consists of, practicing *all* the virtues, including virtues that govern the acquisition and free disposal of privately held wealth, one can readily see why he says that even though Plato tries to recognise the need for self-governance he 'gradually brings [the second *polis*] back to the other form, that is, to the *polis* of *Republic*, where seething class conflict is also controlled by not much more than *sōphrosynē* (1265a4–5).[23] In neither of Plato's ideal *poleis* is the cultivation of leisure activities treated explicitly as the community's end.

The fact that they both end in a condition of constraint, if not of thinly disguised force (*bia*), suggests that, for Aristotle, neither of Plato's ideal states reaches the *terminus ad quem* that uniquely marks off the *polis*. His diagnosis is that Plato misidentifies the sites at which social complexification takes place. For Aristotle the process ensues in the relationships (*koinōniai*) within the household, as we have seen. To be sure, Plato never denies that the household is affected by what goes on elsewhere. On the contrary, in what is arguably the greatest piece of social psychology ever written, *Republic* VIII–IX charts the bad effects of bad constitutions on domestic relationships, and in turn the effect of disordered households on further deterioration of the public sphere. For Aristotle, in contrast, the accent falls on well-managed households as potential sources of political renewal when constitutions go bad. A good householder can emerge from the private sphere to become a good citizen of a reformed *polis*. The household is a robust source of political agency.

Plato's failings can plausibly be viewed as arising from thinking of humans too much as herd and not enough as political animals. This claim

---

[23] On happiness, virtue, and external goods, including private property see *Pol.* VII 1–3; Depew (1991).

Aristotle's Politics and *Plato's* Statesman   251

is hard to miss in Aristotle's definition of the citizen in *Pol.* III 1 and in the discussion of statesmanship and kingship that ensues. This discussion resumes the analysis of the four forms of rule in *Statesman,* whose criticism Aristotle takes as his theme in *Pol.* I 1. Having considered how slave mastery and household management bear on what a *polis* is in *Pol.* I–II, Aristotle takes up the concepts of statesmanship and kingship in *Pol.* III. He begins with a concept that barely makes a ripple in Plato's texts: citizenship. Aristotle defines the citizen (*politēs*) as someone who 'has a share in public decision-making and offices' (*Pol.* III 1, 1275a22–23). It is remarkable that this critic of democracy takes citizenship in democracies to be paradigmatic of the very concept (1275b4–5). The point is to stress what is missing in Plato's political thinking: autonomous agency and cooperative role division in pursuit of a friendship-permeated *koinon ergon* that contrasts with the barely concealed envy and enmity of Plato's ideal *poleis.*

It can even be argued that the very concept of the citizen is not so much underarticulated in Plato's *Statesman* as missing. Just as the notion of a political animal is elided in the transition from herded to governed, the generative trait of citizenship is passed over in Plato's discussion of statesmen and kings. These mistakes have the same root: the *politēs* comes into view only through the notion of a *zōon politikon.* To be sure, except in democracies, active citizenship, and so statesmanship, is open to fewer people. But even the passive citizenship of the out-of-office citizen is construed as a reiterated act of consenting to being ruled by others on a rotational basis. Indeed, under conditions in which the constitution recognises the disproportionately superior birth, usable wealth and especially virtue of a class of aristocrats, a family dynasty, or a king, the citizen consents to being *permanently* ruled as the best way to find and achieve the *koinon sympheron* (*Pol.* III 6, 1279a17). Aristotle goes out of his way to put kingship in as positive a light as he can by making the citizen's choice the deciding factor in distinguishing king from tyrant. Eliding citizenship deprives Plato's preference for kingship, which Aristotle shares on the grounds that kings have the most situation-specific flexibility of its best arguments.

4 *Poleis,* Real and Ideal

Aristotle's portrait of a '*polis* for which we can (only) pray' (*Pol.* VII 4, 1325b38) in *Politics* VII–VIII solves what he regards as a lack of citizenly *philia* in Plato's ideal states, not only by declining to derive political union from craftsmen but also by barring them along with merchants from citizenship altogether. Farming is overwhelmingly dominant. It is to be

252   DAVID J. DEPEW

conducted by forcing slaves or *perioikoi*, who by luck have no claim on citizenship in virtue of ancestry, to do the actual labour. By luck, too, the remainder of the population is said to share free birth, virtue, and external goods so equitably that they may take turns ruling and being ruled without following agreed upon rules for sharing offices as elaborate as those in, for example, Aristotle's 'constitutional regime' *(politeia)*.[24] The result is a *polis* focused on the leisure pursuits described in *Pol.* VIII.[25]

I am not inclined to treat *Pol.* VII–VIII either as nostalgia for the olden days *(ta archeia, Pol.* III 4, 1277b2–3) or as a utopia that may someday come to pass, but as what it textually appears to be: a continuation of the conceptual analysis of the very idea of a *polis* in *Pol.* I–III.[26] This interpretation trades on Aristotle's perception that Plato's political theory begins with an already compromised ideal that conflates concepts that should be more finely differentiated, and so must inevitably resort to constraint to prevent further degeneration. In doing so, the happiness afforded by virtuous activity sufficiently equipped with wealth to use leisure well is checked. Commentators who praise *Politics* for the greater political 'realism' of its middle books – and they are legion, especially where Aristotle's alleged empiricism is played off against Plato's idealism – are tacitly thinking like Platonists. There is no reason to believe that Aristotle regretted the growth in modern times of material abundance, military might, or demotic claims on political participation, or held that constitutions that make correct use of a plethora of external goods – monarchies, aristocracies, or polities – are any less good than an imagined ideal *polis*, or believed that deviant constitutions cannot be reformed by political actors themselves. What determines the correctness of a correct constitution, and even the preference of one deviant constitution over another, is how it integrates whatever free birth, wealth, and virtue – all *prima facie* claims to participation in a political partnership – happen to be on hand at a particular time and place (*Pol.* III 13, 1283a23–42).[27] Politics is as subject to contingencies as any other sublunary phenomenon, but it is open to shaping by deliberated choice.

Constitutions are what turn the *polis* (as distinct from household and village) into *a* particular *polis* (III 15, 1286a13–16). (It is telling that the *polis* of *Pol.* VII does not have one, at least a written one.) In *Statesman*, the

---

[24] *Pol.* III 13, 1284b19–20; IV 6, 1293b33–34; V 7, 1307a7–9.   [25] Depew (1995).

[26] *Pol.* III ends at III 18, 1288b3–6 with an announced transition to *Pol.* VII–VIII. The so-called realistic books IV–VI delay the fulfilment of this promise.

[27] On this topic see Miller (1995).

Aristotle's Politics and *Plato's* Statesman   253

distinction between good and bad constitutions falls between lawfulness and its absence. Aristotle admits that lawfulness marks off *poleis* from alliances and other forms of association (III 4, 1292a32–34), but denies that it distinguishes correct from deviant regimes (III 17, 1288a1–3). Many types of democracy, an unnatural constitutional form, have laws, while the best kinds of kingship, a natural form, have few.[28] Instead, Aristotle redescribes Plato's matrix of constitutional forms in the vocabulary of his own account of the genesis and nature of the *polis*, a vocabulary that prominently includes terms based on what is natural (*kata physin*) and shared (*koinon*). Correct regimes are said to honour and pursue the *koinon sympheron* and are in accord with nature. Incorrect regimes serve the particular advantage of tyrants, oligarchs, or the populist element, the *dēmos*. They are against nature because just claims to political participation are ignored and repressed in them, undermining the common good and citizenly friendship. Aristotle's constitutional theory echoes his theory of the household when he says that there is a whiff of mastery and slavery in deviant constitutions (III 6, 1279a21–22). This is tantamount to claiming that the proper relationship between household and public sphere is eroded in *poleis* with deviant constitutions in ways that recall the condition of Asian urbanisations.

Beginning with the Hellenistic states of Alexander's successors, there have been political systems whose rulers prize, or at least wish to be seen as prizing, leisure activities as intrinsically worthwhile public goods, including the pursuit of scientific knowledge and the production and consumption of tasteful art. The Macedonian Aristotle was an influence on this fashion. Our own regimes institutionalise personal choice in the pursuit of happiness, but tolerate and sometimes even fund art and science, albeit in the hope that systematically acquired knowledge will eventually pay off economically and aesthetic sensitivity will foster ethical behaviour. The difficulty is ensuring that all citizens have enough education, income, and access to the means of communication to share in high-minded leisure pursuits. In the face of just claims to political participation, exclusion from citizenship is an unacceptable solution to this problem. Considerable effort, accordingly, must be devoted to preventing leisure from degenerating into mass entertainment. This is the role of public education. In this respect Aristotle's problems are our problems, and to that extent at least so are his ideals.

---

[28] *Pol.* III 15, 1286a10–15; IV 4, 1291b29–1292a1.

5 Objections and Reflections

My reconstruction of the conceptual core of *Politics* and its relationship to Plato's *Statesman* is open to an objection. I have assumed that Aristotle's promise at *Pol.* I 1, 1252a16–24 to follow 'the customary method' (*hyphēgēmenē methodos*) of analytically breaking down a complex object of inquiry into its least elements (*asyntheta*) in order synthetically to reconstruct it is consistent with, and carried out by, his effort in *Pol.* I 2 to 'observe how things develop naturally from their beginning' until they reach their defining end-state. But Peter Saunders remarks, 'Nothing in I.1 has warned us that the analysis of "smallest parts" is to be historical, in their "natural growth"'.[29] Eckart Schütrumph goes further. With the exception of *Pol.* I 2, the method of *Pol.* I is or is close to Plato's synchronic way of defining by division. Other mentions of 'customary method' in the *corpus* do not have diachronic overtones.[30] Could the received 'analytic-genetic' account of definition endorsed by W. L. Newman in his classic commentary,[31] largely on the warrant of *Pol.* I 2, express little more than too much eagerness to see *Politics* as a coherent whole and an entrenched habit of interpreting Aristotle in the long twilight of Hegel's developmental way of appropriating him?

By recovering the many references and allusions to Plato's texts, Schütrumph has admirably shown that the apple does not fall far from the tree.[32] What differences there are, however, are to my mind both systematic and important. In particular, my account interprets *Politics* in the light of Aristotle's *reform* of Plato's method of division. So viewed, there are developmental aspects in division and divisional aims in developmental trajectories.

The point can be made by looking at a text that at first glance appears inimical to it: Aristotle's series of dichotomous divisions in *Pol.* I 8–11 seems to use *Statesman*'s method to improve on Plato's treatment of economics at *Statesman* 288e–90b. Their aim is to distinguish between various types of property acquisition and exchange. Property acquisition (*ktēsis*) is said to be a proper part of household management (*oikonomikē*). It has two kinds: acquisition of slaves and provisioning (*chrēmatistikē*). Provisioning, too, has two parts: natural provisioning by animal husbandry and provisioning by exchange (*allagē*). Exchange, in turn, has two types: exchange aimed at redressing imbalances between use values directly

---

[29] Saunders (1995, 59) translation.   [30] Schütrumph (1991, 183).
[31] Newman (1887–1903).   [32] Ibid., 78.

Aristotle's Politics and Plato's Statesman 255

available to each householder or region (*metablētikē*) and commercial exchange using money. In turn, monetary exchange can be used either to redress excess and deficient use values across long distances (*kapelikē*) or to make money through charging interest (*obolostatikē*). These illuminating distinctions – arguably the origin of the science of economics – are not aimed at defining property acquisition, provisioning, or even exchange by identifying a final differentia at the end of a long series of dichotomies. On the contrary, Aristotle inveighs against the final money-to-money form that depends on charging interest as unnatural.[33] Instead, division increasingly separates practices that characterise regimes whose approach to production, exchange, and consumption is natural because they are parts of or auxiliary to household management from those that flourish unchecked in deviant constitutions. In this way, division tells an implied story of development towards a norm and of a path of deviation from it. If the developmental side is not as prominent in *Pol.* I 8–11 as it is in *Pol.* I 2 it may simply be because, in *Pol.* I 2, Aristotle is responding to Plato's developmental tale in *Rep.* II–III about how *poleis* emerge from exchange by telling a different story. The point of the implied developmental story about economics in *Pol.* I 8–11 is that Plato's division of exchange cannot reach its *terminus ad quem* because the inventory of traits on which it is based is as incomplete as his genesis of the *polis*. It is not so much that Plato's conception of the *polis* is at odds with Aristotle's, as that he doesn't possess well enough divided concepts to describe, reach, or endorse political ideals they share in principle.

It is reasonable to see *Politics* as conforming to Aristotle's reform of division in his zoological treatises. That reform has a descriptive and an explanatory side (see *HA* I 6, 491a7–14). The descriptive side consists of *HA*'s comprehensive inventory of finely divided traits. The explanatory side is devoted to finding in *PA* environmentally apt functions for these traits in animal kinds and in *GA* showing that these traits acquire their functions only if they emerge in and through an ontogenetic process of differentiation from an initially indeterminate beginning point.[34] If the proper order of development is disturbed, various degrees of malfunction ensue, which Aristotle generally conceives as usurpation of formal by material causes. Usurpations of this sort, which endorse Plato's reiterated disdain for usurpations of soul by body, are Aristotle's warrant for criticising improper subordination of superior to inferior partners in relationships throughout *Pol.* I. The claim that this model can apply to *poleis* only by

---

[33] *Pol.* I 10, 1258b1–7; Meikle (1995).   [34] *GA* II 1, 735a10–25; II 4, 739b34–740a1–24.

256   DAVID J. DEPEW

reducing politics to biology is a red herring. As Schütrumph notes, there is nothing essentially biological about this *methodos*.[35] It is prominently on display in the genealogy of poetic kinds in *Poetics* IV.[36]

A more puzzling issue concerns epistemology. Aristotle distinguishes four types of relationships in *Pol.* I 1, but not four kinds of knowledge of how to govern them. *Statesman* speaks of a single type of knowledge that is sometimes called *epistēmē* and at other times *technē*. So does Aristotle's *Politics*. It is telling that Aristotle does not compare the situation-specific sensitivity of the statesman to the way in which master weavers blend different threads of cloth together, as Plato does (*Statesman* 311b–c). That is not because he is indifferent to situation-specificity. He argues at *EN* I 2, 1094a26–b2 that knowing what crafts are to be practiced in a *polis* and how they are to be regulated cannot itself be a craft at all, even a super-craft, but situation-specific *phronēsis*: practical wisdom in its political form, which is neither *epistēmē* nor *technē* – not *epistēmē*, because *epistēmē* pursues knowledge for its own sake rather than for the sake of giving knowledgably informed orders; and not *technē*, because *technē* countenances steps undertaken for the sake of its products or outcomes rather than actions that are intrinsically noble apart from what does or doesn't result from them.

Aristotle's *phronēsis* places the emphasis on particulars, rather than generalisations. He could have made good use of it in accusing Plato of under differentiating the basic concepts of political science. Appealing to it would have made clear why he himself makes so much of qualitative differences between slaves, wives, children, fellow citizens, and royal subjects in contrast to Plato's quantitative *differentiae*; why he believes that situation-sensitive governance can never be technically applied *epistēmē*; why he insists in *Pol.* I 13 that governance, even of slaves (but not of craftsmen), depends on cultivating role-specific moral virtues in the ruled; and why, in *Pol.* VII–VIII, he intimates that the end-like leisure activities of the *polis* extend beyond entertainment and moral training to pursuing inquiry for its own sake.[37] But that's just the trouble. *Politics* does not make use of his *phronēsis* or closely related terms in *EN* VI. This fact may bolster the suggestion that Aristotle's political theory is not very different from Plato's; he too, it seems, makes use only of *technē* and *epistēmē*. Alternatively, it may suggest either that the epistemological *differentiae* of *EN* VI are already operative in how Aristotle uses *technē* and *epistēmē* in *Politics* or were subsequently elicited in part to make its argument more compelling. The fact that I have refrained

---

[35] See n. 30 above.   [36] Depew (2006).   [37] Depew (1991).

from making use of *EN* VI to explicate *Politics* suggests my sympathy with the second approach.

Interpreting *zōon politikon* as I have done is important in understanding Aristotle's metaphysics of the human person. In its absence, a capacity for participation in political life has for a long time been supposed to be something that all except ontogenetically damaged humans possess purely in virtue of membership in our species. A social pattern of action is replaced with an accessible individual capacity, even incipient urge, to live in states. To realise this *dynamis* an inner drive (often contrasted with Plato's external craftsmanship) is invoked to pull each of us towards our *telos*, thereby smuggling into a mere capacity a quasi-preformationist actualisation according to which a would-be citizen already lurks inside each of us, and simultaneously discounting the manifold actualisations of human politicality in the sense of *Pol.* I 2 that are always already at work in human communities of all sorts. One can hardly blame Aristotle's early modern critics for rejecting this 'Aristotelianism' in favour of treating humans as just what he denied they are: solitary animals. But they too were wrong, since they presupposed the abstract individualism that Aristotle's ontology of the human person rejects.

CHAPTER 13

The Deficiency of Human Nature
The Task of a 'Philosophy of Human Affairs'

Dorothea Frede

1 Introduction: The Problem's Background

The notion that human beings are imperfect in many ways and that their perfection requires special means is commonly associated with Plato rather than with Aristotle. Plato not only treats the objects of the material world as deficient copies of their immaterial and eternal models or 'forms' in general, but displays a pessimistic view of human nature in particular. It must, of course, remain forever a matter of debate in how far Plato shares the view about the poor natural endowment of human beings that he lets the famous sophist Protagoras pronounce in the dialogue he named after him (*Prot.* 320c–324d). But there are good reasons for assuming that Plato at least shared the sophist's diagnosis concerning the natural human endowment in two respects: (i) in comparison with other animals, humans are born in a particularly vulnerable state. They are, by nature, provided neither with food nor with cover nor with the means of self-defence: 'naked, unshod, unbedded, and unarmed' (*Prot.* 321c). According to Protagoras' myth, the poverty of human nature is compensated for only by the 'gift of Prometheus': it is the invention of fire and of certain crafts that ensures the provision of life's necessities. (ii) The Promethean gift of the crafts alone would have been insufficient to ensure the survival of the human race. The formation of communities, as a means of defence and mutual support, required Zeus's special gift of 'political art'. Without the notions of justice and shame, humans would inevitably have destroyed each other. Just like the technical arts, according to the myth in the *Protagoras*, the social arts are not part of the natural human endowment. Their development presupposes training and teaching over many years. It is a task that requires the joint efforts of the entire community.

There are no indications that Aristotle shared either of the two 'Protagorean worries'. He is not concerned with the poor natural endowment of humans, and he does not treat the political art as a 'supernatural gift' that separates humans from other animals. He does so neither in the texts that treat humans as integral parts of nature, nor in his biology, nor in the texts that focus on human affairs, nor in his ethics and politics. If Aristotle displays general confidence in the natural sociability of human beings, this does not mean, however, that he does not regard the ordering of political communities a difficult task.

What problems he sees and how he means to solve them is the topic of this article. The investigation consists of three parts. The first part will point to the reasons for Aristotle's trust in the natural sociability of human beings that makes Protagorean worries seem far-fetched.[1] The second part will discuss certain reservations that Aristotle expresses with respect to the natural sociability of human beings. The third part will investigate the special means that Aristotle regards as necessary to secure the fitness of humans for citizenship.

2 Human Natural Sociability

In contradistinction to Plato, Aristotle sees much more continuity than separation between humans and other animals. For Aristotle sometimes expresses the conviction that there is a kind of *scala naturae* that starts with the lifeless objects in nature, leads over to plants and animals, and ends with human beings. Thus, in *Historia Animalium* VIII 1, 588a4–18 he remarks that, because nature seems to proceed little by little (*kata mikron*), it is sometimes difficult, at first sight, to distinguish between lifeless objects and plants or between plants and animals, so that it is hard to make out exact lines of demarcation. What applies to plants and animals also applies to animals and human beings. In infancy, there is little difference between them, as far as their mental abilities and dispositions of character are concerned. This similarity has been emphasised by specialists in recent years. Animals not only have the technical and provisional skills to plan and organise their lives and to take care of their offspring, they also have character-traits that are very much like human characteristics, especially where the emotions are concerned, so that it seems justifiable to attribute to them at least the vestiges of the virtues of both character and intellect.[2]

---

[1] 'Sociability' is not understood, here, as mere gregariousness, but as the ability to actively participate in the political life of a community. There is no noun that corresponds to the adjective 'political'.

[2] Cf. the discussion in Lennox (1999b), who treats the difference between humans and animals as a matter of degree; a similar view is advocated by Leunissen (2015).

260 DOROTHEA FREDE

While Aristotle seems to assign only a very narrow range of emotions to animals in the *Nicomachean Ethics*, in the *Historia Animalium* he is much more generous. He attributes traces of all the emotions, that we find in humans, to animals, especially in children: 'so in a number of animals we observe gentleness or fierceness, mildness or cross temper, courage and timidity, fear or confidence, high spirit or low cunning' (*HA* VIII 1, 588a15–b, transl. Thompson). Aristotle also acknowledges there that animals possess intellectual abilities that resemble those of human beings:

> ... and with regard to intelligence, something equivalent to sagacity. Some of these qualities in man, as compared with the corresponding qualities in animals, differ only quantitatively; that is to say a man has more of this quality, and an animal has more of some other; other qualities in man are represented by analogous qualities: for instance, just as in man we find craft [*technē*], wisdom [*sophia*] and insight [*synesis*], so in some animals there exists some natural capacity akin to these. (ibid.)

Aristotle does not, of course, entertain any notion that the kinship he observes between natural beings is due to evolutionary processes. But the discovery of such kinship seems to have encouraged him to treat nature as a unity and to attribute principles of character to animals which are at least analogous to those that apply to human beings. Thus, all animals are active beings, and their nature expresses itself in the type of activities that are characteristic of them. To be sure, human beings are in a special position because they alone possess reason. But, with the exception of a few enigmatic references to the extraordinary status of reason in his biological works,[3] Aristotle seems to assume that the development of reason and intelligence is part of the natural endowment and development in human beings, and that reason sets in quite naturally at a certain age.[4] So, while the possession of reason puts man at the top of the animal kingdom, it does not exclude him from the realm of nature.

The continuity between humans and animals is not limited to the emotions and intellectual abilities. It also applies to the conception of man as a social or political animal, a *zōon politikon*. There are two points that deserve special attention. (i) Aristotle acknowledges that that there are other political animals besides man. (ii) Aristotle treats the *polis* as an

---

[3] According to *GA* II 3, 736b28, reason is the only divine element (*theion monon*) and is said to accrue to humans 'from outside' (*thyrathen*). That reason is said to come from outside is due to the fact that it is not contained in the semen and does not develop organically, for there is no organ of reason (ibid., 737a10). But, 'from outside' does not mean that it is bestowed by some supernatural power.

[4] According to *EN* VI 11, 1143b6–9 it is a matter of age (*hēlikia*).

The Task of a 'Philosophy of Human Affairs' 261

organisation that quite naturally evolves in the history of humankind. Both aspects are well known and have been much discussed. A brief review of those salient points will, therefore, suffice at this point.

(i) The conception of the 'political' is used without much elaboration at the beginning of the *Historia Animalium*, where Aristotle turns to the characterisation of the different ways of life that animals lead: He distinguishes between gregarious (*agelaia*) and solitary (*monadika*) animals, and then further singles out animals that have a 'political or social life' (*politika*). The criterion that marks the difference between the merely gregarious and the political animals is quite clear[5]: 'Political creatures are such that have some one common object/work in view [*hōn hen ti kai koinon gignetai pantōn to ergon*]. Such political creatures are man, the bee, the wasp, the ant, and the crane' (*HA* I 1, 487b32–488a12).

That is the gist of Aristotle's explanation of the 'political' character of certain animals. His further discussion of the way of life of the different kinds of political animals explains what the one common function (*ergon*) is: the animals live in unified self-preserving organisations. In the *Politics*, Aristotle adds that human beings are 'more political' than other political animals such as bees, because they are possessed of language. They can, therefore, distinguish and communicate about what is good and what is bad, what is just and what is unjust – and that this is what allows them to form households and city-states (*Pol.* I 2, 1253a7–18). But, while humans possess certain features that single them out from all other animals, their sociability is, nevertheless, a natural condition.

(ii) It should, therefore, come as no surprise that at the beginning of the *Politics*, Aristotle introduces the *polis* as the natural state in human life (*Pol.* I 2).[6] While the household secures reproduction and material survival, and the formation of villages is the natural extension of the family, it is the polis that is the natural aim and end of human sociability. It is only with the formation of the city-state that man reaches the fulfilment of his nature, because it is only the city-state that provides the state of 'autarky', so that humans not only can survive but attain the good life that is characteristic of their nature. Aristotle holds, therefore, that human beings who live apart from a *polis* for other than accidental circumstances must be either superhuman or subhuman creatures. Whether the 'superhuman

---

[5] For a thorough treatment of the textual and conceptual problem connected with this passage cf. Depew (1995). See also Depew (Chapter 12).

[6] 'Nature' (*physis*) and related expressions recur in almost every line of this chapter.

being' refers to the philosopher who leads a life more elevated than ordinary citizens is a question that will be briefly addressed later. The way Aristotle specifies the kind of 'subhuman' persons he has in mind, shows, at any rate, that he does not regard the existence of super- and subhumans as mere hypothetical possibilities. For the declaration that subhuman persons are particularly dangerous because they have weapons (*Pol.* I 2, 1253a32–34) indicates that Aristotle is not speaking about barbarians living far beyond the range of civilisation or about mythical creatures like Polyphemus, but has in mind gangs of pirates and marauding mercenaries who present a permanent threat, not only to travellers outside the city-borders, but also to small and badly defended communities.

For people within the 'human range', life in a city-state is the natural *telos*.[7] Why this should be so, and what the salient points of the 'autarky' of city-life are, Aristotle does not explain any further at this point. But he must have more in mind than the greater material diversity that is provided by a larger community. A *polis* is not just a community that satisfies more refined material needs on the basis of extended commercial exchange, as Plato first suggests in response to the objection to a minimal life in a 'city of pigs' (*Rep.* II 372d). The difference between 'mere life' and the 'good life' in the case of humans consists in the opportunity to develop and activate the human intellectual potential to the full. For man is not only a political but also a rational political animal. And it is the development of practical reason that depends in a significant way on communal life, as Aristotle's remarks about the importance of language (*logos*) indicate. The ability of human beings to form the concepts of good and bad, of just and unjust, is due to a natural predisposition. But that they do in fact develop them and employ them in the right way in their daily encounters is not predetermined by nature, but is the result of life in a sufficiently sophisticated community. The *polis* is, therefore, a community that provides the opportunity both to acquire and to employ the right conception of what it is to live a proper human life. This opportunity is twofold: it consists in the proper moral and intellectual education of the citizens, and in the chance to apply one's abilities within the community. The difference between man and beast is, then, not just a matter of degree. There is, rather, a deep divide between them. Animals are, by nature, incapable of obtaining happiness because they lack reason and, therefore, do not plan and

---

[7] Aristotle, similarly, speaks of the natural development of tragedy from early improvised beginnings to its full maturity (*Poet.* 4, 1449a9–19).

The Task of a 'Philosophy of Human Affairs' 263

organise their way of life in a conscious way. Nor do they acquire the virtues of character; for the development of such virtues requires practical reason. What organisation animals are capable of is conditioned by instinct, not by reason. That is why life in a beehive or in a flock of cranes functions automatically and is not based on decisions, even if their 'rulers' do exert a kind of 'foresight' for the whole. But what the *telos*, i.e. 'the good', for each type of animal consists in is determined by its nature, and the *telos* is attained in due course, if the external circumstances permit it.

3 The Limitations of Human Sociability

The appearance of a natural continuity between man and beast seems to speak for the assumption that there is a natural basis of Aristotle's ethics and politics, and, therefore, some interpreters presuppose that the fact that Aristotle attributes a natural function and *telos* to human beings speaks for a 'biologistic' foundation of his practical philosophy. But it takes little reflection to recognise that biological study and observations of human activities are not very informative, when it comes to determining the nature of the human good. For, while animals have a fixed way of life that they follow by instinct, so that it is possible to determine the natural way of life of a wolf or an elephant, of a dolphin or a sea anemone, no such fixed conditions exist in the case of human beings. As a closer look will show, there is no natural uniformity to the human *telos*, as there is in the case of other living organisms; and teleology is not a determining force, but only an explanatory principle.

There is, first of all, the fact that Aristotle regards as natural certain distinctions within the human species. Thus, he treats slavery as a natural phenomenon on the ground that slaves have no practical reason to take care of their own lives, and are, therefore, fit only for the kind of heavy labour that is an indispensable factor in human culture. The critique of Aristotle's extensive defence of the view that slaves are the natural property of their masters and represent no more than living tools (*Pol.* I 3–8) is not limited to the moral outrage that the justification of slavery provokes in Aristotle's readers. It also causes severe problems for his anthropology. For how can there be members of a species that do not share the essential and definitory property of that species, namely reason, and are, therefore, by nature incapable of a happy life? The different aspects of this theory have been dealt with by various authors in recent decades, and will be passed over here.[8]

---

[8] References are confined here to Schofield (1990), Smith (1991), Heath (2008), Karbowski (2013).

Women are also by nature not fit for citizenship proper, according to Aristotle. For, although they are born free and possess practical reason, they are supposedly unable to partake in politics because their *phronēsis* is limited and lacks political authority; it is *akyros* (*Pol.* I 12–13). The meaning and justification of this restriction is still a matter of controversy. The explanation, first introduced by Fortenbaugh in 1975, that women are incapable of controlling their emotions, still has its adherents.[9] But it overlooks the fact that women would thereby be depicted as natural acratics and incapable of virtue; for lack of control of one's emotion is the hallmark of *akrasia* (cf. *EN* VII 1, 1145b12). But, this explanation clearly contradicts the ascription of virtue to women in many places in Aristotle.[10] If Aristotle holds that women's practical reason 'lacks authority', it must be because he regards it as insufficient to rule over the household or to engage in public affairs.[11]

Slaves and women are not the only exceptions from the natural designation of citizenship. For, although Aristotle at first presents it as a matter of natural development that human beings not only live in families, but that families extend themselves to form villages, and that villages unite in city-states (*Pol.* I 2), he later admits that this development does not happen everywhere, but does so only under certain conditions. The proper order of a city-state is not settled by nature, nor is it attained on the basis of natural instinct and predispositions. It is based on human decisions and planning, and, therefore, it does not work automatically everywhere, as it does in the case of bees forming beehives. While in nature things happen either necessarily or for the most part (*hōs epi to poly*), there is no such regularity in the case of human nature.

For the ability to form cities is not distributed evenly by nature. The citizens of a polis must have certain qualities that are not shared by the inhabitants of all parts of the earth. Climate, according to Aristotle, makes a lot of difference. As he sees it, neither the nations of the earth's colder nor its hotter parts are able to form proper city-states (*Pol.* VII 7). The inhabitants of the cold parts of Europe allegedly are full of spirit (*thymos*), but deficient in intelligence (*dianoia*) and craft knowledge (*technē*). Though they remain free, they are 'unpoliticisable' (*apoliteuta*) (328a26) and incapable of ruling their neighbours. The people in Asia, on the other

---

[9] For a critical discussion cf. Deslauriers (2003; 2009).

[10] Cf. *EN* VIII 7, 1158a17–19; *Pol.* I 13, 1260b13–20 et pass. It also ignores the fact that *akyros* is never used in the sense of *akratēs*. On *akyros* cf. Frede (2018).

[11] Aristotle's distinctions between the kind of *phronēsis* and virtues required for the rulers and the ruled is a special topic. Cf. *Pol.* III 4, 1277b13–29.

The Task of a 'Philosophy of Human Affairs'   265

hand, the Persians, and perhaps also the Egyptians, have souls inspired by craft-knowledge and intelligence, but they lack spirit. They live the lives of slaves in permanence because they accept tyranny voluntarily: lack of spirit lets them accept life in a hereditary monarchy (*Pol.* III 14). It is only the Greeks who, thanks to their intermediary location, possess both the spirit and the intelligence that is necessary for the formation of city-states and the life of free citizens (VII 7, 1327b29–33).

But this condition is not fulfilled equally among the Greeks either (ibid., 1327b33–38). This concession is to account for the fact that the Greek city-states have quite different constitutions (*politeiai*: forms of government), a fact that is amply witnessed by the descriptions and critical discussions of the 'correct' and the 'deviant' forms of government that fill many of the books in the *Politics*. Comments on that multiformity must be kept at a minimum here, but there are no less than six forms of government in city states, three correct forms: kingship, aristocracy, and polity (a modified form of democracy), and three deviant forms: tyranny, oligarchy, and radical democracy. The criterion that separates the correct and the deviant forms of government is simple: the correct forms serve the common good (*to koinēi sympheron*); the deviant forms serve only the interest of the ruler or ruling class (*Pol.* III 6–7).

Finally and most importantly: Human beings are not by nature virtuous, nor do they develop their social qualities naturally with age, but they are ambivalent (*epamphoterizousin*), as Aristotle states near the end of the *Politics* (VII 13, 1332b1–11). They can turn to the better, but also to the worse, although some are by nature better endowed than others. But all humans require a carefully orchestrated moral and intellectual education, and training from infancy on, even in the best of cities. In addition, they require the right external conditions to apply their moral skills in a community that is organised in a sufficiently sophisticated way so as to provide them with the opportunity to acquire both the virtues of character and the virtues of the intellect. That is why Aristotle regards the ability to live in a polis as the *conditio sine qua non* of happiness and treats life in a city as man's natural *telos*. For it is only in a city-state that man can realise his best potential and reach his natural perfection ('the best').

But, while the three correct forms of constitution all serve the common good or advantage, none of them is identical with the *one*, the very best form that Aristotle has in mind when he speaks of the *polis* as the natural *telos* of human nature. That the common good is not necessarily identical with *the* human good is indicated by the remark that, although there are many different forms of city-states, there is 'only one that is by nature

266   DOROTHEA FREDE

everywhere the best' (*mia monon pantachou kata physin hē aristē*) (*EN* V 7, 1135a5). That this is just not an *obiter dictum* is confirmed by the fact that, in the *Politics*, Aristotle distinguishes between three kinds of 'best constitutions'. There is the best one, the 'city of our prayers' (*kat' euchēn*) (*Pol.* II 1, 1260b29–36), but that does not exist yet even among the well-governed cities. Besides the very best one, there is also the best constitution under normal circumstances, and there is the best under less than good conditions (IV 1, 1288b19–37). Aristotle justifies the need to study all these forms of constitutions, because it is the task of political science, just like it is in medicine and gymnastics, to study not just the best conditions, but also the less good conditions. But, as far as the quality of life in the city is concerned, he leaves no doubt that only the social life in the by nature best city will render human life perfect – and that that best city does not yet exist. That is why Aristotle not only discusses and criticises the conceptions of the best states by other authors at length in book II of the *Politics*, but also promises to present his own design of such a city, a task that he turns to in books VII and VIII.

To readers of the *Nicomachean Ethics* these reservations concerning all existing states may come as a surprise; for the discussion of happiness (*eudaimonia*) as the human *telos* suggests that the good, even the perfect life, is within human reach. The self-assured tone of the investigation of the human good in the *Nicomachean Ethics* seems not to leave room for doubts concerning its feasibility. Indeed, the *Nicomachean Ethics* start with a reference to a political 'master science of life' (*kyriōtatē kai malista architektonikē*) (*EN* I 2) which takes care of its order by providing the appropriate laws for the education and the conduct of the citizens and represents the target everyone should aim for.

The question is, then, whether Aristotle is about to provide the science that he introduces in such glowing terms, and whether he regards himself as its 'architect'. There are good reasons for denying that such are his intentions in the *Nicomachean Ethics*. For he clearly does not take on the task of providing the laws that order the life of the citizens, what they should learn, what they should do and abstain from. Instead, he indicates only in outline (*typōi*) what happiness is and what conditions it is based on: the different kinds of virtue and their opposites, the nature of friendship, of pleasure, and so on. In other words, Aristotle provides the philosophical underpinnings of such a master science, but not political science itself. That is the kind of 'help' he promises to give to the project of making human beings good (*EN* II 2, 1104a10f). That such are his intentions is confirmed by the fact that he repeatedly refers to particular points of

The Task of a 'Philosophy of Human Affairs' 267

interest for students in his audience with an interest in politics and legislation.[12] These references suggest that he expects those of his students with sufficient ability and ambition to acquire that science, to engage actively in politics and to apply, as far as possible, the results of his philosophical analysis of the conditions of the best life.

4 The Task of a Philosophy of Human Affairs and the Best Constitution

That Aristotle regards his philosophical work as only half done at the end of the *Nicomachean Ethics* emerges when he turns to the question of the education of the citizens and treats the guidance by good laws as the crucial factor in that respect (*EN* X 9, 1179b31–1180a5). For he assigns to the laws the authority not only to establish the rules and order in a city, but also to provide the right kind of moral habituation of the citizens from early age on and throughout their adult life (1180a5–1180b23). While Aristotle has so far analysed the concepts on which political science is based, he now turns to a practical question of fundamental importance: Who is to educate the legislators?

As it turns out, Aristotle shares Plato's pessimism with respect to the educators in the existing states, as expressed in the *Protagoras* (319b–320b) and the *Meno* (90a–94e). As Aristotle explains in terms that must be intentional reminders of Plato's contentions, political knowledge and virtue are not taught in any of the existent states (*EN* X 9, 1180b28–1181a24). For neither do the practitioners of politics know how to pass on their art to others, nor is it taught by the self-proclaimed teachers of politics, the sophists. The justification of Aristotle's verdict is also very much in line with Plato's critical assessment. Like Plato, Aristotle does not deny that there are gifted politicians, but claims that they act only on the basis of a certain skill and experience rather than by reason and principle; for they neither speak nor write about such matters. In addition, none of the gifted statesmen are able to make statesmen of their own sons or any of their friends – a thing one would expect that they should do if only they could. The sophists receive even worse grades than the politicians: they neither know what kind of thing politics is, because they have no experience in it, nor do they know what politics is about. Otherwise they would not put it at the same level as rhetoric or treat it as even inferior to it.

---

[12] Cf. *EN* I 3, 1095a2–6; 13, 1102a7–26; VII 11, 1152b1–3.

268   DOROTHEA FREDE

Though Aristotle shares Plato's pessimism about existent states, he clearly does not regard the matter as hopeless. For he treats the study of the constitutions and their laws as a programme of training for future statesmen with the proviso that, just as in the case of medicine, it is not sufficient to study written work, it is also necessary to acquire sufficient experience and judgement. The acquisition of such experience and judgement is not to come from an active engagement in politics. Instead, Aristotle refers to the 'collections of constitutions and laws' as the material that provides the adequate background for such study. They will provide students with the knowledge of what is good and bad about different constitutions and what enactments will suit what circumstances. The collections of constitutions and laws referred to are, no doubt, the collection of the constitutions of 158 city-states that Aristotle must have compiled with the help of various members of his school. Of that work that is mentioned in the ancient lists of his works,[13] only a fragment has been discovered in the British Library in the late nineteenth century: The Constitution of the Athenians. It is a clear witness to the thoroughness of the procedure. For it contains two parts: Its first part is an investigation into the history of the Athenian constitution, its second part analyses the institutions in Aristotle's own time.[14]

The very fact that Aristotle went to such lengths in collecting material for the study of legislation explains the role he assigned to himself with respect to the master science: He regarded himself not a legislator nor a statesman, but as the teacher and instructor of future legislators and politicians. This self-assessment is confirmed by the final section, which concludes the *Nicomachean Ethics*. There Aristotle deplores the fact that his predecessors have left the subject of legislation unexamined, and he promises to make up for that lack himself: 'It is best, therefore, that we should ourselves study it, and in general study the question of the constitution, in order to complete to the best of our ability the philosophy of human affairs' (*hopōs he peri ta anthrōpeia philosophia teleiothēi*) (*EN* X 9, 1181b12–15). And that completion, as Aristotle makes clear, is to come from a careful study of the subject of politics that he is going to provide for his disciples in his own *Politics*:

> First then, if anything has been said well in detail by our predecessors, let us try to review it; then in the light of the constitutions that we have collected let us study what sorts of influence preserve and destroy states, and to what

---

[13] Cf. Diogenes Laertius, *LEP* V 27, 1: 'Constitutions of 158 cities, in general and in particular, democratic, oligarchic, aristocratic, tyrannical'.
[14] Cf. Rhodes (1981).

The Task of a 'Philosophy of Human Affairs'   269

causes it is due that some are well and others ill administered. When these matters have been studied we shall perhaps be more likely to see with a comprehensive view, which constitution is best, and how each must be ordered, and what laws and customs it must use, if it is to be best. Let us make a beginning of our investigation. (ibid., 1181b15–24)

This concluding section of the *Nicomachean Ethics* is often not treated with the attention it deserves. Some commentators regard it as a mere bridge to the *Politics*, and some editors have even treated it as spurious.[15] One reason for suspicion is the claim that his predecessors have left the subject of legislation unexamined. For has not Plato devoted an overabundance of time to the laws in his *Laws*? And is not Aristotle's critical evaluation of Plato's and other authors' conceptions of the order of ideal states in *Politics* II a clear witness to the fact that the subject had not been left unexamined? Reflection shows why these objections are beside the point. Aristotle does not deny that others have reflected on the ideal forms of states, and he does not deny that Plato, in particular, has written extensively on that subject.[16] But neither Plato nor any of the other authors have engaged in an analysis of the basic principles of legislation as such, or investigated what laws will fit what types of constitutions. And that is a deficiency that Aristotle intends to make up for and indeed does make up for in his investigations of the different factors that preserve and destroy the different forms of constitutions in the *Politics*. For, as he sees it, that type of study will provide future legislators with the kind of experience that makes them capable of designing the laws that are suitable for the different kinds of community, including the best possible one.[17]

A further reason for suspicion concerns Aristotle's promise that the study of the principles of legislation will complete the 'philosophy of human affairs' (*hē peri ta anthrōpeia philosophia*), sometimes translated as 'the philosophy of human nature', as in Ross. The phrase is indeed peculiar, for linguistic as well as for factual reasons. First, the adjective *anthrōpeios*, instead of *anthrōpinos*, is rarely used by Aristotle.[18] Second, the construction *philosophia peri* plus the accusative, rather than the genitive, is unusual. There are, however, good reasons that justify that combination.

---

[15] Susemihl brackets it, in his 1887 edition; and Stewart (1892) expresses strong reservations in his commentary against it.

[16] In fact, Aristotle complains that Plato's *Laws* for the most part consists of laws (*Pol.* II 6, 1265a1).

[17] This explains why the *Politics* not only deals with the different types of constitutions, but also goes to great lengths to work out the factors that preserve and destroy even the deviant kinds of constitutions of radical democracy, oligarchy and tyranny in a more or less realistic manner, in the so-called empirical books IV–VI of the *Politics*.

[18] Manuscript Lb has the more usual '*anthrōpinē*'.

The adjective *anthrōpeios* is used by Aristotle twice elsewhere, in each case in contrasts to '*theios*'.[19] Third, there is a parallel to the *peri* plus accusative in the famous passage in the *Parts of Animals* I 5 that compares the elevated status of the study of the eternal and divine (*pros tēn peri ta theia philosophian*) with the pedestrian study of perishable plants and animals (645a4). Aristotle insinuates there that the scarcity of information on the heavenly objects is counterbalanced by the wealth of observations that are available in biology and by the fact that even lowly animals, like all things in nature, have their own beauty.[20] There is, then, no reason to suspect the phrase in *EN* X 9 that points out that ethics and politics belong to the same discipline and are the subject of a philosophical investigation.

Aristotle has good reasons to emphasise that he is concerned with a philosophy about 'things human', for this affirmation counterbalances the exalted role attributed to the theoretical life in the previous two chapters *EN* X 7 and 8. The contrast drawn there between the 'divine' happiness that consists in theorising only and the second-rate happiness represented by human occupations *prima facie* suggests that the secondary kind of happiness is not a subject worth a philosopher's attention. This is not the occasion for entering into the much debated question of why Aristotle makes such a sharp divide between the theoretical form of life and the second-rate practical human life, even to the extent that a theoretician will share common human concerns only to the degree that is necessary for his survival. But some suggestions concerning that piece of text are in order here.

That the text contains a distinction between the theoretical and the practical life is only in keeping with Aristotle's promise to discuss the theoretical life later (*EN* I 4, 1096a4–5). There is a similar promise in the *Eudemian Ethics* (*EE* I 1, 1214a12–14), but, even if its last book had originally been in a less truncated state, there is no indication that it contained a proper discussion of the theoretical life. As a temporary stop gap, Aristotle seems to have inserted in the *Nicomachean Ethics* X a piece of text he had written earlier. Traces of such a text can indeed be found in the *Politics* VII 2–3, where Aristotle draws a similarly sharp contrast between the theoretical and the practical life.[21] If he inserted that ready-to-hand

---

[19] *EN* X 4, 1175a4: 'all things humans are incapable of being constantly active'; *Protrepticus* 104, 2: 'the (merely) human life'.

[20] The adjective '*anthrōpeios*' is used frequently by Plato and other authors of the classical age.

[21] He there refers to a controversy (*Pol.* VII 2, 1324b25), and there are good reasons for the assumption that the depiction of the philosopher who is not even part of the city was part of Aristotle's contribution to a debate within the Academy, whether or not philosophers had the obligation to partake in politics.

The Task of a 'Philosophy of Human Affairs'

text, he must have done so with the intention of mitigating the contrast between the two types of life. For, given the fact that the *EN* is concerned with human happiness from book I on *anthrōpinē eudaimonia*, and based on a fully fledged account of human virtue, it would be bizarre if the upshot of that long investigation should consist of the recommendation to focus on divine objects as much as possible and to bother with human affairs only to the degree that is absolutely necessary.

Some editorial emendations here and there would have sufficed to mitigate the contrast between the two kinds of life. While the study of divine and eternal things is most happy-making for those with sufficient interest and ability to pursue such topics, philosophers depend on a community that not only guarantees peace and justice, but also sufficient education, and that sees to it that there is such a thing as philosophy (*EN* VI 13, 1145a6–11). As Aristotle points out in his discussion of friendship, the community of philosophers is particularly valuable (IX 1, 1164b2–6), and philosophising is one of the pastimes of true friends who spend their lives together (*symphilosophein*) (IX 12, 1172a5).

That Aristotle did not have the time to carry out the intended revision and to present a 'compatibilist' evaluation of the theoretical and the practical life is suggested by the abruptness with which the subject of the divine life is dropped at the beginning of *EN* X 9. The search for the education of the legislators simply ignores pure *theoria* just as much as it ignores the preceding denigration of the concern with political affairs as 'unleisurely' (X 7, 1177b4–15). Instead, Aristotle encourages his students to engage in extended studies of the different kinds of constitutions in order to see what destroys and preserves the different kinds of constitutions and to find out which constitution is best and how it must be ordered. For this very reason he insists that what he is doing is philosophy, albeit the philosophy concerning human affairs, just as he had occasionally mentioned the fact that he is concerned with philosophical questions before.[22]

Aristotle makes no pretence in the *Politics* to be a politician himself. What he does is just to give help to those with an interest, ambition, and the potential to become politicians, by instructing them on the basic philosophical principles of their discipline, by continuing 'the philosophy concerning human affairs'. That is what he hopes to achieve when he promises, in *EN* II 2, 1104a10–11, that he is not just concerned with theory, like in his other treatises, but wants to 'give what help he can' to

---

[22] That he is engaged in philosophical investigations is indicated several times, cf. *EN* III 1, 1109b30–35; VII 11, 1152b1–3; *Pol.* III 8, 1279b10–16; 12, 1282b14–23 *et pass.*

make people good. The help consists in conveying to his audience the kind of knowledge that enables them to fulfil the task of legislators:

> For legislators make citizens good by forming habits in them, and this is the wish of every legislator, and those who do not miss their mark, and it is in this that a good constitution differs from a bad one. (*EN* II 1, 1103b2)

The promise at the beginning of the *EN* that the master science of politics will provide the good life through laws that will regulate all aspects of the life of the citizens leaves us with the question of whether happiness, the human *telos*, will be attained only in that very best city-state, or whether the discussion in the *Politics* of the three types of proper constitutions is to be regarded as a sign that there is happiness also in 'ordinary' forms of state, provided that they are ruled by law and aim for the common good. The evidence concerning this question is ambiguous. On the one hand there is the promise of a 'best state' as the objective of the master science – and the condition of the human good per se (*t'anthrōpinon agathon*) (*EN* I 1, 1094b7). The need of a proper conception of the best constitution also justifies Aristotle's design of his own conception of the best form of state at the end of the *Politics*:

> Anyone who intends to investigate the best constitution in the proper way must first determine which life is most choiceworthy, since if this remains unclear, what the best constitution is must also remain unclear. (*Pol.* VII 1, 1323a14–17, transl. Reeve)

And, indeed, Aristotle's design of an ideal state is a fairly detailed sketch of a community, a sketch that he intended to supplement with a programme for the education of the citizens of his best state.[23]

On the other hand, the fact that Aristotle discusses extensively the different forms of constitutions suggests that he presupposes that the citizens of all proper forms of state will have the opportunity to lead a happy life. And the fact that he explicitly distinguishes between three senses of 'best constitution' seems to speak for the assumption that there are degrees of happiness in the different types. As mentioned before, there is the absolutely best state that Aristotle calls 'the city of our prayers' (*Pol.* II 1, 1260b27) that is the aim of his investigation, there is the best state under the usual conditions, and there is the best state under certain less good conditions (IV 1, 1288a21–30). Aristotle justifies the need to study them all

---

[23] The educational programme is not carried out beyond the musical education of children. This is perhaps an indication that Aristotle realised that legislation and education should be, rather, the practitioners' task.

The Task of a 'Philosophy of Human Affairs'   273

on the ground that a statesman, like a trainer, should be able to give instructions not only for the very best constitution, but also for the others: 'For one should not study only what is best, but also what is possible and similarly what is easier and more attainable by all' (1288b37–39). As he adds, a statesman should be able to help the existing constitutions. And, though Aristotle sticks to the condition that the city-state is the perfect community if its organisation aims not only for common life but for 'beautiful actions' and makes them the condition of living well and happily (III 9, 1281a1–4), he does not seem to regard this condition fulfilled only in that very best state that is not yet to be found. Most forms of constitution give their citizens the opportunity to perform virtuous acts, and Aristotle nowhere claims that good persons should engage in politics only in the best state and in no other. Although he affirms that a good citizen can be a good human being only in a good state, there is no suggestion that this condition is fulfilled only in the best kind of state. All proper forms of political communities aim for the common good and require their citizens to act in accordance with justice and the laws.

But why, then, does Aristotle require that his students not only study at length the less than perfect constitutions that exist in reality, but also insist that they realise that there is one form that is by nature the best, even if it is nowhere to be found? First, Aristotle does not assume that his best state cannot be realised. It may be unlikely, but not impossible that there will be the kind of 'middle of the road' society ruled by an aristocracy of the mind that is both able and willing to rule and be ruled in turn, and to treat each other with fairness and justice in the way Aristotle envisages.[24] Second, and more importantly, Aristotle regards it as necessary for students of politics to know what is best, what to aim for when it comes to engaging in practical politics, in legislation, as well as in the administration of a state. He may not expect the realisation of his ideal, but he expects that those with the talent, the ambition, and the opportunity will act for the best under the given circumstances. That is why it is necessary to engage in the 'philosophy of human affairs'. There is the need for legislators and educators who are both able and willing to keep the citizens on the straight and narrow path of

---

[24] Aristotle's depiction of the 'city of our prayers' shows that speculations that Alexander the Great was the addressee of his advice are wide off the mark. Whatever the later much romanticised personal relationship may have been between Aristotle and his former pupil, Aristotle makes perfectly clear that his ideal is the small *polis* that lives in peace with its neighbours; for he deeply disapproved of conquests and the suppression of other states (*Pol.* VII 2, 1324b22–41) Whether he believed in the future of the autonomous city-state while Alexander was forging an empire must remain a matter of speculation.

274   DOROTHEA FREDE

virtue, even if this aim can be achieved only to a limited degree. As Aristotle once pointed out, the truly good man will make the best of the circumstances he finds himself in, just like an army-general makes the best military use of the army at his command, and the shoemaker makes the best shoes out of the hides that are given to him (*EN* I 10, 1100b35–1101a6). What is true of those other craftsmen is also true of the politician: he makes the best of the population of his city-state, but, in order to do so, he must know what the very best as such is, and what is best under the given circumstances. To achieve even that much presupposes that the politicians are well-versed in the philosophy of human affairs.

Bibliography

ARISTOTLE'S WORKS

APo *Posterior Analytics*
  – Translated by Hugh Tredennick, in: Aristotle II (Loeb Classical Library), Cambridge, MA, 1960.

Cat. *Categories*
  – Translation with Notes by J. L. Ackrill. Oxford: Clarendon, 1963.

DA *De Anima*
  – Translation with an Introduction and Commentary by Christopher Shields. Oxford: Clarendon, 2016.
  – Translated by Robert Hicks. Cambridge University Press, 1907.
  – *Aristotle's De Anima: Books II and III with Certain Passages from Book I*. Translation by David Hamlyn. Oxford: Clarendon, 1968.
  – *On the Soul.* Translated by W. S. Hett, in: Aristotle VIII (Loeb Classical Library), Cambridge, MA, 1957.

DC *De Caelo*
  – *On the Heavens.* Translated by William Guthrie. Cambridge, MA: Harvard University Press, 1939.
  – *On the Heavens I & II*. Translation with an Introduction and Commentary by Stuart Leggatt. Warminster: Aris & Philipps, 1995.

DI *De Interpretatione*
  – *On Interpretation*. Translation with Notes by J. L. Ackrill. Oxford: Clarendon, 1963.

EE *Eudemian Ethics*
  – Translated by J. Solomon. *The Complete Works of Aristotle*. Edited by Jonathan Barnes. Vol. II. Princeton University Press, 1984, 1922–81.
  – Translated by H. Rackham, in Aristotle in XXIII Volumes, Vol. XX, Cambridge, MA: Harvard University Press, 1981.

EN	*Nicomachean Ethics*
	– Translation with Historical Introduction by Christopher Rowe. Philosophical Introduction and Commentary by Sarah Broadie. Oxford University Press, 2002.
	– Translation with Introduction, Notes and Glossary by Irwin Terence. Indianapolis, IN: Hackett, 1999.
	– Translated by Harris Rackham. Cambridge, MA: Harvard University Press, 1934.
	– Translated by William David Ross. *The Complete Works of Aristotle.* Edited by Jonathan Barnes. Vol. II. Princeton University Press, 1984, 1729–867.
GA	*Generation of Animals*
	– Translated by A. L. Peck, in: Aristotle XIII (Loeb Classical Library), Cambridge, MA, 1943.
Gen. et Corr.	*De Generatione et Corruptione*
	– Translated by E. S. Forst, in: Aristotle III (Loeb Classical Library), Cambridge, MA, 1955.
HA	*History of Animals*
	– Books I–III. Translated by A. L. Peck, in: Aristotle IX (Loeb Classical Library), Cambridge, MA, 1965.
	– Books IV–VI. Translated by A. L. Peck, in: Aristotle X (Loeb Classical Library), Cambridge, MA, 1970.
	– Books VII–X. Translated by D. M. Balme, in: Aristotle XI (Loeb Classical Library), Cambridge, MA, 1991.
	– Translated by D. W. Thompson. *The Complete Works of Aristotle.* Edited by Jonathan Barnes. Vol. II. Princeton University Press, 1984, 774–993.
IA	*De Incessu Animalium*
	– *Progression of Animals.* Translated by E. S. Forster, in: Aristotle XII (Loeb Classical Library), Cambridge, MA, 1961.
Insomn.	*De Insomnis*
	– *On Dreams.* Translated by W. S. Hett, in: Aristotle VIII (Loeb Classical Library), Cambridge, MA, 1957.
MA	*Movement of Animals*
	– Translated by E. S. Forster, in: Aristotle XII (Loeb Classical Library), Cambridge, MA, 1961.
Mem.	*De Memoria et Reminiscentia*
	– *On Memory.* Translation with Interpretive Summaries by R. Sorabji, 2nd ed., University of Chicago Press, 2004.
Met.	*Metaphysics*
	– Translated by W. D. Ross. *The Complete Works of Aristotle.* Edited by Jonathan Barnes. Vol. II. Princeton University Press, 1984, 1552–728.
Meteor.	*Meteorologica*
	– Translated by H. D. P. Lee, in: Aristotle VII (Loeb Classical Library), Cambridge, MA, 1952.

Bibliography

PA *On the Parts of Animals*
  - Translation with Introduction and Commentary by James G. Lennox. Oxford: Clarendon, 2001.
  - Translated by A. L. Peck, in: Aristotle XII (Loeb Classical Library), Cambridge, MA, 1961.
  - Translated by W. Ogle. *The Complete Works of Aristotle*. Edited by Jonathan Barnes. Vol. I. Princeton University Press 1984,
  - *De Partibus Animalium I / De Generatione Animalium I (with passages from II. 1–3)*. Translated by D. M. Balme (Clarendon Aristotle Series), Oxford: Clarendon, 1972.

Phys. *Physics*
  - Translated by R. P. Hardie and R. K. Gaye. *The Works of Aristotle*. Vol. II. Ed. W. D. Ross. Oxford: Clarendon, 1970.

PN *Parva Naturalia*
  - Translated by W. S. Hett, in: Aristotle VIII (Loeb Classical Library), Cambridge, MA, 1957.

Poet. *Poetics*
  - Translation and Commentary by Stephen Halliwell. Chapel Hill, NC: The University of North Carolina Press, 1987.

Pol. *Politics*
  - Translated by B. Jowett. *The Complete Works of Aristotle*. Edited by Jonathan Barnes. Vol. II. Princeton University Press, 1984, 1986–2129.
  - *Books I and II*. Translated by Trevor Saunders. Oxford: Clarendon Press, 1995.
  - Translated by Carnes Lord. University of Chicago Press, 1984.
  - Translated by C. D. C. Reeve. Indianapolis, IN: Hackett, 1998.

Resp. *De Respiratione*
  - *On Breath*. Translated by W. S. Hett, in: Aristotle VIII (Loeb Classical Library), Cambridge, MA, 1957.

Rhet. *Rhetoric*
  - Translated by J. H. Freese, in: Aristotle XII (Loeb Classical Library), Cambridge, MA, 1926.

SE *On Sophistical Refutations*
  - Translated by E. S. Forster, in: Aristotle III (Loeb Classical Library), Cambridge, MA, 1955.

Sens. *Sense and Sensibilia*
  - Translated by J. I. Beare. *The Complete Works of Aristotle*. Edited by Jonathan Barnes. Princeton University Press, 693–714.

Somn. *De Somno et Vigilia*
  - *On Sleep and Waking*. Translated by W. S. Hett, in: Aristotle VIII (Loeb Classical Library), Cambridge, MA, 1957.

Top. *Topics*
  - Translated by Edward S. Forster, in: Aristotle II (Loeb Classical Library), Cambridge, MA, 1960.

278 *Bibliography*

GENERAL BIBLIOGRAPHY

Adkins, Arthur William Hope 1991. 'The Connection between Aristotle's Ethics and Politics', in David Keyt and Fred Miller (eds.) *A Companion to Aristotle's Politics*. Oxford: Blackwell, 75–93.

Alston, William P. 1964. *Philosophy of Language*. Englewood Cliffs, NJ: Prentice-Hall.

Annas, Julia 1977. 'Plato and Aristotle on Friendship and Altruism', *Mind* 86: 532–54.

2005. 'Virtue Ethics: What Kind of Naturalism?', in Stephen Gardiner (ed.) *Virtue Ethics, Old and New*. Ithaca, NY: Cornell University Press, 11–29.

Anton, John 1995. 'Aristotle on the Nature of *Logos*', *Philosophical Inquiry* 18: 1–30.

Arendt, Hannah 1958. *The Human Condition*. University of Chicago Press.

Ax, Wolfram 1978. 'Ψόφος, φωνή and διάλεκτος als Grundbegriffe aristotelischer Sprachreflexion', *Glotta* 56: 245–71.

Ayers, Michael 1968. *The Refutation of Determinism*. London: Methuen.

Baker, Samuel 2015. 'The Concept of *Ergon*: Towards an Achievement Interpretation of Aristotle's "Function Argument"', *Oxford Studies in Ancient Philosophy* 48: 227–66.

Balme, David 1987. 'The Place of Biology in Aristotle's Philosophy', in Allan Gotthelf and James Lennox (eds.) *Philosophical Issues in Aristotle's Biology*. Cambridge University Press, 13–16.

Barney, Rachel 2006. 'The Sophistic Movement', in Mary Louise Gill and Pierre Pellegrin (eds.) *A Companion to Ancient Philosophy*. Oxford: Blackwell, 77–101.

2008. 'Aristotle's Argument for a Human Function', *Oxford Studies in Ancient Philosophy* 34: 293–344.

Bar-On, Dorit 2004. *Speaking My Mind: Expression and Self-Knowledge*. Oxford: Clarendon Press.

Bayertz, Kurt 2012. *Der aufrechte Gang. Eine Geschichte des anthropologischen Denkens*. München: Beck.

Bodson, Liliane 1996. 'Some of Aristotle's Writings about Bird Behavior and Issues Still Current in Comparative Psychology', *International Journal of Comparative Psychology* 9: 26–41.

Bordt, Michael 2011. 'Why Aristotle's God Is Not the Unmoved Mover', *Oxford Studies in Ancient Philosophy* XL: 91–109.

Bostock, David 2000. *Aristotle's Ethics*. Oxford University Press.

Boyle, Matthew 2017. 'A Different Kind of Mind?', in Kristin Andrews and Jacob Beck (eds.) *The Routledge Handbook of Philosophy of Animal Minds*. London: Routledge, 109–18.

Boyle, Matthew and Lavin, Douglas 2010. 'Goodness and Desire', in S. Tenenbaum (ed.) *Desire, Practical Reason, and the Good*. New York, NY: Oxford University Press, 161–201.

Bibliography 279

Brandom, Robert 1994. *Making It Explicit*. Cambridge, MA: Harvard University Press.

2002. 'Non-Inferential Knowledge, Perceptual Experience and Secondary Qualities', in N. Smith (ed.) *Reading McDowell*. London: Routledge, 92–105.

Brentano, Franz 1874. *Psychology from an Empirical Point of View*. Translated by A. C. Rancurello, D. B. Terrell and L. McAlister. Introduction by P. Simons. London: Routledge 1995.

Brittain, Charles and Brennan, Tad 2002. *Simplicius: On Epictetus Handbook 27–53*. Ancient Commentators on Aristotle. London: Duckworth.

Broadie, Sarah 1991. *Ethics with Aristotle*. New York, NY: Oxford University Press.

1996. '*Nous* and Nature in *De Anima* III', in *Proceedings of the Boston Area Colloquium in Ancient Philosophy* 12: 163–76.

Broadie, Sarah and Rowe, Christopher 2002. *Aristotle, Nicomachean Ethics, Translation, Introduction, and Commentary*. Oxford University Press.

Buddensiek, Friedemann 1999. *Die Theorie des Glücks in Aristoteles' Eudemischer Ethik*. Göttingen: Vandenhoeck & Ruprecht.

Burnyeat, Myles 1980. 'Aristotle on Learning to Be Good', in Amélie Oksenberg Rorty (ed.) *Essays on Aristotle's Ethics*. Berkeley, CA: University of California Press, 69–92.

2002. '*De Anima* II 5', *Phronesis* 47: 1–64.

2003. 'Introduction: Aristotle on the Foundations of Sublunary Physics', in Frans De Haas and Jaap Mansfeld (eds.) *Aristotle's On Generation and Corruption I (Symposium Aristotelicum)*. Oxford: Clarendon Press, 7–24.

2008. *Aristotle's Divine Intellect: The Aquinas Lecture 2008*. Milwaukee, WI: Marquette University Press.

Carson, Scott 2003. 'Aristotle on Meaning and Reference', *History of Philosophy Quarterly* 20: 319–37.

Cashdollar, Stanford 1973. 'Aristotle's Account of Incidental Perception', *Phronesis* 18(1): 156–75.

Casmann, Otto 1594. *Psychologia Anthropologica, Sive Animae Humanae Doctrina*. Hanau: Fischer.

Caston, Victor 1996a. 'Aristotle on the Relation of the Intellect to the Body: Commentary on Broadie', *Proceedings of the Boston Area Colloquium in Ancient Philosophy* 12: 177–92.

1996b. 'Why Aristotle Needs Imagination', *Phronesis* 41(1): 20–55.

1998. 'Aristotle and the Problem of Intentionality', *Philosophy and Phenomenological Research* 58(2): 249–98.

1999. 'Aristotle's Two Intellects: A Modest Proposal', *Phronesis* 44(3): 199–227.

Charlton, William 1987. 'Aristotle on the Place of Mind in Nature', in Allan Gotthelf and James Lennox (eds.) *Philosophical Issues in Aristotle's Biology*. Cambridge University Press, 409–23.

Cho, Dae-Ho 2003. *Ousia und Eidos in der Metaphysik und Biologie des Aristoteles*. Stuttgart: Steiner.

280 *Bibliography*

2012. 'Lautäußerungen der Vögel in der aristotelischen *Historia Animalium*', *Antike Naturwissenschaft und ihre Rezeption* 22: 11–38.

Clark, Stephen 1975. *Aristotle's Man. Speculations upon Aristotelian Anthropology*. Oxford: Clarendon Press.

Clayton, N. S., Griffiths, D. P., and Dickinson, A. 2000. 'Declarative and Episodic-Like Memory in Animals: Personal Musings of a Scrub Jay', in Cecilia Heyes and Ludwig Huber (eds.) *The Evolution of Cognition*. Cambridge, MA: The MIT Press, 273–88.

Cohoe, Caleb 2016. 'When and Why Understanding Needs *Phantasmata*: A Moderate Interpretation of Aristotle's *De Memoria* and *De Anima* on the Role of Images in Intellectual Activities', *Phronesis* 61(3): 337–72.

Coles, Andrew 1997. 'Animal and Childhood Cognition in Aristotle's Biology and the *Scala Naturae*', in Wolfgang Kullmann and Sabine Föllinger (eds.) *Aristotelische Biologie. Intentionen, Methoden, Ergebnisse*. Stuttgart: Steiner, 287–323.

Connell, Sophia 2016. *Aristotle on Female Animals*. Cambridge University Press.

Coope, Ursula 2012. 'Why Does Aristotle Think That Ethical Virtue Is Required for Practical Wisdom?', *Phronesis* 57(2): 142–63.

Cooper, John M. 1977. 'Friendship and the Good in Aristotle', *The Philosophical Review* 86(3): 290–315.

1990. 'Political Animals and Civic Friendship', in Günther Patzig (ed.) *Aristoteles' 'Politik'*. Göttingen: Vandenhoeck & Ruprecht, 220–41.

2004. *Knowledge, Nature, and the Good*. Princeton University Press.

2010. 'Political Community and the Highest Good', in James Lennox and Robert Bolton (eds.) *Being, Nature, and Life: Essays in Honor of Allan Gotthelf*. Cambridge University Press, 212–64.

Corcilius, Klaus 2009. 'How Are Episodes of Thought Initiated According to Aristotle?', in Gerd Van Riel and Pierre Destrée (eds.) *Ancient Perspectives on Aristotle's De Anima*. Leuven University Press, 1–17.

Corcilius, Klaus and Gregoric, Pavel 2010. 'Separability vs. Difference: Parts and Capacities of the Soul in Aristotle', *Oxford Studies in Ancient Philosophy* 39: 81–119.

Curzer, Howard 2005. 'How Good People Do Bad Things. Aristotle on the Misdeeds of the Virtuous', *Oxford Studies in Ancient Philosophy* 28: 233–56.

2012. *Aristotle and the Virtues*. Oxford University Press.

Davidson, Donald 1982. 'Rational Animals', *Dialectica* 36(4): 317–28.

1997. 'Seeing through Language', in John Preston (ed.) *Thought and Language*. Cambridge University Press, 15–27.

Depew, David 1991. 'Politics, Music, and Contemplation in Aristotle's Ideal State', in David Keyt and Fred Miller (eds.) *A Companion to Aristotle's Politics*. Oxford: Blackwell, 346–80.

1995. 'Humans and Other Political Animals in Aristotle's *History of Animals*', *Phronesis* 40: 156–81.

Bibliography

2006. 'From Hymn to Tragedy: Aristotle's Genealogy of Poetic Kinds', in Eric Csapo and Margaret Miller (eds.) *The Origins of Theater in Ancient Greece and Beyond: From Ritual to Drama*. Cambridge University Press, 126–49.

Deslauriers, Marguerite 2003. 'Aristotle on the Virtues of Slaves and Women', *Oxford Studies in Ancient Philosophy* 25: 213–31.

2009. 'Sexual Difference in Aristotle's Politics and His Biology', *Classical World* 102: 215–30.

Diogenes Laertius 1925. *LEP. Lives of Eminent Philosophers*. Translated by R. D. Hicks (Loeb Classical Library), Cambridge, MA: Harvard University Press.

Drefcinski, Shane 1996. 'The Fallible *Phronimos*', *Ancient Philosophy* 16: 139–53.

Dretske, Fred 2004. 'Seeing, Believing, and Knowing', in Robert Schwartz (ed.) *Perception*. Oxford: Blackwell, 268–86.

Everson, Stephen 1997. *Aristotle on Perception*. Oxford University Press.

Falcon, Andreas and Leunissen, Mariska 2015. 'The Scientific Role of *Eulogos* in Aristotle's Cael ii 12', in David Ebrey (ed.) *Theory and Practice in Aristotle's Natural Science*. Cambridge University Press, 217–40.

Fermani, Arianna 2014. '*To Kakon Pollachôs Legetai*: The Plurivocity of the Notion of Evil in Aristotelian Ethics', in Claudia Baracchi (ed.) *The Bloomsbury Companion to Aristotle*. New York: Bloomsbury, 241–59.

Fitch, W. Tecumseh 2010. *The Evolution of Language*. Cambridge University Press.

Foot, Philippa 2001. *Natural Goodness*. Oxford: Clarendon Press.

Fortenbaugh, William 1975. *Aristotle on Emotion: A Contribution to Philosophical Psychology, Rhetoric, Poetics, Politics, and Ethics*. London: Duckworth.

1977. 'Aristotle on Slaves and Women', in Jonathan Barnes, Malcolm Schofield and Richard Sorabji (eds.) *Articles on Aristotle 2: Ethics and Politics*. London: Duckworth, 135–39.

2006. *Aristotle's Practical Side: On His Psychology, Ethics, Politics and Rhetoric*. Leiden: Brill.

Foster, Susanne 1997. 'Aristotle and Animal *Phronesis*', *Philosophical Inquiry* 19: 27–38.

Frede, Dorothea 1992. 'The Cognitive Role of *Phantasia* in Aristotle', in Martha C. Nussbaum and Amélie Oksenberg Rorty (eds.) *Essays on Aristotle's De Anima*. Oxford: Clarendon, 279–95.

2005. 'Citizenship in Aristotle's *Politics*', in Richard Kraut and Steven Skultety (eds.) *Aristotle's Politics: Critical Essays*. Lanham: Rowman & Littlefield, 167–84.

2006. 'Pleasure and Pain in Aristotle's Ethics', in Richard Kraut (ed.) *The Blackwell Guide to Aristotle's Nicomachean Ethics*. Oxford: Blackwell, 255–75.

2015. 'Aristotle's Virtue Ethics', in Lorraine Besser-Jones and Michael Slote (eds.) *The Routledge Companion to Virtue Ethics*. New York: Routledge, 17–29.

282 *Bibliography*

2018. 'Equal But Not Equal: Plato and Aristotle on Women as Citizens', in Georgios Anagnostopoulos and Gerasimos Santas (eds.) *Democracy, Equality, and Justice in Ancient Greece: Historical and Philosophical Perspectives.* Cham: Springer, 287–306.

Frede, Michael 1996. 'Aristotle's Rationalism', in Michael Frede and Gisela Striker (eds.) *Rationality in Greek Thought.* Oxford: Clarendon Press, 157–73.

2008. 'Aristotle on Thinking', *Rhizai* 5(2): 287–301.

Frey, Christopher 2018, 'Aristotle on the Intellect and Limits of Natural Science', in John Sisko (ed.) *Philosophy of Mind in Antiquity.* London: Routledge, 160–74.

Gallagher, Robert 2011. 'Aristotle on *Eidei Diapherontoi*', *British Journal for the History of Philosophy* 19: 363–84.

Garver, Eugene 2011. *Aristotle's Politics: Living Well and Living Together.* University of Chicago Press.

Geach, Peter 1956. 'Good and Evil', *Analysis* 17: 35–42.

1977. *The Virtues.* Cambridge University Press.

Gelber, Jessica 2017. 'Females in Aristotle's Embryology', in Andrea Falcon and David Lefebvre (eds.) *Aristotle's Generation of Animals: A Critical Guide.* Cambridge University Press, 171–87.

Gill, Mary Louise and Pellegrin, Pierre (eds.) 2006. *A Companion to Ancient Philosophy.* Oxford: Blackwell.

Glock, Hans-Johann 1996. *A Wittgenstein Dictionary.* Oxford: Blackwell.

2003. *Quine and Davidson on Language, Thought and Reality.* Cambridge University Press.

2009. 'Can Animals Act for Reasons?', *Inquiry* 52: 323–54.

2012. 'The Anthropological Difference', in Constantin Sandis and Mark J. Cain (eds.) *Human Nature.* Cambridge University Press, 105–31.

2013. 'Animal Minds: A Non-Representationalist Approach', *American Philosophical Quarterly* 50: 213–32.

Goodey, Christopher 1996. 'On Aristotle's "Animal Capable of Reason"', *Ancient Philosophy* 16: 389–403.

Gosling, J. C. B. and Taylor, C. C. W. 1982. *The Greeks on Pleasure.* Oxford: Clarendon Press.

Gotthelf, Allan 2012. 'Historiae I: Plantarum et Animalium', in Allan Gotthelf (ed.) *Teleology, First Principles, and Scientific Method in Aristotle's Biology.* Oxford University Press, 307–42.

Granger, Herbert 1985. 'The Scala Naturae and the Continuity of Kinds', *Phronesis* 30: 181–200.

Grimaldi, William 1980. '*Semeion, Tekmerion, Eikos* in Aristotle's Rhetoric', *American Journal of Philology* 101: 383–98.

Hacker, Peter M. S. 2007. *Human Nature: The Categorical Framework.* Oxford: Wiley-Blackwell.

2013. *The Intellectual Powers: A Study of Human Nature.* Oxford: Wiley-Blackwell.

Bibliography

Hacker-Wright, John 2009. 'Human Nature, Personhood, and Ethical Naturalism', *Philosophy* 84: 413–27.

Hard, Robin and Gill, Christopher (eds.) 2014. *Epictetus: Discourses, Fragments, Handbook*. Oxford University Press.

Harte, Verity 2014. 'The *Nicomachean Ethics* on Pleasure', in Ronald Polansky (ed.) *The Cambridge Companion to Aristotle's Nicomachean Ethics*. Cambridge University Press, 288–318.

Hayduck, Michael (ed.) 1897. *Ioannis Philoponi in Aristotelis de anima libros commentaria* (= *Commentaria in Aristotelem Graeca* 15). Berlin: Reimer.

Heath, Malcolm 2008. 'Aristotle on Natural Slavery', *Phronesis* 53: 243–70.

Henry, Devin 2007. 'How Sexist Is Aristotle's Developmental Biology?', *Phronesis* 52: 251–69.

   2013. 'Optimality Reasoning in Aristotle's Natural Teleology', *Oxford Studies in Ancient Philosophy* 45: 225–63.

Henry, Devin and Nielsen, Karen Margrethe (eds.) 2015. *Bridging the Gap between Aristotle's Science and Ethics*. Cambridge University Press.

Hitz, Zena 2011. 'Aristotle on Self-Knowledge and Friendship', *Philosopher's Imprint* 11(12): 1–28.

Hoffmann, Magdalena 2010. *Der Standard des Guten bei Aristoteles. Regularität im Unbestimmten*. Freiburg: Alber.

Horn, Christoph 2006. '*Epieikeia*: The Competence of the Perfectly Just Person in Aristotle', in Burkhard Reis and Stella Haffmans (eds.) *The Virtuous Life in Greek Ethics*. Cambridge University Press, 142–66.

   2016. 'Individual Competence and Collective Deliberation in Aristotle's *Politics*', in Cinzia Arruzza and Dimitri Nikulin (eds.) *Philosophy and Political Power in Antiquity*. Leiden: Brill, 94–113.

Hursthouse, Rosalind 1999. *On Virtue Ethics*. Oxford University Press.

   2004. 'On the Grounding of the Virtues in Human Nature', in Jan Szaif and Matthias Lutz-Bachmann (eds.) *Was ist das für den Menschen Gute? What is Good for a Human Being?* Berlin: De Gruyter, 263–75.

   2013. 'Neo-Aristotelian Ethical Naturalism', in Hugh LaFollette (ed.), *The International Encyclopedia of Ethics*. Malden: Wiley, 3571–80.

Irwin, Terence 1985. 'Permanent Happiness: Aristotle and Solon', *Oxford Studies in Ancient Philosophy* 3: 89–124.

Jaeger, Werner 1947. *Paideia. Die Formung des griechischen Menschen*. Berlin: De Gruyter.

James, William 1890. *The Principles of Psychology*, Vol. 1. New York: Holt and Macmillan.

Jansen, Ludger 2010. 'Vernünftiger Rede fähig. Das Menschenbild des Aristoteles', in Ludger Jansen and Christoph Jedan (eds.) *Philosophische Anthropologie in der Antike*. Frankfurt am Main: Ontos, 157–84.

Johansen, Thomas 1997. *Aristotle on the Sense-Organs*. Cambridge University Press.

   2012. *The Powers of Aristotle's Soul*. Oxford University Press.

Johnson, Monte Ransome 2005. *Aristotle on Teleology*. Oxford University Press.

Bibliography

Kahn, Charles 1992. 'Aristotle on Thinking', in Martha C. Nussbaum and Amélie Oksenberg Rorty (eds.) *Essays on Aristotle's De Anima*. Oxford: Clarendon, 359–80.

Karbowski, Joseph 2012. 'Slaves, Women, and Aristotle's Natural Teleology', *Ancient Philosophy* 32: 323–50.

2013. 'Aristotle's Scientific Inquiry into Natural Slavery', *Journal of the History of Philosophy* 51: 331–53.

2014. 'Aristotle on the Deliberative Abilities of Women', *Apeiron* 47: 435–60.

Keil, Geert 2012. 'Beyond Assimilationism and Differentialism. Comment on Glock', *Deutsches Jahrbuch Philosophie* 4: *Welt der Gründe*. Hamburg: Meiner, 914–22.

Kelley, Laura A. and Kelley, Jennifer L. 2014. 'Animal Visual Illusion and Confusion: The Importance of a Perceptual Perspective', *Behavioral Ecology* 25(3): 450–63.

Kenny, Anthony J. P. 1975. *Will, Freedom and Power*. Oxford: Blackwell.

1989. *The Metaphysics of Mind*. Oxford: Clarendon Press.

2010. 'Concepts, Brains, and Behaviour', *Grazer Philosophische Studien* 81: 105–13.

Keyt, David 1987. 'Three Fundamental Theorems in Aristotle's *Politics*', *Phronesis* 32: 54–79.

1991. 'Three Basic Theorems in Aristotle's Politics', in David Keyt and Fred Miller (eds.) *A Companion to Aristotle's Politics*. Oxford: Blackwell, 118–41.

1993. 'Aristotle and Anarchism', *Reason Papers* 18: 133–52.

Kontos, Pavlos 2014. 'The Non-Virtuous Intellectual States in Aristotle's Ethics', *Oxford Studies in Ancient Philosophy* 47: 205–44.

Kosman, Aryeh 2004. 'Aristotle on the Desirability of Friends', *Ancient Philosophy* 24: 135–54.

Kraut, Richard 2002. *Aristotle: Political Philosophy*, Oxford University Press.

Kretzmann, Norman 1974. 'Aristotle on Spoken Sound Significant by Convention', in John Corcoran (ed.), *Ancient Logic and Its Modern Interpretations*, Dordrecht: Springer, 3–21.

Kullmann, Wolfgang 1974. *Wissenschaft und Methode. Interpretationen zur aristotelischen Theorie der Naturwissenschaften*. Berlin: De Gruyter.

1991. 'Man as a Political Animal in Aristotle' in David Keyt and Fred Miller (eds.) *A Companion to Aristotle's Politics*. Oxford: Blackwell, 94–117.

Künne, Wolfgang 1995. 'Sehen', *Logos* 2: 103–21.

Labarrière, Jean-Louis 1984. 'Imagination Humaine et Imagination Animale chez Aristote', *Phronesis* 29: 17–49.

1990. 'De la Phronêsis Animale', in Daniel Devereux and Pierre Pellegrin (eds.) *Biologie, Logique et Métaphysique chez Aristote*. Paris: Editions CNRS, 405–28.

1993a. 'Aristote et l'Éthologie', *Revue Philosophique de la France et de l'Étranger* 2: 281–300.

1993b. 'Aristote et la Question du Langage Animal', *Mètis* 8: 247–60.

2004. *Langage, Vie Politique et Mouvement des Animaux: Études Aristotéliciennes*. Paris: J. Vrin.

Bibliography

2005a. 'De la *Phronêsis* Animale chez Aristote', in Jean-Louis Labarrière, *La Condition Animale. Études sur Aristote et les Stoïciens*. Louvain-la-Neuve: Peeters, 121–48.

2005b. *La Condition Animale. Études sur Aristote et les Stoïciens*. Louvain-la-Neuve: Peeters.

Lennox, James G. 1980, 'Aristotle on Genera, Species, and "The More and the Less"', *Journal of the History of Biology* 13(2): 321–46.

1987. 'Kinds, Forms of Kinds and the More and Less in Aristotle's Biology', in Allan Gotthelf and James Lennox (eds.) *Philosophical Issues in Aristotle's Biology*. Cambridge University Press, 339–59.

1991. 'Between Data and Demonstration: The *Analytics* and the *Historia Animalium*', in Alan Bowen (ed.) *Science and Philosophy in Classical Greece*. New York: Garland, 261–95.

1996. 'Aristotle's Biological Development: The Balme Hypothesis', in William Wians (ed.) *Aristotle's Philosophical Development: Problems and Prospects*. Lanham, MD: Rowman & Littlefield, 229–48.

1999a. 'The Place of Mankind in Aristotle's Zoology', *Philosophical Topics* 27 (1): 1–16.

1999b. 'Aristotle on the Biological Roots of Human Virtue', repr. Devin Henry and Karen Margrethe Nielsen (eds.) 2015. *Bridging the Gap between Aristotle's Science and Ethics*. Cambridge University Press, 193–213.

2001a. 'Nature Does Nothing in Vain . . .', in James G. Lennox (ed.) *Aristotle's Philosophy of Biology: Studies in the Origins of Life*. Cambridge University Press, 205–23.

2001b. *Aristotle's Philosophy of Biology*. Cambridge University Press.

2005. 'Getting a Science Going: Aristotle on Entry Level Kinds', in Gereon Wolters (ed.) *Homo Sapiens und Homo Faber*. Berlin: De Gruyter, 87–100.

2009. 'Aristotle on Mind and the Science of Nature', in Marietta Rossetto, Michael Tsianikas, George Couvalis and Maria Palaktsoglou (eds.) *Greek Research in Australia: Proceedings of the Eighth Biennial International Conference of Greek Studies*. Adelaide: Flinders University, 1–18.

2010a. 'Bios, Praxis and the Unity of Life', in Sabine Föllinger (ed.) *Was ist 'Leben'? Aristoteles' Anschauungen zur Entstehung und Funktionsweise von Leben*. Stuttgart: Steiner, 239–59.

2010b. '*Bios* and Explanatory Unity in Aristotle's Biology', in David Charles (ed.) *Definition in Ancient Greek Philosophy*. Oxford University Press, 329–55.

Leunissen, Mariska 2010. *Explanation and Teleology in Aristotle's Science of Nature*. Cambridge University Press.

2015. 'Aristotle on Knowing Natural Science for Sake of Living Well', in Devin Henry and Karen Margrethe Nielsen (eds.) *Bridging the Gap between Aristotle's Science and Ethics*. Cambridge University Press, 214–31.

2018. 'Order and Method in *Aristotle's Generation of Animals* 2', in Andrea Falcon and David Lefebvre (eds.) *Aristotle's Generation of Animals: A Critical Guide*. Cambridge University Press, 56–74.

Bibliography

Liu, Irene 2010. 'Love Life: Aristotle on Living Together with Friends', *Inquiry* 53: 579–601.

Lloyd, Geoffrey 1978. 'The Empirical Basis of the Physiology of the Parva Naturalia', in G. E. R. Lloyd and G. E. L. Owen (eds.) *Aristotle on Mind and the Senses*. Cambridge University Press, 215–40.

1991. 'Aristotle's Zoology and His Metaphysics: The Status Quaestionis. A Critical Review of Some Recent Theories', in Geoffrey Lloyd (ed.) *Methods and Problems in Greek Science*. Cambridge University Press, 373–97.

1996. 'The Relationship of Psychology to Zoology', in Geoffrey Lloyd (ed.) *Aristotelian Explorations*. Cambridge University Press, 38–66.

Lorenz, Hendrik 2006. *The Brute Within. Appetitive Desire in Plato and Aristotle.* Oxford University Press.

Lurz, Robert 2009. 'The Philosophy of Animal Minds: An Introduction', in Robert Lurz (ed.) *The Philosophy of Animal Minds*. Cambridge University Press, 1–14.

MacIntyre, Alasdair 2007. *After Virtue: A Study in Moral Theory*. University of Notre Dame Press.

Maslin, Keith 2001. *An Introduction to the Philosophy of Mind*. Oxford: Blackwell.

McCready-Flora, Ian 2013. 'Aristotle and the Normativity of Belief', *Oxford Studies in Ancient Philosophy* 44: 67–98.

2014. 'Aristotle's Cognitive Science: Belief, Affect and Rationality', *Philosophy and Phenomenological Research* 89: 394–435.

McDowell, John 1994. *Mind and World*. Cambridge, MA: Harvard University Press.

1995. 'Two Sorts of Naturalism', in Rosalind Hursthouse and Philippa Foot (eds.) *Virtues and Reasons*. Oxford: Clarendon Press, 149–80.

1996. *Mind and World*. Cambridge, MA: Harvard University Press.

McGrew, William C., Schiefenhövel, Wulf and Marchant, Linda F. (eds.) 2013. *The Evolution of Human Handedness*. Annals of the New York Academy of Sciences 1288. Hoboken: Wiley-Blackwell.

Meikle, Scott 1995. *Aristotle's Economic Thought*. Oxford: Clarendon Press.

Menn, Stephen 2012. 'Aristotle's Theology', in Christopher Shields (ed.) *The Oxford Handbook of Aristotle*. Oxford University Press, 422–66.

Meyer, Martin 2006. 'Der Mensch als Maß und Muster. Anthropozentrische Momente der aristotelischen Biologie', *Antike Naturwissenschaft und ihre Rezeption* 16: 19–34.

2011. 'Aristoteles über die anatomischen Voraussetzungen des Sprechens', *Antike Naturwissenschaft und ihre Rezeption* 21: 37–54.

2015. *Aristoteles und die Geburt der biologischen Wissenschaft*. Wiesbaden: Springer.

Mill, John S. 1843. *A System of Logic*. London: Longmans, Green and Co, 1911.

Miller, Fred 1995. *Nature, Justice, and Rights in Aristotle's Politics*. Oxford University Press.

Bibliography

2013. 'The Rule of Reason', in Marguerite Deslauriers and Pierre Destrée (eds.) *The Cambridge Companion to Aristotle's Politics*. Cambridge University Press, 38–66.

Modrak, Deborah 1987. *Aristotle: The Power of Perception*. University of Chicago Press.

    1994. 'Aristotle: Women, Deliberation, and Nature', in Bat-Ami Bar On (ed.) *Engendering Origins*. Albany, NY: SUNY Press, 207–22.

Moss, Jessica 2012. *Aristotle on the Apparent Good*. Oxford University Press.

    2014. 'Right Reason in Plato and Aristotle: On the Meaning of *Logos*', *Phronesis* 59: 181–230.

    2017. 'Aristotle's Ethical Psychology', in Christopher Bobonich (ed.) *The Cambridge Companion to Ancient Ethics*. Cambridge University Press, 124–43.

Mulcahy, Nicholas J. and Call, Josep 2006. 'Apes Save Tools for Future Use', *Science* 312: 1038–40.

Mulgan, Richard 1974. 'Aristotle's Doctrine that Man is a Political Animal', *Hermes* 102: 438–45.

    1977. *Aristotle's Political Theory: An Introduction for Students of Political Theory*. Oxford University Press.

Mulhern, John 2008. '*Kakia* in Aristotle', in Ineke Sluiter and Ralph Mark Rosen (eds.) *Kakos. Badness and Anti-Value in Classical Antiquity*. Leiden: Brill, 233–54.

Müller, Anselm Winfried 2004. 'Aristotle's Conception of Ethical and Natural Virtue: How the Unity Thesis Sheds Light on the Doctrine of the Mean', in Jan Szaif and Matthias Lutz-Bachmann (eds.) *Was ist das für den Menschen Gute? What Is Good for a Human Being?* Berlin: De Gruyter, 18–53.

Müller, Jörn 2006. *Physis und Ethos. Der Naturbegriff bei Aristoteles und seine Relevanz für die Ethik*. Würzburg: Königshausen & Neumann.

    2016. 'Natur, Funktion und Moral. Die Verschränkung von Deskriptivität und Normativität im *physis*-Begriff bei Aristoteles', in Marko Fuchs and Annett Wienmeister (eds.) *Funktion und Normativität bei Aristoteles und Darwin*. University of Bamberg Press, 21–63.

Nagle, Brendan 2006. *The Household as the Foundation of Aristotle's Polis*. Cambridge University Press.

Newman, William 1887–1903. *The Politics of Aristotle*. Oxford: Clarendon.

Newmyer, Stephen T. 2016. *The Animal and the Human in Ancient and Modern Thought: The 'Man Alone of Animals' Concept*. New York: Routledge.

Noriega-Olmos, Simon 2013. *Aristotle's Psychology of Signification: A Commentary on De Interpretatione 16a3–18*. Berlin: De Gruyter.

Nussbaum, Martha Craven 1978. *Aristotle's De Motu Animalium*. Princeton University Press.

    1983. 'The "Common Explanation" of Animal Motion', in Paul Moraux and Jürgen Wiesner (eds.) *Zweifelhaftes im Corpus Aristotelicum. Studien zu einigen Dubia*. Berlin: De Gruyter, 116–56.

288   *Bibliography*

2001. *The Fragility of Goodness: Luck and Ethics in Greek Tragedy and Philosophy*. Revised Edition. Cambridge University Press.

Osborne, Catherine 2007. *Dumb Beasts and Dead Philosophers*. Oxford University Press.

Pakaluk, Michael 2005. *Aristotle's Nicomachean Ethics: An Introduction*. Cambridge University Press.

Pasnau, Robert 1999. *Thomas Aquinas: Commentary on Aristotle's De anima, translation with introduction and notes*. New Haven: Yale University Press.

Pearson, Giles 2012. *Aristotle on Desire*. Cambridge University Press.

Pellegrin, Pierre 1985. 'Aristotle: A Zoology without Species', in Allan Gotthelf (ed.) *Aristotle on Nature and Living Things*. Pittsburgh, PA: Mathesis, 95–115.

    1987. 'Logical Difference and Biological Difference: The Unity of Aristotle's Thought', in Allan Gotthelf and James Lennox (eds.) *Philosophical Issues in Aristotle's Biology*. Cambridge University Press, 313–38.

Penn, Derek C., Holyoak, Keith J. and Povinelli, Daniel J. 2008. 'Darwin's Mistake. Explaining the Discontinuity between Human and Nonhuman Minds', *Behavioral and Brain Sciences* 31, 109–78.

Penn, Derek C. and Povinelli, Daniel J. 2012. 'The Human Enigma', in Keith J. Holyoak and Robert G. Morrison (eds.) *The Oxford Handbook of Thinking and Reasoning*. Oxford University Press, 529–42.

Philoponus. *On Aristotle On the Intellect (de Anima 3.4-8)*. Translated by William Charlton. 2014. London: Bloomsbury Academic.

Plato 1997a. *Complete Works*. Edited by J. M. Cooper and D. S. Hutchinson. Indianapolis: Hackett.

    1997b. 'Rep.' Republic. Translated by G. M. A. Grube, revised by C. D. C. Reeve, in Plato, *Complete Works*, 971–1223.

    1997c. 'Statesman'. Translated by C. J. Rowe, in Plato, *Complete Works*, 294–358.

Plutarch 1957. 'De Sollertia Animalium', in Plutarch, *Moralia, Vol. XII*. Translated by H. Cherniss and W. C. Helmbold (Loeb Classical Library). Cambridge, MA: Harvard University Press.

Polansky, Ronald 2007. *Aristotle's De Anima*. Cambridge University Press.

Premack, David 2007. 'Human and Animal Cognition: Continuity and Discontinuity', *Proceedings of the National Academy of Science* 105(35), 13861–67.

Quine, Willard Van Orman 1960. *Word and Object*. Cambridge, MA: MIT Press.

Rabbås, Øyvind 2015. 'Eudaimonia, Human Nature, and Normativity. Reflections on Aristotle's Project in *Nicomachean Ethics* Book I', in Øyvind Rabbås, Eyjólfur Kjalar Emilsson, Hallvard Fossheim and Miira Tuominen (eds.) *The Quest for the Good Life. Ancient Philosophers on Happiness*. Oxford University Press, 88–112.

Rapp, Christof 2014. 'Aristotle and the Cosmic Game of Dice. A Conundrum in De Caelo II.12', *Rhizomata* 2: 161–86.

Reader, Soren 2000. 'New Directions in Ethics: Naturalism, Reasons and Virtue', *Ethical Theory and Moral Practice* 3: 341–64.

Bibliography

Rhodes, Peter 1981. *A Commentary on the Aristotelian 'Athenaion Politeia'*. Oxford University Press.

Rödl, Sebastian 2007. *Self-Consciousness*. Cambridge, MA: Harvard University Press.

Salkever, Stephen 1990. *Finding the Mean: Theory and Practice in Aristotelian Political Philosophy*. Princeton University Press.

Sauvé Meyer, Susan 2016. 'Aristotle on Moral Motivation', in Iakovos Vasiliou (ed.) *Moral Motivation: A History*. Oxford University Press, 45–66.

Scheiter, Krisanna 2012. 'Images, Appearances, and *Phantasia* in Aristotle', *Phronesis* 57(3): 251–78.

Schofield, Malcolm 1990. 'Ideology and Philosophy in Aristotle's Theory of Slavery', in Günther Patzig (ed.) *Aristoteles' 'Politik'*. Göttingen: Vandenhoeck & Ruprecht, 1–27.

   1992. 'Aristotle on the Imagination', in Martha C. Nussbaum and Amélie Oksenberg Rorty (eds.) *Essays on Aristotle's De Anima*. Oxford: Clarendon, 249–77.

   1999. *Saving the City: Issues in Ancient Philosophy*. London: Routledge.

Schütrumpf, Eckart 1991. *Aristoteles Politik, Buch I*. Berlin: Akademie-Verlag.

Scott, Dominic 2010. 'One Virtue or Many? Aristotle's Politics 1.13 and the Meno', in Verity Harte et al. (eds.) *Aristotle and the Stoics. Reading Plato, BICS* Supplement 107. University of London Institute of Classical Studies, 101–22.

   2015. *Levels of Argument: A Comparative Study of Plato's Republic and Aristotle's Nicomachean Ethics*. Oxford University Press.

Seed, Amanda and Tomasello, Michael 2010. 'Primate Cognition', *Topics on Cognitive Science* 2: 407–19.

Segev, Mor 2017. 'Aristotle on Nature, Human Nature and Human Understanding', *Rhizomata* 5(2): 177–209.

Shields, Christopher 2007. *Aristotle*. London: Routledge.

   2011. 'Perfecting Pleasures: The Metaphysics of Pleasure in *Nicomachean Ethics* X', in Jon Miller (ed.) *Aristotle's Nicomachean Ethics: A Critical Guide*. Cambridge University Press, 191–210.

   2015. 'The Science of the Soul in Aristotle's Ethics', in Devin Henry and Karen Margrethe Nielsen (eds.) *Bridging the Gap between Aristotle's Science and Ethics*. Cambridge University Press, 232–54.

Smith, Nicholas 1991. 'Aristotle's Theory of Natural Slavery', in David Keyt and Fred Miller (eds.) *A Companion to Aristotle's Politics*. Oxford: Blackwell, 142–55.

Smith Pangle, Lorraine 2003. *Aristotle and the Philosophy of Friendship*. Cambridge University Press.

Smyth, Herbert Weir 1920. *Greek Grammar*. Cambridge, MA: Harvard University Press.

Sorabji, Richard 1993. *Animal Minds and Human Morals. The Origins of the Western Debate*. Ithaca, NY: Cornell University Press.

Stewart, John A. 1892. *Notes on the Nicomachean Ethics*. Oxford: Clarendon Press.

Strawson, Peter F. 1971. *Logico-Linguistic Papers*. London: Methuen.

290   *Bibliography*

Sturgeon, Nicholas 2006. 'Ethical Naturalism', in David Copp (ed.) *Ethical Theory*. Oxford University Press, 91–101.

Susemihl, Franz 1887. *Aristotelis Ethica Nicomachea*. Leipzig: Teubner.

Tomasello, Michael 2014. *A Natural History of Human Thinking*. Cambridge, MA: Harvard University Press.

Tomasello, Michael and Rakoczy, Hannes 2003. 'What Makes Human Cognition Unique? From Individual to Shared to Collective Intentionality', *Mind and Language* 18: 121–47.

Trott, Adriel 2014. *Aristotle on the Nature of Community*. Cambridge University Press.

van der Eijk, Philip 1997. 'The Matter of Mind: Aristotle on the Biology of "Psychic" Processes and the Bodily Aspects of Thinking', in Wolfgang Kullmann and Sabine Föllinger (eds.) *Aristotelische Biologie. Intentionen, Methoden, Ergebnisse*. Stuttgart: Steiner, 231–58.

van Schaik, Carel P. 2016. *The Primate Origins of Human Nature*. Hoboken: Wiley.

Vogler, Candace 2013. 'Natural Virtue and Proper Upbringing', in Julia Peters (ed.) *Aristotelian Ethics in Contemporary Perspective*. New York: Routledge, 145–57.

Wallies, Max (ed.) 1891. *Alexandri Aphrodisiensis in Aristotelis topicorum libros octo commentaria (= Commentaria in Aristotelem Graeca* 2.2). Berlin: Reimer.

Ward, Julie 2009. 'Is Human a Homonym for Aristotle?', *Apeiron* 41: 75–98.

Warren, James 2014. *The Pleasures of Reason in Plato, Aristotle, and the Hellenistic Hedonists*. Cambridge University Press.

Wedin, Michael 1988. *Mind and Imagination in Aristotle*. New Haven, CT: Yale University Press.

1989. 'Aristotle on the Mechanics of Thought', *Ancient Philosophy* 9(1): 67–86.

Wheeler, Mark 1999. 'Semantics in Aristotle's *Organon*', *Journal of the History of Philosophy* 37(2): 191–226.

White, Alan 1972. 'Mind–Brain Analogies', *Canadian Journal of Philosophy* 1: 457–72.

Whiting, Jennifer 2002. 'Locomotive Soul: The Parts of Soul in Aristotle's Scientific Works', *Oxford Studies in Ancient Philosophy* 22: 141–200.

2006. 'The Nicomachean Account of *Philia*', in Richard Kraut (ed.) *The Blackwell Guide to Aristotle's Nicomachean Ethics*. Oxford: Blackwell, 276–304.

Witt, Charlotte 1998. 'Form, Normativity, and Gender in Aristotle: A Feminist Perspective', in Cynthia Freeland (ed.) *Feminist Interpretations of Aristotle*. University Park, PA: Penn State University Press, 118–37.

Wittgenstein, Ludwig 1953. *Philosophical Investigations*. Translated by G. E. M. Anscombe, P. M. S. Hacker and J. Schulte, 4th, revised edition by P. M. S. Hacker and J. Schulte. Oxford: Wiley-Blackwell, 2009.

Zirin, Ronald 1980. 'Aristotle's Biology of Language', *Transactions of the American Philological Association* 10: 325–47.

Index

accident, accidental property, 30, 36–37, 131, 134, 193, 244

action, agency, 10, 34, 66–68, 70, 72–73, 79–84, 87, 89–94, 103, 111, 115, 126–28, 132–33, 164, 168, 176, 178–79, 186–90, 196, 200, 202, 204, 206–9, 211–12, 216, 231, 243, 245, 250, 256–57, 267, 273

   divine, 69–70

   in humans vs. in animals, 5, 10–11, 13, 31, 69, 137, 142, 181

actuality, actualisation, 38, 41, 100–3, 148, 150, 168, 170, 179, 182–83, 189, 192–99, 257

additive vs. transformative theories.

   see transformation thesis

aisthēsis. see perception

aisthētikon, 33, 107, 144, 172, 174

akrasia. see incontinence

Alexander the Great, 253, 273

ambidextrousness, 131, 141

ambiguity, 12, 14–15

analogy, 6–7, 14, 40, 47, 58, 66, 74, 85–90, 107, 109, 112–13, 117, 122, 128–31, 155, 164, 169, 172, 174–75, 180, 188, 202, 260

anatomy, 108, 111, 119, 132, 135

Anaxagoras, 46–48, 110, 142, 212

animal minds, philosophy/question of, 5, 13, 142–43, 146, 150

animal, political, 4, 10, 26–27, 48, 114–15, 122, 158, 160, 182, 221–26, 237–39, 241, 244–45, 251, 257, 260–62

animal, rational, 3–4, 8, 25–28, 63–65, 158, 180, 182, 234, 236

animals, anarchic/leaderless, 244

Annas, Julia, 166, 187

anthropocentrism, 119–20, 123, 128

anthropological difference, 2, 4–7, 10–15, 51, 126, 135, 138, 140–60

anthropology, history of the word, 1

anticipation, 5, 9, 142

apes. *see* primates

Aquinas, 5, 8, 71, 104, 144, 155

aretē, 163, 167–69, 174, 176–77, 179–80, 204–9, 213, 215, 217, 231 (*see also* excellence)

artefacts, 16, 57, 164, 167–72, 180

as-ifness, 13–14, 157

assimilationism vs. differentialism, 5–7, 11–15, 143, 145, 155

autarky, 247, 261–62

Baker, Samuel, 169, 171

belief, 13, 45, 61, 65, 69, 143, 145, 150–51, 153–54, 157, 233

bios. see form of life/way of life

bios theōrētikos. see contemplative life

bipedalism, 3, 27–28, 35, 42, 99–100, 110, 124, 141, 235, 242, 244

blood, 99, 104, 109, 112, 233

bodily parts, 32, 112, 118, 136, 138, 175

borderline cases, 15

Bordt, Michael, 90

Bostock, David, 168, 178

Boyle, Matthew, 8–9

brain, 41, 100, 108–9, 147, 149–50, 152

Brandom, Robert, 8, 150, 156

Brentano, Franz, 144, 147

Broadie, Sarah, 102, 168, 207, 232

Burnyeat, Myles, 40–41, 69, 73, 101

calculation, 31, 55, 65–67, 74, 105–6, 126–28, 137, 177

capacity approach to the mind, 143, 147–50

Cartesian dualism, 147, 149

Casmann, Otto, 1

causation, 100, 103, 106, 116, 127–28, 132, 149–50, 157, 174, 188–89, 247, 255

celestial bodies, 77–80, 86–88, 92

change, 36–40, 42, 102–3, 105–7, 111, 149, 170–71

character, 92, 95, 112, 115, 132, 136, 138, 178, 190, 200–1, 204–6, 210, 212–13, 215–16, 229, 231–32, 259–60, 263, 265

Charlton, William, 102, 105, 123

291

292 Index

choice, 106, 137, 209, 239, 252
citizens, 227, 246, 249–52, 256–57
city, city-state. *see* state
classification, biological, 6, 15, 120–21, 134
cognition, 8–9, 11, 15, 40, 44–48, 50–52,
  54–57, 60–62, 64, 69–72, 74–76, 106,
  111–13, 127–28, 130, 142, 148–49, 151,
  153–54, 158–59, 193, 212, 217, 224–25,
  228–29
Coles, Andrew, 34, 123
common good, 26, 253, 265–66, 272–73
communication, 11, 27, 46, 48, 51, 53–54,
  129–30, 158–60, 197–98, 224, 239, 244,
  246–47, 253, 261
constitution, political, 115–16, 212–13, 227,
  238–39, 241, 243, 250–53, 255, 265–66,
  268–69, 271–73
contemplation, 35, 41, 58–59, 70, 73, 75, 166,
  181, 195–98, 206–8, 216
contemplative life, 35, 58–59, 95–96, 166,
  180–81, 195–96, 216, 270
continence, 208–9, 215
continuity (in nature, between animals and
  humans), 5–7, 14–15, 83, 121, 123,
  259–61, 263
conventions, 11, 46, 49–50, 52–55, 115, 130,
  159–60, 224, 228
Cooper, John M., 26, 32, 114, 197–98, 221
cosmology, 77–96, 136
cosmos, 51, 77–78, 86, 88, 95, 105, 110
Curzer, Howard, 200, 203, 209–10, 214–17

Darwin, Charles, 15
Davidson, Donald, 5, 8, 127, 150
decision, 7, 65, 69, 126–27, 137, 176, 239, 263
definition, Aristotle's account of, 3–5, 25–31,
  36–37, 41–43, 120, 124–25, 140, 242
deliberation, 7, 9, 11, 35, 44, 60, 65–71, 75,
  113–14, 117, 126–27, 129–30, 136–38,
  142, 181, 229–30, 232, 236, 239, 246–47,
  252
Depew, David, 12, 50, 122, 132, 221, 223–24,
  226, 239, 250, 252, 256, 261
Descartes, René, 5, 144–45, 147
desire, 9, 45–46, 58, 60–61, 64, 69–76, 81–83,
  93, 95, 104–6, 114, 119, 127–28, 144–45,
  170, 175–76, 178, 183, 201, 203–4, 209,
  228, 231, 249
development, 1, 95, 113, 115, 166, 170, 217,
  245–46, 248, 254–55, 258, 260,
  262–64
diathesis. see disposition
dichotomy, 28, 124–25, 240, 242–43
difference, gradual vs. categorical, quantitive vs.
  qualitative. *see* gradualism

differentia specifica. see definition, Aristotle's
  account of
digestion, 34, 157
dihairesis, 3, 124
Diogenes of Sinope, 28, 242
discontinuity, 5–7
disposition, 47, 72, 92, 109, 125, 132, 163,
  171–73, 175–80, 224, 228, 245, 259
diversity, coordinated, 225–30
divine, 7, 32–33, 39–45, 60, 65, 69–70, 75, 79,
  85–92, 94–96, 109–11, 119–20, 136, 166,
  174, 180–82, 214–16, 233, 244, 260,
  270–71
Drefcinski, Shane, 200, 209
dualisers, dualise, 6, 121, 265

earth, 32, 78, 82–83, 85–89, 91, 93, 264
economy, economics, 238, 241, 247–48, 254–55
education, 176, 201, 248, 253, 258, 262,
  265–67, 271–73
emotion, 5, 71–72, 74, 91, 142–43, 150, 157,
  202, 205, 224–25, 228–30, 234–35,
  259–60, 264
enkrateia. see continence
entelecheia. see actuality
epieikēs, 200–2, 206, 208, 211–12, 216–17
epistēmē, 35, 99, 256–57
epistēmonikon, 34–35, 177
equivocation, 12, 44, 53, 57, 156, 169, 172, 180,
  233, 235
ergon. see function
essence, 3, 25, 27–33, 35–36, 38–42, 120, 122,
  131, 136, 163, 181, 233, 243
essential definition, 3–4, 44, 138, 239–40
essentialism, 6, 120–22, 126, 133–34, 140, 147
essentialism, teleological, 118, 131–38
ethology, 132–33, 142
eudaimonia. see happiness
evolution, biological, 1, 15, 142, 260–61
excellence, 92, 164, 167–68, 177, 201, 206–7,
  210, 212–14, 216–17, 231
exceptionalism, anthropological, 5, 7
explanation, 3, 25, 27, 29–32, 34–35, 37, 46, 55,
  77, 128, 149, 263

fallibility, 45, 144, 200–2, 205, 211–12, 217
female. *see* women
fixed stars, 78–79, 85–88, 90
Foot, Philippa, 165–66
form (in contrast to matter), 58, 100–1, 125,
  133–34, 171, 180
form of life/way of life, 19, 59, 89, 95, 107, 111,
  114–15, 118, 132–38, 216, 221–24,
  226–27, 234, 242–43, 261, 263, 270
Fortenbaugh, William, 45, 61, 75, 230, 232, 264

Index

293

free citizens, 208, 229–31, 236, 245–46, 252, 264
friendship, 5, 59, 182–99, 210, 216, 239, 251, 253, 266, 271
function, 5, 32, 34, 37, 92, 108, 110–11, 118, 132–38, 157, 163–72, 174–81, 206–8, 222–36, 245–46, 255, 261, 263
functionalism (about virtue, about biology), 163–72, 179–81, 243, 255

Geach, Peter, 166–67
genus proximum. see definition, Aristotle's account of
geocentrism, 78, 86
Gill, Mary Louise, 105
Glock, Hans-Johann, 13–14
God, 39, 41–42, 44–45, 90–91, 94–95, 173, 194, 198–99, 208, 216
god-like. *see* divine
gods, 58, 60, 69–70, 75, 173, 214, 233, 244
good life, 34–35, 137, 261, 272
goodness, 49, 168, 173, 185, 189, 193–94, 197, 201, 204, 210, 215, 236
government. *see* constitution, political
gradualism, 5–6, 10–13, 16, 121–23, 126, 130, 138, 143, 150, 259, 262
Granger, Herbert, 6
great chain of being, 6, 143
gregariousness, 10–11, 26, 50, 58, 114, 121–22, 221–24, 226, 245, 259, 261
growth, 34, 37–38, 102–3, 106–7, 113–14, 123, 136, 144, 174, 254

Hacker, Peter M. S., 145, 147, 159
hands, 5, 7, 32, 35, 46–48, 110–11, 135–36, 141–42
happiness, 5, 75, 82, 85, 89–93, 95, 137, 190–91, 195–97, 206–8, 227, 232–34, 236–37, 241, 249–50, 252–53, 262–63, 265–66, 270–73
Harte, Verity, 188
health, 52, 80–82, 84–85, 92, 188–89, 195, 203, 207
heaven, 78–79, 85–88, 270
hexis. see disposition
hierarchy, 2, 8, 30–31, 34–36, 47, 136, 144, 155, 222, 228, 230–31, 235, 241, 248
highest good, highest end, 81–82, 84–89, 93–94
Hobbes, Thomas, 239
homonymy. *see* equivocation
horismos, 27
household, 26, 48, 113, 226–27, 229–30, 235, 238, 241, 245–48, 250–55, 261, 264
human condition, 77, 94, 119–20, 200

human-animal difference. *see* anthropological difference
human-animal studies, 5
hylomorphism, 100, 102–4, 106, 125, 134

ideal state. *see* state
idion. see peculiarity
imagination, 8–10, 13, 33, 41, 45, 58–61, 64–71, 75–76, 105–6, 127–31, 136–38, 144, 199
incontinence, 75, 215, 264
infallibility. *see* fallibility
intellect, 3, 7, 17, 20, 25, 32, 34–42, 44–45, 50, 69–70, 85–86, 90–92, 94–95, 101–7, 112, 122–23, 130–31, 135, 143–47, 150, 158, 166, 176, 180–82, 187, 192–99, 202, 260
intelligence, 6, 35, 46–48, 55, 79, 110–13, 123, 128, 136, 142, 145, 176, 223–24, 226, 248, 260, 264–65
intentionality, 144, 147, 150–51

Johansen, Thomas, 101
justice, 11, 26–27, 48–51, 173, 176, 184, 193, 198, 209, 211, 214, 216, 226, 234, 239, 258, 261–62, 271, 273

kalos kagathos, kalokagathia, 200–1, 204–5, 207, 216
kata mikron, 6, 259
kata physin, 217, 227, 231, 253, 266
Kenny, Anthony, 145–46, 148–49, 159
kind, biological. *see* species
kind, natural, 50–51, 222, 232, 236
kinēsis. see motion, movement
knowledge, 8, 34–35, 37, 40–41, 44, 53, 59, 69, 71, 99–100, 105, 116, 119, 154–55, 175, 205–8, 229, 253, 256, 264–65, 267–68, 272
koinon ergon, 122, 224, 251, 261
koinon sympheron, 11, 246, 251, 253, 265
Kosman, Aryeh, 195

Labarrière, Jean-Louis, 44–45, 49, 52, 111, 127, 129–30, 224
language, 8, 11, 45–46, 49–50, 53–58, 122, 129–30, 142–43, 145–46, 148, 150, 153, 156, 158–60, 261–62
laughter, 5, 142, 240
law(s). *see* legislation, legislator
legislation, legislator, 2, 22, 49, 72, 115–16, 208, 211, 216, 227, 239, 248–50, 252–53, 266–69, 271–74
leisure, 208, 241, 247, 249–50, 252–53, 256, 271
Lennox, James, 1, 111, 132, 134, 234

Leunissen, Mariska, 88, 107
lingualism, 158
Liu, Irene, 197
locomotion, 34, 37–38, 100, 102–3, 105–9, 144, 155, 172, 242
logistikon, 34–35, 106, 177
logos, 3–4, 8–9, 11, 26–27, 34, 45–48, 50, 55, 57, 61–63, 74, 79, 114, 120, 122–23, 129, 131, 150, 158–59, 168, 180, 205, 226, 232, 235, 244, 247–48, 262
love, 71, 183–91, 193, 195, 202, 210

MacIntyre, Alasdair, 166–67
master science. *see* political science
mathematics, 36–38, 55, 70–72, 99, 102, 104
matter of degree. *see* gradualism
McCready-Flora, Ian C., 158–59
McDowell, John, 8, 101, 150, 155–56
meaning (semantic), 12, 14, 16, 45, 49, 51–54, 63, 101, 122, 129, 159
memory, 5, 9, 13, 41, 60–63, 68, 71, 112, 118, 126–27, 129, 150
metaphor, metaphorical speech, 6, 49, 169, 171–72, 175, 239
metaphysics, 2, 6–7, 27, 30–31, 99, 122, 125, 140, 200, 217, 257
Miller, Fred, 239
mind/the mental, notion of, 144–50
money, 56, 82, 115, 195, 210–11, 254–55
morality, 2, 11–12, 72, 103, 165–68, 187, 200–2, 205–7, 210–12, 215–17, 226, 245–47, 249, 256, 262–63, 265, 267
Moss, Jessica, 46, 61, 67, 177
motion, movement, 8, 33–34, 45, 51, 55–56, 58, 63, 66, 71, 78–79, 81, 83, 85–92, 105–8, 118, 127–28, 131, 135–36, 144, 173–74, 233

natural science, 4, 7, 33, 36–38, 42, 99, 101–6, 111–12, 123
nature
  does nothing in vain, 11, 26, 32, 47–48, 50–51, 132, 198, 225–27, 234
  second nature, 166, 179
noētikon, noein, 32–33, 39, 44, 66, 69, 102, 136
nous. see intellect
Nussbaum, Martha, 128, 166, 200
nutrition, 34, 61, 75, 100, 111, 114–16, 132–33, 136, 172, 174

orektikon, 61, 107, 144, 176
Osborne, Catherine, 45, 54, 127
ousia. see substance

pain, 11, 26–27, 45, 48, 51, 58, 60, 72–73, 76, 82, 150, 152, 209–10
Pakaluk, Michael, 168, 178–79
parts of the soul. *see* soul
peculiarity, 3–5, 7, 10–12, 25–27, 29, 31–32, 35, 45, 49–50, 60–61, 64–65, 69, 75, 108, 126, 131, 135, 137, 140–42, 160, 182, 194, 199, 240
peculiarity criterion, 61, 75
Peirce, Charles Sanders, 160
Pellegrin, Pierre, 28, 120–21
perception, 8, 13–14, 16, 33–34, 37–41, 45, 48, 58, 60–69, 71, 75–76, 100, 102, 106–8, 127, 129, 136, 143–45, 150–57, 232
perfection, 44, 58, 200, 211–12, 236, 258, 265
perfection, moral, 200–17
persuasion, 45, 72, 74
phantasia. see imagination
phantasmata, 9, 33, 60, 64–71, 126
phantastikon, 33, 144
philosophers, 201, 249–50, 262, 270–71
philosophy of human affairs, 2, 137, 235, 267–74
phonē. see voice
phronēsis. see wisdom, practical
phronimos, 110–12, 200–3, 205, 212, 216–17
physics, 4, 25, 35–38, 42, 54, 101
physiology, 1, 33, 41, 118–20, 124–25, 132–35, 142, 149–50, 152
planets, 78–79, 86–92
plants, 6, 15, 18, 37, 58, 61, 75, 77, 83–84, 86–88, 91–93, 101–2, 107, 109, 113, 136, 144, 146, 151, 165, 172–74, 180, 259, 270
Plato, 28, 45, 54, 74, 83, 85, 91, 124, 150, 164–66, 168, 170–72, 200–2, 205, 207–8, 217, 227, 240–42, 244–46, 248–59, 262, 267–70
pleasure, 11, 26–27, 48, 51, 58, 60, 64, 68, 70, 72–73, 76, 92, 94–95, 114, 157, 184–99, 202–4, 209–11, 247, 249, 266
Plutarch, 157
poiēsis, 34
polis. see state
political science, 266, 268, 272
politicality, 12, 221, 227, 257
politician, 22, 145, 267–68, 271, 274
potentiality, 38–39, 41, 58, 92, 100, 137, 148–49, 175, 179, 250, 262, 265, 271
praxis. see action, agency
primates, 100, 121, 141, 152
prohairesis. see deliberation, decision, choice
Promethean gift, 258
pros hen ambiguity, 12, 14
psychē, psyche, 128, 144, 232

Index

psychology, 2, 13–14, 54, 60–76, 101, 104, 118–20, 124–25, 127–28, 130, 132–34, 144, 164, 171–72, 187, 215, 221–22, 225, 228, 235, 239, 250

quantitative vs. qualitative difference. *see* gradualism

Rabbås, Øyvind, 9
rationality, reason
practical, 34, 103, 105–6, 136, 200, 202, 205, 263–64
theoretical, 35, 103, 105–6, 136, 232
reasonable resignation, 81–82, 86, 93
regularity, 78–79, 86–87, 90, 132, 264
reproduction, 92, 94, 100, 113, 115, 144, 165–66, 222–24, 245–46, 261
role division, 21, 221–25, 227–31, 234–35, 239, 245–46, 251
ruler, 113, 216, 222, 227–28, 230, 232–36, 240, 244, 246, 263–65

Sauvé Meyer, Susan, 190
scala naturae, 6, 15, 121, 123, 136, 259
Schofield, Malcolm, 228, 236, 245
science of human nature, 3–4
seeing. *see* perception
self-control, 145, 206, 250
self-mover, 78
self-sufficiency, 113–14, 195, 241, 247
sensation, 8, 34, 144
shame, 72–73, 202, 205–6, 211, 258
similarity, 15, 31, 57, 112, 166
slave, slavery, 49, 74, 222, 227–37, 240, 244–47, 251–54, 256, 263–65
sleep, 41, 68, 71
sociability, 259–67 (*see also* gregariousness)
sophists, 115, 258, 267
sōphrosynē. *see* self-control
Sorabji, Richard, 45, 123, 128, 150–51
species, 6, 9, 51, 84, 99, 116, 124–25, 129, 132, 134, 137, 144, 172, 223–26, 242–44, 255
speech, 8, 10–11, 26–27, 44–59, 62–63, 122, 129–30, 133–35, 148, 158–60, 181, 198, 226, 235, 247
spheres (cosmology), 78–79, 85–90, 92, 228
spoudaios, 168, 200–4, 208–9, 212–17
state, 11–12, 26, 48–52, 57–58, 113–16, 166, 201, 221, 226–30, 234–36, 238–39, 241, 245–53, 255–57, 260–62, 264–70, 272–74
statesman, 227–28, 240, 242, 244, 246, 251, 256, 267–68, 272–73
Stoics, stoicism, 157, 200, 212, 217
sublunary beings, sublunary realm, 82–86, 88, 94, 228, 252

substance, 3, 27, 29, 37, 50, 90, 100, 103, 120, 125, 147–50, 163–64, 169–73, 175–76, 179–80
survival, 92, 133, 223, 234, 241, 258, 261, 270
syllogism, 55, 65, 126–28
symbol, 46, 49–50, 52–59, 62–64, 130, 146, 148, 160

technē, 6, 34–35, 47, 175, 256–57, 260, 264
teleology, 79, 104, 110, 115, 118, 131–38, 165, 167, 169–70, 225, 227, 229–31, 234, 243, 257, 262–63, 265–66, 272
telos. *see* teleology
theology, 4, 25, 35–36, 39–42
theoretical life. *see* contemplative life
theōria. *see* contemplation
thymos, 61, 64, 264
thyrathen (from outside), 7, 123, 260
tongue, 51, 53, 129, 133–35
tool, 35, 46–47, 56, 231, 263
transformation thesis, 7–16, 143, 155–57, 194
truth, 8, 34, 44, 55–56, 59, 69, 77, 150–51, 156, 177, 202–5, 213, 233
two-footed/two-legged. *see* bipedalism

understanding, 33–35, 38–42, 44, 46, 129, 193, 228
uniqueness. *see* peculiarity
universals, anthropological, 140
unmoved mover, 78, 86, 90, 106, 173
upright posture, 5, 7, 32–34, 42, 100, 109–11, 135–36, 141, 181, 229, 244

vagueness, 14–16
virtue ethics, 164–65, 167, 179
virtue, intellectual, 95, 112, 171, 173, 176–79, 205, 246–47, 265
voice, 11, 26–27, 48, 50–54, 63, 122, 129–30, 157, 159
voluntariness, 67–69, 75, 166, 178, 202, 206, 209, 265

wisdom, 6, 63, 112, 129, 155, 174–75, 177, 205, 216, 260
wisdom, practical, 34–35, 44, 47, 55, 75, 172, 177, 205, 213, 233, 256, 264
Wittgenstein, Ludwig, 147–48
women, 200, 222, 227–37, 246, 264
words, 52–57, 130, 159

zoology, zoological investigation, 4, 25, 29, 42, 99, 104, 107–13, 116–17, 132, 221, 223–27, 242, 245, 255
zōon logon echon. *see* animal, rational
zōon politikon. *see* animal, political

CPSIA information can be obtained
at www.ICGtesting.com
Printed in the USA
LVHW022125170121
676736LV00004B/38